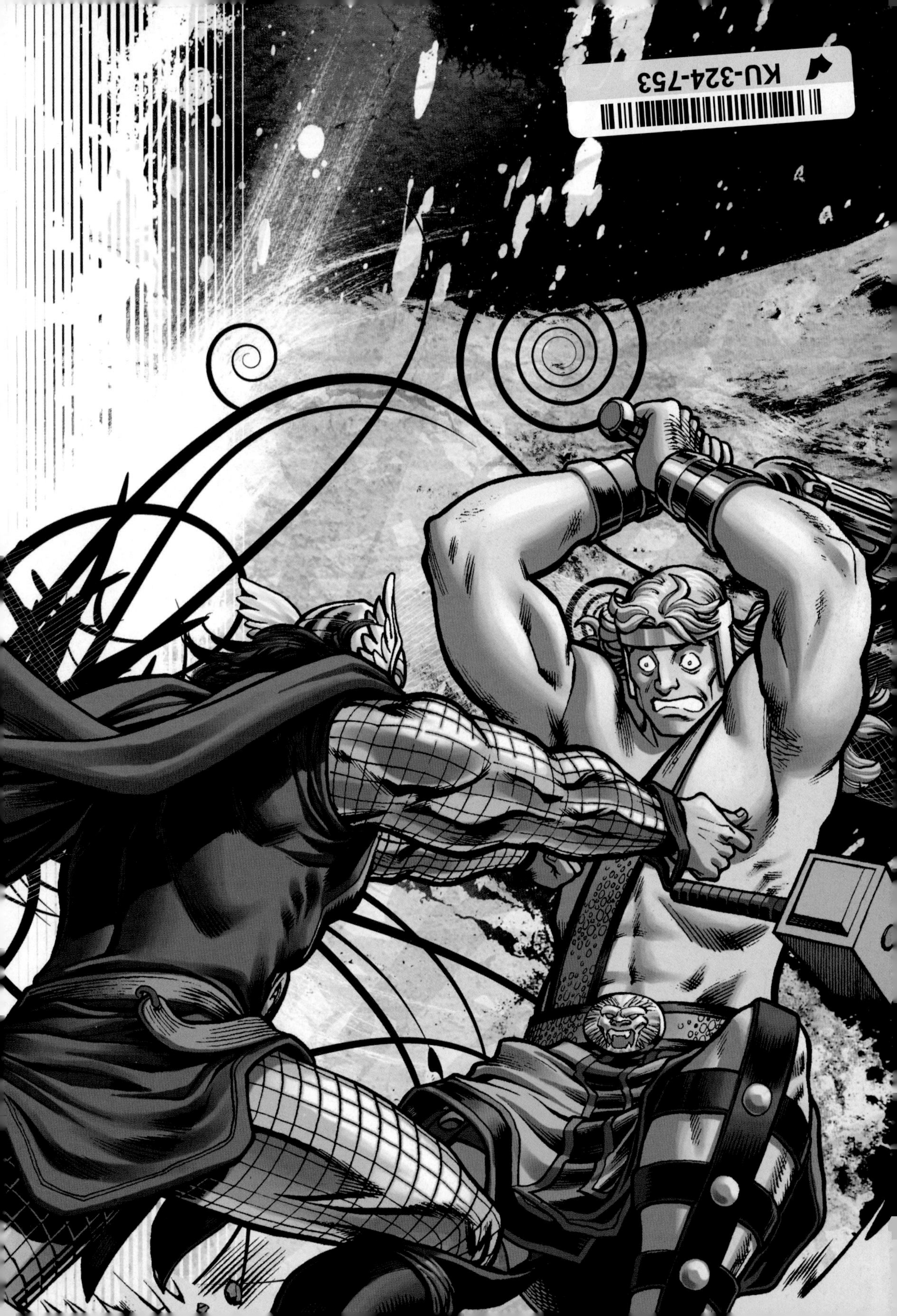

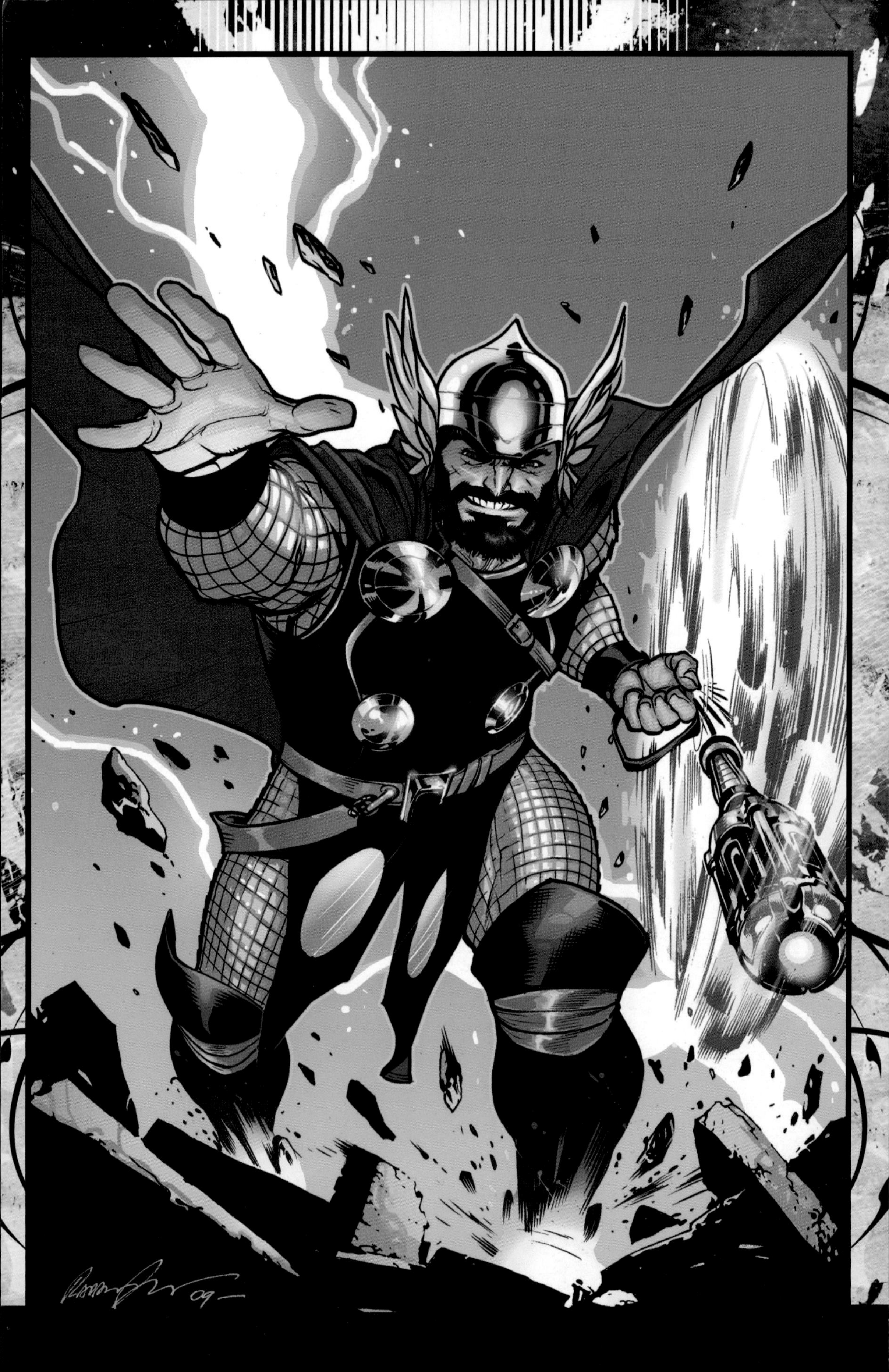

INCREDIBLE HERCULES #132

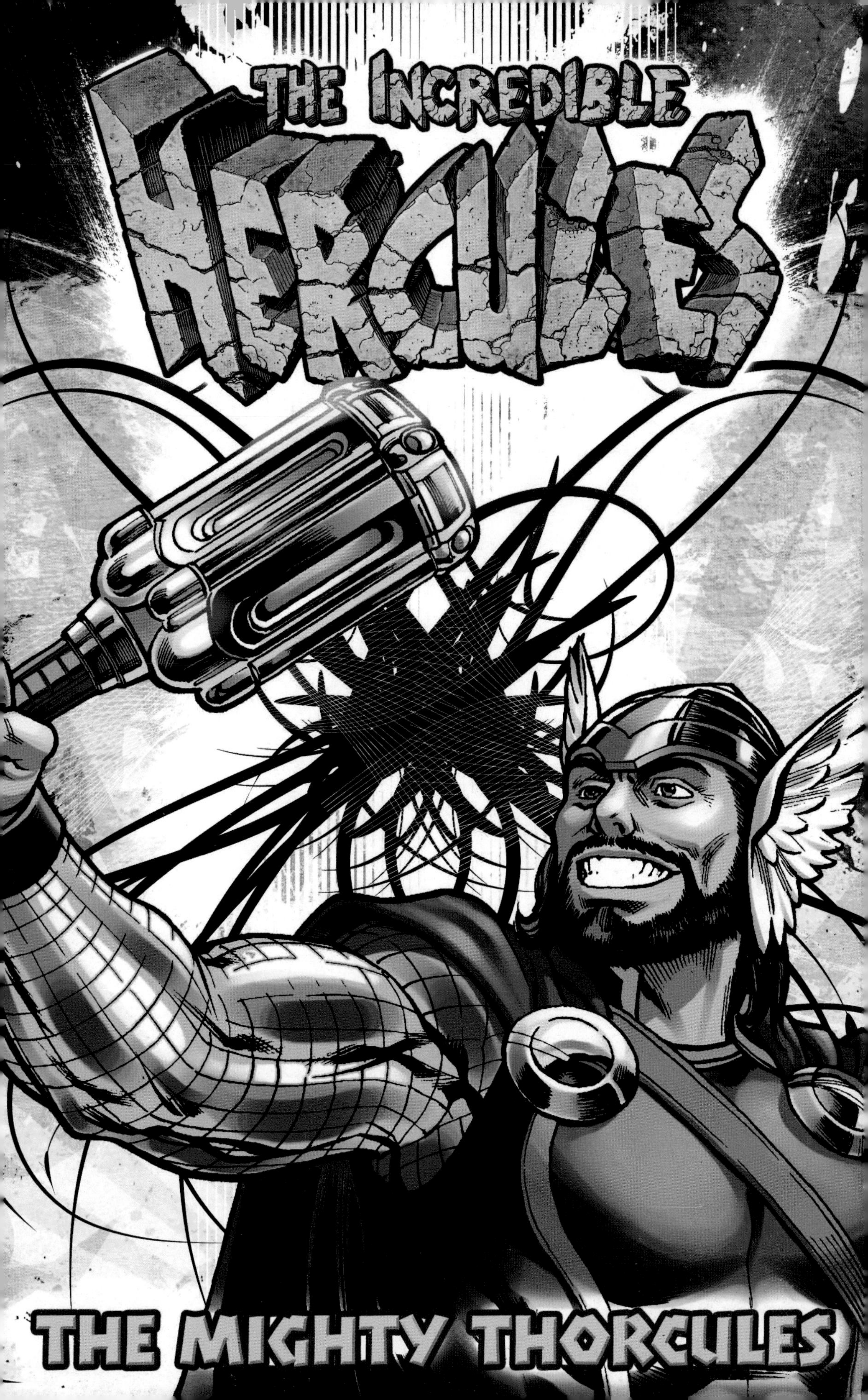
THE INCREDIBLE
HERCULES
THE MIGHTY THORCULES

THE INCREDIBLE HERCULES

Writers: **GREG PAK** & **FRED VAN LENTE**

Pencils (Issues #132, #134 & #136): **REILLY BROWN**

Inks (Issues #132, #134 & #136): **NELSON DECASTRO**

Art (Issues #133, #135 & #137): **RODNEY BUCHEMI**

Colorists: **GUILLEM MARI, EMILY WARREN, GURU EFX, ULISES ARREOLA**

& **SOTOCOLOR'S A. STREET**

Letterer: **SIMON BOWLAND**

Cover Artist: **RAFAEL ALBUQUERQUE** with **JOHN RAUCH** (cover colors, #136 & #137)

Assistant Editor: **JORDAN D. WHITE**

Associate Editor: **NATHAN COSBY**

Editor: **MARK PANICCIA**

Collection Editor: **CORY LEVINE**

Assistant Editors: **ALEX STARBUCK** & **JOHN DENNING**

Editors, Special Projects: **JENNIFER GRÜNWALD** & **MARK D. BEAZLEY**

Senior Editor, Special Projects: **JEFF YOUNGQUIST**

Senior Vice President of Sales: **DAVID GABRIEL**

Editor in Chief: **JOE QUESADA**

Publisher: **DAN BUCKLEY**

Executive Producer: **ALAN FINE**

INCREDIBLE HERCULES: THE MIGHTY THORCULES. Contains material originally published in magazine form as INCREDIBLE HERCULES #132-137. First printing 2009. Hardcover ISBN# 978-0-7851-3831-0. Softcover ISBN# 978-0-7851-3677-4. Published by MARVEL PUBLISHING, INC., a subsidiary of MARVEL ENTERTAINMENT, INC. OFFICE OF PUBLICATION: 417 5th Avenue, New York, NY 10016. Copyright © 2009 and 2010 Marvel Characters, Inc. All rights reserved. Hardcover: $19.99 per copy in the U.S. (GST #R127032852). Softcover: $14.99 per copy in the U.S. (GST #R127032852). Canadian Agreement #40668537. All characters featured in this issue and the distinctive names and likenesses thereof, and all related indicia are trademarks of Marvel Characters, Inc. No similarity between any of the names, characters, persons, and/or institutions in this magazine with those of any living or dead person or institution is intended, and any such similarity which may exist is purely coincidental. **Printed in the U.S.A.** ALAN FINE, EVP - Office Of The Chief Executive Marvel Entertainment, Inc. & CMO Marvel Characters B.V.; DAN BUCKLEY, Chief Executive Officer and Publisher - Print, Animation & Digital Media; JIM SOKOLOWSKI, Chief Operating Officer; DAVID GABRIEL, SVP of Publishing Sales & Circulation; DAVID BOGART, SVP of Business Affairs & Talent Management; MICHAEL PASCIULLO, VP Merchandising & Communications; JIM O'KEEFE, VP of Operations & Logistics; DAN CARR, Executive Director of Publishing Technology; JUSTIN F. GABRIE, Director of Publishing & Editorial Operations; SUSAN CRESPI, Editorial Operations Manager; ALEX MORALES, Publishing Operations Manager; STAN LEE, Chairman Emeritus. For information regarding advertising in Marvel Comics or on Marvel.com, please contact Mitch Dane, Advertising Director, at mdane@marvel.com. For Marvel subscription inquiries, please call 800-217-9158. Manufactured between 11/9/09 and 12/9/09 (hardcover) and 11/9/09 and 4/14/10 (softcover) by R.R. DONNELLEY INC., SALEM, VA, USA.

THOR THE MIGHTY!

A CLASSIC ORIGIN, WITH COMMENTARY BY THE INCREDIBLE HERCULES

OOH!! I TRIPPED...
IT'S A SECRET CHAMBER! BUT THERE'S NOTHING INSIDE... EXCEPT THAT GNARLED WOODEN STICK--LIKE AN ANCIENT CANE!
IN HELPLESS ANGER, DON BLAKE STRIKES THE USELESS CANE AGAINST THE IMMOVABLE BOULDER, AND, AS HE DOES SO...
WHA--?!!

DR. DONALD BLAKE. OUR HERO, LADIES AND GENTLEMEN.

IMPRESSED BY STICKS. HOW'D THIS GUY EARN AN M.D.? (PROBABLY CHEATED)

A WUSS WITH RUBBER BAND ARMS TRIES TO SMASH A BOULDER WITH A STICK... TRULY, ONE OF THE GREATEST ORIGIN STORIES EVER TOLD.

THE CANE!! IT HAS BECOME A MIGHTY HAMMER!! AND I HAVE BEEN TRANSFORMED INTO--INTO--WAIT! THERE ARE WORDS INSCRIBED ON THE HAMMER!!
"WHOSOEVER HOLDS THIS HAMMER, IF HE BE WORTHY, SHALL POSSESS THE POWER OF... THOR"
THOR!! THE LEGENDARY GOD OF THUNDER!! THE MIGHTIEST WARRIOR OF ALL MYTHOLOGY!! THIS IS HIS HAMMER!! AND I--I AM THOR!!!

WHAT DOES HE NOTICE FIRST? THE CAPE? THE WINGED HELMET? THAT HE CAN WALK?

NO, OF COURSE NOT. LET'S READ THE SIDE OF THIS MALLET.

"OBJECTS IN HAMMER MAY BE CLOSER THAN THEY APPEAR"

AND THE MORAL OF THE STORY, KIDS? EVEN WHEN TRANSFORMED BY NORWEGIAN HOODOO, A WEENIE IS ALWAYS A WEENIE, AND NOWHERE NEAR AS AWESOME AS A REAL HERO, LIKE... GEE, I DON'T KNOW... ME!

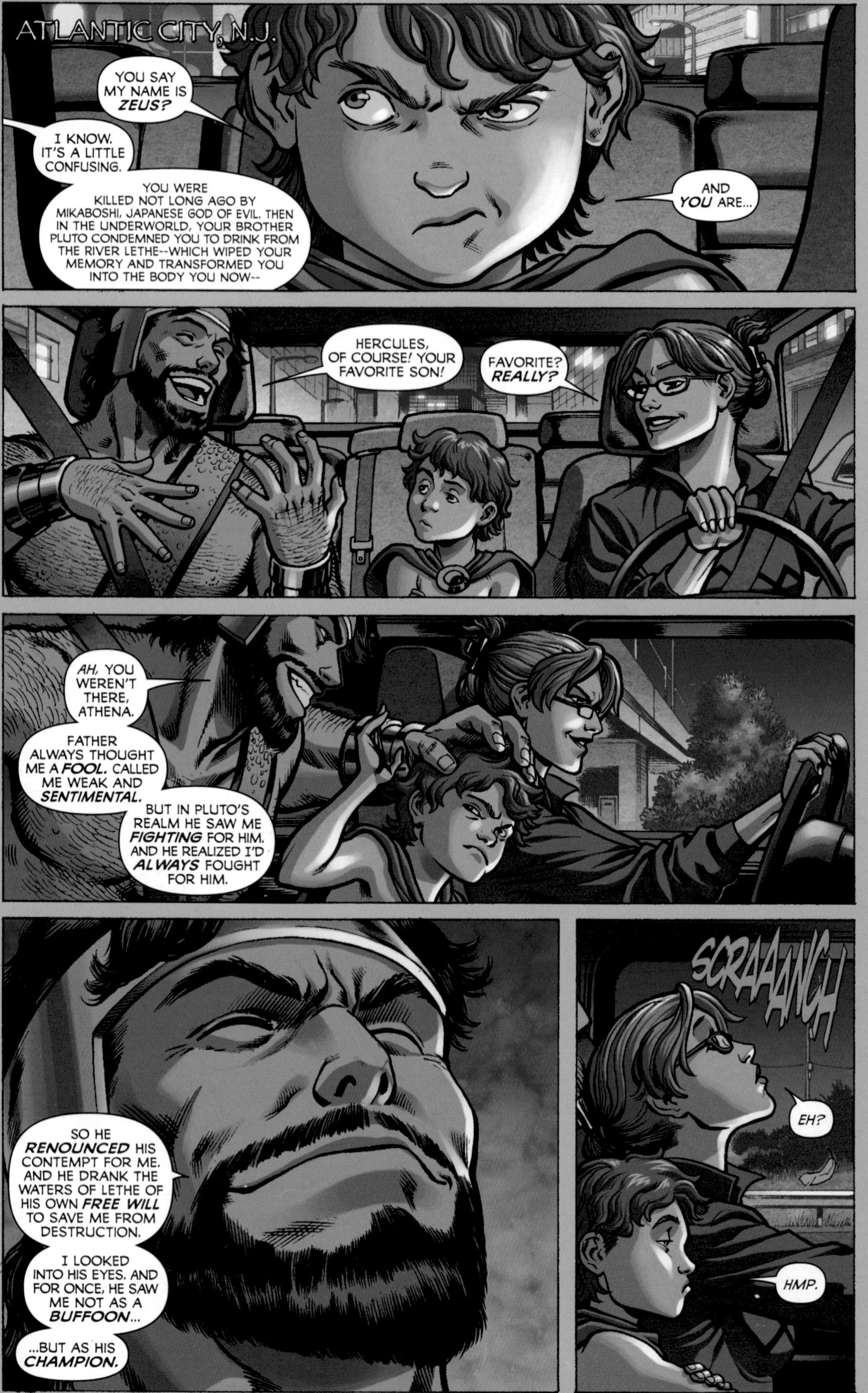
ATLANTIC CITY, N.J.
YOU SAY MY NAME IS *ZEUS?*
I KNOW. IT'S A LITTLE CONFUSING.
YOU WERE KILLED NOT LONG AGO BY MIKABOSHI, JAPANESE GOD OF EVIL. THEN IN THE UNDERWORLD, YOUR BROTHER PLUTO CONDEMNED YOU TO DRINK FROM THE RIVER LETHE--WHICH WIPED YOUR MEMORY AND TRANSFORMED YOU INTO THE BODY YOU NOW--
AND *YOU* ARE...
HERCULES, OF COURSE! YOUR FAVORITE SON!
FAVORITE? *REALLY?*
AH, YOU WEREN'T THERE, ATHENA.
FATHER ALWAYS THOUGHT ME A *FOOL.* CALLED ME WEAK AND *SENTIMENTAL.*
BUT IN PLUTO'S REALM HE SAW ME *FIGHTING* FOR HIM. AND HE REALIZED I'D *ALWAYS* FOUGHT FOR HIM.
SO HE *RENOUNCED* HIS CONTEMPT FOR ME. AND HE DRANK THE WATERS OF LETHE OF HIS OWN *FREE WILL* TO SAVE ME FROM DESTRUCTION.
I LOOKED INTO HIS EYES. AND FOR ONCE, HE SAW ME NOT AS A *BUFFOON*...
...BUT AS HIS *CHAMPION.*
SCRAAANCH
EH?
HMP.

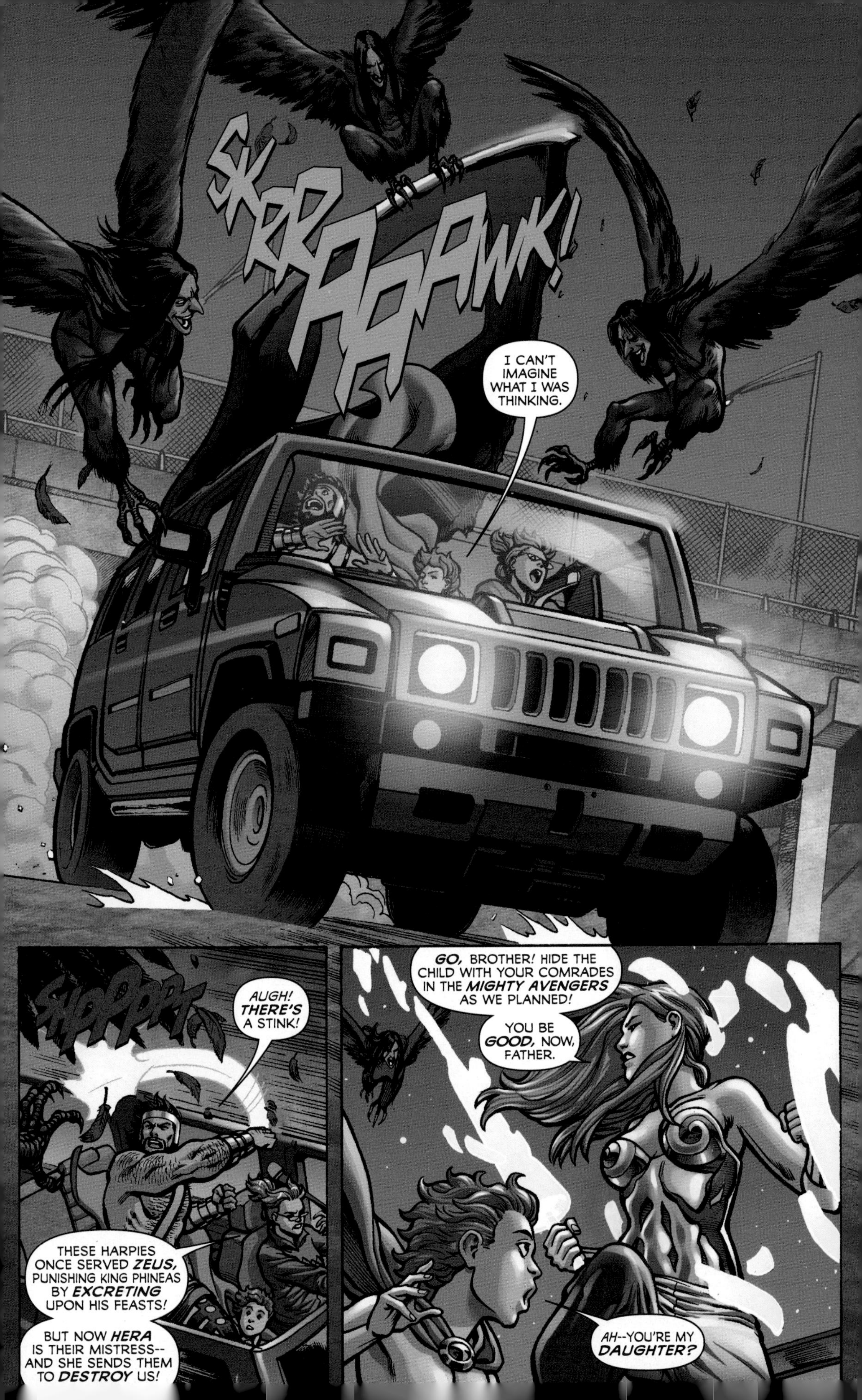
SKRRAAAWK!
I CAN'T IMAGINE WHAT I WAS THINKING.
AUGH! **THERE'S** A STINK!
THESE HARPIES ONCE SERVED **ZEUS,** PUNISHING KING PHINEAS BY **EXCRETING** UPON HIS FEASTS!
BUT NOW **HERA** IS THEIR MISTRESS-- AND SHE SENDS THEM TO **DESTROY** US!
GO, BROTHER! HIDE THE CHILD WITH YOUR COMRADES IN THE **MIGHTY AVENGERS** AS WE PLANNED!
YOU BE **GOOD,** NOW, FATHER.
AH--YOU'RE MY **DAUGHTER?**

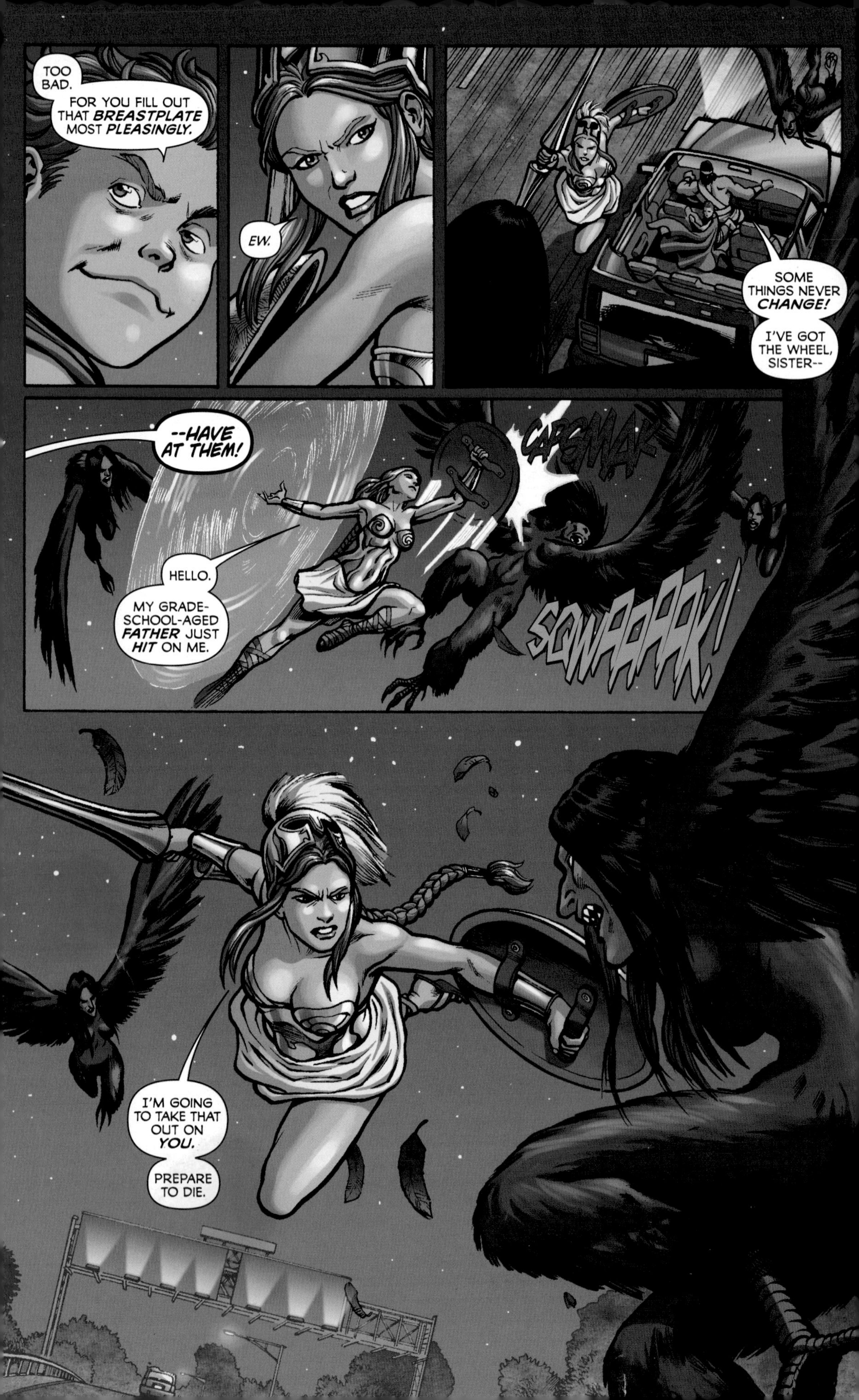
TOO BAD.
FOR YOU FILL OUT THAT BREASTPLATE MOST PLEASINGLY.
EW.
SOME THINGS NEVER CHANGE!
I'VE GOT THE WHEEL, SISTER--
--HAVE AT THEM!
CARSMAK
HELLO.
MY GRADE-SCHOOL-AGED FATHER JUST HIT ON ME.
SQWAAAAK!
I'M GOING TO TAKE THAT OUT ON YOU.
PREPARE TO DIE.

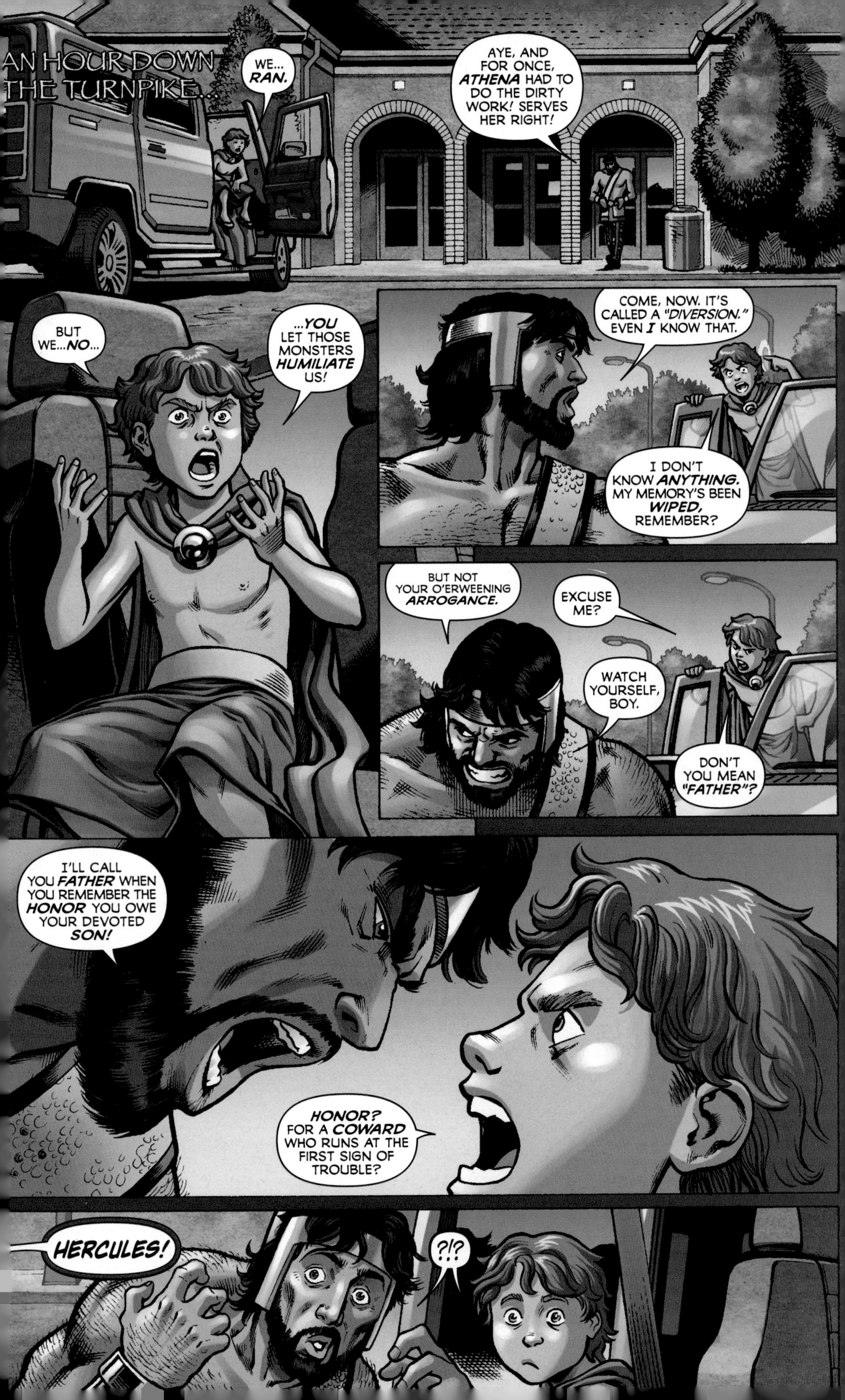
AN HOUR DOWN THE TURNPIKE...
WE... RAN.
AYE, AND FOR ONCE, ATHENA HAD TO DO THE DIRTY WORK! SERVES HER RIGHT!
BUT WE...NO...
...YOU LET THOSE MONSTERS HUMILIATE US!
COME, NOW. IT'S CALLED A "DIVERSION." EVEN I KNOW THAT.
I DON'T KNOW ANYTHING. MY MEMORY'S BEEN WIPED, REMEMBER?
BUT NOT YOUR O'ERWEENING ARROGANCE.
EXCUSE ME?
WATCH YOURSELF, BOY.
DON'T YOU MEAN "FATHER"?
I'LL CALL YOU FATHER WHEN YOU REMEMBER THE HONOR YOU OWE YOUR DEVOTED SON!
HONOR? FOR A COWARD WHO RUNS AT THE FIRST SIGN OF TROUBLE?
HERCULES!
?!?

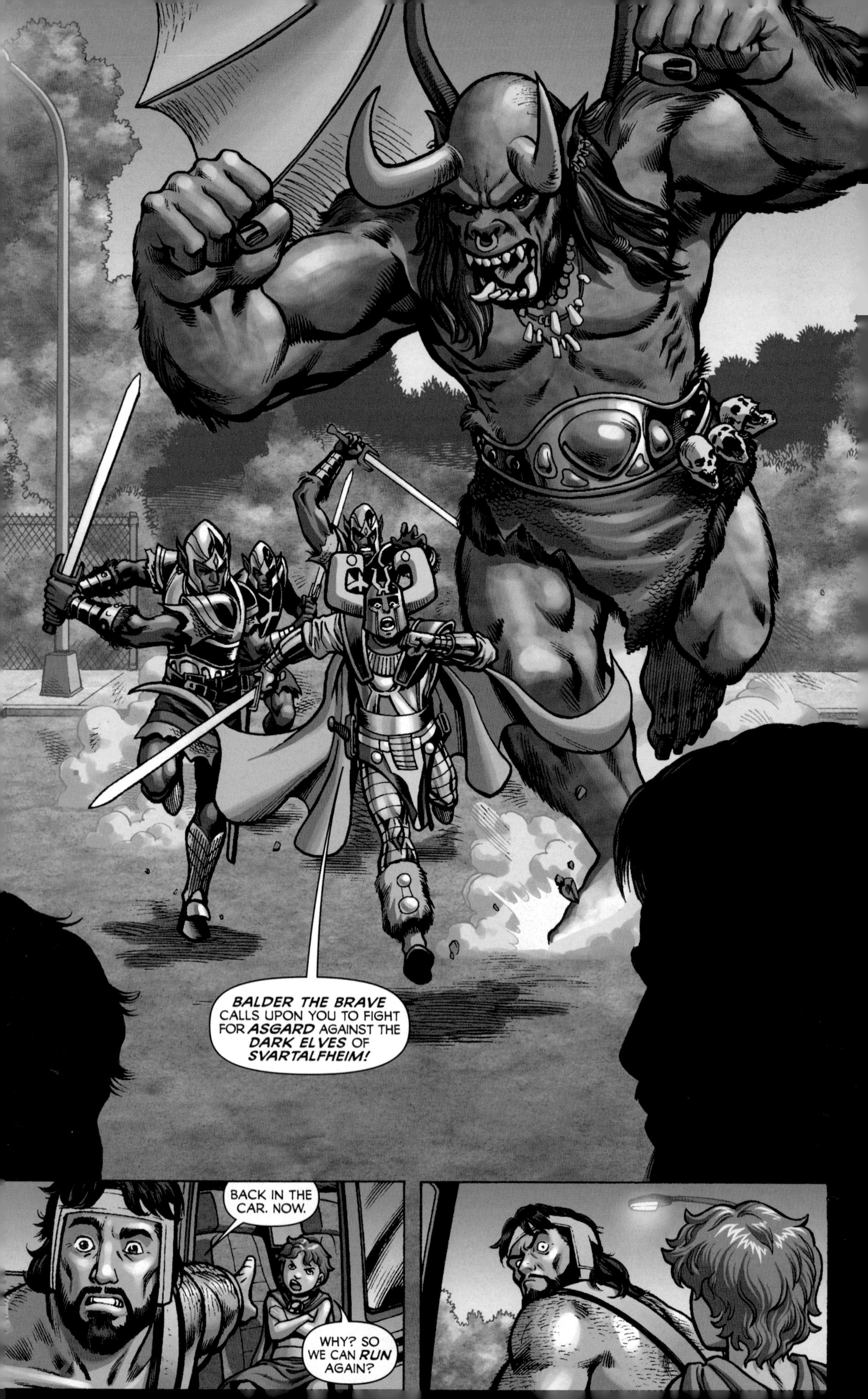
BALDER THE BRAVE CALLS UPON YOU TO FIGHT FOR ASGARD AGAINST THE DARK ELVES OF SVARTALFHEIM!
BACK IN THE CAR. NOW.
WHY? SO WE CAN RUN AGAIN?

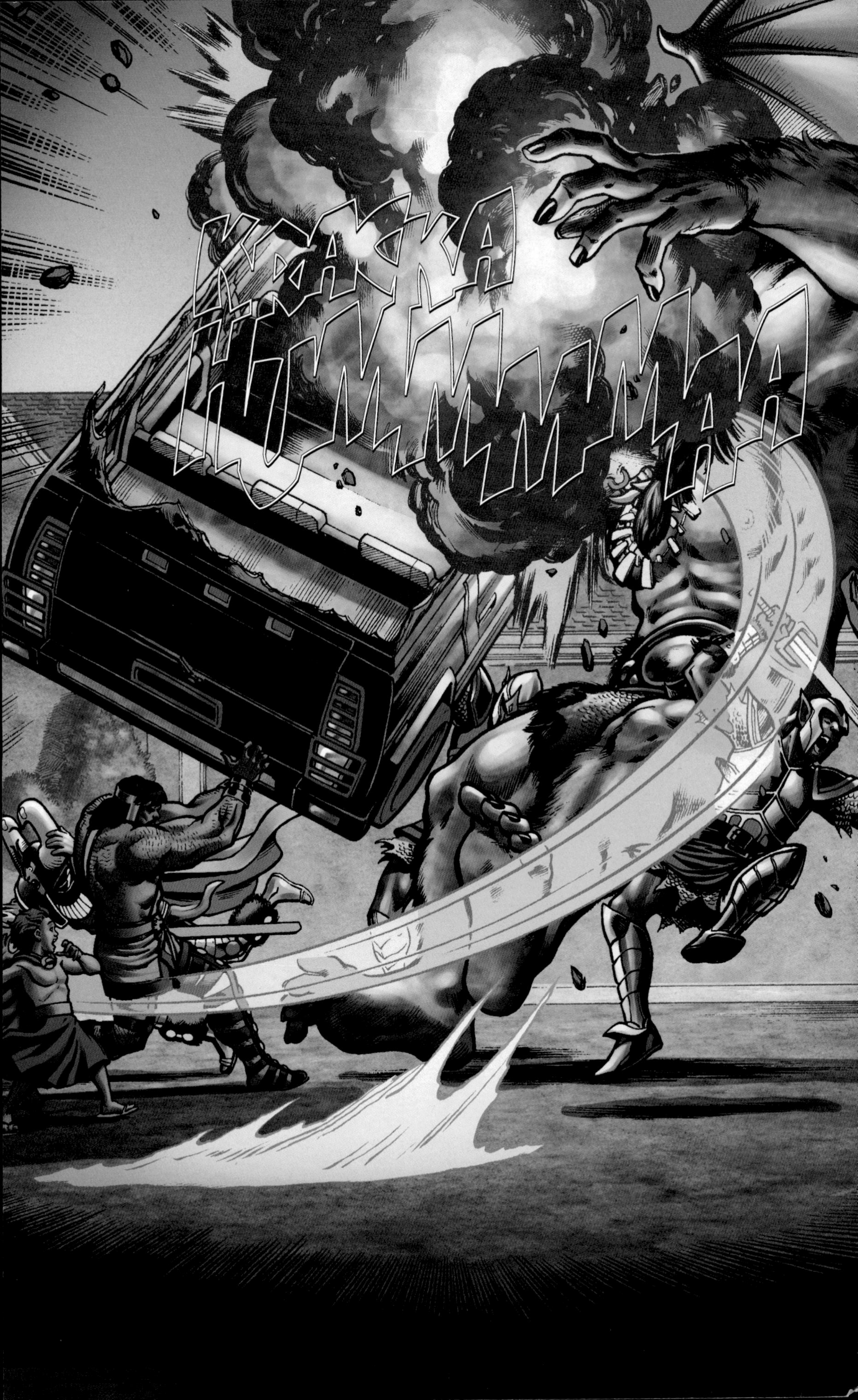
KRAKKA
HOMMMMMA

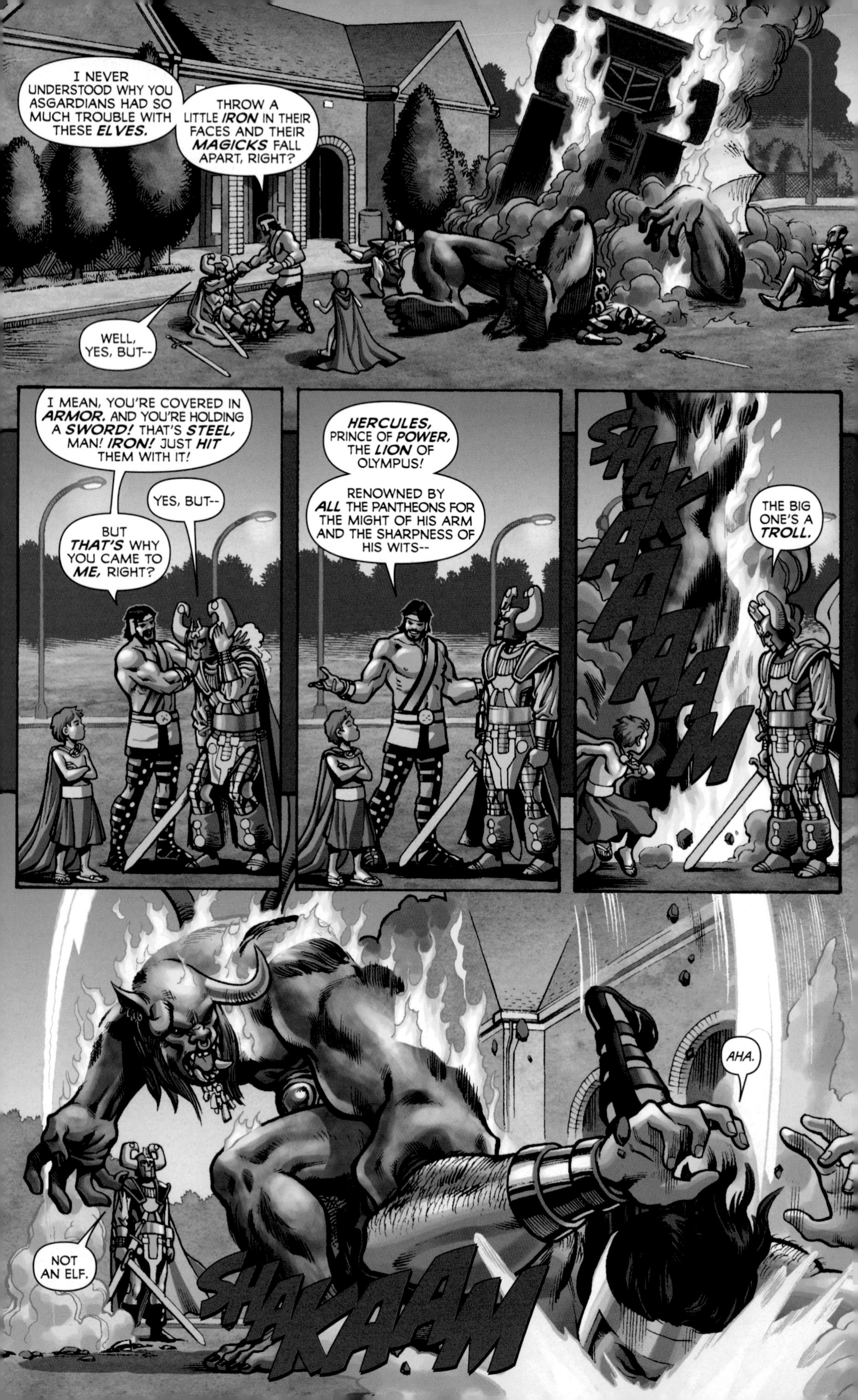
I NEVER UNDERSTOOD WHY YOU ASGARDIANS HAD SO MUCH TROUBLE WITH THESE ELVES.
THROW A LITTLE IRON IN THEIR FACES AND THEIR MAGICKS FALL APART, RIGHT?
WELL, YES, BUT--
I MEAN, YOU'RE COVERED IN ARMOR. AND YOU'RE HOLDING A SWORD! THAT'S STEEL, MAN! IRON! JUST HIT THEM WITH IT!
YES, BUT--
BUT THAT'S WHY YOU CAME TO ME, RIGHT?
HERCULES, PRINCE OF POWER, THE LION OF OLYMPUS!
RENOWNED BY ALL THE PANTHEONS FOR THE MIGHT OF HIS ARM AND THE SHARPNESS OF HIS WITS--
SHAKAAAAAAM
THE BIG ONE'S A TROLL.
AHA.
NOT AN ELF.
SHAKAAM

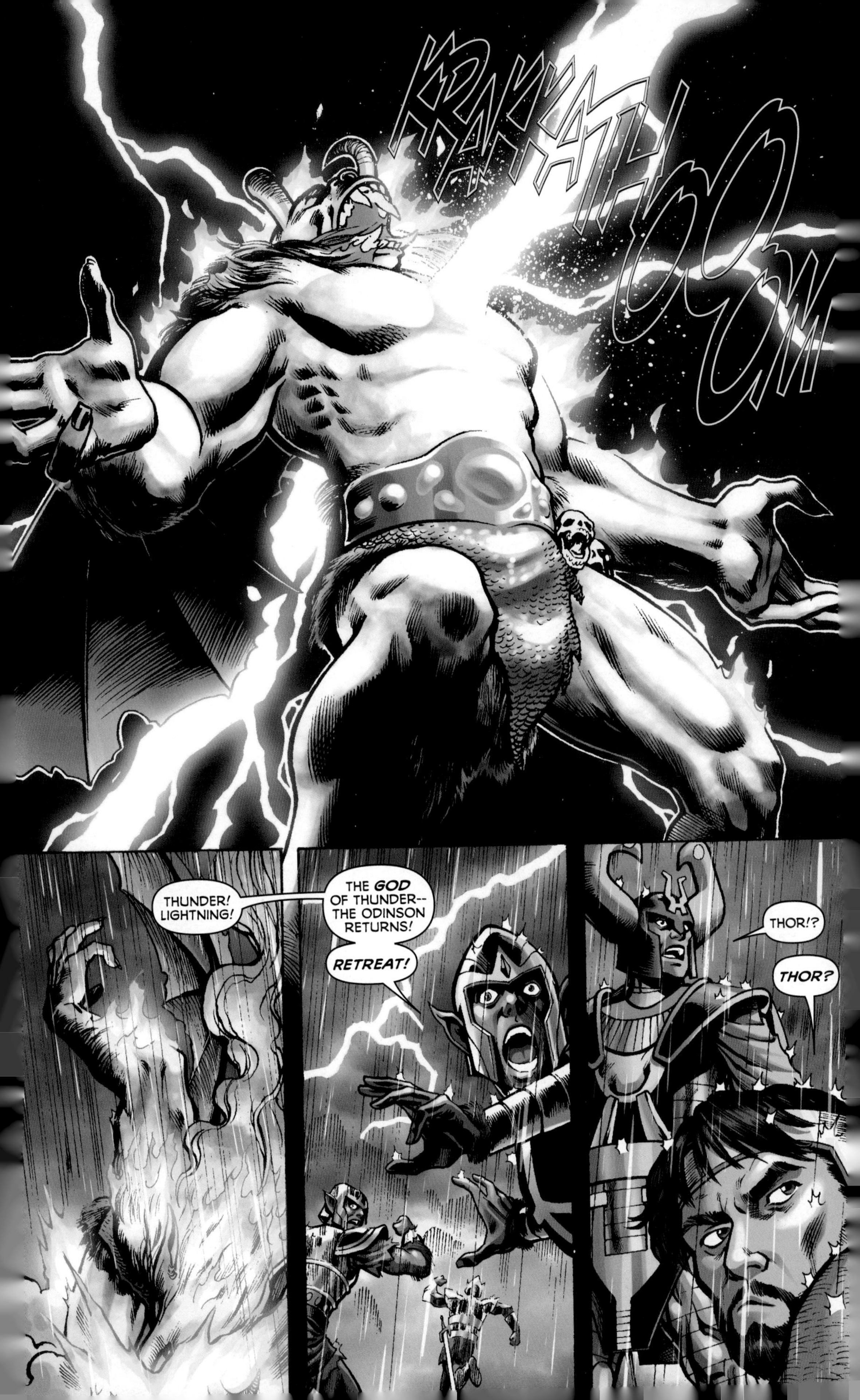
THUNDER! LIGHTNING!
THE GOD OF THUNDER-- THE ODINSON RETURNS!
RETREAT!
THOR!?
THOR?

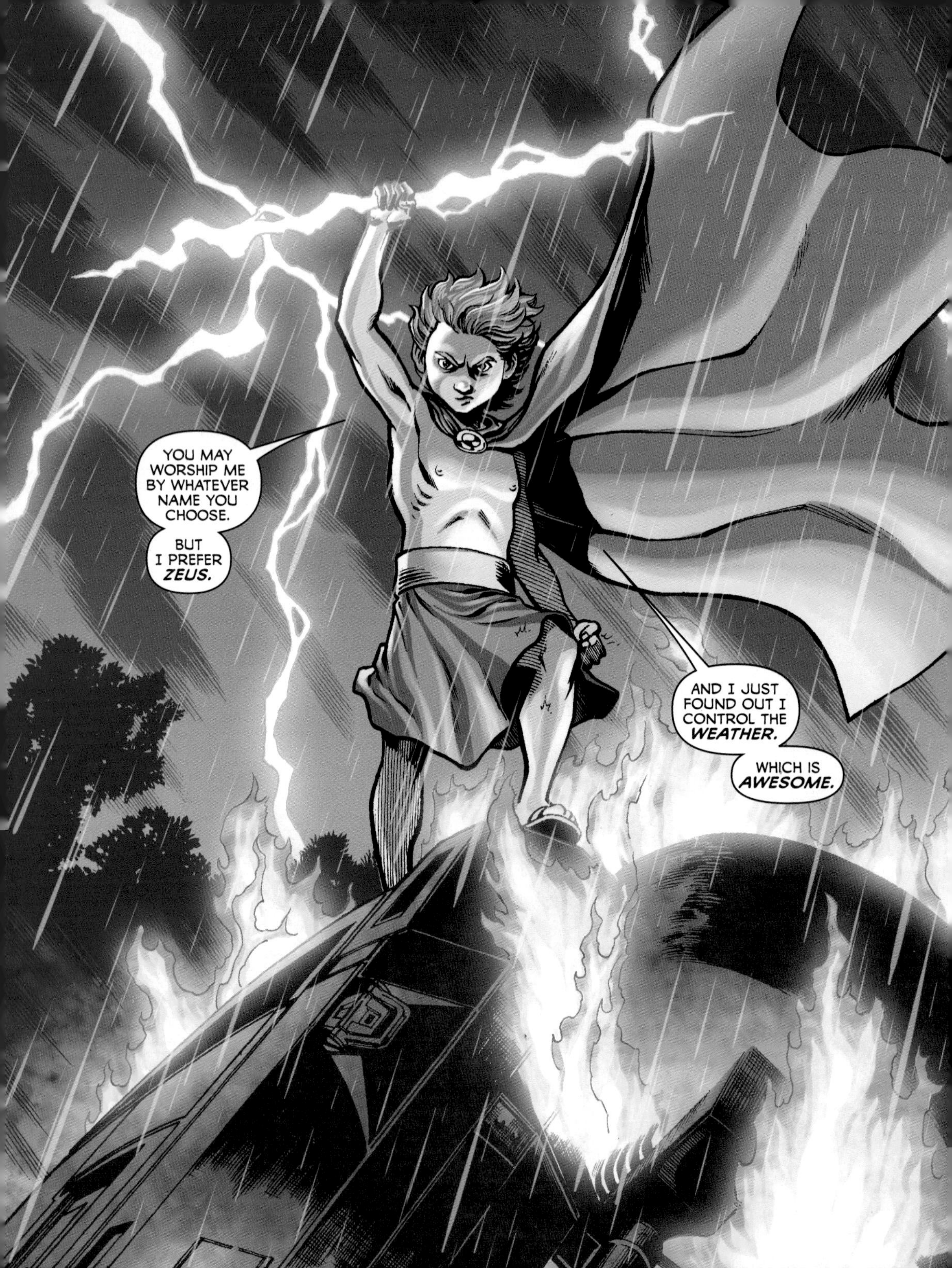
YOU MAY WORSHIP ME BY WHATEVER NAME YOU CHOOSE.
BUT I PREFER *ZEUS.*
AND I JUST FOUND OUT I CONTROL THE *WEATHER.*
WHICH IS *AWESOME.*

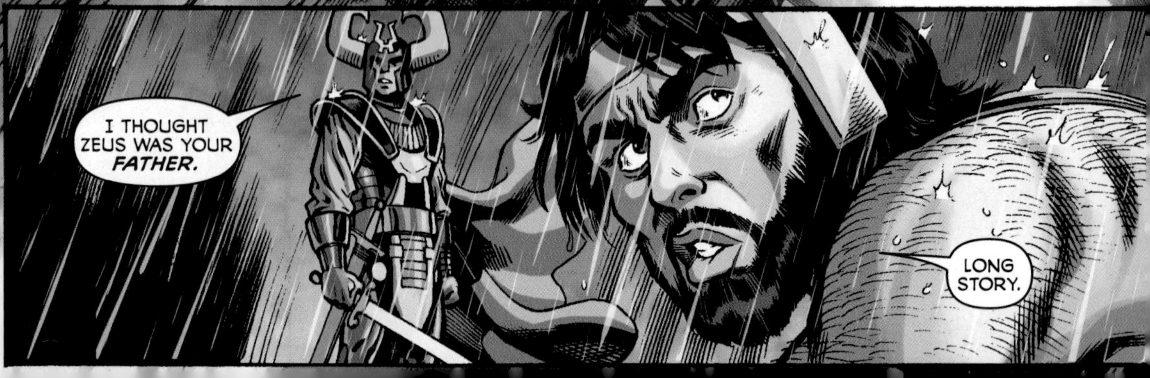
I THOUGHT ZEUS WAS YOUR *FATHER.*
LONG STORY.

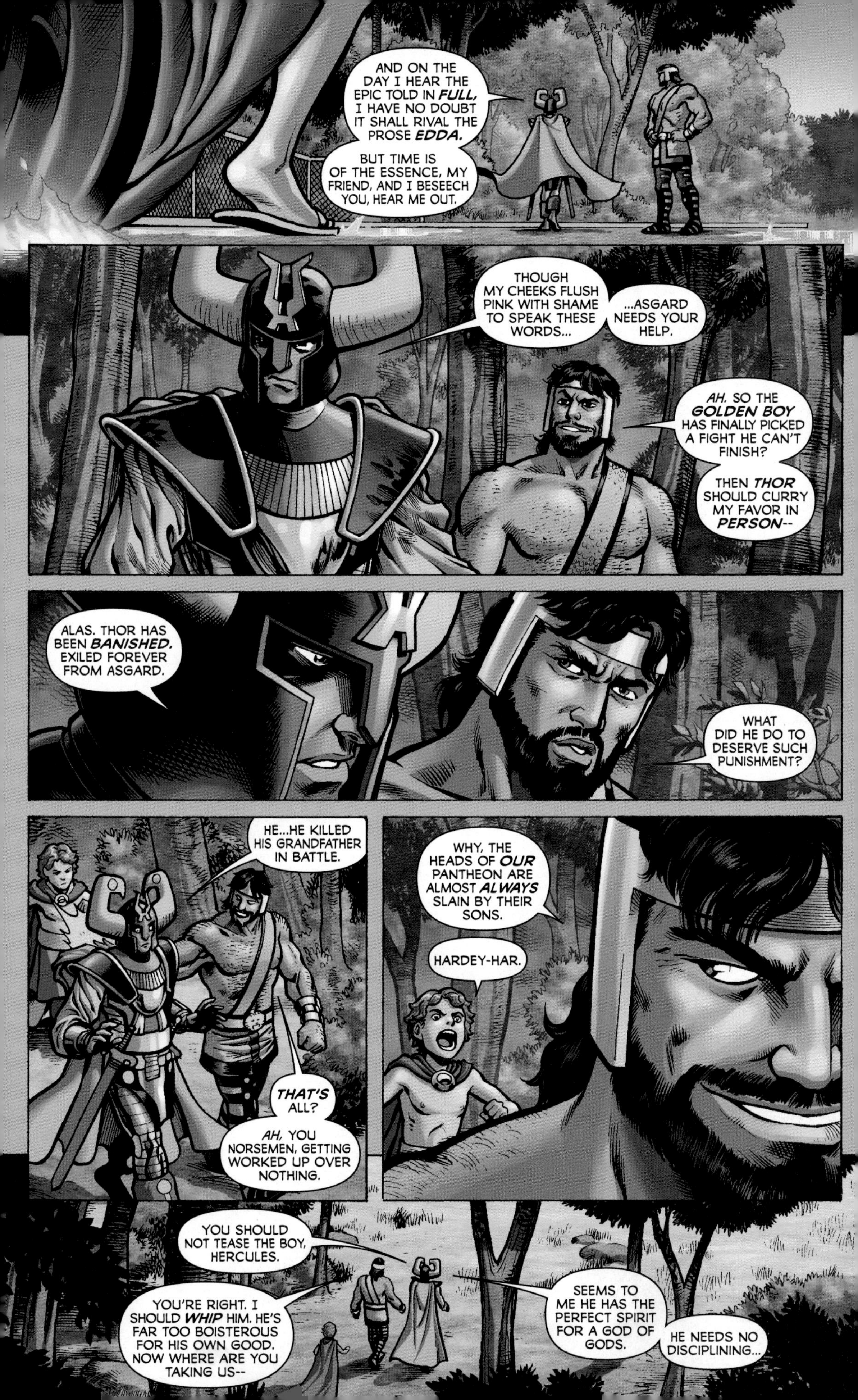
AND ON THE DAY I HEAR THE EPIC TOLD IN FULL, I HAVE NO DOUBT IT SHALL RIVAL THE PROSE EDDA.
BUT TIME IS OF THE ESSENCE, MY FRIEND, AND I BESEECH YOU, HEAR ME OUT.
THOUGH MY CHEEKS FLUSH PINK WITH SHAME TO SPEAK THESE WORDS...
...ASGARD NEEDS YOUR HELP.
AH. SO THE GOLDEN BOY HAS FINALLY PICKED A FIGHT HE CAN'T FINISH?
THEN THOR SHOULD CURRY MY FAVOR IN PERSON--
ALAS. THOR HAS BEEN BANISHED. EXILED FOREVER FROM ASGARD.
WHAT DID HE DO TO DESERVE SUCH PUNISHMENT?
HE...HE KILLED HIS GRANDFATHER IN BATTLE.
THAT'S ALL?
AH, YOU NORSEMEN, GETTING WORKED UP OVER NOTHING.
WHY, THE HEADS OF OUR PANTHEON ARE ALMOST ALWAYS SLAIN BY THEIR SONS.
HARDEY-HAR.
YOU SHOULD NOT TEASE THE BOY, HERCULES.
YOU'RE RIGHT. I SHOULD WHIP HIM. HE'S FAR TOO BOISTEROUS FOR HIS OWN GOOD. NOW WHERE ARE YOU TAKING US--
SEEMS TO ME HE HAS THE PERFECT SPIRIT FOR A GOD OF GODS.
HE NEEDS NO DISCIPLINING...

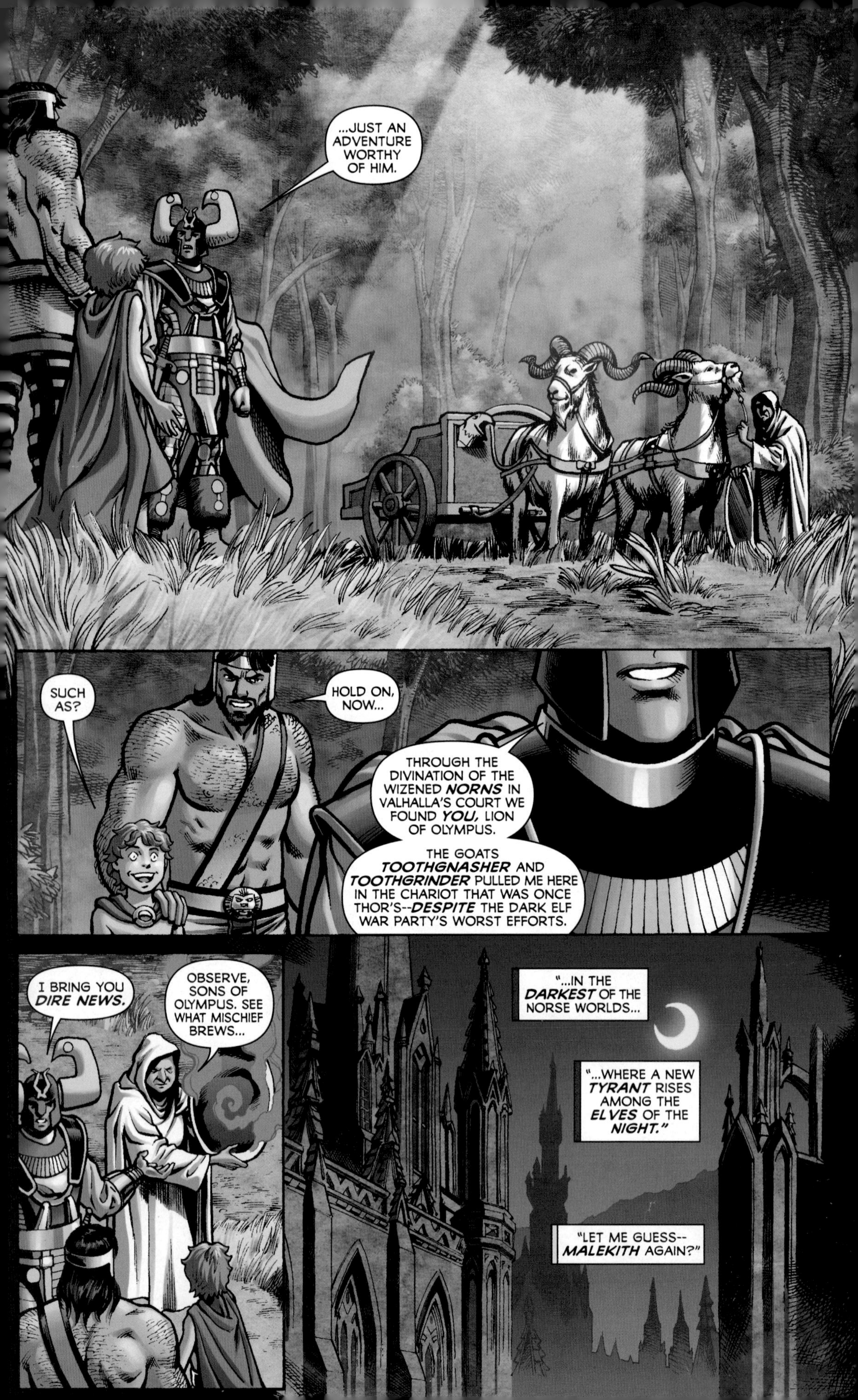
...JUST AN ADVENTURE WORTHY OF HIM.
SUCH AS?
HOLD ON, NOW...
THROUGH THE DIVINATION OF THE WIZENED NORNS IN VALHALLA'S COURT WE FOUND YOU, LION OF OLYMPUS.
THE GOATS TOOTHGNASHER AND TOOTHGRINDER PULLED ME HERE IN THE CHARIOT THAT WAS ONCE THOR'S--DESPITE THE DARK ELF WAR PARTY'S WORST EFFORTS.
I BRING YOU DIRE NEWS.
OBSERVE, SONS OF OLYMPUS. SEE WHAT MISCHIEF BREWS...
"...IN THE DARKEST OF THE NORSE WORLDS...
"...WHERE A NEW TYRANT RISES AMONG THE ELVES OF THE NIGHT."
"LET ME GUESS-- MALEKITH AGAIN?"

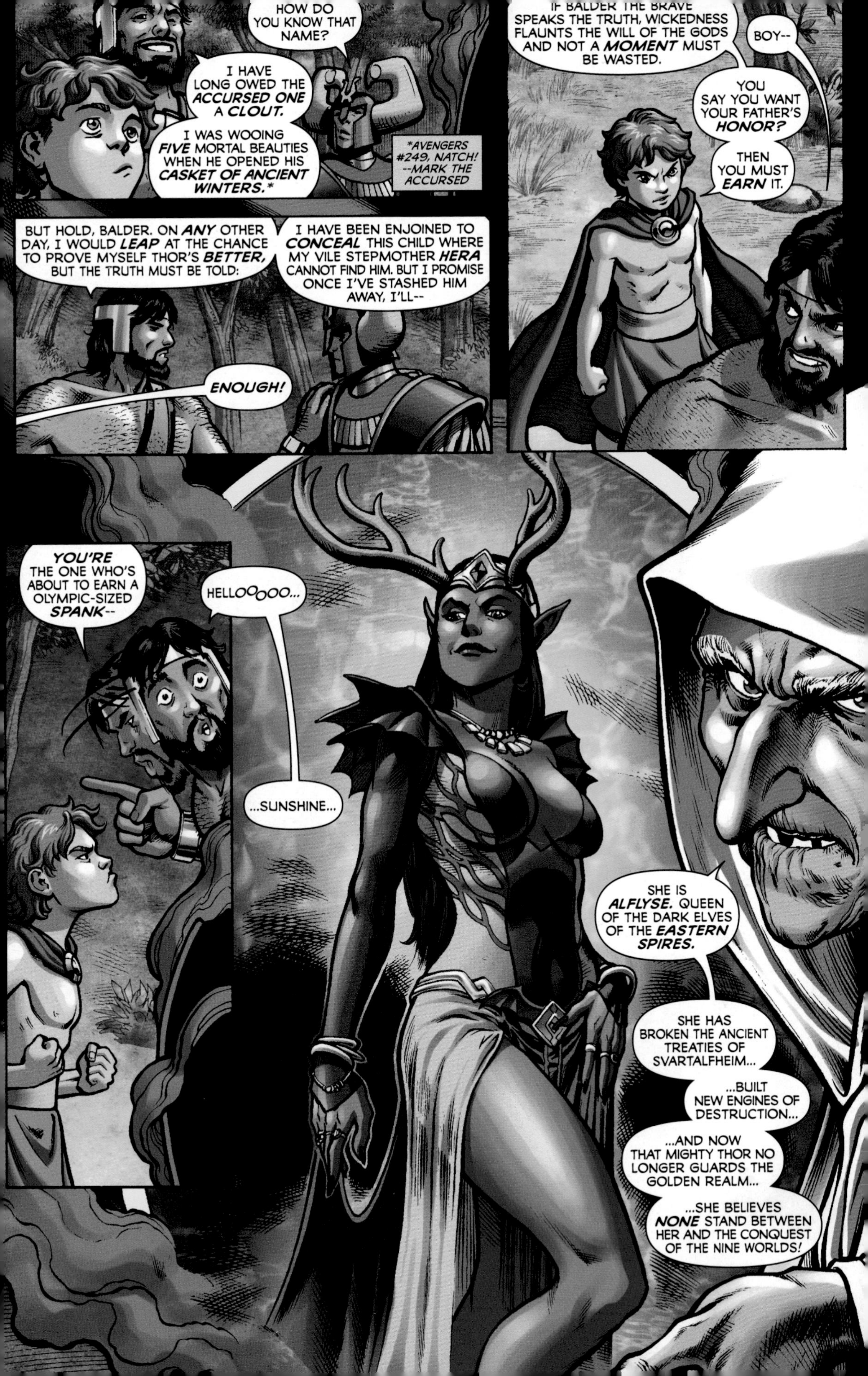

HOW DO YOU KNOW THAT NAME?
I HAVE LONG OWED THE ACCURSED ONE A CLOUT.
I WAS WOOING FIVE MORTAL BEAUTIES WHEN HE OPENED HIS CASKET OF ANCIENT WINTERS.*
*AVENGERS #249, NATCH! --MARK THE ACCURSED
IF BALDER THE BRAVE SPEAKS THE TRUTH, WICKEDNESS FLAUNTS THE WILL OF THE GODS AND NOT A MOMENT MUST BE WASTED.
BOY--
YOU SAY YOU WANT YOUR FATHER'S HONOR?
THEN YOU MUST EARN IT.
BUT HOLD, BALDER. ON ANY OTHER DAY, I WOULD LEAP AT THE CHANCE TO PROVE MYSELF THOR'S BETTER, BUT THE TRUTH MUST BE TOLD:
I HAVE BEEN ENJOINED TO CONCEAL THIS CHILD WHERE MY VILE STEPMOTHER HERA CANNOT FIND HIM. BUT I PROMISE ONCE I'VE STASHED HIM AWAY, I'LL--
ENOUGH!
YOU'RE THE ONE WHO'S ABOUT TO EARN A OLYMPIC-SIZED SPANK--
HELLOOOOO...
...SUNSHINE...
SHE IS ALFLYSE. QUEEN OF THE DARK ELVES OF THE EASTERN SPIRES.
SHE HAS BROKEN THE ANCIENT TREATIES OF SVARTALFHEIM...
...BUILT NEW ENGINES OF DESTRUCTION...
...AND NOW THAT MIGHTY THOR NO LONGER GUARDS THE GOLDEN REALM...
...SHE BELIEVES NONE STAND BETWEEN HER AND THE CONQUEST OF THE NINE WORLDS!

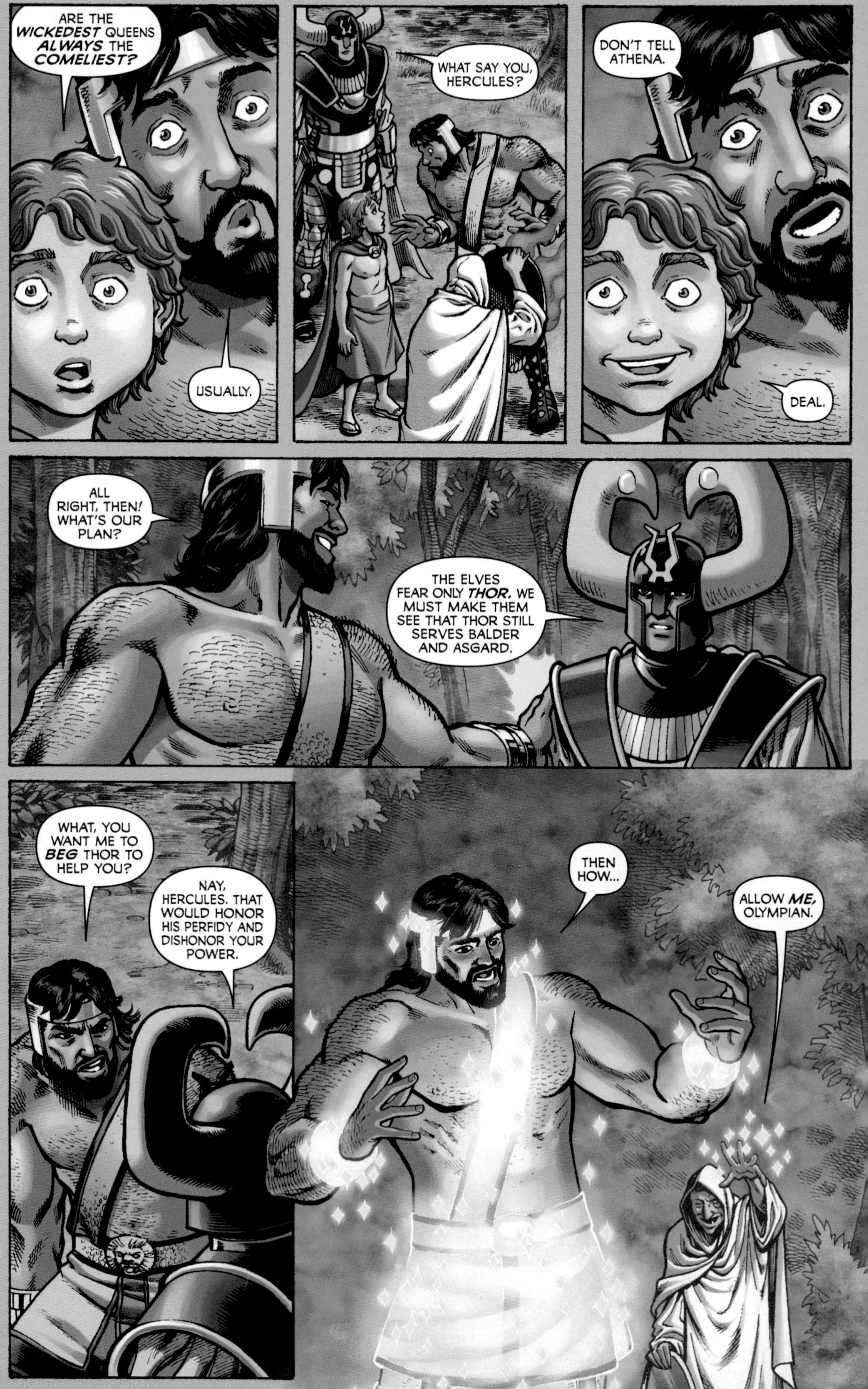

ARE THE ***WICKEDEST*** QUEENS ***ALWAYS*** THE ***COMELIEST?***
USUALLY.
WHAT SAY YOU, HERCULES?
DON'T TELL ATHENA.
DEAL.
ALL RIGHT, THEN! WHAT'S OUR PLAN?
THE ELVES FEAR ONLY ***THOR.*** WE MUST MAKE THEM SEE THAT THOR STILL SERVES BALDER AND ASGARD.
WHAT, YOU WANT ME TO ***BEG*** THOR TO HELP YOU?
NAY, HERCULES. THAT WOULD HONOR HIS PERFIDY AND DISHONOR YOUR POWER.
THEN HOW...
ALLOW ***ME,*** OLYMPIAN.

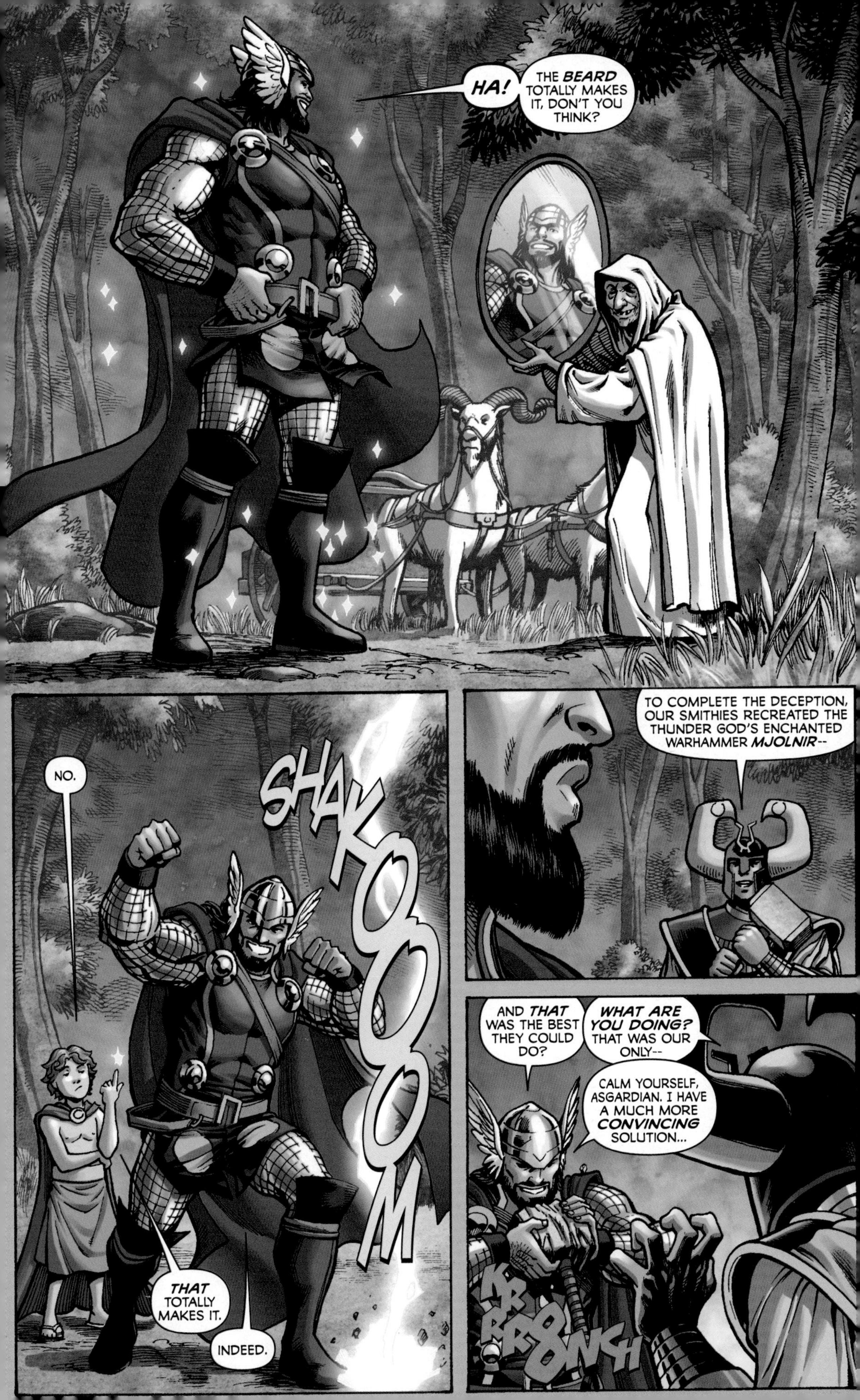
HA!
THE BEARD TOTALLY MAKES IT, DON'T YOU THINK?
NO.
SHAKOOOOOM
THAT TOTALLY MAKES IT.
INDEED.
TO COMPLETE THE DECEPTION, OUR SMITHIES RECREATED THE THUNDER GOD'S ENCHANTED WARHAMMER MJOLNIR--
AND THAT WAS THE BEST THEY COULD DO?
WHAT ARE YOU DOING? THAT WAS OUR ONLY--
CALM YOURSELF, ASGARDIAN. I HAVE A MUCH MORE CONVINCING SOLUTION...
KRRRRONCH

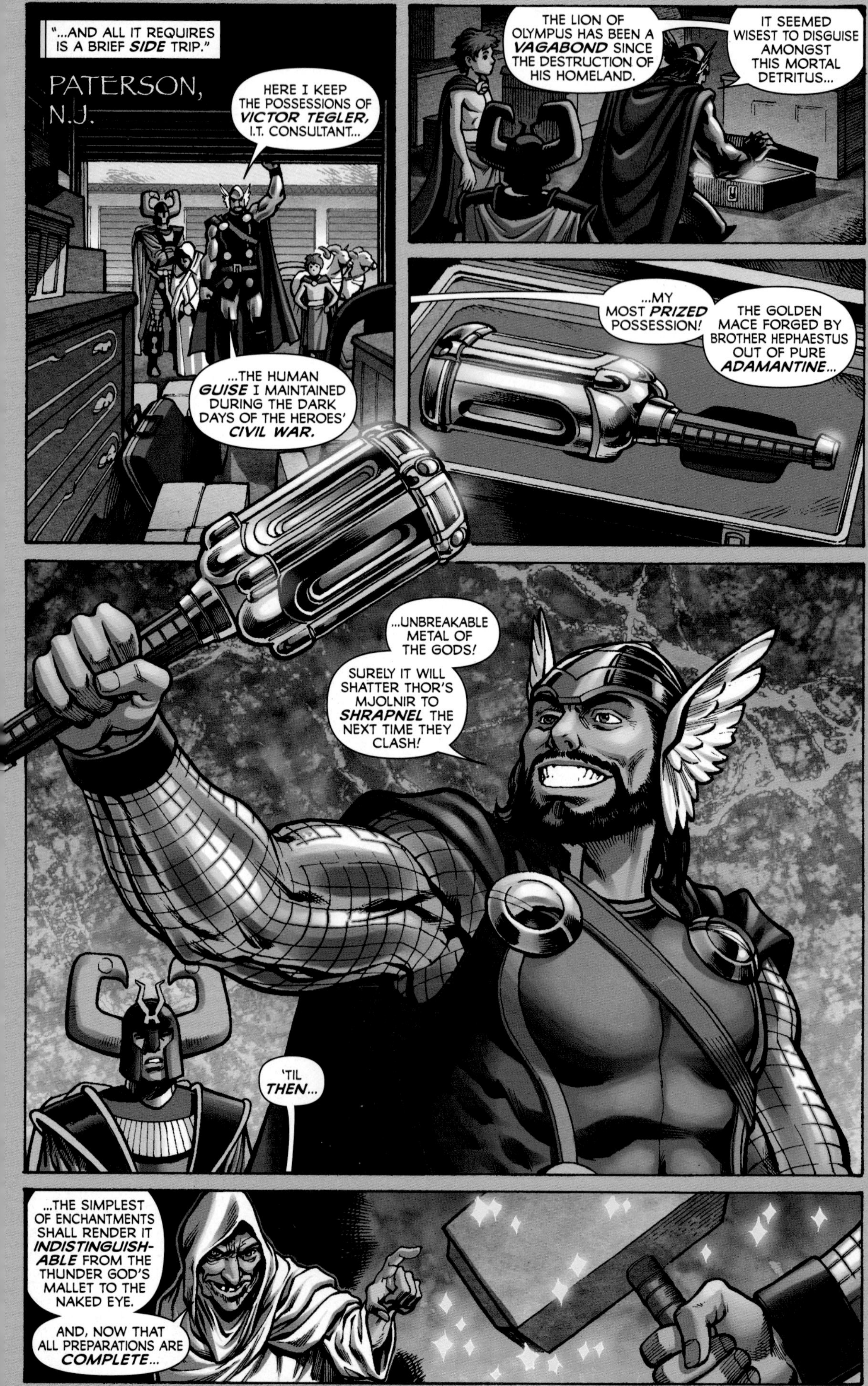
"...AND ALL IT REQUIRES IS A BRIEF SIDE TRIP."
PATERSON, N.J.
HERE I KEEP THE POSSESSIONS OF VICTOR TEGLER, I.T. CONSULTANT...
...THE HUMAN GUISE I MAINTAINED DURING THE DARK DAYS OF THE HEROES' CIVIL WAR.
THE LION OF OLYMPUS HAS BEEN A VAGABOND SINCE THE DESTRUCTION OF HIS HOMELAND.
IT SEEMED WISEST TO DISGUISE AMONGST THIS MORTAL DETRITUS...
...MY MOST PRIZED POSSESSION!
THE GOLDEN MACE FORGED BY BROTHER HEPHAESTUS OUT OF PURE ADAMANTINE...
...UNBREAKABLE METAL OF THE GODS!
SURELY IT WILL SHATTER THOR'S MJOLNIR TO SHRAPNEL THE NEXT TIME THEY CLASH!
'TIL THEN...
...THE SIMPLEST OF ENCHANTMENTS SHALL RENDER IT INDISTINGUISH-ABLE FROM THE THUNDER GOD'S MALLET TO THE NAKED EYE.
AND, NOW THAT ALL PREPARATIONS ARE COMPLETE...

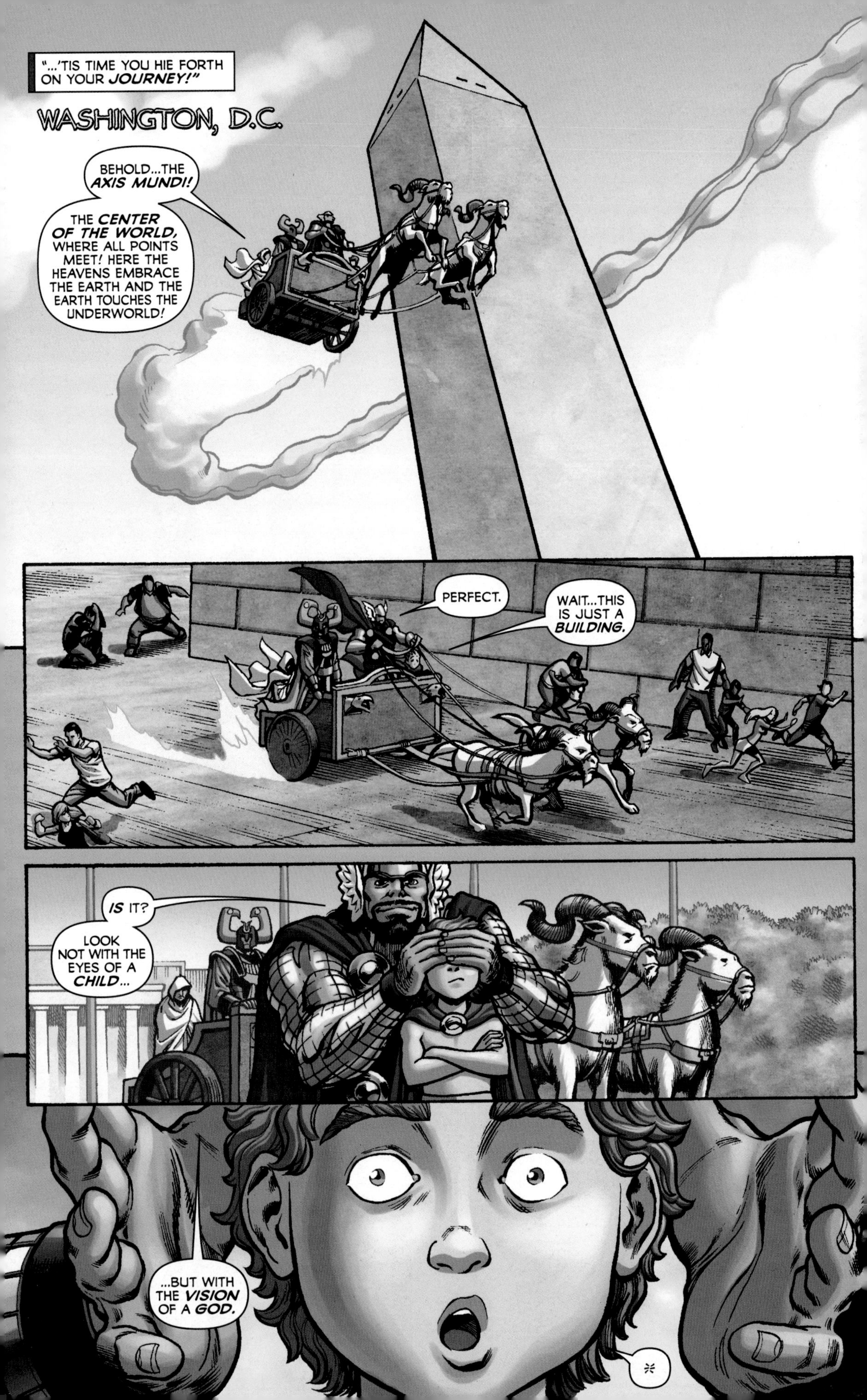

"...'TIS TIME YOU HIE FORTH ON YOUR JOURNEY!"
WASHINGTON, D.C.
BEHOLD...THE AXIS MUNDI!
THE CENTER OF THE WORLD, WHERE ALL POINTS MEET! HERE THE HEAVENS EMBRACE THE EARTH AND THE EARTH TOUCHES THE UNDERWORLD!
PERFECT.
WAIT...THIS IS JUST A BUILDING.
IS IT?
LOOK NOT WITH THE EYES OF A CHILD...
...BUT WITH THE VISION OF A GOD.

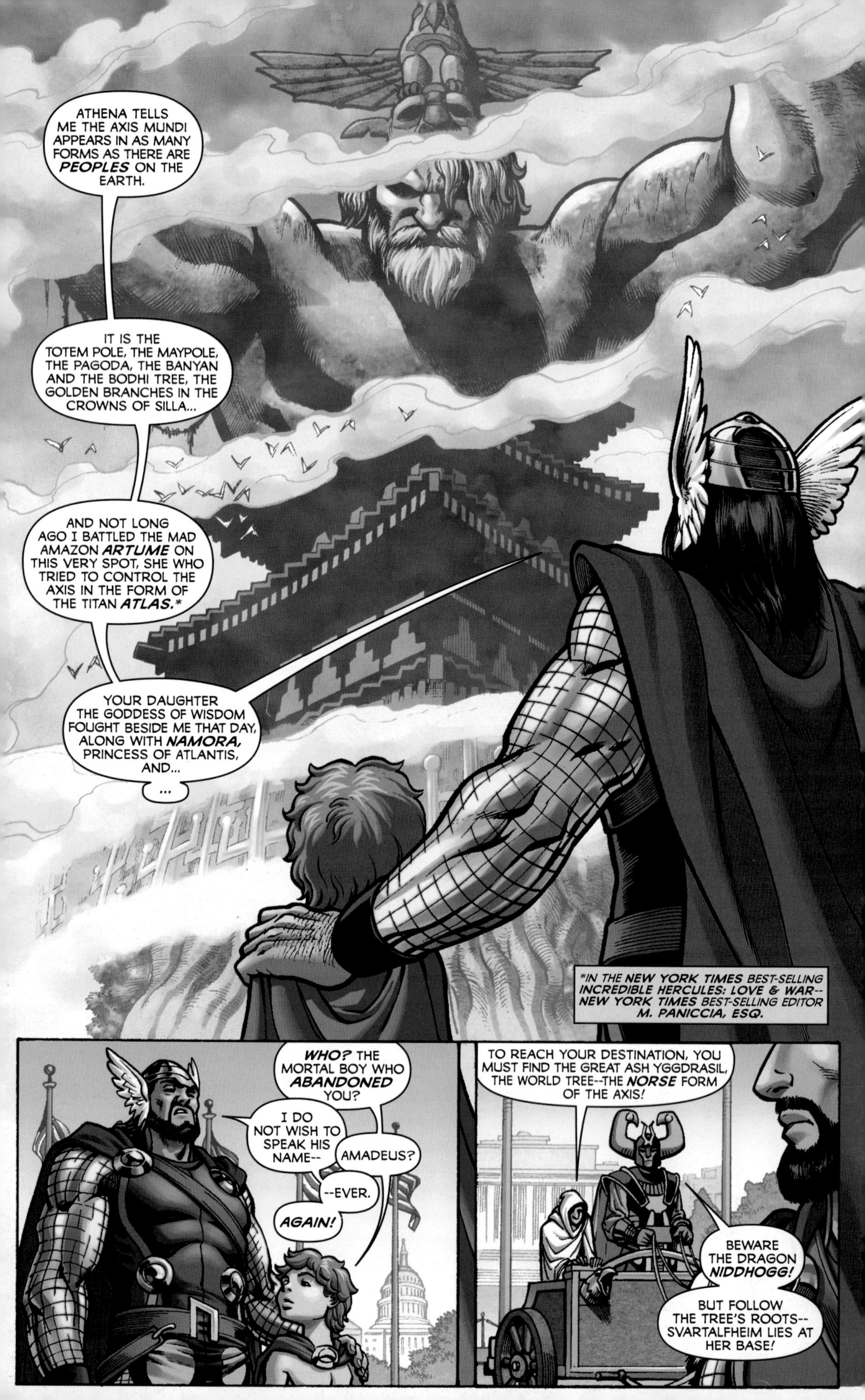
ATHENA TELLS ME THE AXIS MUNDI APPEARS IN AS MANY FORMS AS THERE ARE PEOPLES ON THE EARTH.
IT IS THE TOTEM POLE, THE MAYPOLE, THE PAGODA, THE BANYAN AND THE BODHI TREE, THE GOLDEN BRANCHES IN THE CROWNS OF SILLA...
AND NOT LONG AGO I BATTLED THE MAD AMAZON ARTUME ON THIS VERY SPOT, SHE WHO TRIED TO CONTROL THE AXIS IN THE FORM OF THE TITAN ATLAS.*
YOUR DAUGHTER THE GODDESS OF WISDOM FOUGHT BESIDE ME THAT DAY, ALONG WITH NAMORA, PRINCESS OF ATLANTIS, AND...
...
*IN THE NEW YORK TIMES BEST-SELLING INCREDIBLE HERCULES: LOVE & WAR-- NEW YORK TIMES BEST-SELLING EDITOR M. PANICCIA, ESQ.
WHO? THE MORTAL BOY WHO ABANDONED YOU?
I DO NOT WISH TO SPEAK HIS NAME--
AMADEUS?
--EVER.
AGAIN!
TO REACH YOUR DESTINATION, YOU MUST FIND THE GREAT ASH YGGDRASIL, THE WORLD TREE--THE NORSE FORM OF THE AXIS!
BEWARE THE DRAGON NIDDHOGG!
BUT FOLLOW THE TREE'S ROOTS-- SVARTALFHEIM LIES AT HER BASE!

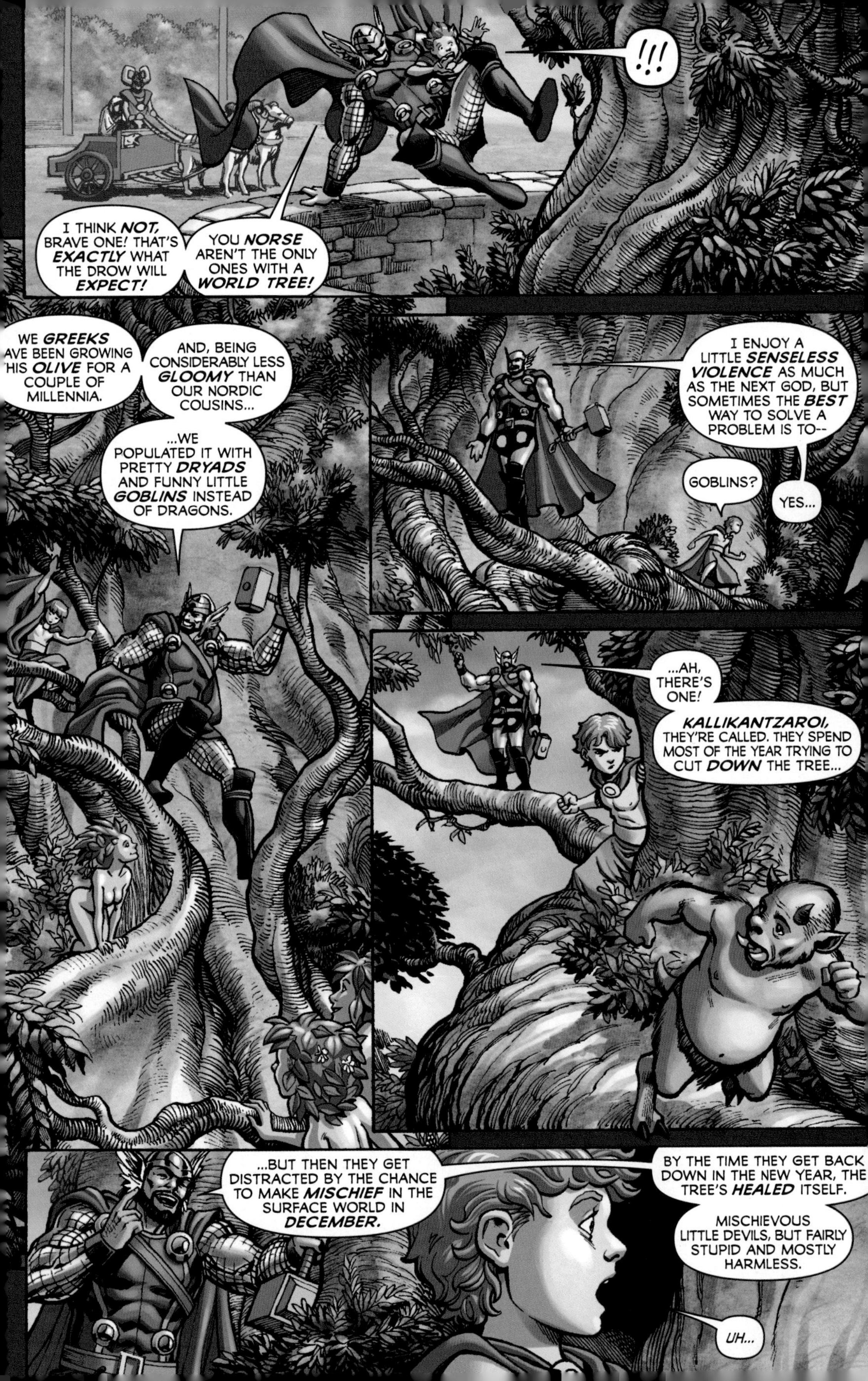
!!!
I THINK NOT, BRAVE ONE! THAT'S EXACTLY WHAT THE DROW WILL EXPECT!
YOU NORSE AREN'T THE ONLY ONES WITH A WORLD TREE!
WE GREEKS HAVE BEEN GROWING THIS OLIVE FOR A COUPLE OF MILLENNIA.
AND, BEING CONSIDERABLY LESS GLOOMY THAN OUR NORDIC COUSINS...
...WE POPULATED IT WITH PRETTY DRYADS AND FUNNY LITTLE GOBLINS INSTEAD OF DRAGONS.
I ENJOY A LITTLE SENSELESS VIOLENCE AS MUCH AS THE NEXT GOD, BUT SOMETIMES THE BEST WAY TO SOLVE A PROBLEM IS TO--
GOBLINS?
YES...
...AH, THERE'S ONE!
KALLIKANTZAROI, THEY'RE CALLED. THEY SPEND MOST OF THE YEAR TRYING TO CUT DOWN THE TREE...
...BUT THEN THEY GET DISTRACTED BY THE CHANCE TO MAKE MISCHIEF IN THE SURFACE WORLD IN DECEMBER.
BY THE TIME THEY GET BACK DOWN IN THE NEW YEAR, THE TREE'S HEALED ITSELF.
MISCHIEVOUS LITTLE DEVILS, BUT FAIRLY STUPID AND MOSTLY HARMLESS.
UH...

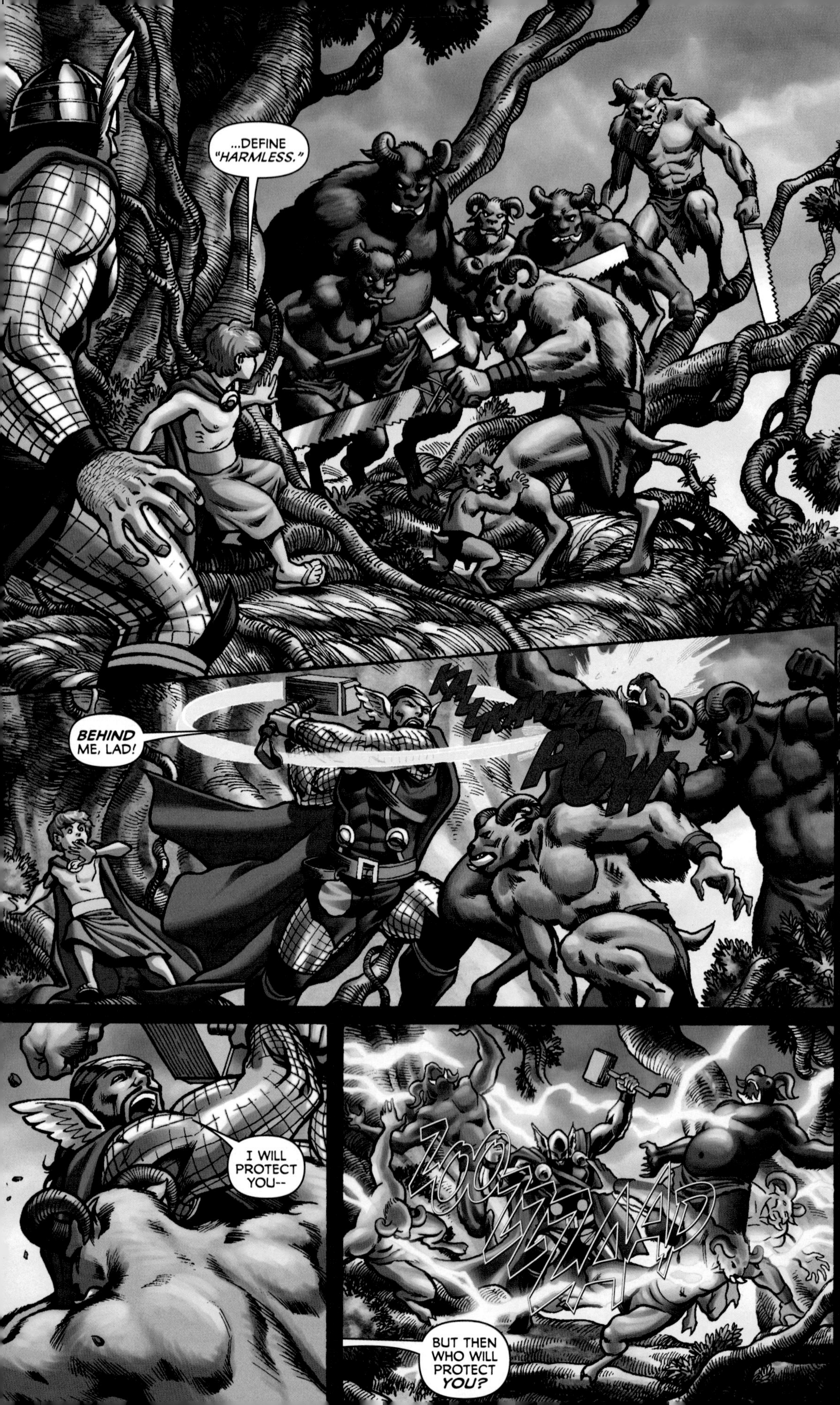
...DEFINE "*HARMLESS.*"
BEHIND ME, LAD!
POW
I WILL PROTECT YOU--
BUT THEN WHO WILL PROTECT *YOU?*

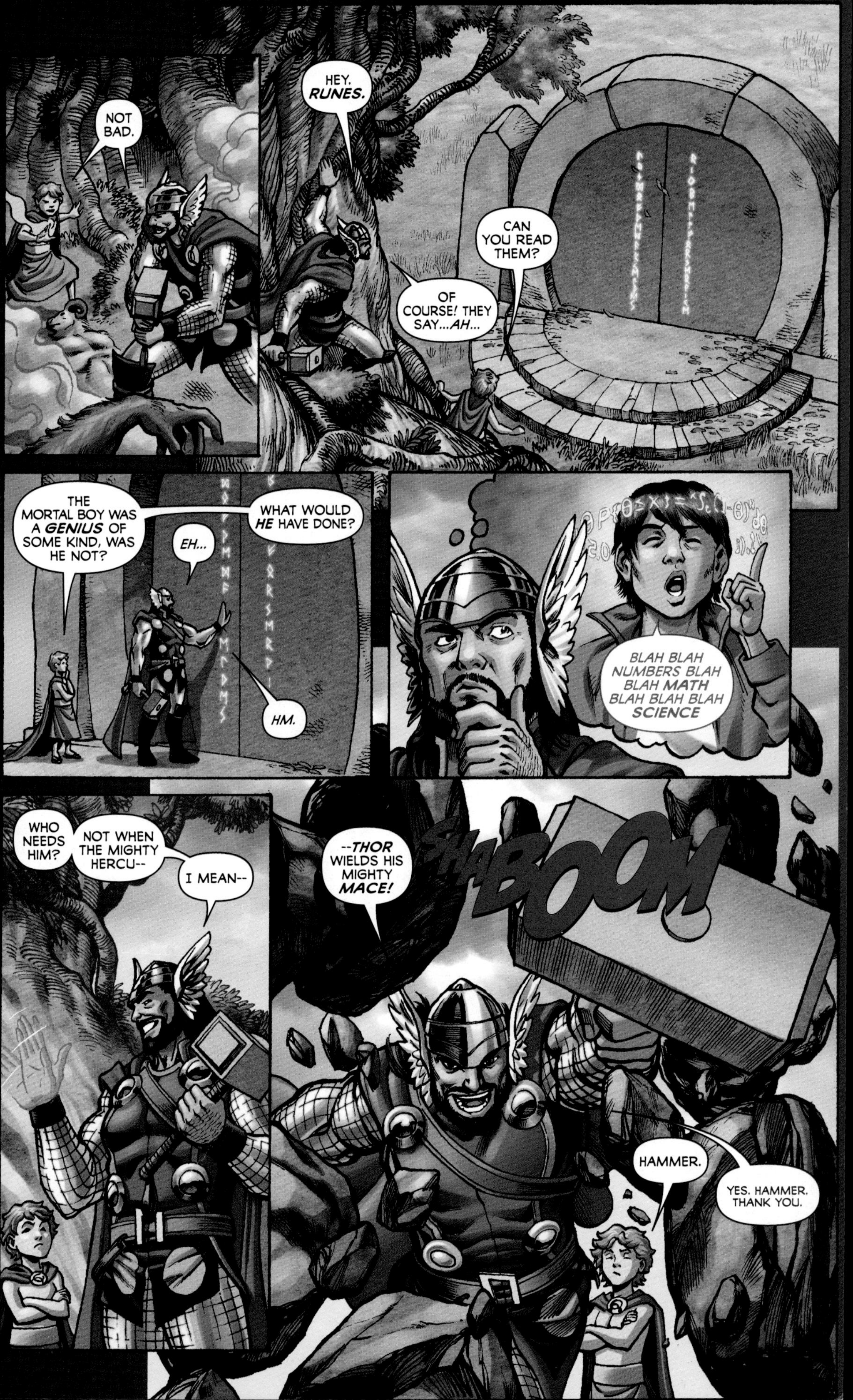
NOT BAD.
HEY. RUNES.
CAN YOU READ THEM?
OF COURSE! THEY SAY...AH...
THE MORTAL BOY WAS A GENIUS OF SOME KIND, WAS HE NOT?
WHAT WOULD HE HAVE DONE?
EH...
HM.
BLAH BLAH NUMBERS BLAH BLAH MATH BLAH BLAH BLAH SCIENCE
WHO NEEDS HIM?
NOT WHEN THE MIGHTY HERCU--
I MEAN--
--THOR WIELDS HIS MIGHTY MACE!
SHABOOM
HAMMER.
YES. HAMMER. THANK YOU.

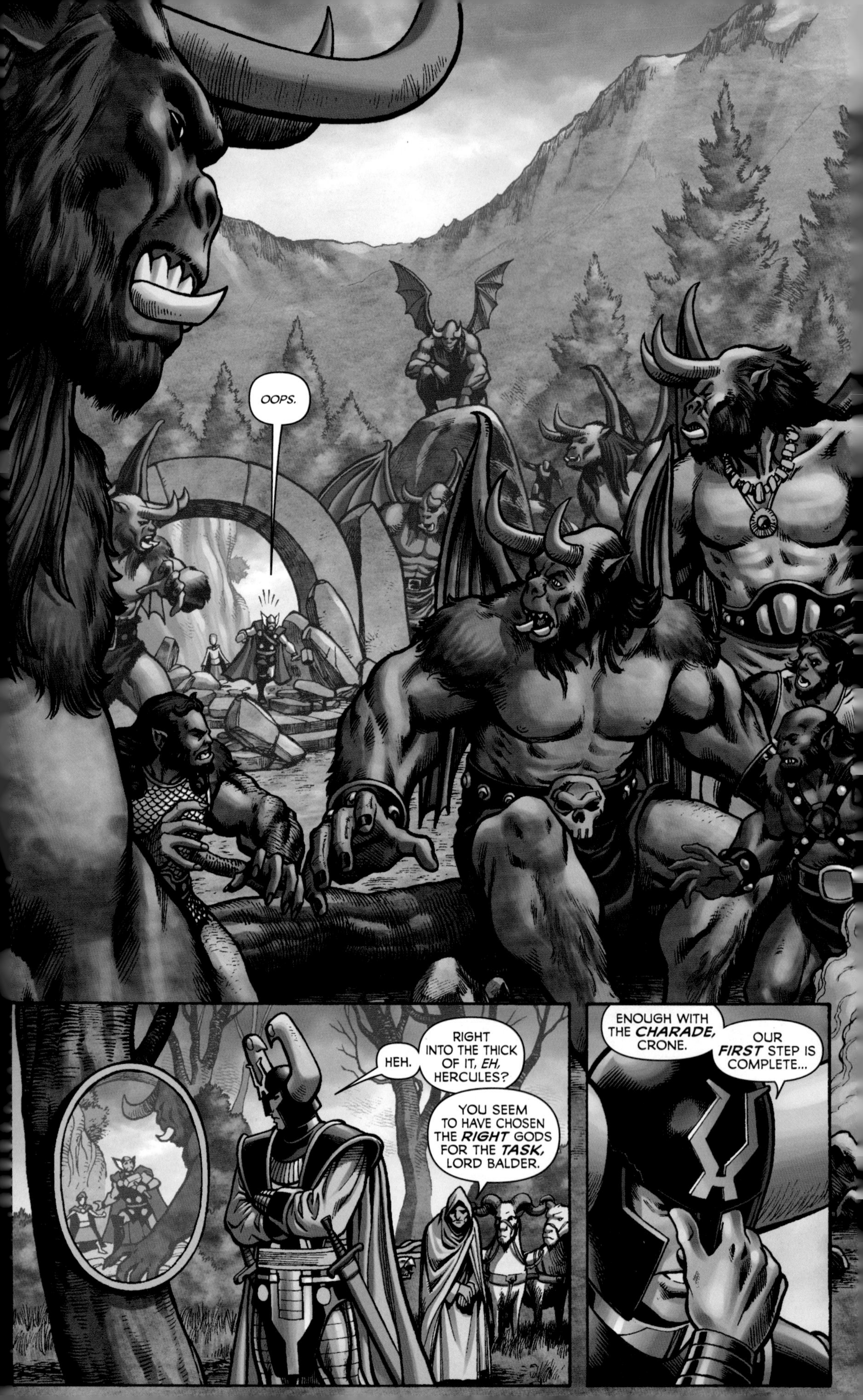

OOPS.
HEH.
RIGHT INTO THE THICK OF IT, *EH,* HERCULES?
YOU SEEM TO HAVE CHOSEN THE ***RIGHT*** GODS FOR THE ***TASK,*** LORD BALDER.
ENOUGH WITH THE ***CHARADE,*** CRONE.
OUR ***FIRST*** STEP IS COMPLETE...

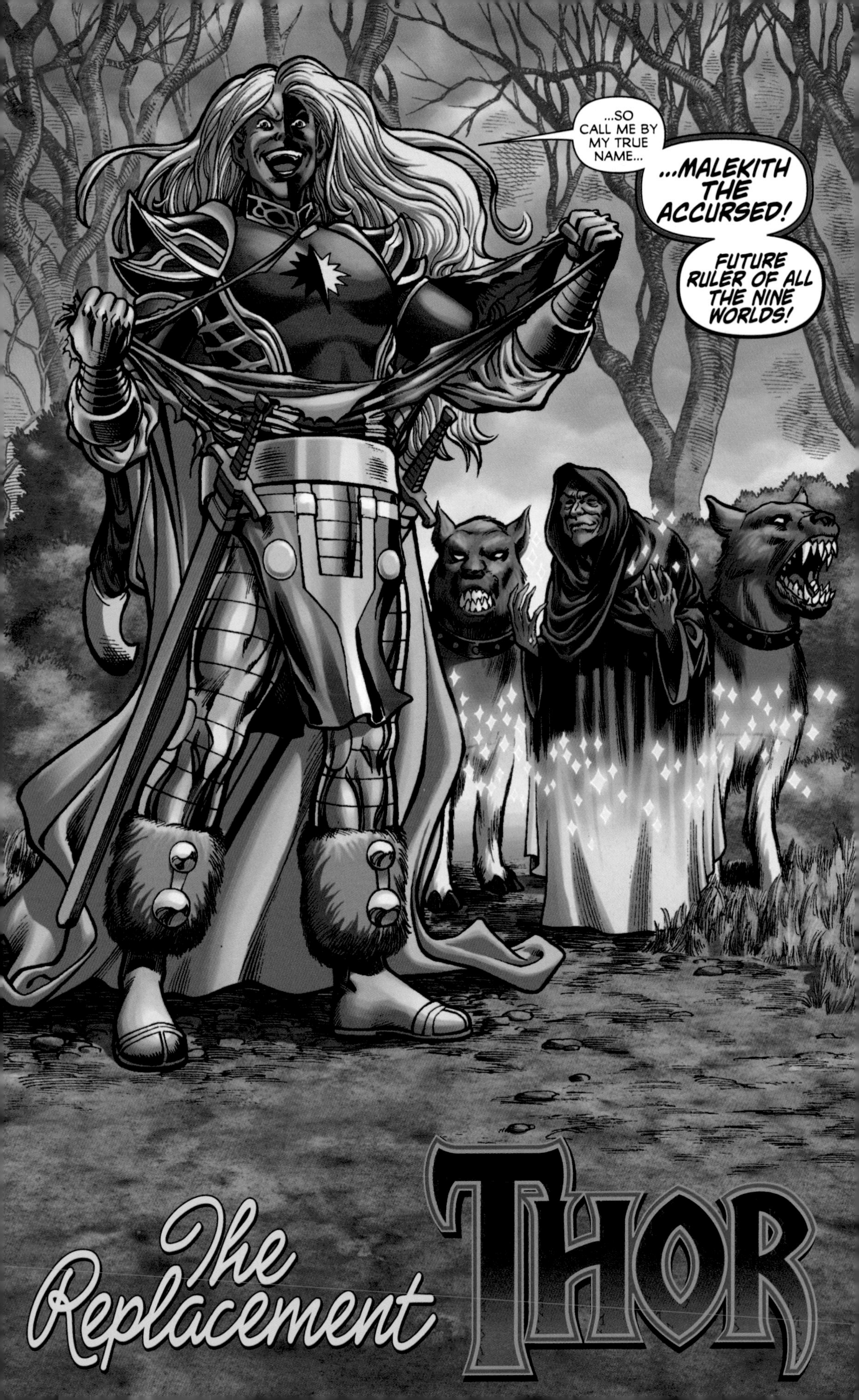
...SO CALL ME BY MY TRUE NAME...
...MALEKITH THE ACCURSED!
FUTURE RULER OF ALL THE NINE WORLDS!
The Replacement THOR

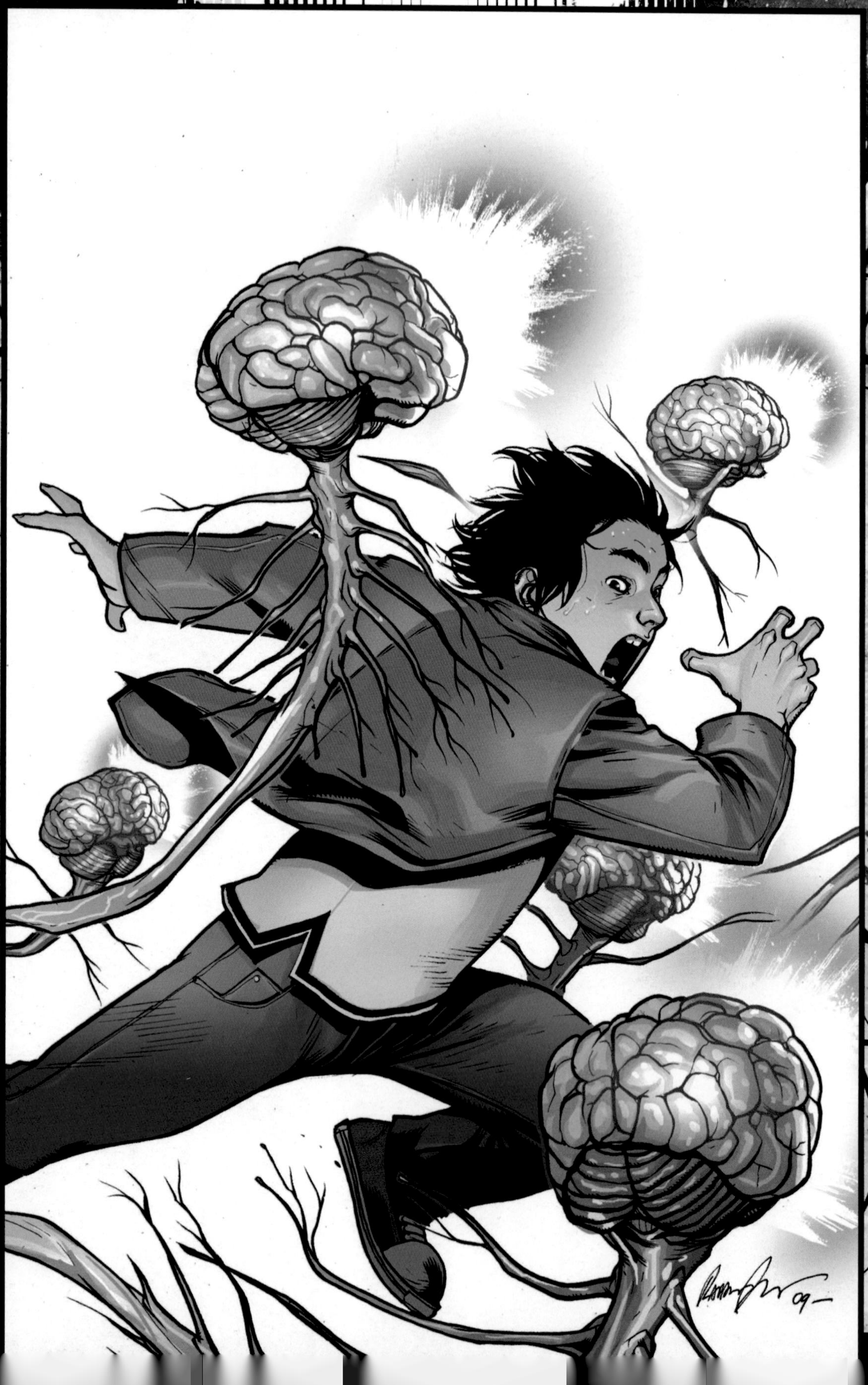

EXCELLO SOAP PROUDLY PRESENTS

BRAIN FIGHT 2009

1. The helicarrier Hercules and Amadeus Cho stole was originally built to do battle with whom?

2. One of the alien gods slain by the Skrulls was Hadith the Omen-Maker, worshipped by the Queega of the Quolan system, which first appeared where?

3. The winner of the "Name-Cho's-Pup" competition hailed from what country?

4. "Artume" is the Etruscan name for what Roman goddess?

5. Young Heracles killed his music teacher with what?

6. In the battle between the Dark Avengers and the Olympus Group, who did Noh-Varr fight to a standstill?

7. Who shot craps in the Stygian Casino?

8. Hercules and his dead counterpart fought inside a painting by what 15th century Dutch artist?

EMAIL YOUR ANSWERS to BRAINFIGHT@EXCELLOSOAP.COM to become eligible for THESE FABULOUS PRIZES:

THIRD PRIZE: Be named the SEVENTH SMARTEST HUMAN IN THE WORLD!

SECOND PRIZE: Have your house blown up so you throw in with the demi-god HERCULES, then abandon him when you learn that said demi-god's big sister, ATHENA, goddess of wisdom, might have been involved in blowing up the house and that the little sister you thought died in the explosion turns out to be alive, so you try and find her and solve your parents' murder at the same time!

FIRST PRIZE: All of the above, just like AMADEUS CHO!

THIS IS NOT A REAL CONTEST. OBVIOUSLY, YOU ARE NOT THE 7TH SMARTEST PERSON ON EARTH.

BADUMP

UNHH--?

?

SOMEBODY LEFT A **BOOK** BEHIND.

DON'T REMEMBER ANYONE SITTING **NEXT** TO ME, THOUGH.

MUST'VE GOT ON **AND** OFF **AFTER** I FELL ASLEEP...

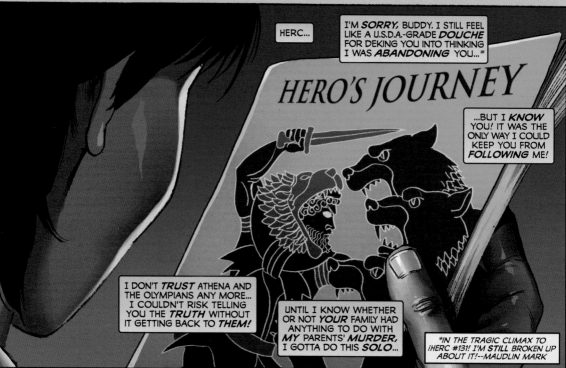

HERC...

I'M **SORRY**, BUDDY. I STILL FEEL LIKE A U.S.D.A.-GRADE **DOUCHE** FOR DEKING YOU INTO THINKING I WAS **ABANDONING** YOU...*

HERO'S JOURNEY

...BUT I **KNOW** YOU! IT WAS THE ONLY WAY I COULD KEEP YOU FROM **FOLLOWING** ME!

I DON'T **TRUST** ATHENA AND THE OLYMPIANS ANY MORE... I COULDN'T RISK TELLING YOU THE **TRUTH** WITHOUT IT GETTING BACK TO **THEM!**

UNTIL I KNOW WHETHER OR NOT **YOUR** FAMILY HAD ANYTHING TO DO WITH **MY** PARENTS' **MURDER**, I GOTTA DO THIS **SOLO**...

*IN THE TRAGIC CLIMAX TO iHERC #13?! I'M **STILL** BROKEN UP ABOUT IT!--MAUDLIN MARK

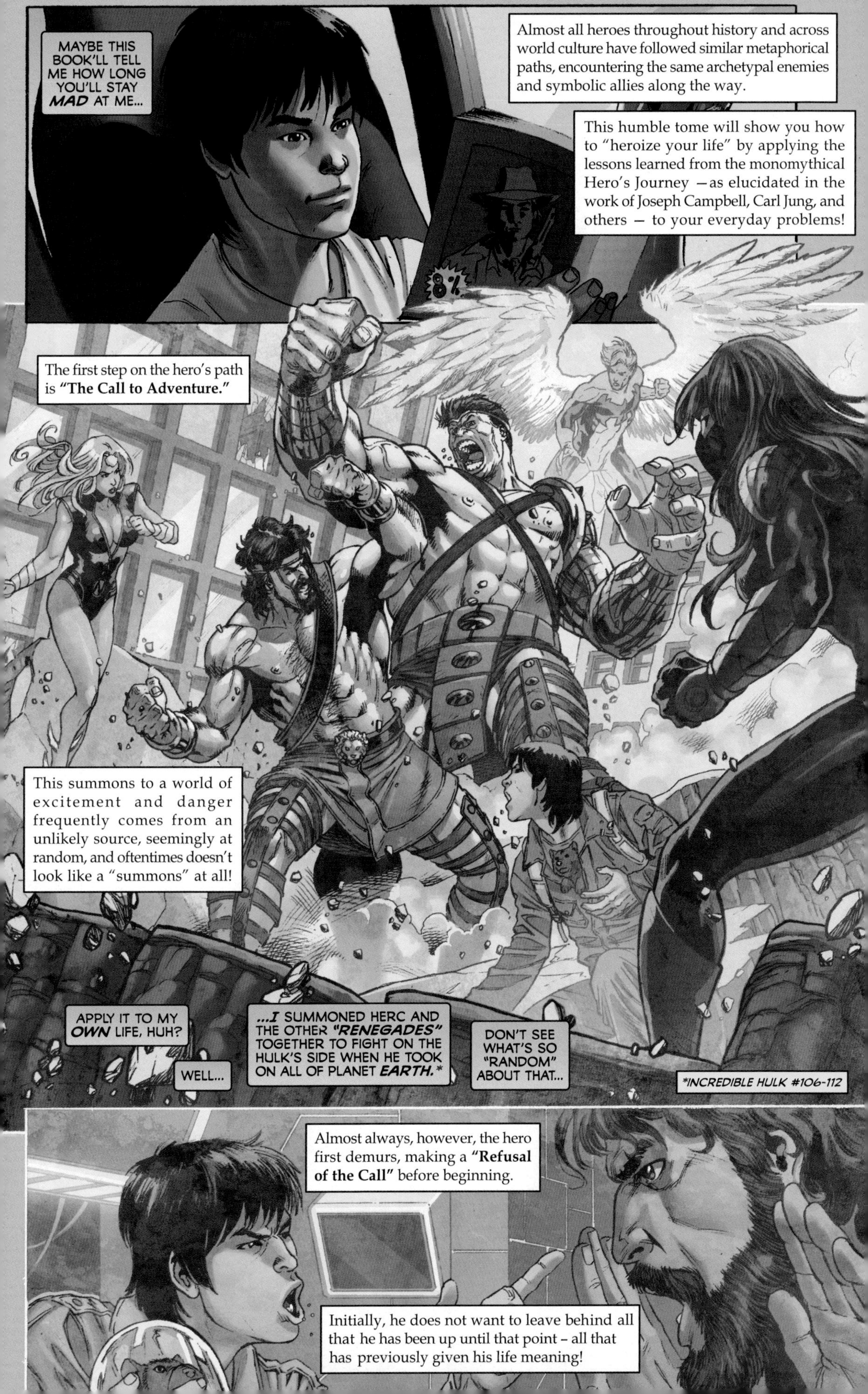
MAYBE THIS BOOK'LL TELL ME HOW LONG YOU'LL STAY *MAD* AT ME...
Almost all heroes throughout history and across world culture have followed similar metaphorical paths, encountering the same archetypal enemies and symbolic allies along the way.
This humble tome will show you how to "heroize your life" by applying the lessons learned from the monomythical Hero's Journey —as elucidated in the work of Joseph Campbell, Carl Jung, and others — to your everyday problems!
8%
The first step on the hero's path is **"The Call to Adventure."**
This summons to a world of excitement and danger frequently comes from an unlikely source, seemingly at random, and oftentimes doesn't look like a "summons" at all!
APPLY IT TO MY *OWN* LIFE, HUH?
WELL...
...*I* SUMMONED HERC AND THE OTHER *"RENEGADES"* TOGETHER TO FIGHT ON THE HULK'S SIDE WHEN HE TOOK ON ALL OF PLANET *EARTH.**
DON'T SEE WHAT'S SO "RANDOM" ABOUT THAT...
**INCREDIBLE HULK #106-112*
Almost always, however, the hero first demurs, making a **"Refusal of the Call"** before beginning.
Initially, he does not want to leave behind all that he has been up until that point – all that has previously given his life meaning!

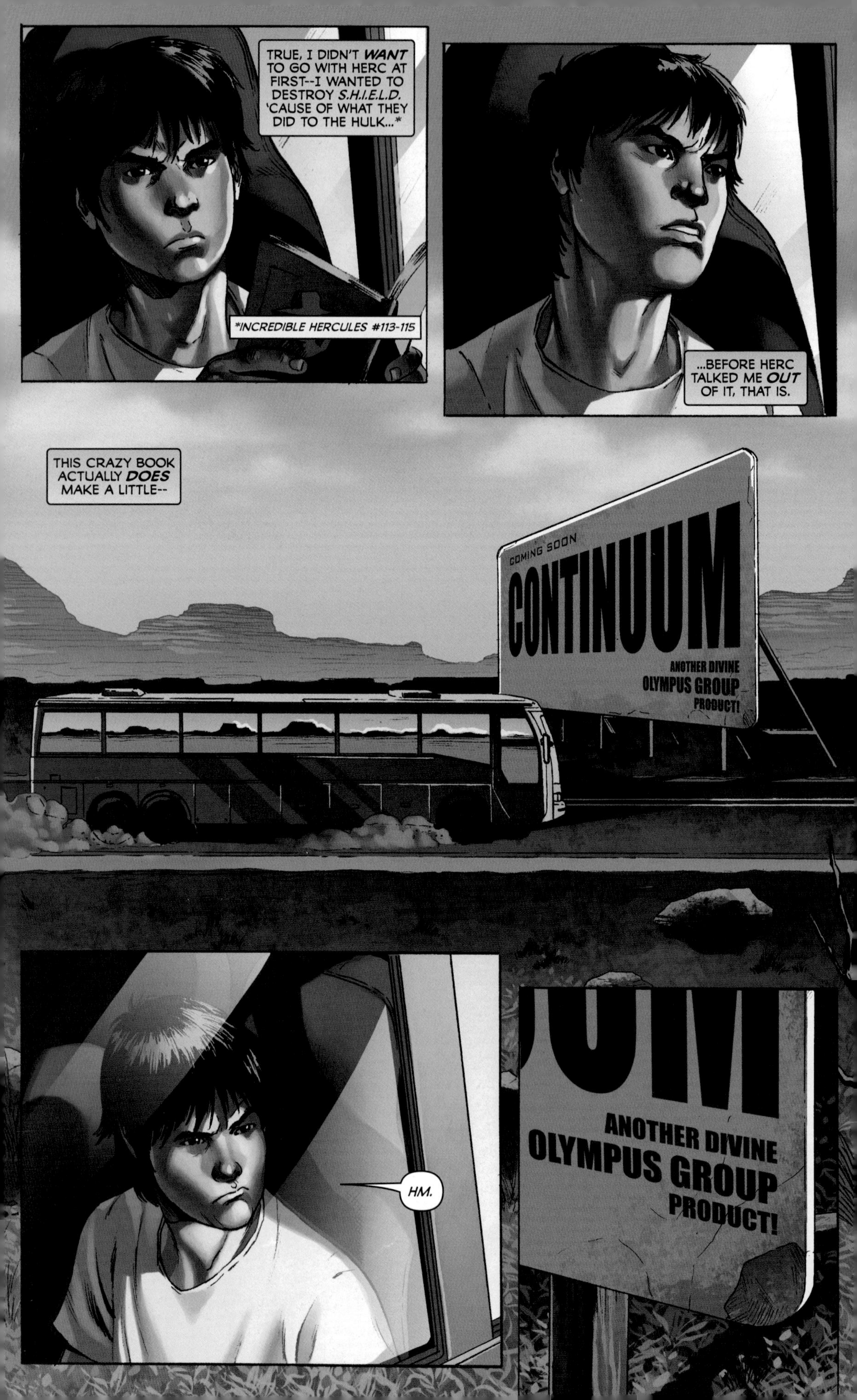
TRUE, I DIDN'T WANT TO GO WITH HERC AT FIRST--I WANTED TO DESTROY S.H.I.E.L.D. 'CAUSE OF WHAT THEY DID TO THE HULK...*
*INCREDIBLE HERCULES #113-115
...BEFORE HERC TALKED ME OUT OF IT, THAT IS.
THIS CRAZY BOOK ACTUALLY DOES MAKE A LITTLE--
COMING SOON
CONTINUUM
ANOTHER DIVINE OLYMPUS GROUP PRODUCT!
HM.
ANOTHER DIVINE OLYMPUS GROUP PRODUCT!

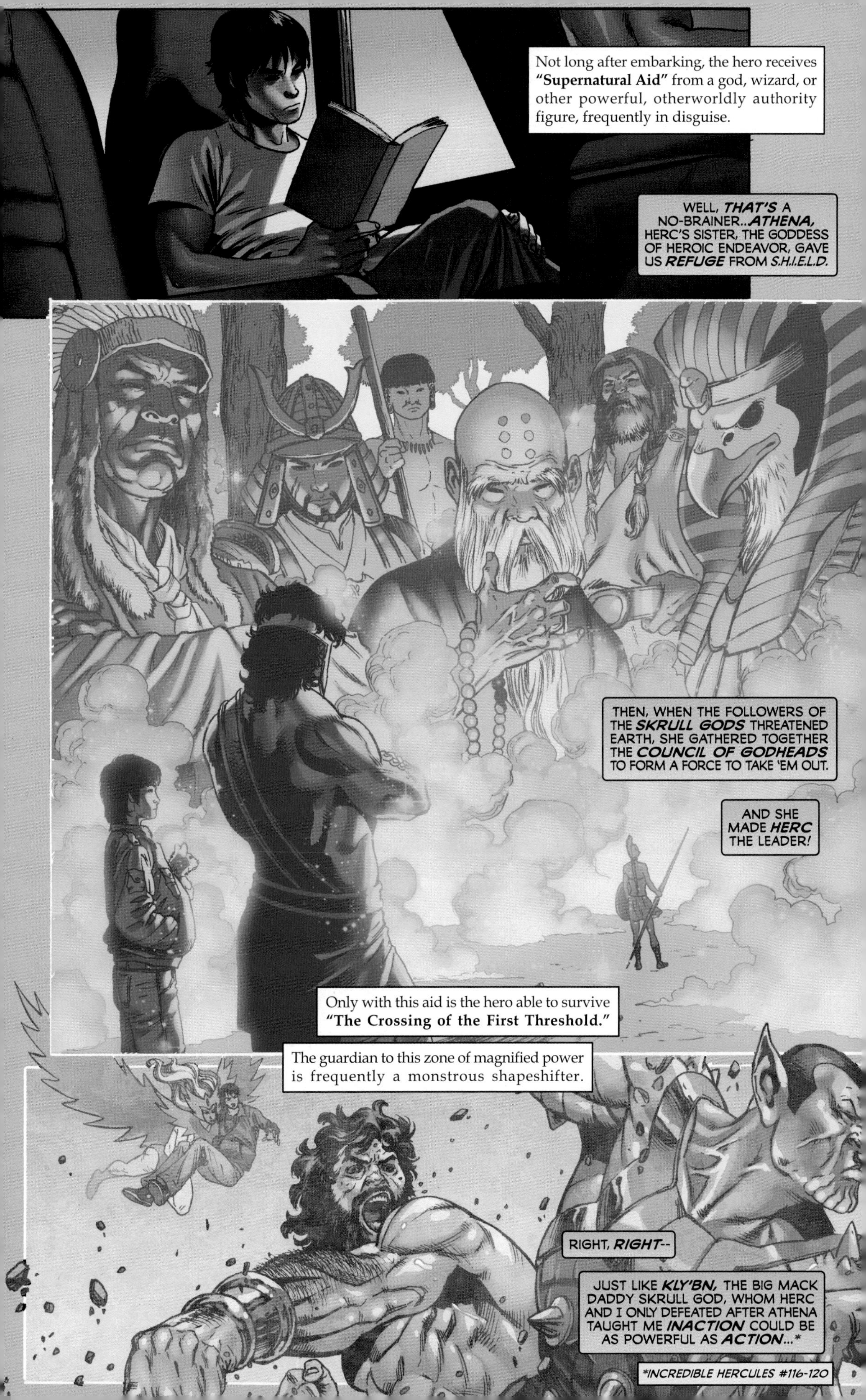
Not long after embarking, the hero receives "Supernatural Aid" from a god, wizard, or other powerful, otherworldly authority figure, frequently in disguise.
WELL, THAT'S A NO-BRAINER...ATHENA, HERC'S SISTER, THE GODDESS OF HEROIC ENDEAVOR, GAVE US REFUGE FROM S.H.I.E.L.D.
THEN, WHEN THE FOLLOWERS OF THE SKRULL GODS THREATENED EARTH, SHE GATHERED TOGETHER THE COUNCIL OF GODHEADS TO FORM A FORCE TO TAKE 'EM OUT.
AND SHE MADE HERC THE LEADER!
Only with this aid is the hero able to survive "The Crossing of the First Threshold."
The guardian to this zone of magnified power is frequently a monstrous shapeshifter.
RIGHT, RIGHT--
JUST LIKE KLY'BN, THE BIG MACK DADDY SKRULL GOD, WHOM HERC AND I ONLY DEFEATED AFTER ATHENA TAUGHT ME INACTION COULD BE AS POWERFUL AS ACTION...*
*INCREDIBLE HERCULES #116-120

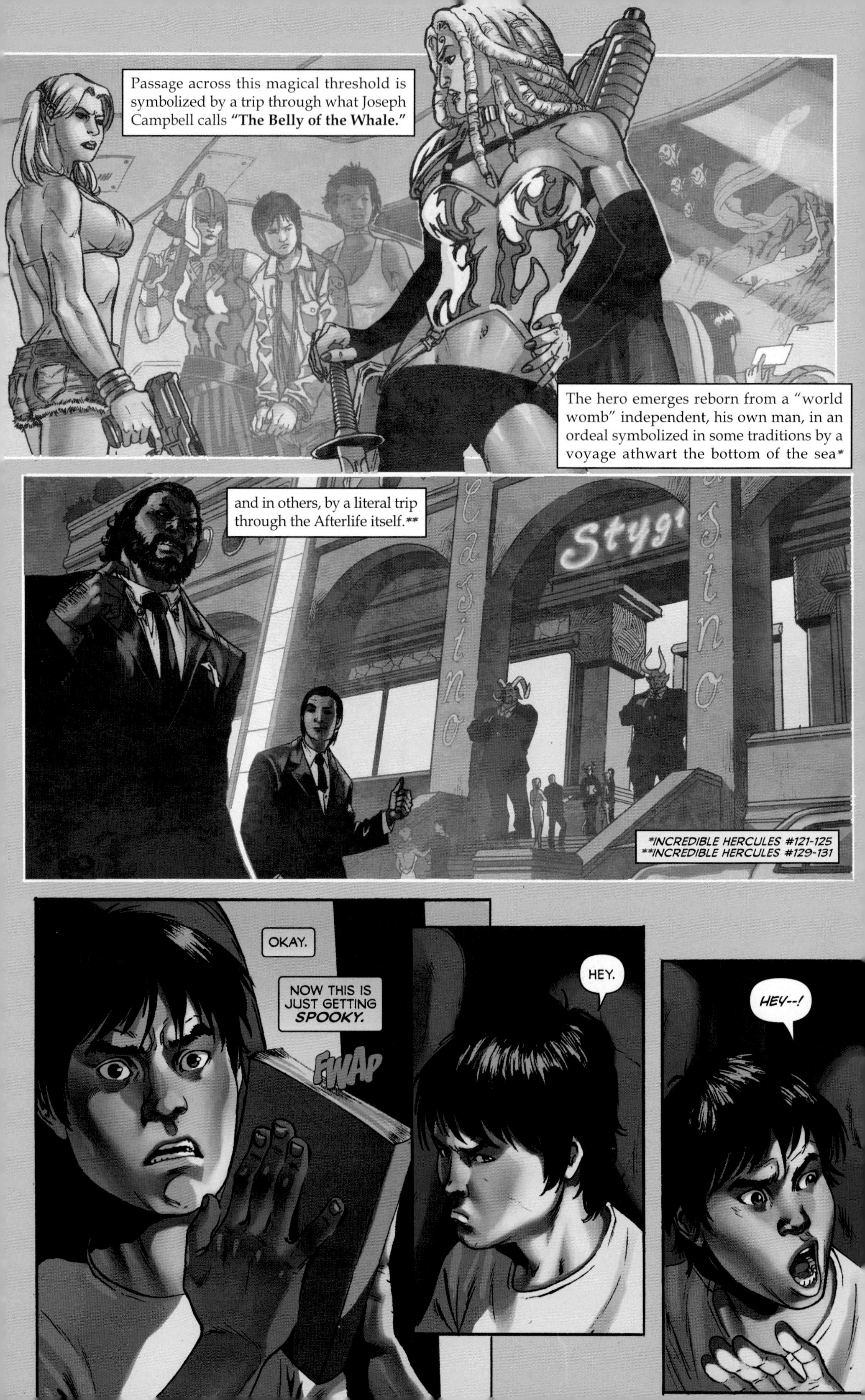
Passage across this magical threshold is symbolized by a trip through what Joseph Campbell calls **"The Belly of the Whale."**
The hero emerges reborn from a "world womb" independent, his own man, in an ordeal symbolized in some traditions by a voyage athwart the bottom of the sea*
and in others, by a literal trip through the Afterlife itself.**
Styg
Casino
Casino
*INCREDIBLE HERCULES #121-125
**INCREDIBLE HERCULES #129-131
OKAY.
NOW THIS IS JUST GETTING *SPOOKY.*
FWAP
HEY.
HEY--!

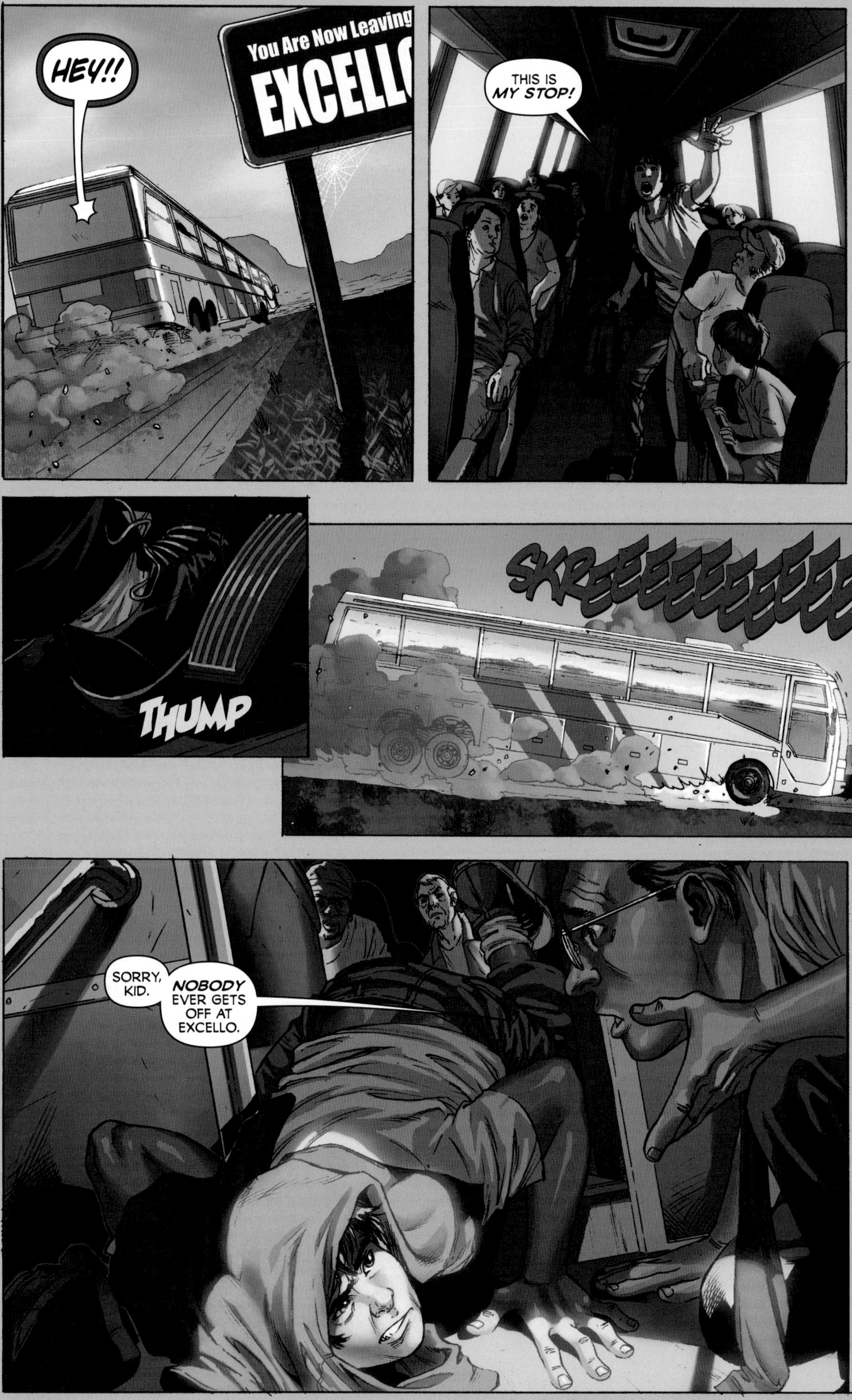
HEY!!
You Are Now Leaving
EXCELL
THIS IS MY STOP!
THUMP
SKREEEEEEEEEEE
SORRY, KID.
NOBODY EVER GETS OFF AT EXCELLO.

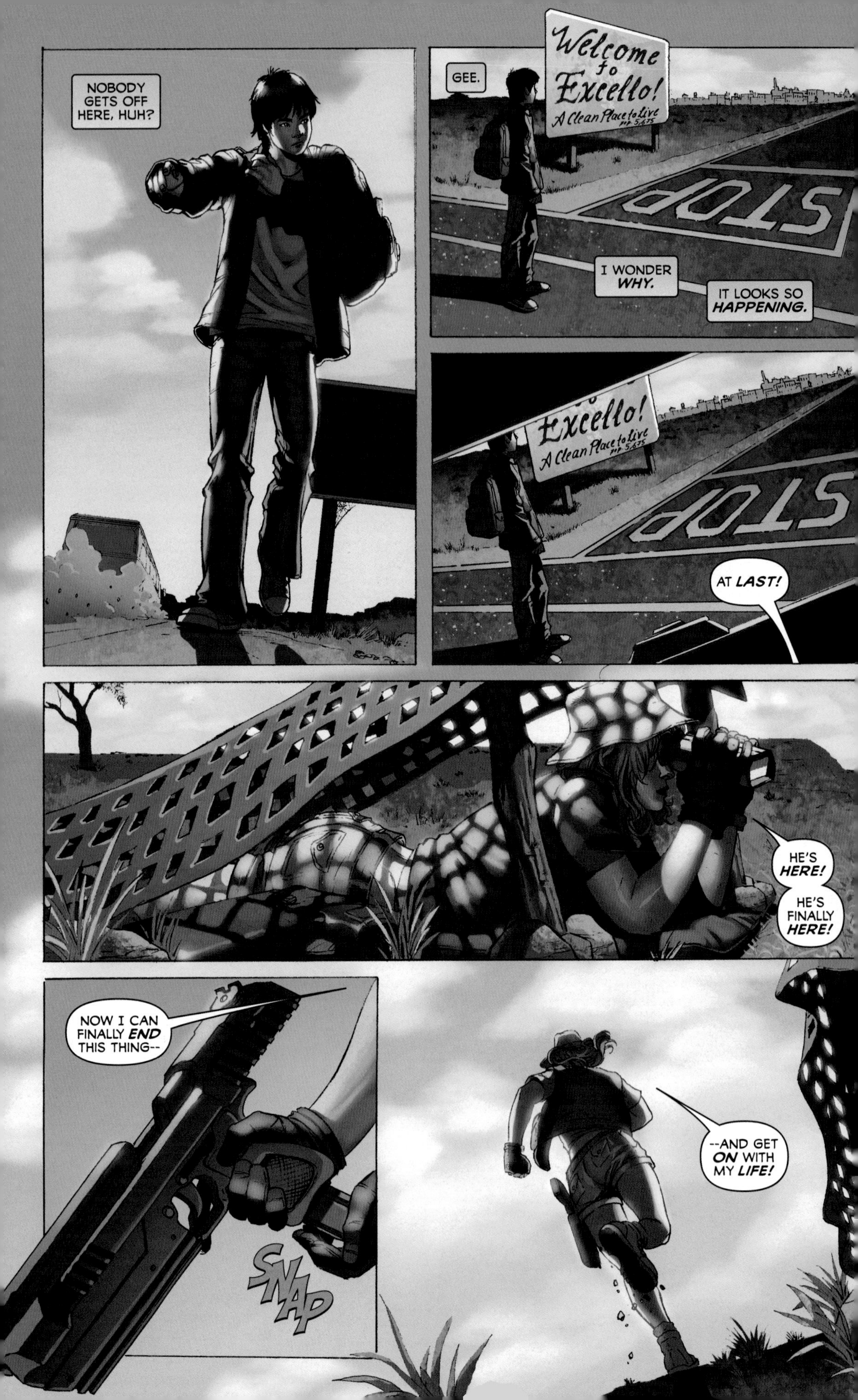
NOBODY GETS OFF HERE, HUH?
Welcome to Excello! A Clean Place to Live POP 5,675
GEE.
STOP
I WONDER WHY.
IT LOOKS SO HAPPENING.
Excello! A Clean Place to Live POP 5,675
STOP
AT LAST!
HE'S HERE!
HE'S FINALLY HERE!
NOW I CAN FINALLY END THIS THING--
SNAP
--AND GET ON WITH MY LIFE!

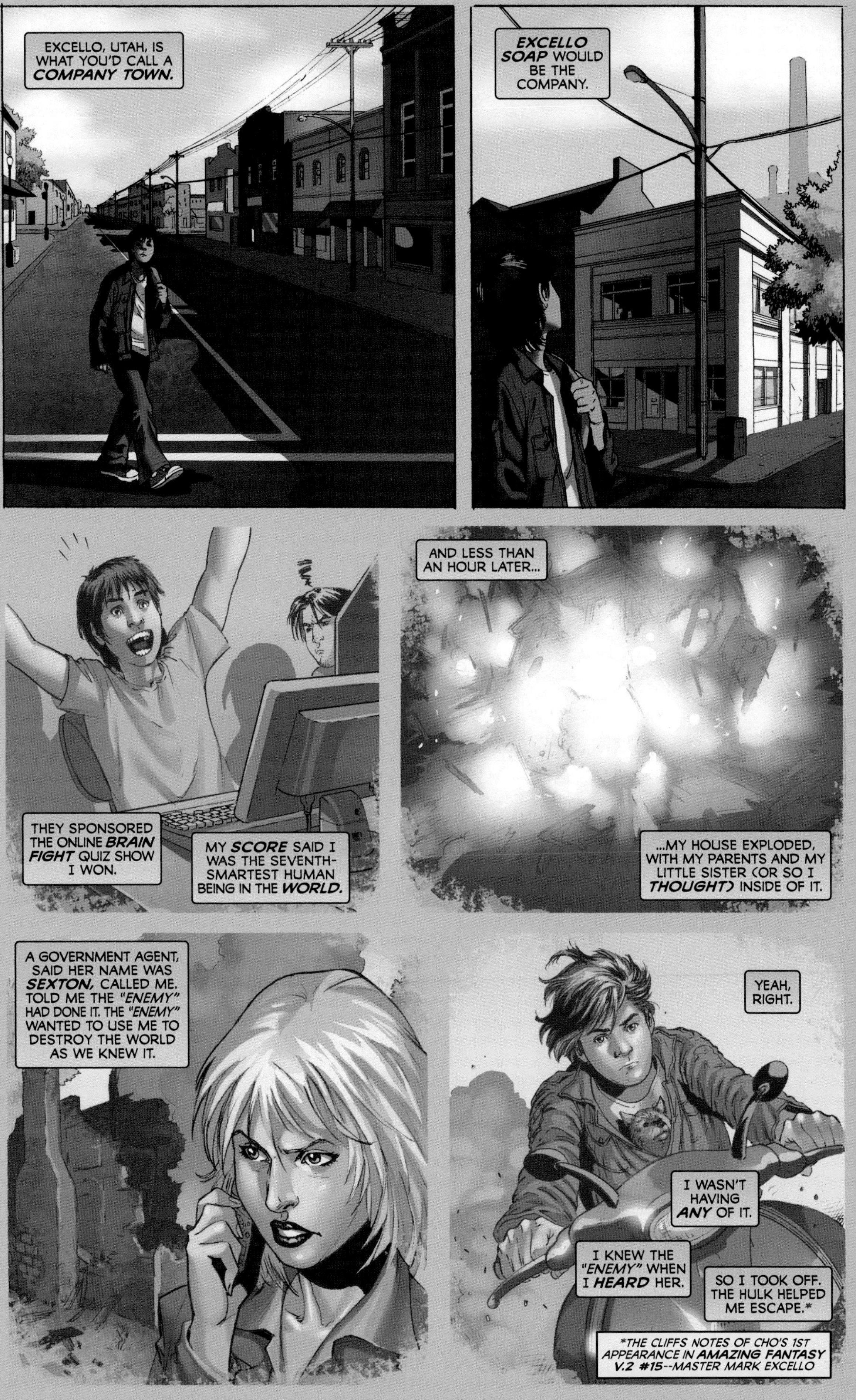
EXCELLO, UTAH, IS WHAT YOU'D CALL A COMPANY TOWN.
EXCELLO SOAP WOULD BE THE COMPANY.
THEY SPONSORED THE ONLINE BRAIN FIGHT QUIZ SHOW I WON.
MY SCORE SAID I WAS THE SEVENTH-SMARTEST HUMAN BEING IN THE WORLD.
AND LESS THAN AN HOUR LATER...
...MY HOUSE EXPLODED, WITH MY PARENTS AND MY LITTLE SISTER (OR SO I THOUGHT) INSIDE OF IT.
A GOVERNMENT AGENT, SAID HER NAME WAS SEXTON, CALLED ME. TOLD ME THE "ENEMY" HAD DONE IT. THE "ENEMY" WANTED TO USE ME TO DESTROY THE WORLD AS WE KNEW IT.
YEAH, RIGHT.
I WASN'T HAVING ANY OF IT.
I KNEW THE "ENEMY" WHEN I HEARD HER.
SO I TOOK OFF. THE HULK HELPED ME ESCAPE.*
*THE CLIFFS NOTES OF CHO'S 1ST APPEARANCE IN AMAZING FANTASY V.2 #15--MASTER MARK EXCELLO

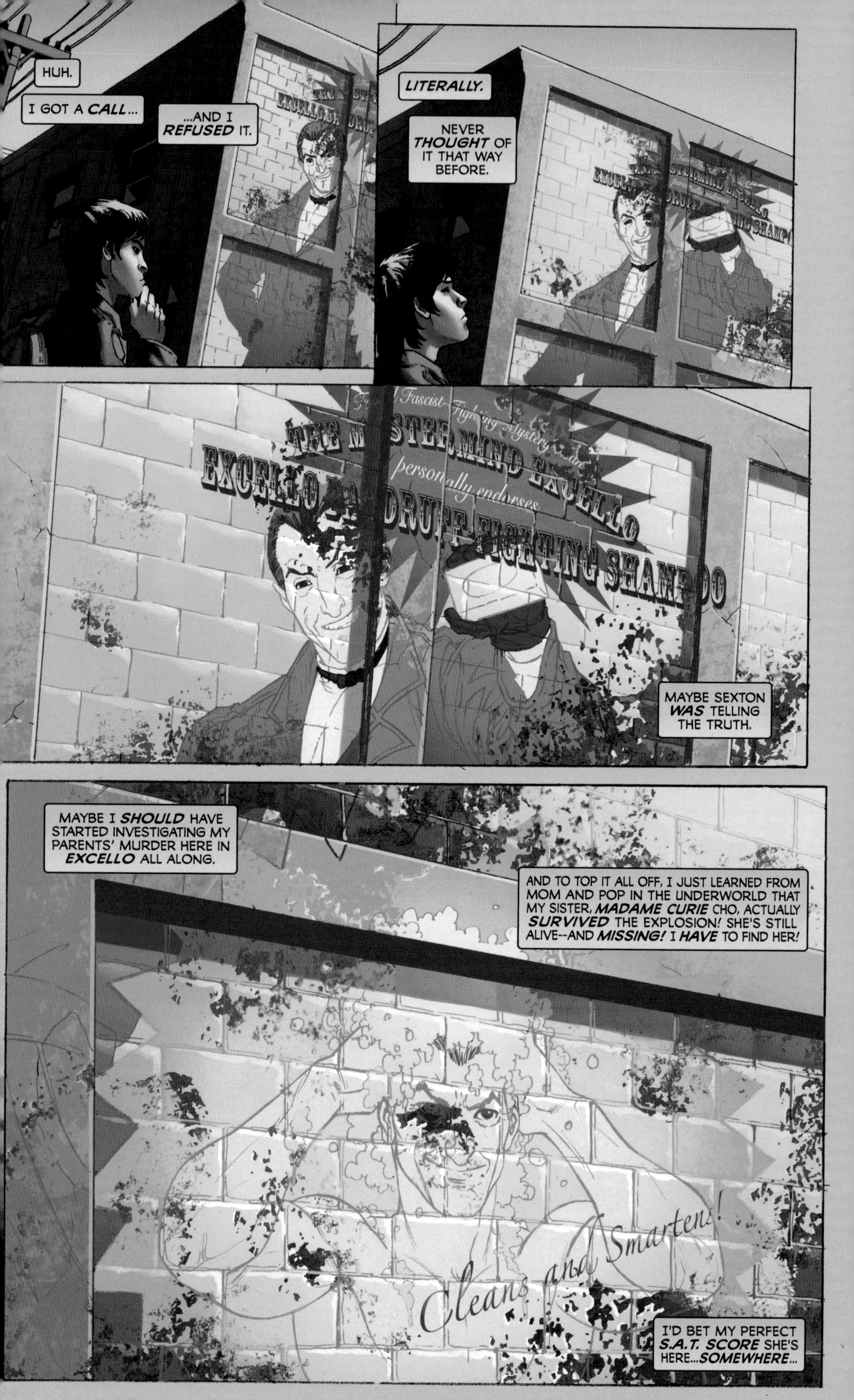
HUH.
I GOT A CALL...
...AND I REFUSED IT.
LITERALLY.
NEVER THOUGHT OF IT THAT WAY BEFORE.
THE MASTERMIND EXCELLO
personally endorses
EXCELLO DANDRUFF-FIGHTING SHAMPOO
MAYBE SEXTON WAS TELLING THE TRUTH.
MAYBE I SHOULD HAVE STARTED INVESTIGATING MY PARENTS' MURDER HERE IN EXCELLO ALL ALONG.
AND TO TOP IT ALL OFF, I JUST LEARNED FROM MOM AND POP IN THE UNDERWORLD THAT MY SISTER, MADAME CURIE CHO, ACTUALLY SURVIVED THE EXPLOSION! SHE'S STILL ALIVE--AND MISSING! I HAVE TO FIND HER!
Cleans and Smartens!
I'D BET MY PERFECT S.A.T. SCORE SHE'S HERE...SOMEWHERE...

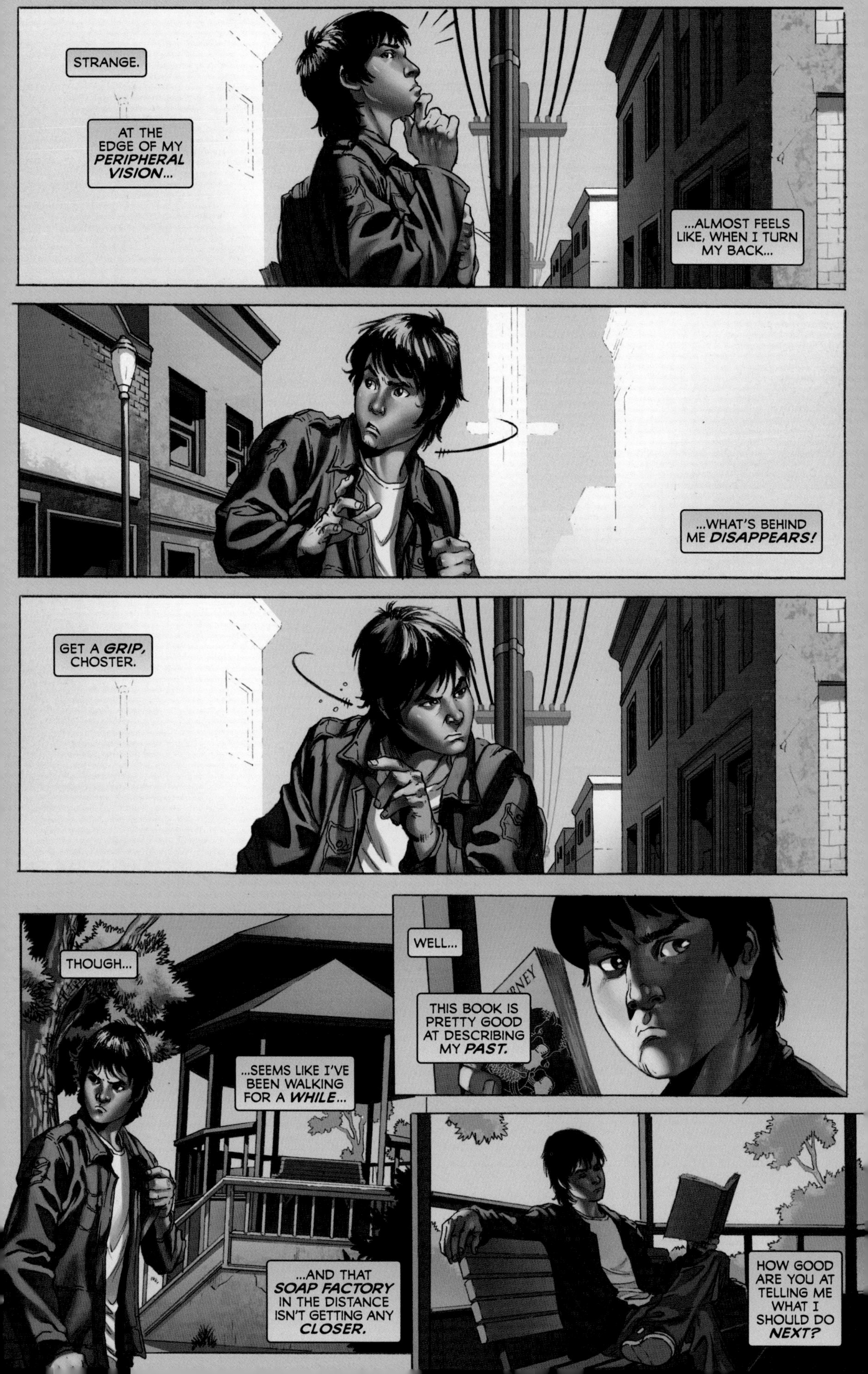
STRANGE.
AT THE EDGE OF MY PERIPHERAL VISION...
...ALMOST FEELS LIKE, WHEN I TURN MY BACK...
...WHAT'S BEHIND ME DISAPPEARS!
GET A GRIP, CHOSTER.
THOUGH...
...SEEMS LIKE I'VE BEEN WALKING FOR A WHILE...
...AND THAT SOAP FACTORY IN THE DISTANCE ISN'T GETTING ANY CLOSER.
WELL...
THIS BOOK IS PRETTY GOOD AT DESCRIBING MY PAST.
HOW GOOD ARE YOU AT TELLING ME WHAT I SHOULD DO NEXT?

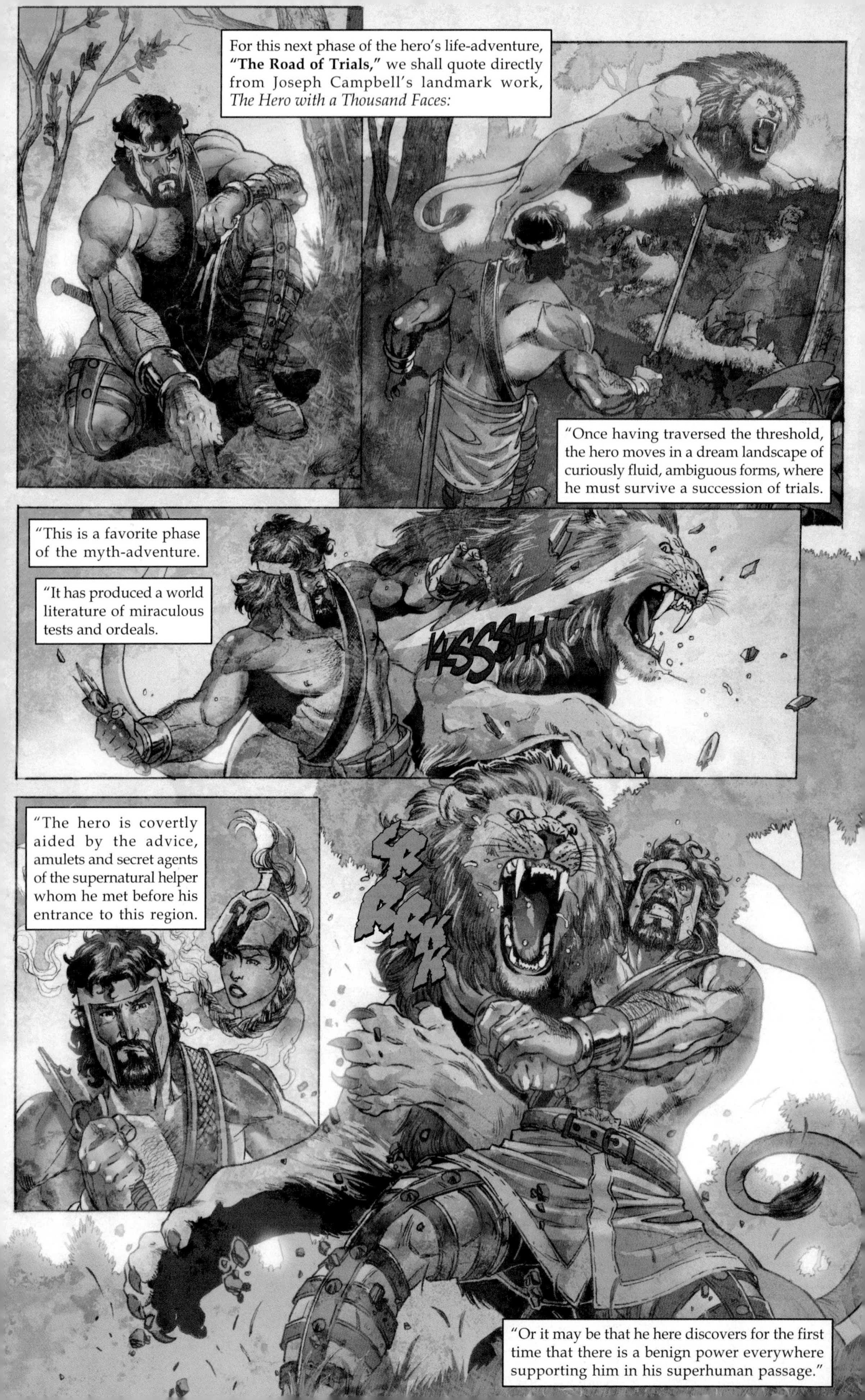
For this next phase of the hero's life-adventure, "The Road of Trials," we shall quote directly from Joseph Campbell's landmark work, *The Hero with a Thousand Faces:*
"Once having traversed the threshold, the hero moves in a dream landscape of curiously fluid, ambiguous forms, where he must survive a succession of trials.
"This is a favorite phase of the myth-adventure.
"It has produced a world literature of miraculous tests and ordeals.
KSSSHH
"The hero is covertly aided by the advice, amulets and secret agents of the supernatural helper whom he met before his entrance to this region.
"Or it may be that he here discovers for the first time that there is a benign power everywhere supporting him in his superhuman passage."

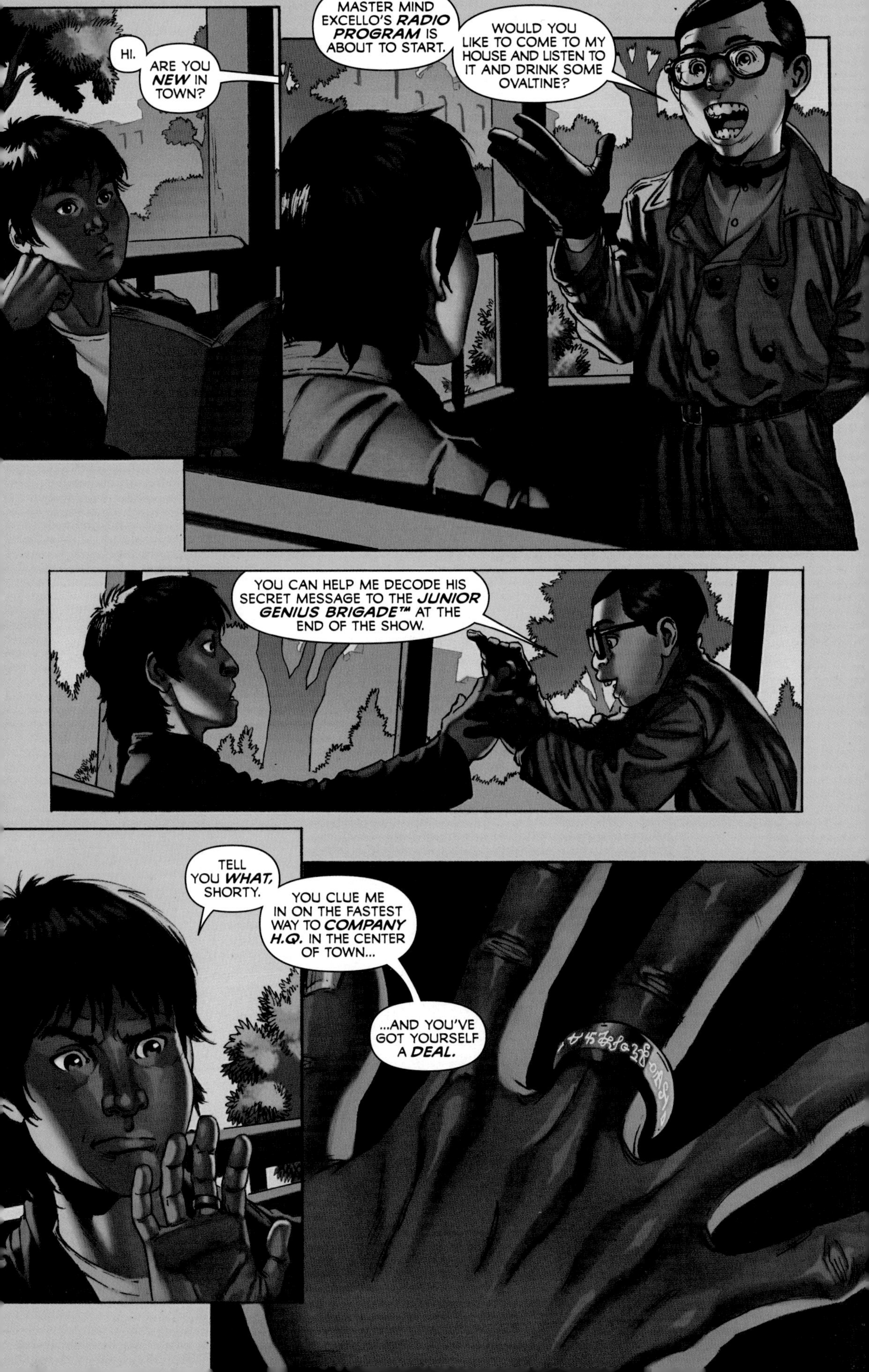
HI.
ARE YOU NEW IN TOWN?
MASTER MIND EXCELLO'S RADIO PROGRAM IS ABOUT TO START.
WOULD YOU LIKE TO COME TO MY HOUSE AND LISTEN TO IT AND DRINK SOME OVALTINE?
YOU CAN HELP ME DECODE HIS SECRET MESSAGE TO THE JUNIOR GENIUS BRIGADE™ AT THE END OF THE SHOW.
TELL YOU WHAT, SHORTY.
YOU CLUE ME IN ON THE FASTEST WAY TO COMPANY H.Q. IN THE CENTER OF TOWN...
...AND YOU'VE GOT YOURSELF A DEAL.

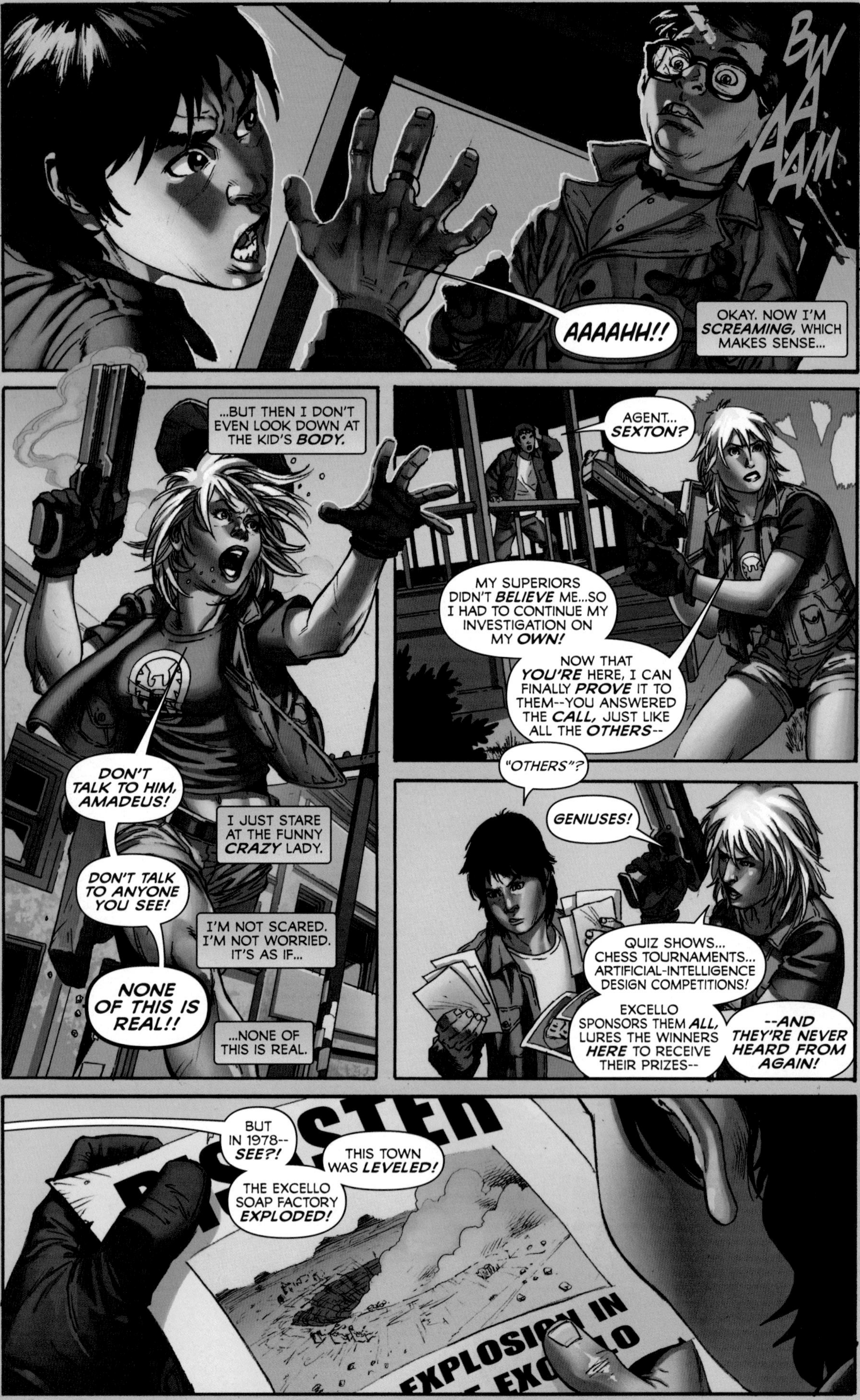
BWAAAAM
AAAAHH!!
OKAY. NOW I'M SCREAMING, WHICH MAKES SENSE...
...BUT THEN I DON'T EVEN LOOK DOWN AT THE KID'S BODY.
DON'T TALK TO HIM, AMADEUS!
I JUST STARE AT THE FUNNY CRAZY LADY.
DON'T TALK TO ANYONE YOU SEE!
I'M NOT SCARED. I'M NOT WORRIED. IT'S AS IF...
NONE OF THIS IS REAL!!
...NONE OF THIS IS REAL.
AGENT... SEXTON?
MY SUPERIORS DIDN'T BELIEVE ME...SO I HAD TO CONTINUE MY INVESTIGATION ON MY OWN!
NOW THAT YOU'RE HERE, I CAN FINALLY PROVE IT TO THEM--YOU ANSWERED THE CALL, JUST LIKE ALL THE OTHERS--
"OTHERS"?
GENIUSES!
QUIZ SHOWS... CHESS TOURNAMENTS... ARTIFICIAL-INTELLIGENCE DESIGN COMPETITIONS!
EXCELLO SPONSORS THEM ALL, LURES THE WINNERS HERE TO RECEIVE THEIR PRIZES--
--AND THEY'RE NEVER HEARD FROM AGAIN!
BUT IN 1978-- SEE?!
THIS TOWN WAS LEVELED!
THE EXCELLO SOAP FACTORY EXPLODED!

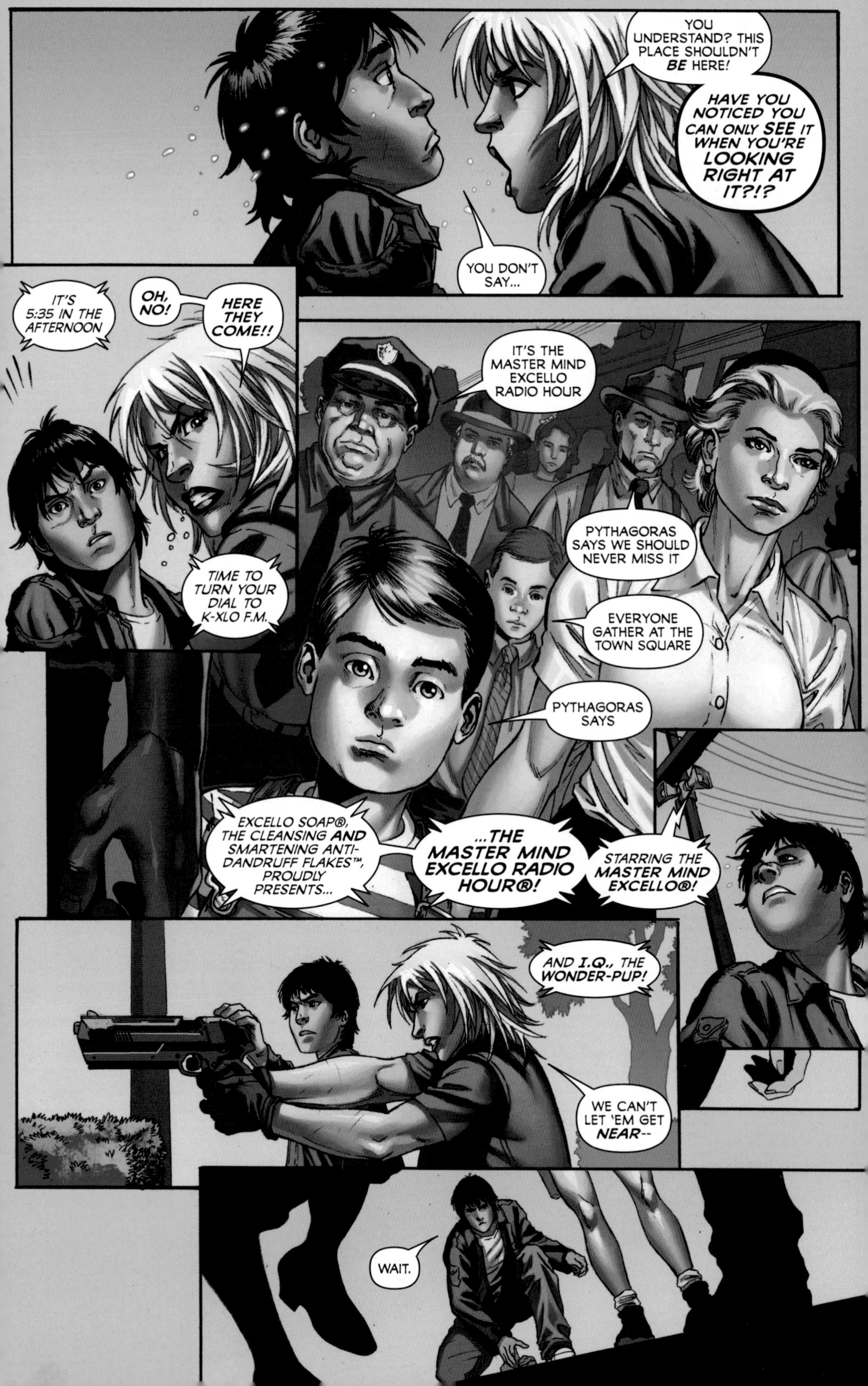
YOU UNDERSTAND? THIS PLACE SHOULDN'T BE HERE!
HAVE YOU NOTICED YOU CAN ONLY SEE IT WHEN YOU'RE LOOKING RIGHT AT IT?!?
YOU DON'T SAY...
IT'S 5:35 IN THE AFTERNOON
OH, NO!
HERE THEY COME!!
TIME TO TURN YOUR DIAL TO K-XLO F.M.
IT'S THE MASTER MIND EXCELLO RADIO HOUR
PYTHAGORAS SAYS WE SHOULD NEVER MISS IT
EVERYONE GATHER AT THE TOWN SQUARE
PYTHAGORAS SAYS
EXCELLO SOAP®, THE CLEANSING AND SMARTENING ANTI-DANDRUFF FLAKES™, PROUDLY PRESENTS...
...THE MASTER MIND EXCELLO RADIO HOUR®!
STARRING THE MASTER MIND EXCELLO®!
AND I.Q., THE WONDER-PUP!
WE CAN'T LET 'EM GET NEAR--
WAIT.

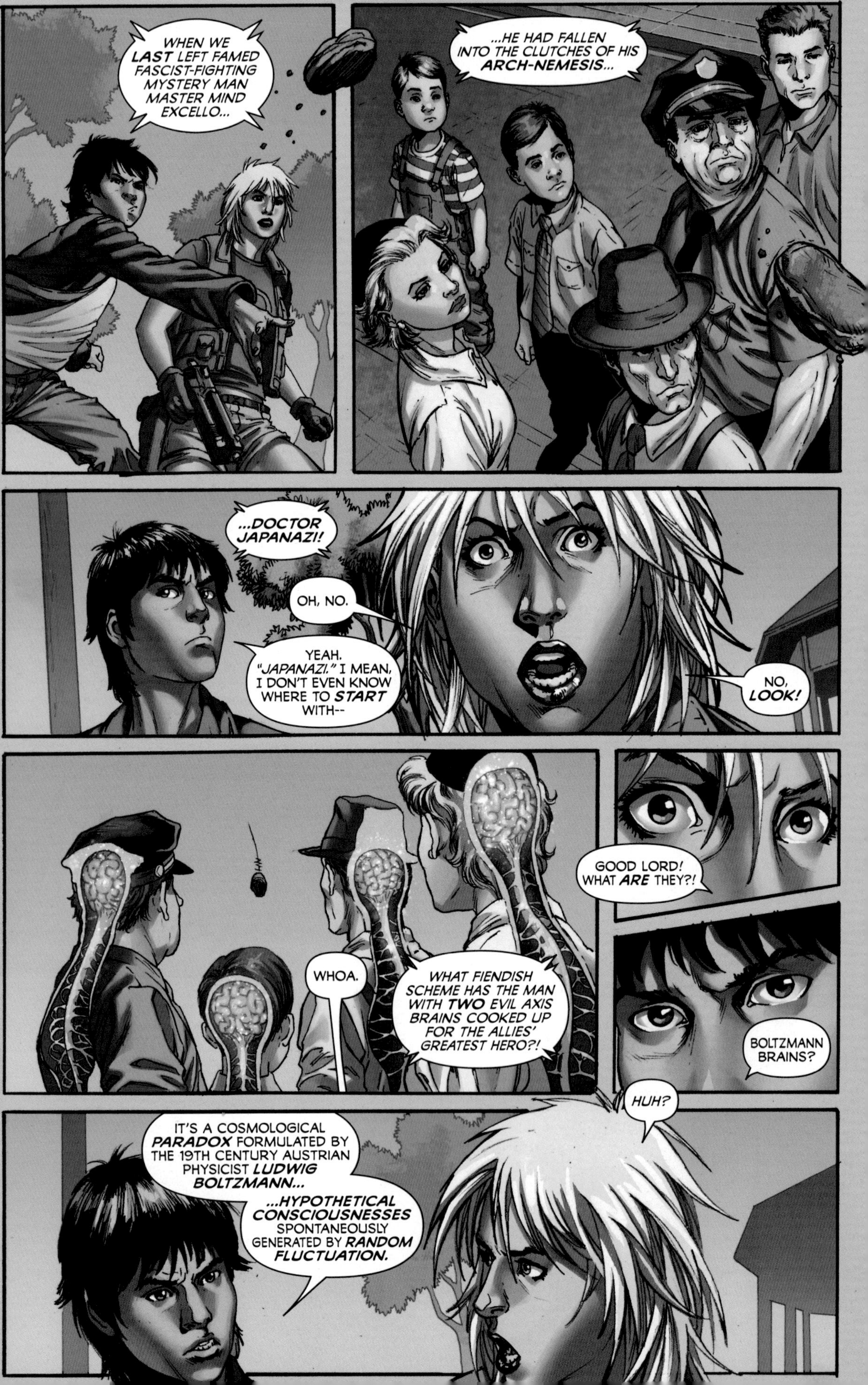
WHEN WE LAST LEFT FAMED FASCIST-FIGHTING MYSTERY MAN MASTER MIND EXCELLO...
...HE HAD FALLEN INTO THE CLUTCHES OF HIS ARCH-NEMESIS...
...DOCTOR JAPANAZI!
OH, NO.
YEAH. "JAPANAZI." I MEAN, I DON'T EVEN KNOW WHERE TO START WITH--
NO, LOOK!
WHOA.
WHAT FIENDISH SCHEME HAS THE MAN WITH TWO EVIL AXIS BRAINS COOKED UP FOR THE ALLIES' GREATEST HERO?!
GOOD LORD! WHAT ARE THEY?!
BOLTZMANN BRAINS?
HUH?
IT'S A COSMOLOGICAL PARADOX FORMULATED BY THE 19TH CENTURY AUSTRIAN PHYSICIST LUDWIG BOLTZMANN...
...HYPOTHETICAL CONSCIOUSNESSES SPONTANEOUSLY GENERATED BY RANDOM FLUCTUATION.

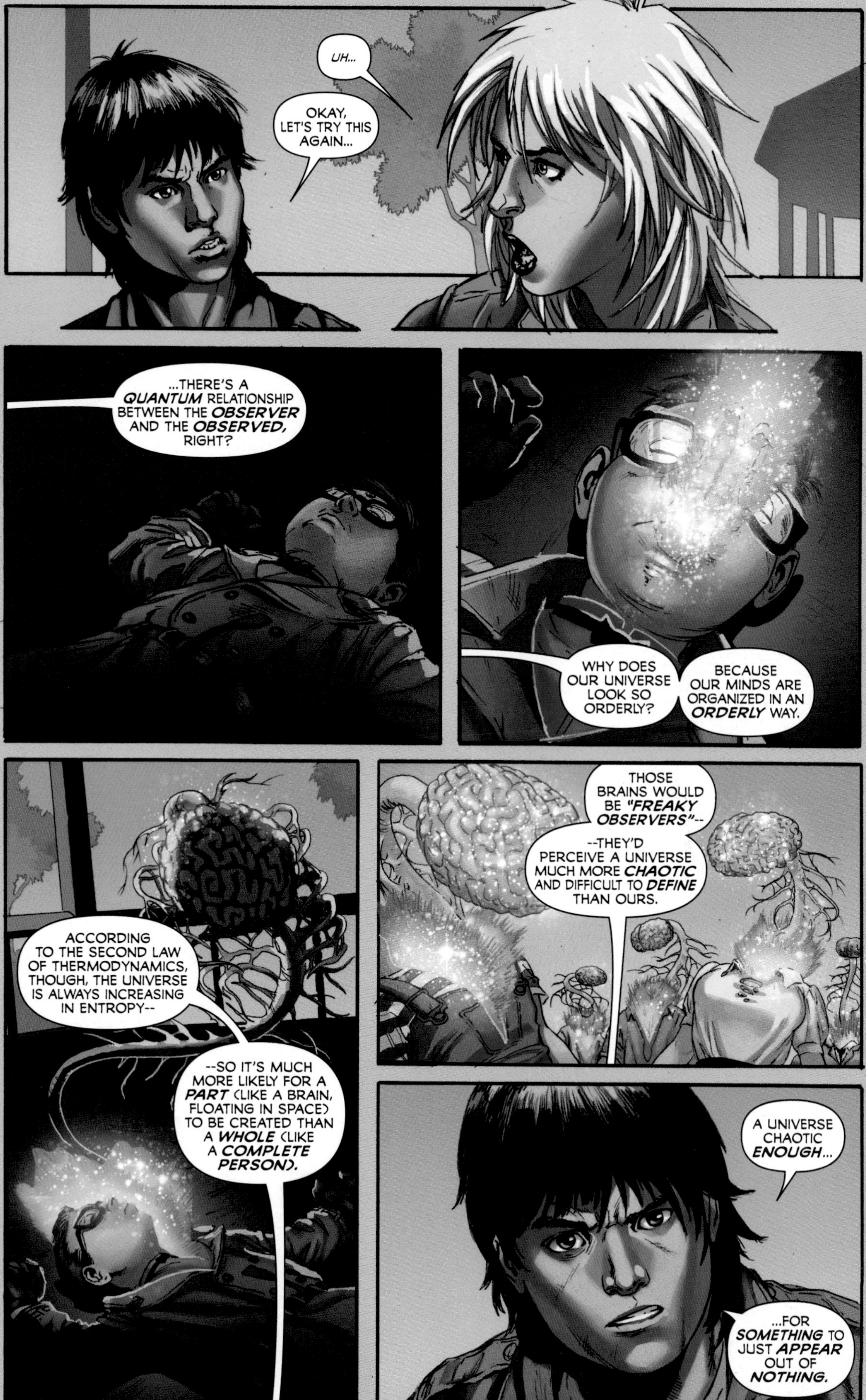
UH...
OKAY, LET'S TRY THIS AGAIN...
...THERE'S A QUANTUM RELATIONSHIP BETWEEN THE OBSERVER AND THE OBSERVED, RIGHT?
WHY DOES OUR UNIVERSE LOOK SO ORDERLY?
BECAUSE OUR MINDS ARE ORGANIZED IN AN ORDERLY WAY.
ACCORDING TO THE SECOND LAW OF THERMODYNAMICS, THOUGH, THE UNIVERSE IS ALWAYS INCREASING IN ENTROPY--
--SO IT'S MUCH MORE LIKELY FOR A PART (LIKE A BRAIN, FLOATING IN SPACE) TO BE CREATED THAN A WHOLE (LIKE A COMPLETE PERSON).
THOSE BRAINS WOULD BE "FREAKY OBSERVERS"--
--THEY'D PERCEIVE A UNIVERSE MUCH MORE CHAOTIC AND DIFFICULT TO DEFINE THAN OURS.
A UNIVERSE CHAOTIC ENOUGH...
...FOR SOMETHING TO JUST APPEAR OUT OF NOTHING.

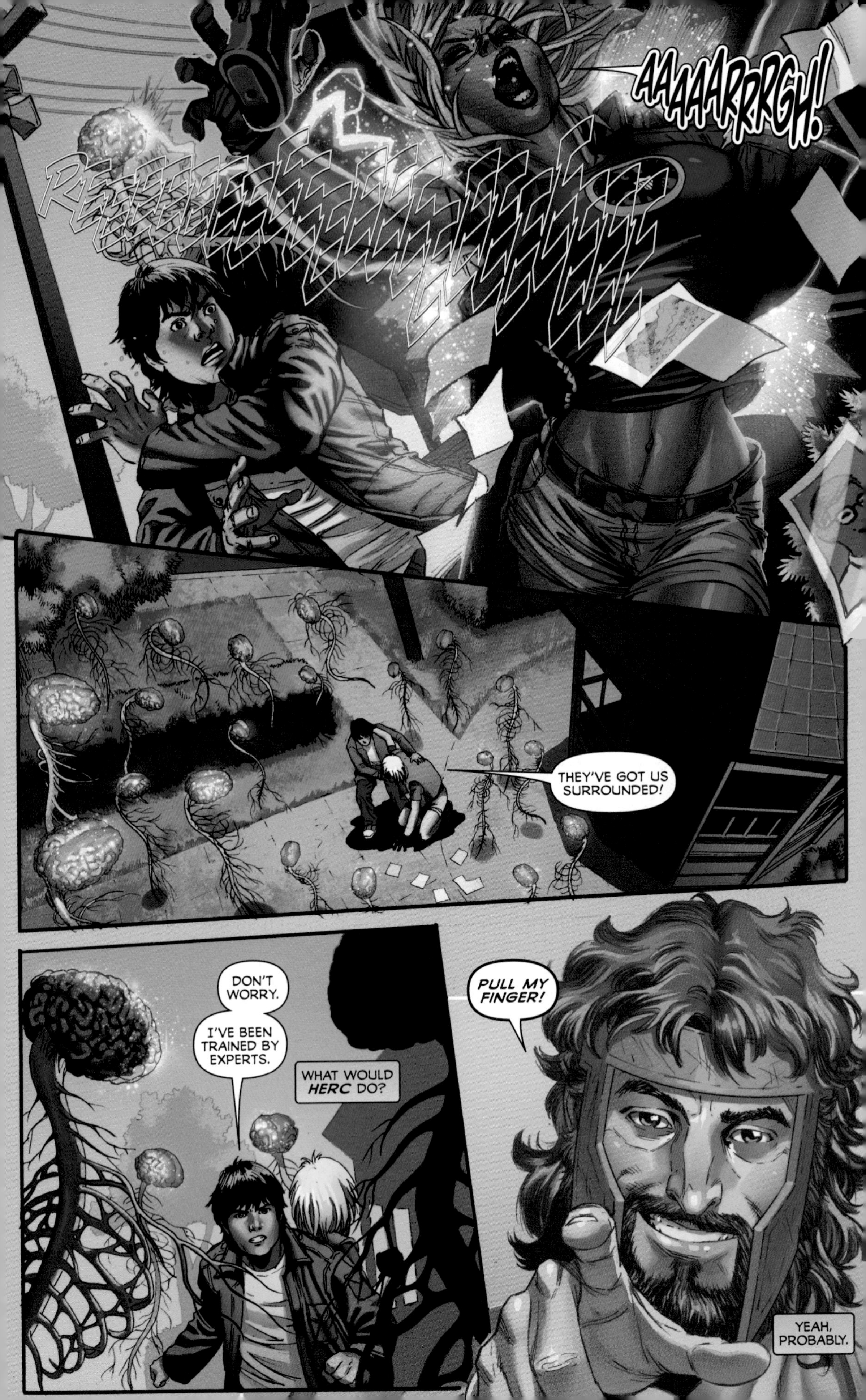
AAAAARRRGH!
THEY'VE GOT US SURROUNDED!
DON'T WORRY.
I'VE BEEN TRAINED BY EXPERTS.
WHAT WOULD *HERC* DO?
PULL MY FINGER!
YEAH, PROBABLY.

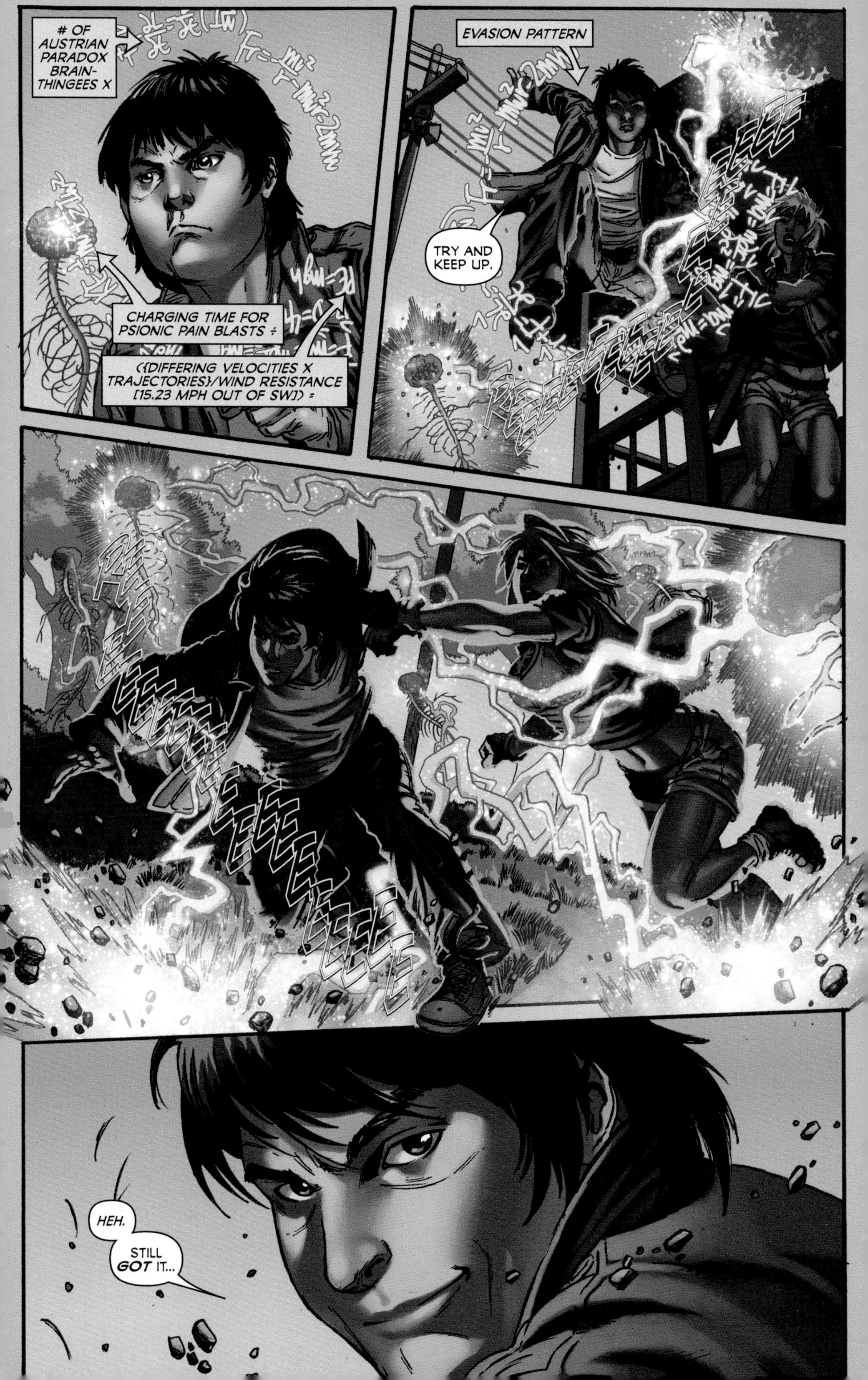

OF AUSTRIAN PARADOX BRAIN-THINGEES X
CHARGING TIME FOR PSIONIC PAIN BLASTS ÷
({DIFFERING VELOCITIES X TRAJECTORIES}/WIND RESISTANCE [15.23 MPH OUT OF SW]) =
EVASION PATTERN
TRY AND KEEP UP.
HEH.
STILL GOT IT...

WHAT...

WE DIDN'T *MOVE*...

BUT MY *CALCULATIONS* WERE ALL--

GAAAAAHHH!!

TOTALLY SCREWED.

TH-THIS TOWN...

MADE OF...

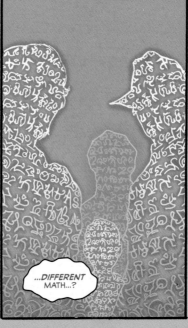

...DIFFERENT MATH...?

HOW...HOW IS THAT...

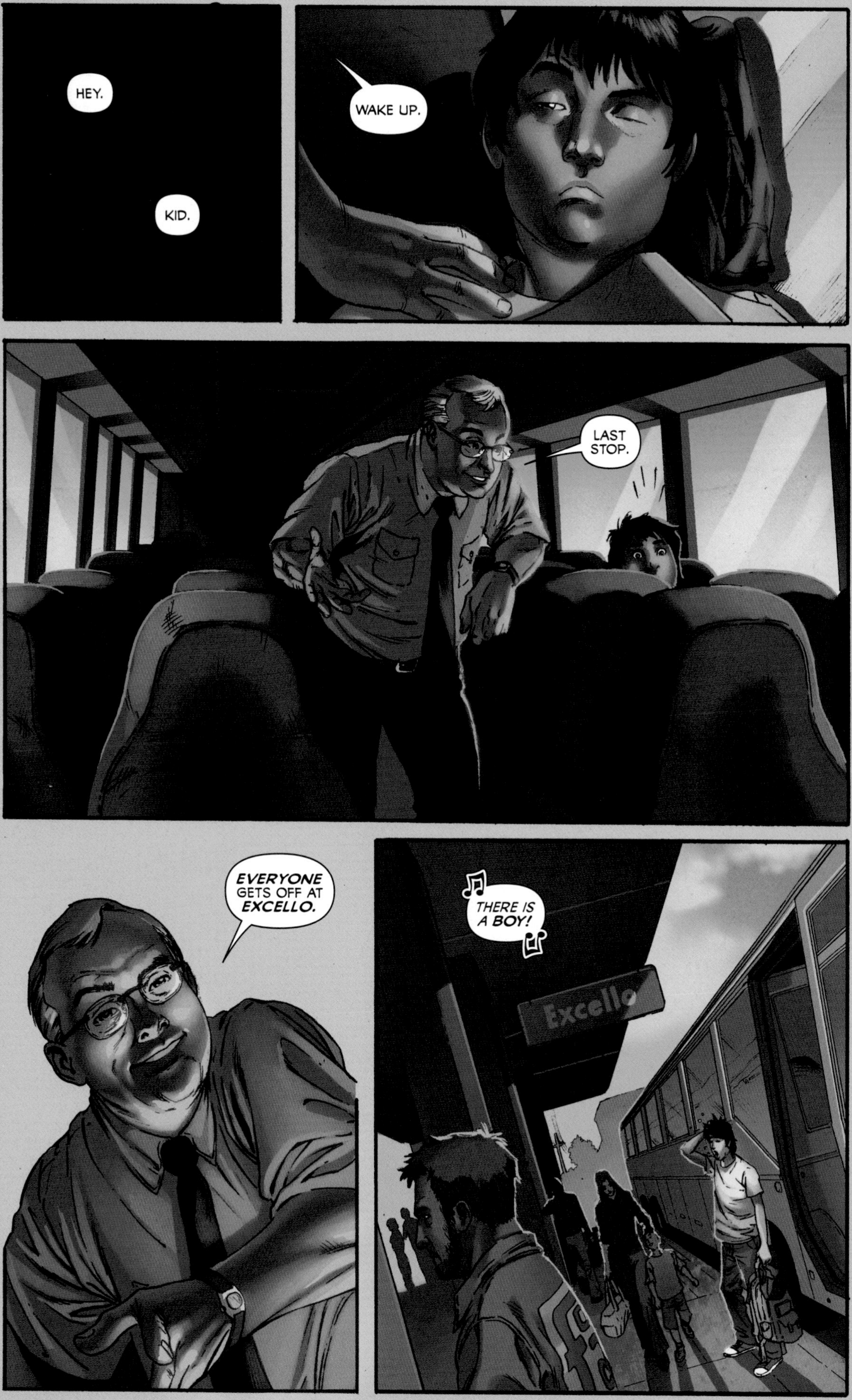
HEY.
KID.
WAKE UP.
LAST STOP.
EVERYONE GETS OFF AT *EXCELLO.*
THERE IS A BOY!
Excello

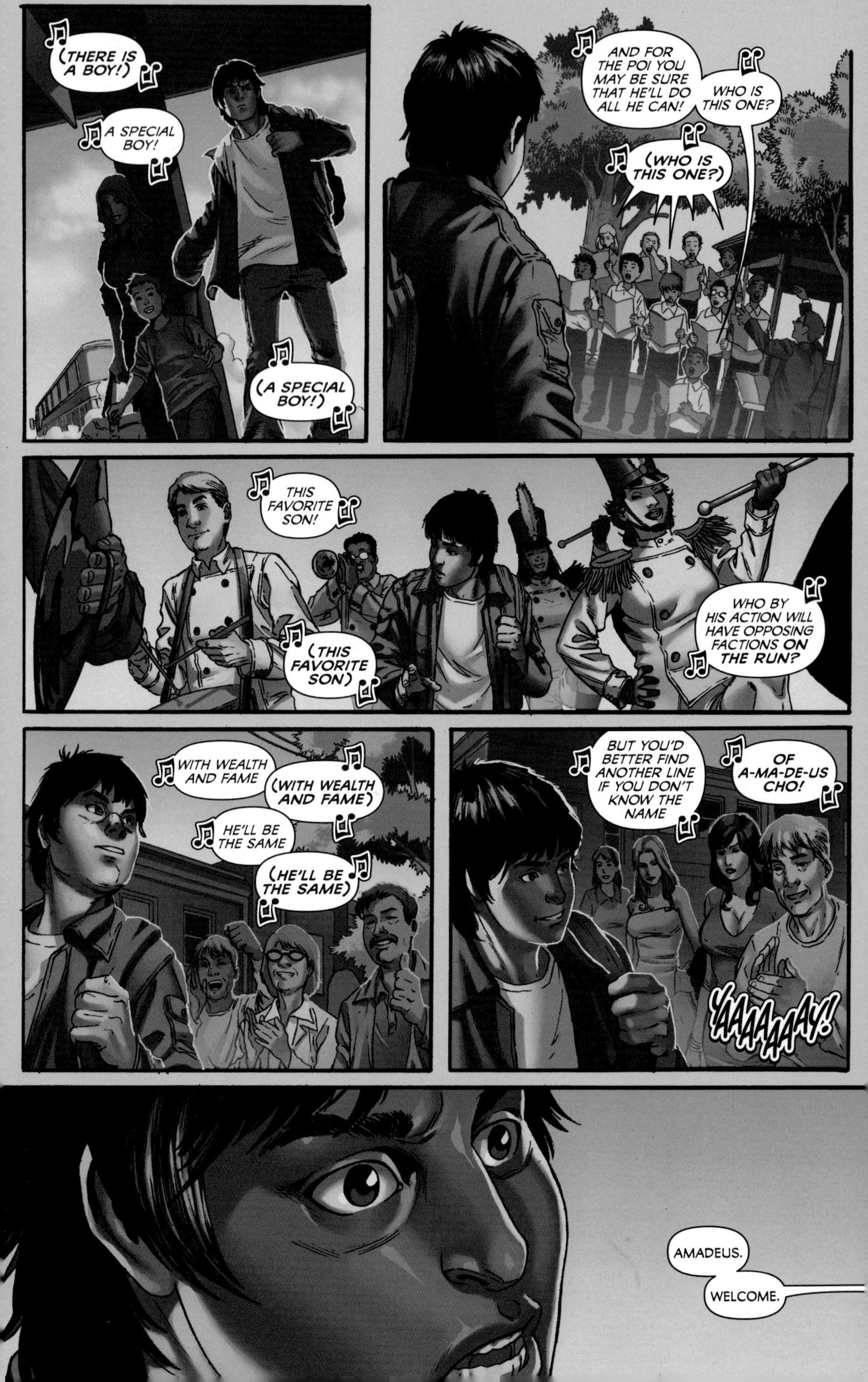
(THERE IS A BOY!)
A SPECIAL BOY!
(A SPECIAL BOY!)
AND FOR THE POI YOU MAY BE SURE THAT HE'LL DO ALL HE CAN!
WHO IS THIS ONE?
(WHO IS THIS ONE?)
THIS FAVORITE SON!
(THIS FAVORITE SON)
WHO BY HIS ACTION WILL HAVE OPPOSING FACTIONS ON THE RUN?
WITH WEALTH AND FAME
(WITH WEALTH AND FAME)
HE'LL BE THE SAME
(HE'LL BE THE SAME)
BUT YOU'D BETTER FIND ANOTHER LINE IF YOU DON'T KNOW THE NAME
OF A-MA-DE-US CHO!
YAAAAAAAY!
AMADEUS.
WELCOME.

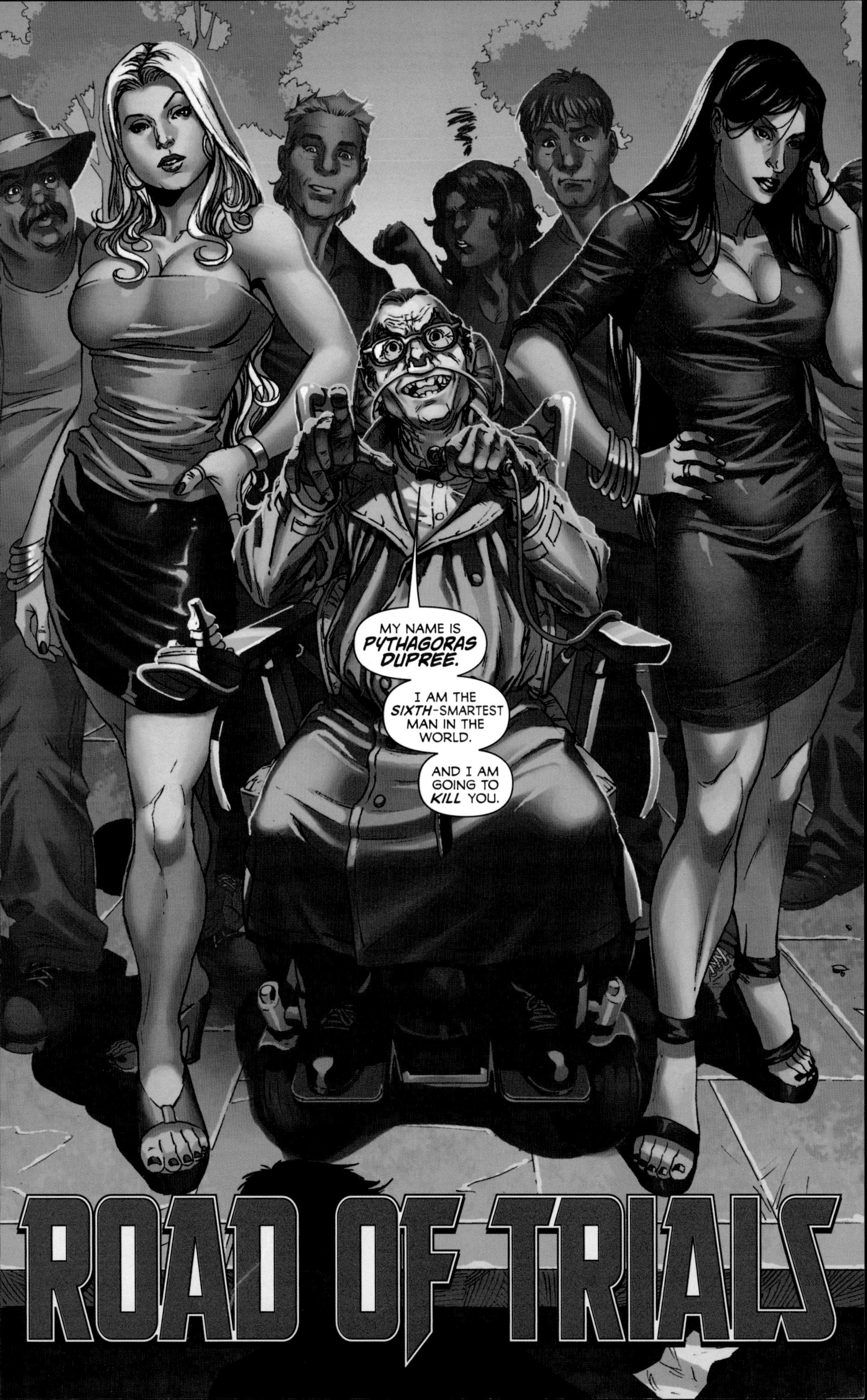
MY NAME IS PYTHAGORAS DUPREE.
I AM THE SIXTH-SMARTEST MAN IN THE WORLD.
AND I AM GOING TO KILL YOU.
ROAD OF TRIALS

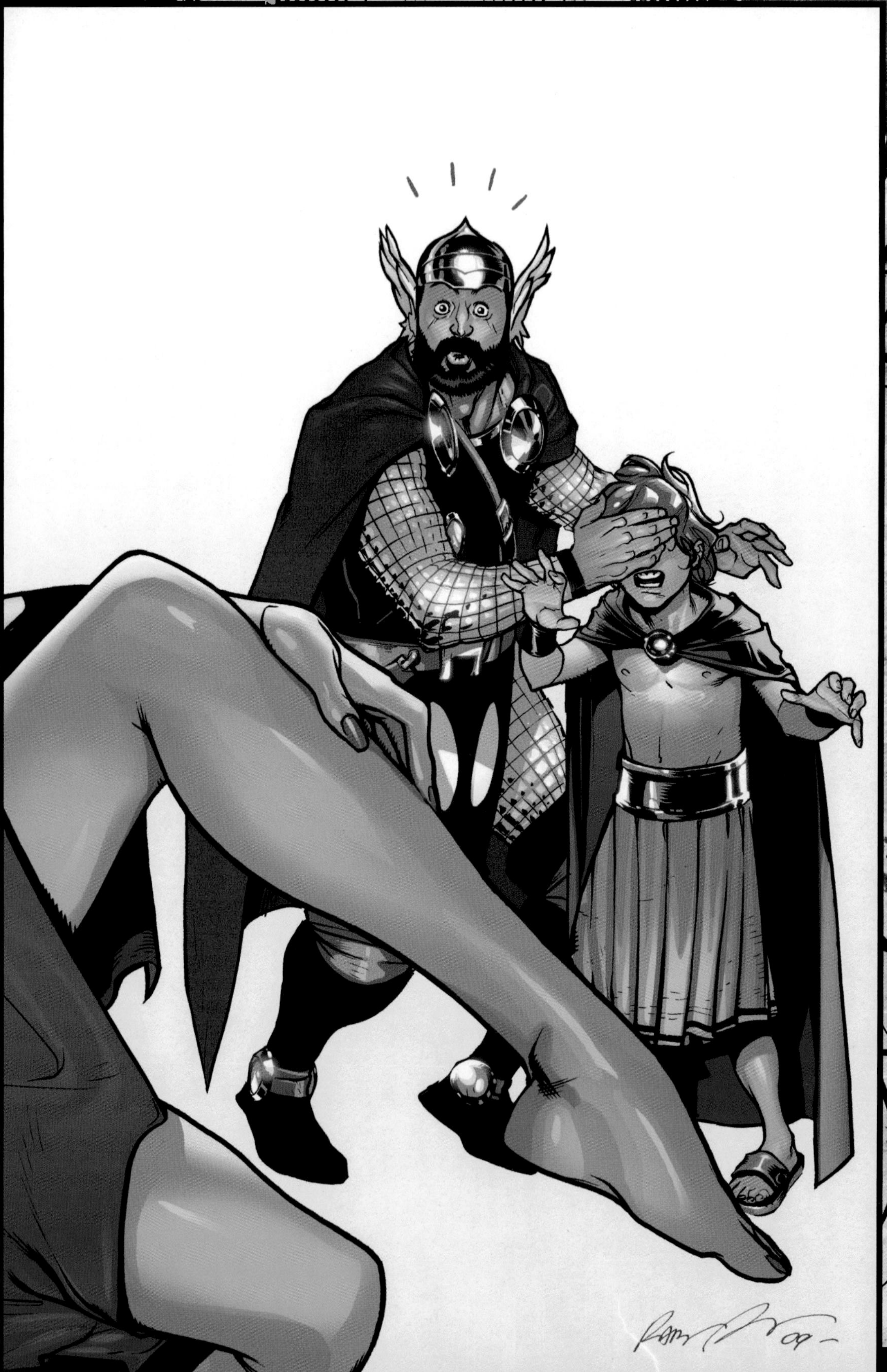

FASHION

FAUX PASGARDIAN

CUTTING EDGE COUTURE CUT-DOWN BY
THE INCREDIBLE HERCULES

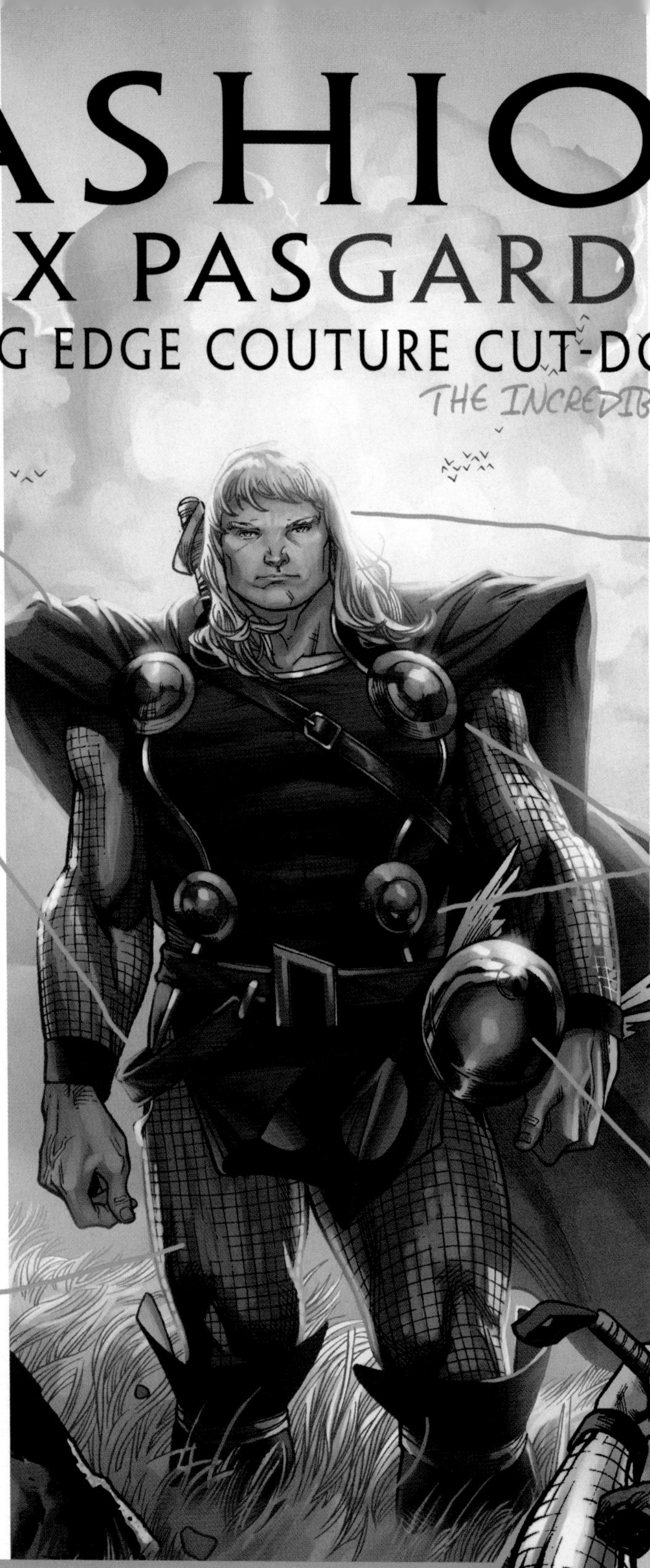

Nice shoulderpads. Did the 80's JUST hit Asgard?
Thor: Goldilocks of Thunder.
Is this strap for his god-wallet? Has he got a god-hacky sack?
Thor's got Thipples! Can you milk those?
REAL men wear skirts.
Protective helmet. Lot of baseball played on the Rainbow Bridge?

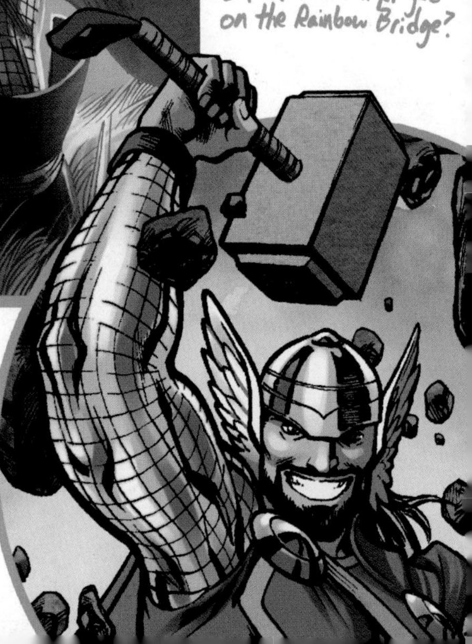

BOTTOM LINE: No self-respecting Olympian would be caught dead in Asgardian garb, unless they were impersonating Thor alongside their amnesiac child-father.

Doesn't look too bad with a beard, though.

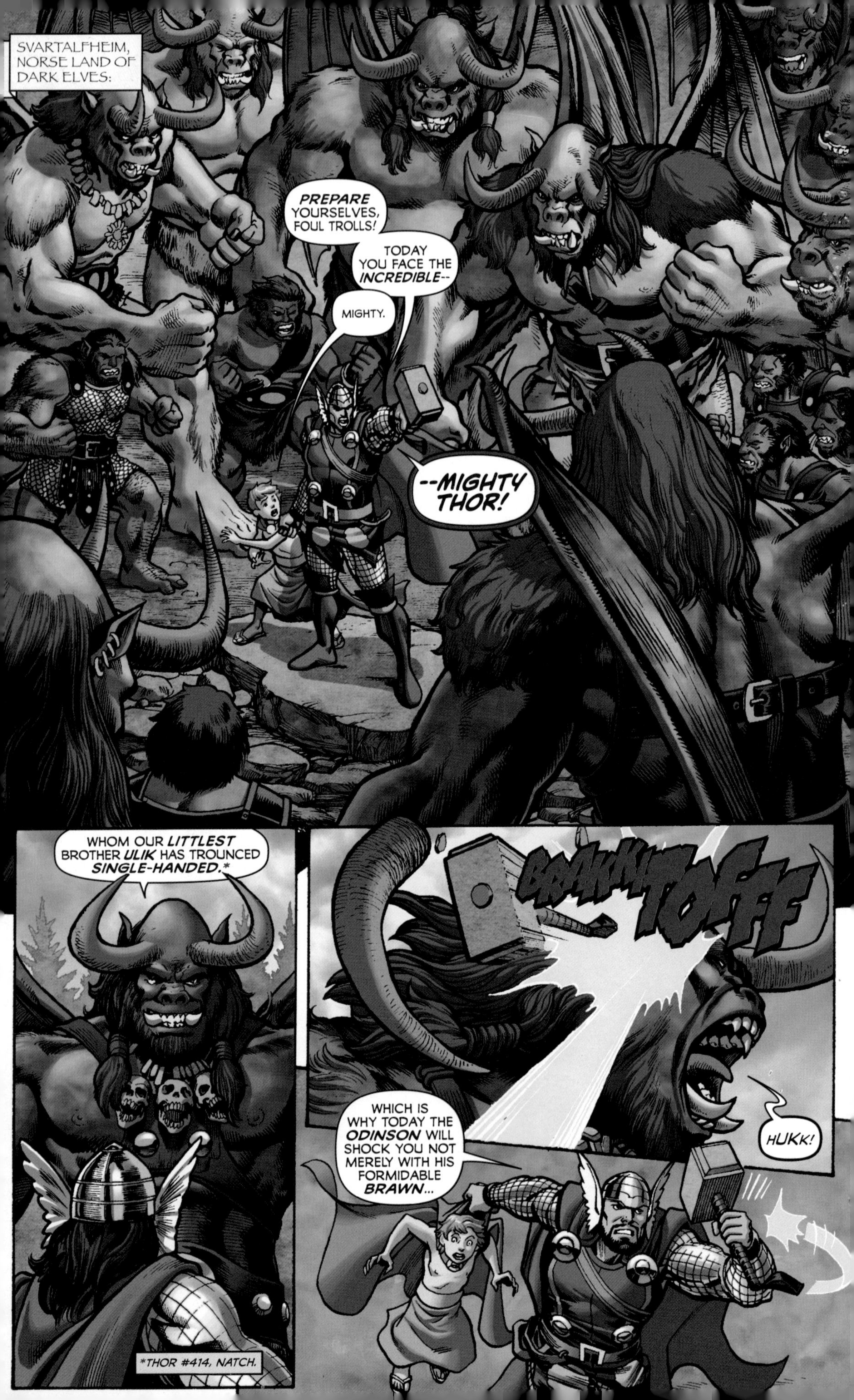
SVARTALFHEIM, NORSE LAND OF DARK ELVES:
PREPARE YOURSELVES, FOUL TROLLS!
TODAY YOU FACE THE INCREDIBLE--
MIGHTY.
--MIGHTY THOR!
WHOM OUR LITTLEST BROTHER ULIK HAS TROUNCED SINGLE-HANDED.*
*THOR #414, NATCH.
BRAKK TOFFF
HUKK!
WHICH IS WHY TODAY THE ODINSON WILL SHOCK YOU NOT MERELY WITH HIS FORMIDABLE BRAWN...

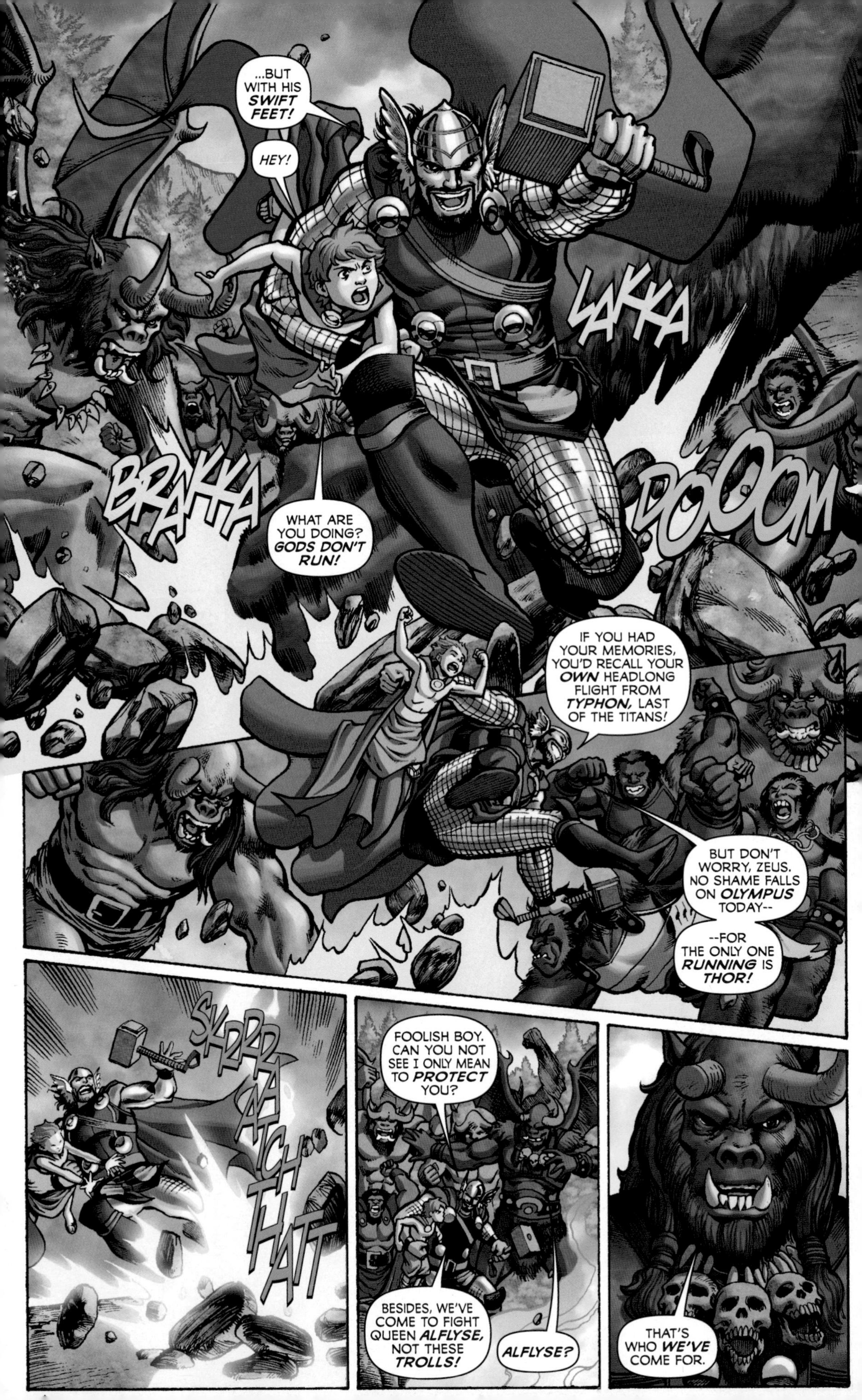
...BUT WITH HIS SWIFT FEET!
HEY!
LAKKA
BRAKKA
WHAT ARE YOU DOING? GODS DON'T RUN!
DOOOOM
IF YOU HAD YOUR MEMORIES, YOU'D RECALL YOUR OWN HEADLONG FLIGHT FROM TYPHON, LAST OF THE TITANS!
BUT DON'T WORRY, ZEUS. NO SHAME FALLS ON OLYMPUS TODAY--
--FOR THE ONLY ONE RUNNING IS THOR!
SKRRRA
THATCH
THATT
FOOLISH BOY. CAN YOU NOT SEE I ONLY MEAN TO PROTECT YOU?
BESIDES, WE'VE COME TO FIGHT QUEEN ALFLYSE, NOT THESE TROLLS!
ALFLYSE?
THAT'S WHO WE'VE COME FOR.

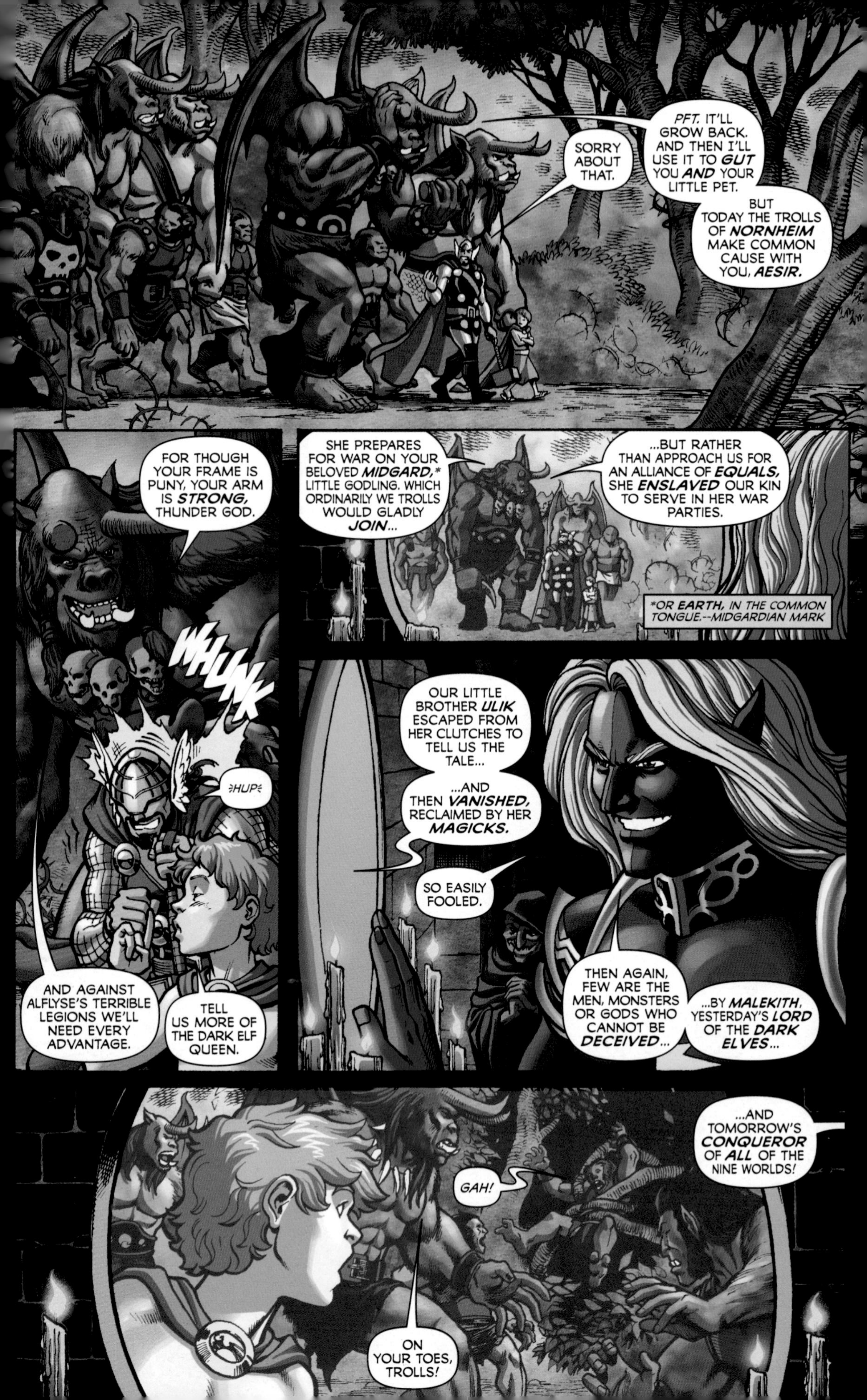

SORRY ABOUT THAT.
PFT. IT'LL GROW BACK. AND THEN I'LL USE IT TO GUT YOU AND YOUR LITTLE PET.
BUT TODAY THE TROLLS OF NORNHEIM MAKE COMMON CAUSE WITH YOU, AESIR.
FOR THOUGH YOUR FRAME IS PUNY, YOUR ARM IS STRONG, THUNDER GOD.
WHUNK
HUP
AND AGAINST ALFLYSE'S TERRIBLE LEGIONS WE'LL NEED EVERY ADVANTAGE.
TELL US MORE OF THE DARK ELF QUEEN.
SHE PREPARES FOR WAR ON YOUR BELOVED MIDGARD,* LITTLE GODLING. WHICH ORDINARILY WE TROLLS WOULD GLADLY JOIN...
...BUT RATHER THAN APPROACH US FOR AN ALLIANCE OF EQUALS, SHE ENSLAVED OUR KIN TO SERVE IN HER WAR PARTIES.
*OR EARTH, IN THE COMMON TONGUE.--MIDGARDIAN MARK
OUR LITTLE BROTHER ULIK ESCAPED FROM HER CLUTCHES TO TELL US THE TALE...
...AND THEN VANISHED, RECLAIMED BY HER MAGICKS.
SO EASILY FOOLED.
THEN AGAIN, FEW ARE THE MEN, MONSTERS OR GODS WHO CANNOT BE DECEIVED...
...BY MALEKITH, YESTERDAY'S LORD OF THE DARK ELVES...
...AND TOMORROW'S CONQUEROR OF ALL OF THE NINE WORLDS!
GAH!
ON YOUR TOES, TROLLS!

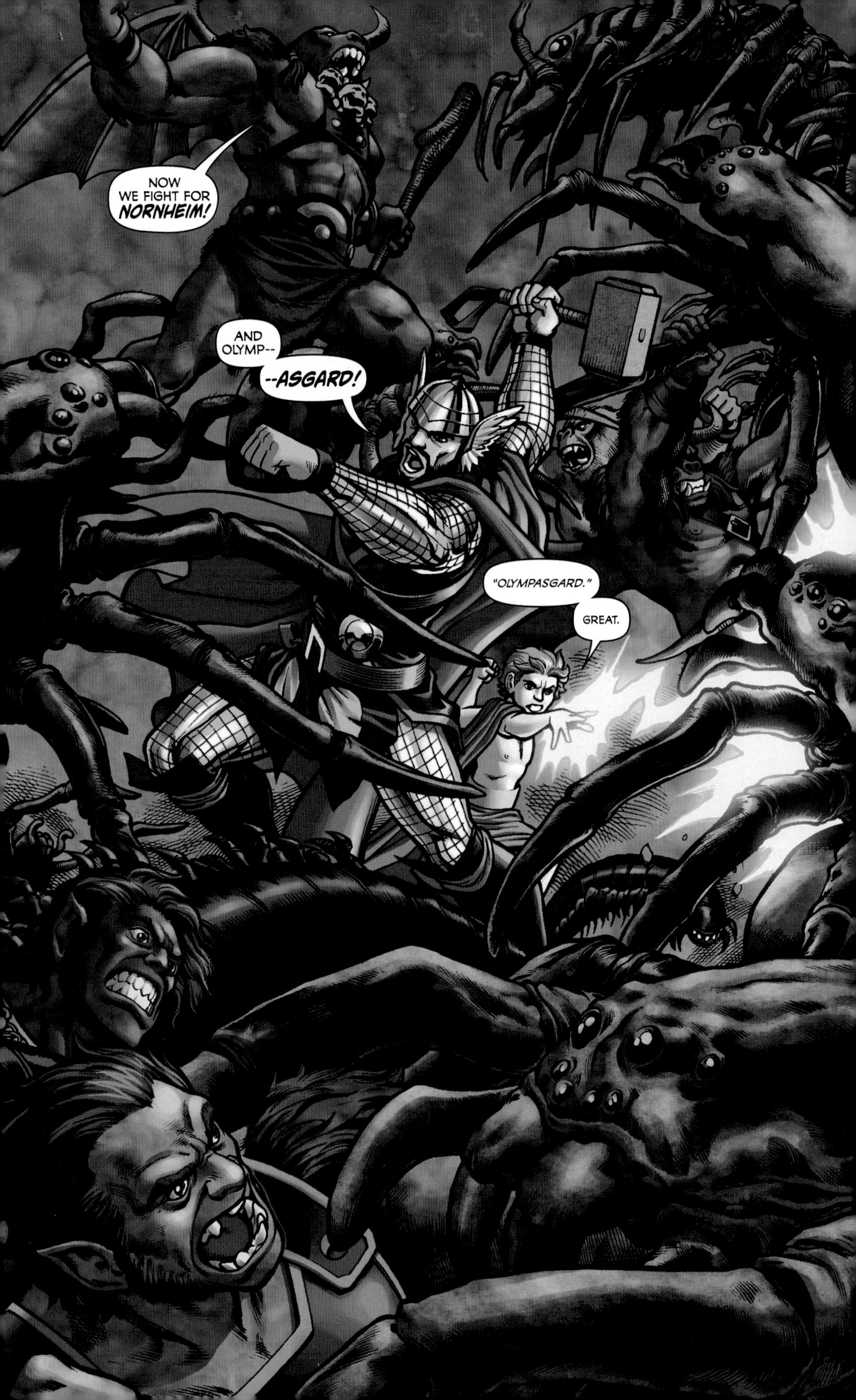
NOW WE FIGHT FOR NORNHEIM!
AND OLYMP--
--ASGARD!
"OLYMPASGARD."
GREAT.

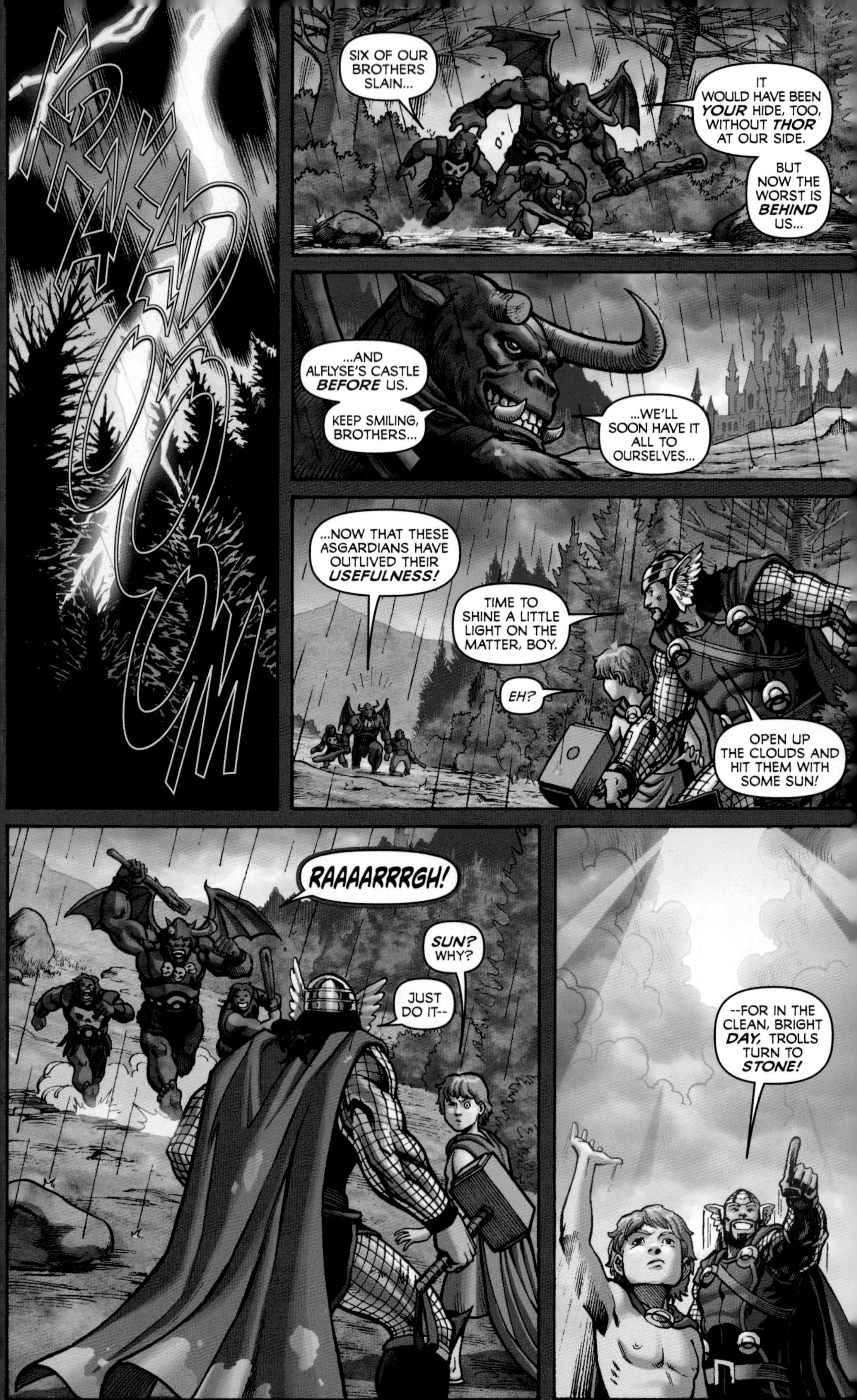
KRAKADOOOM
SIX OF OUR BROTHERS SLAIN...
IT WOULD HAVE BEEN YOUR HIDE, TOO, WITHOUT THOR AT OUR SIDE.
BUT NOW THE WORST IS BEHIND US...
...AND ALFLYSE'S CASTLE BEFORE US.
KEEP SMILING, BROTHERS...
...WE'LL SOON HAVE IT ALL TO OURSELVES...
...NOW THAT THESE ASGARDIANS HAVE OUTLIVED THEIR USEFULNESS!
TIME TO SHINE A LITTLE LIGHT ON THE MATTER, BOY.
EH?
OPEN UP THE CLOUDS AND HIT THEM WITH SOME SUN!
RAAAARRRGH!
SUN? WHY?
JUST DO IT--
--FOR IN THE CLEAN, BRIGHT DAY, TROLLS TURN TO STONE!

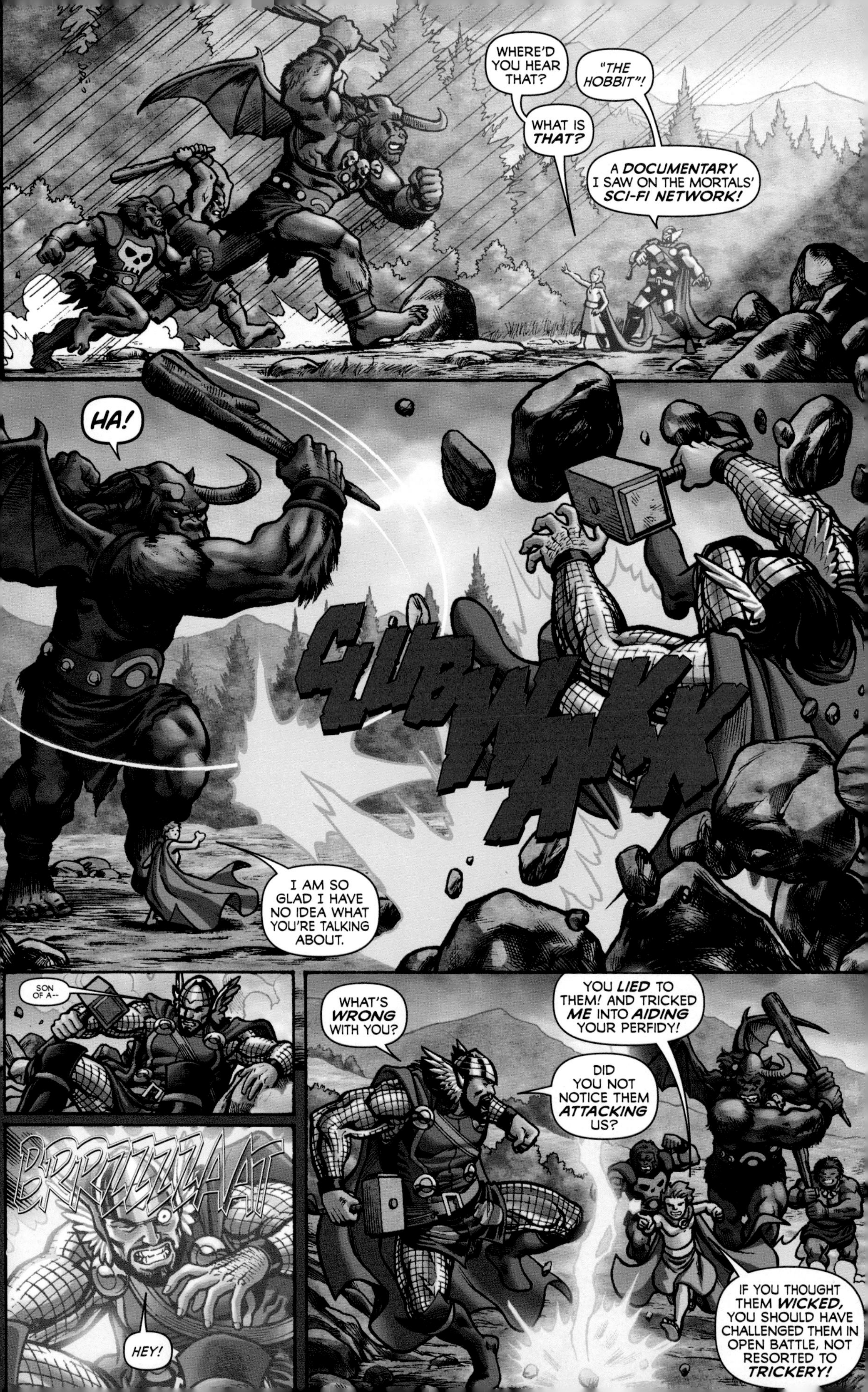
WHERE'D YOU HEAR THAT?
"THE HOBBIT"!
WHAT IS THAT?
A DOCUMENTARY I SAW ON THE MORTALS' SCI-FI NETWORK!
HA!
CLUBWAKKK
I AM SO GLAD I HAVE NO IDEA WHAT YOU'RE TALKING ABOUT.
SON OF A--
BRRZZZZAAT
HEY!
WHAT'S WRONG WITH YOU?
YOU LIED TO THEM! AND TRICKED ME INTO AIDING YOUR PERFIDY!
DID YOU NOT NOTICE THEM ATTACKING US?
IF YOU THOUGHT THEM WICKED, YOU SHOULD HAVE CHALLENGED THEM IN OPEN BATTLE, NOT RESORTED TO TRICKERY!

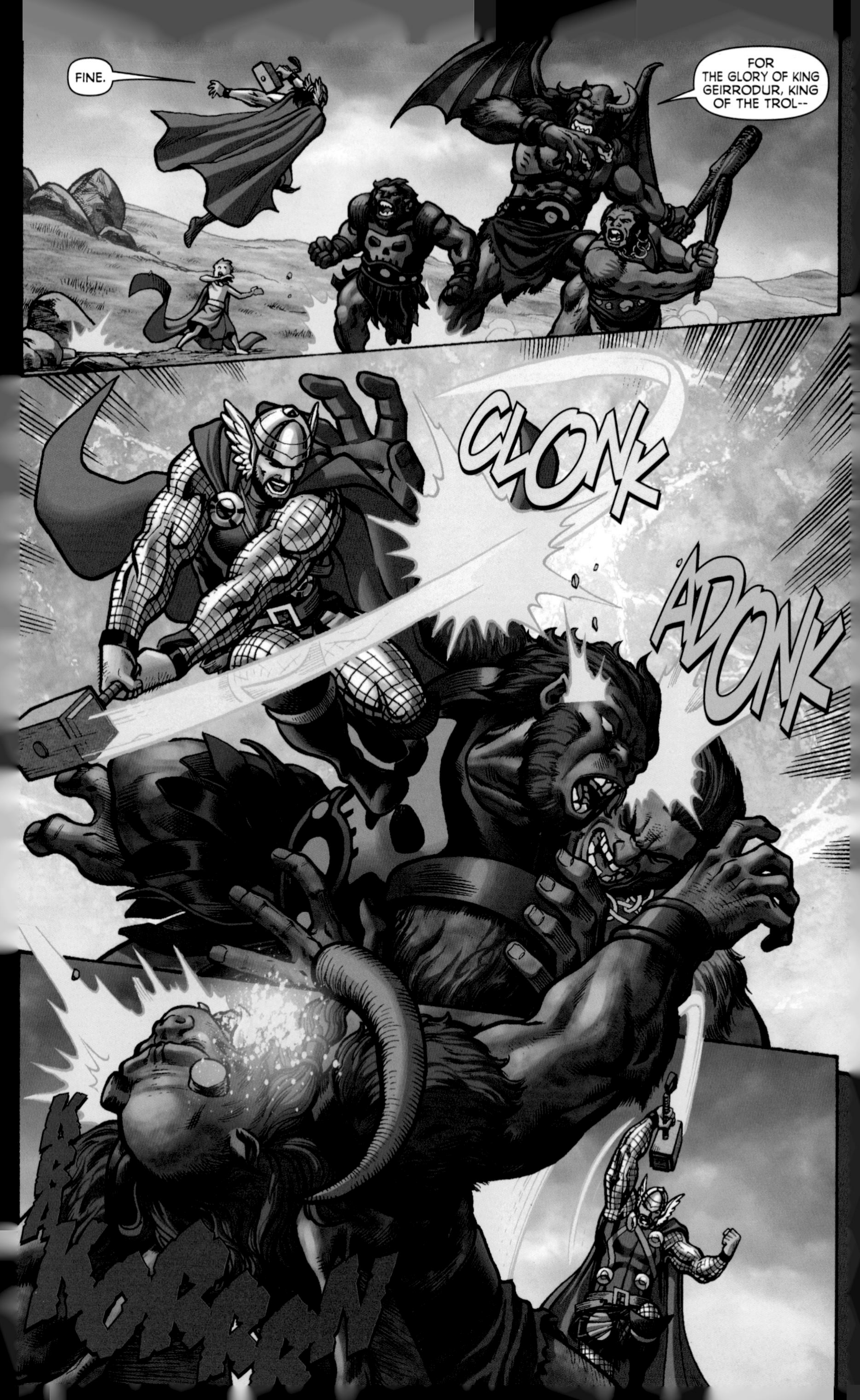
FINE.
FOR THE GLORY OF KING GEIRRODUR, KING OF THE TROL--
CLONK
ADONK

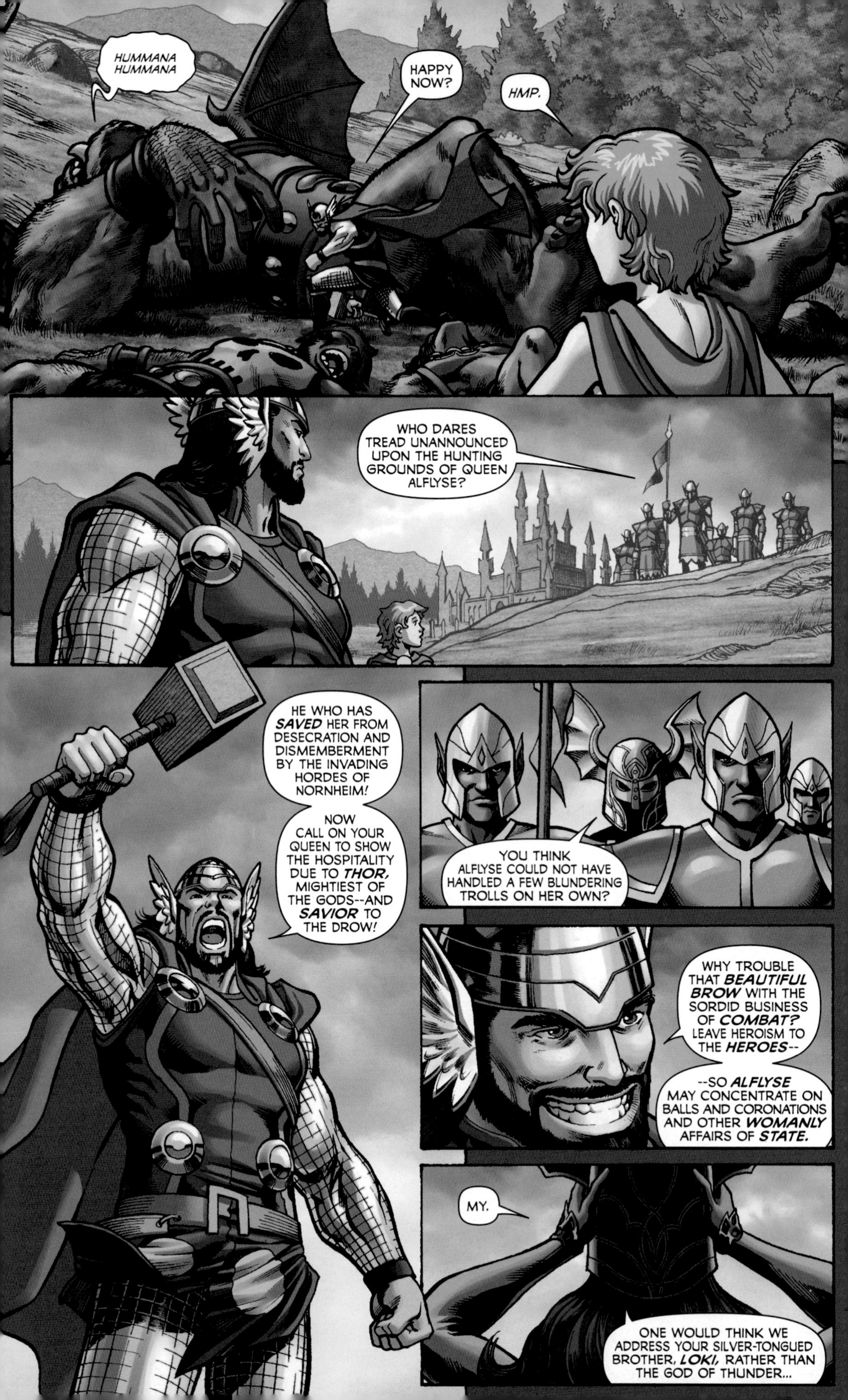
HUMMANA HUMMANA
HAPPY NOW?
HMP.
WHO DARES TREAD UNANNOUNCED UPON THE HUNTING GROUNDS OF QUEEN ALFLYSE?
HE WHO HAS SAVED HER FROM DESECRATION AND DISMEMBERMENT BY THE INVADING HORDES OF NORNHEIM!
NOW CALL ON YOUR QUEEN TO SHOW THE HOSPITALITY DUE TO THOR, MIGHTIEST OF THE GODS--AND SAVIOR TO THE DROW!
YOU THINK ALFLYSE COULD NOT HAVE HANDLED A FEW BLUNDERING TROLLS ON HER OWN?
WHY TROUBLE THAT BEAUTIFUL BROW WITH THE SORDID BUSINESS OF COMBAT? LEAVE HEROISM TO THE HEROES--
--SO ALFLYSE MAY CONCENTRATE ON BALLS AND CORONATIONS AND OTHER WOMANLY AFFAIRS OF STATE.
MY.
ONE WOULD THINK WE ADDRESS YOUR SILVER-TONGUED BROTHER, LOKI, RATHER THAN THE GOD OF THUNDER...

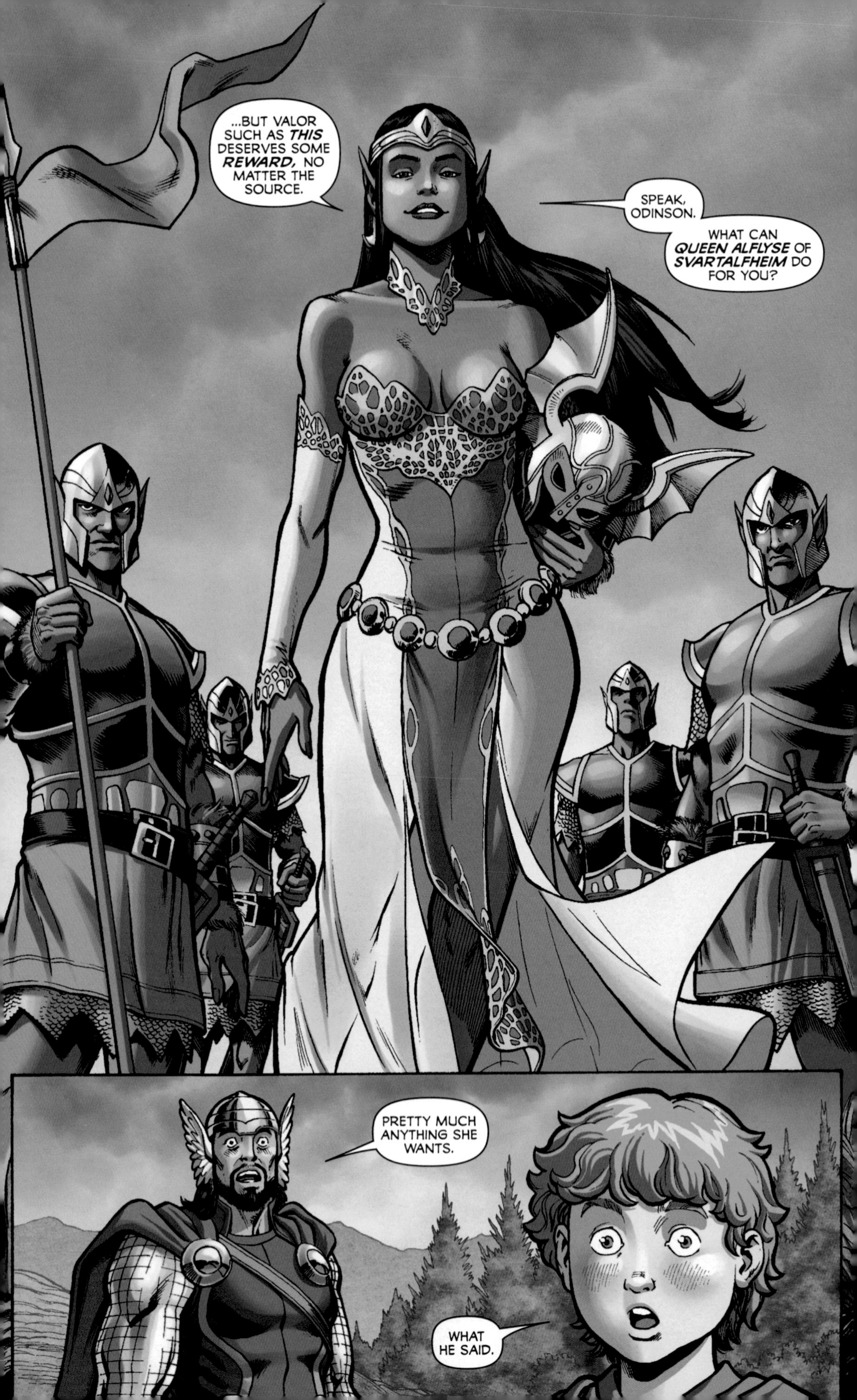
...BUT VALOR SUCH AS *THIS* DESERVES SOME *REWARD,* NO MATTER THE SOURCE.
SPEAK, ODINSON.
WHAT CAN *QUEEN ALFLYSE* OF *SVARTALFHEIM* DO FOR YOU?
PRETTY MUCH ANYTHING SHE WANTS.
WHAT HE SAID.

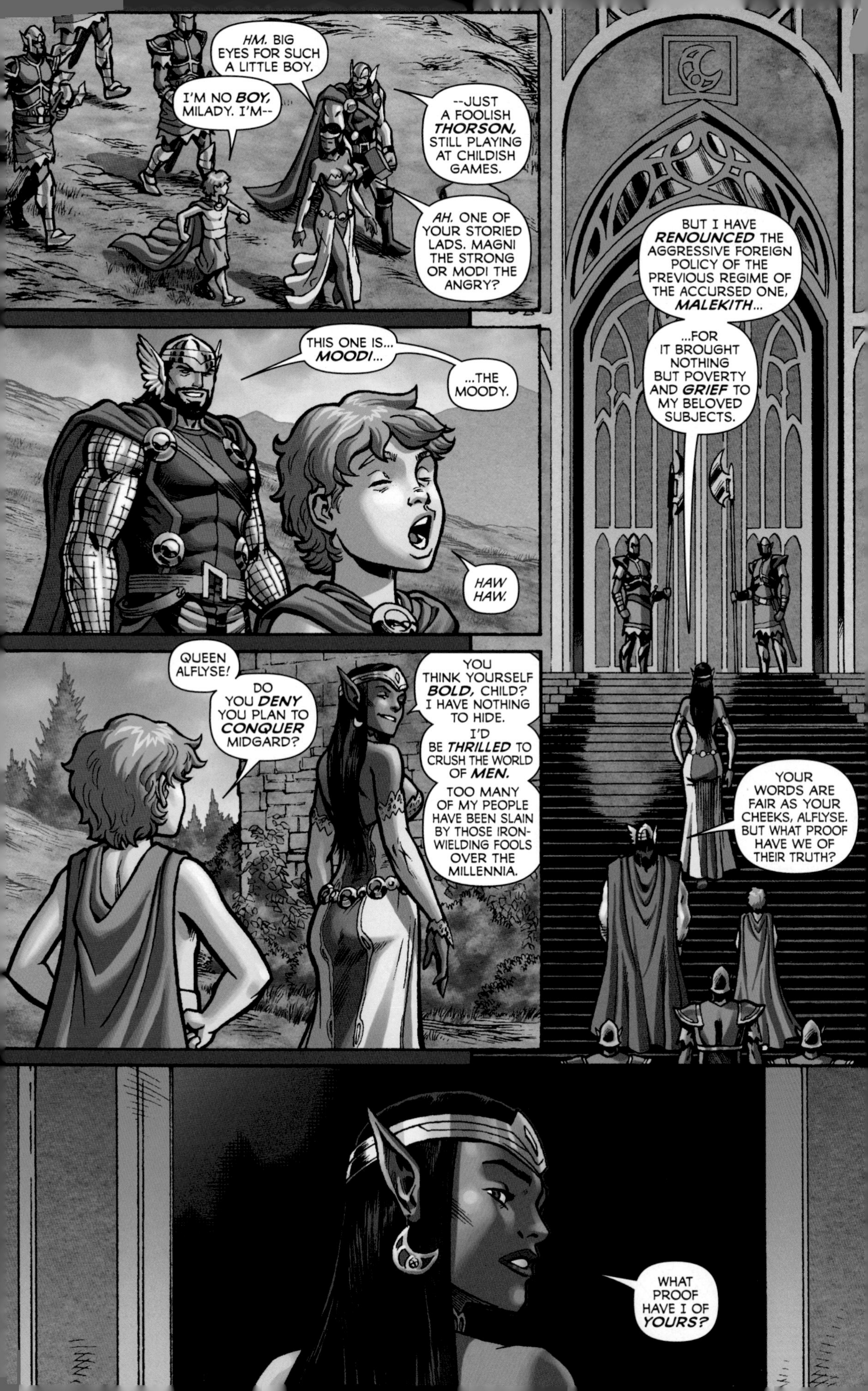
HM. BIG EYES FOR SUCH A LITTLE BOY.
I'M NO BOY, MILADY. I'M--
--JUST A FOOLISH THORSON, STILL PLAYING AT CHILDISH GAMES.
AH. ONE OF YOUR STORIED LADS. MAGNI THE STRONG OR MODI THE ANGRY?
THIS ONE IS... MOODI...
...THE MOODY.
HAW HAW.
QUEEN ALFLYSE!
DO YOU DENY YOU PLAN TO CONQUER MIDGARD?
YOU THINK YOURSELF BOLD, CHILD? I HAVE NOTHING TO HIDE.
I'D BE THRILLED TO CRUSH THE WORLD OF MEN.
TOO MANY OF MY PEOPLE HAVE BEEN SLAIN BY THOSE IRON-WIELDING FOOLS OVER THE MILLENNIA.
BUT I HAVE RENOUNCED THE AGGRESSIVE FOREIGN POLICY OF THE PREVIOUS REGIME OF THE ACCURSED ONE, MALEKITH...
...FOR IT BROUGHT NOTHING BUT POVERTY AND GRIEF TO MY BELOVED SUBJECTS.
YOUR WORDS ARE FAIR AS YOUR CHEEKS, ALFLYSE. BUT WHAT PROOF HAVE WE OF THEIR TRUTH?
WHAT PROOF HAVE I OF YOURS?

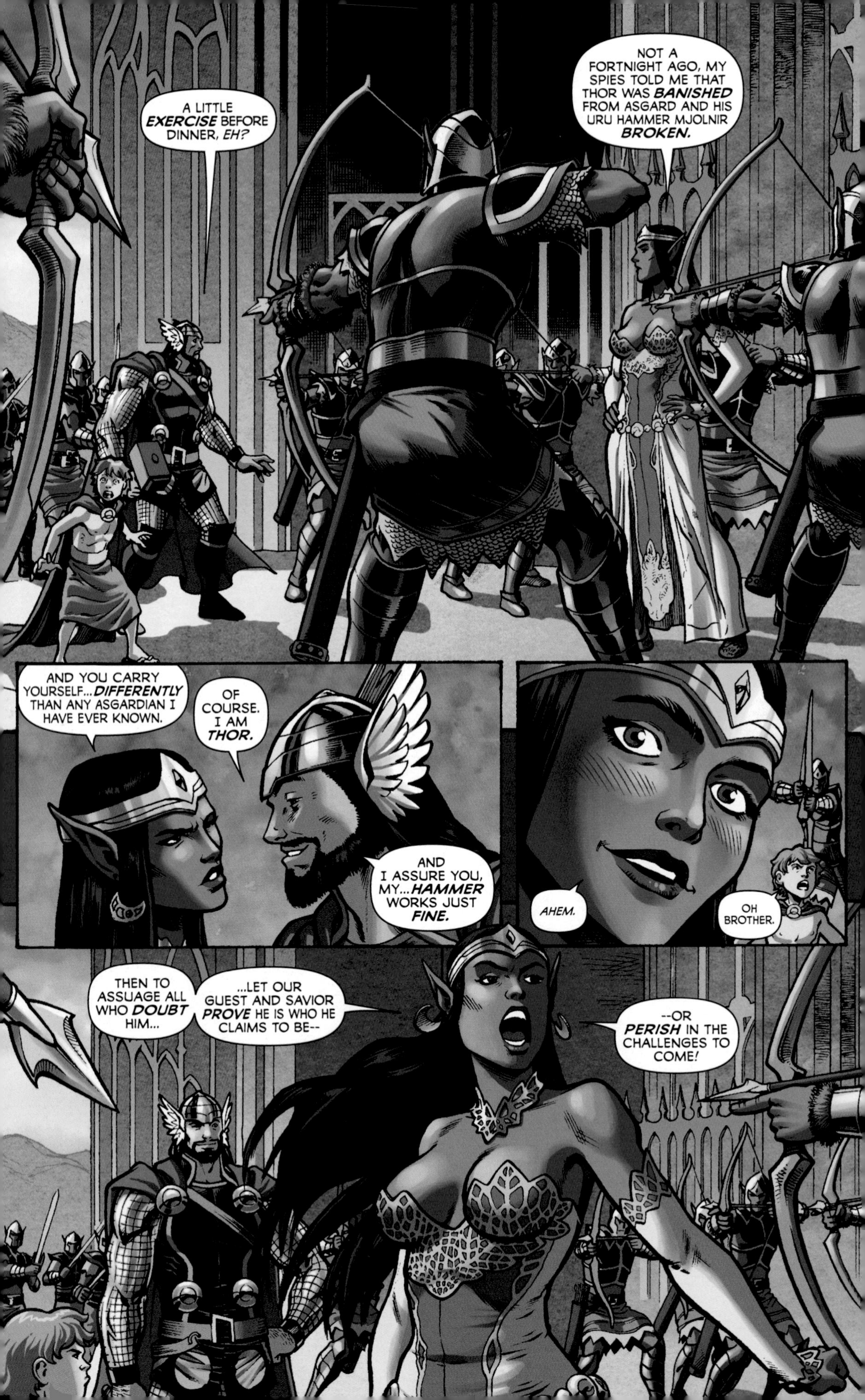
A LITTLE EXERCISE BEFORE DINNER, EH?
NOT A FORTNIGHT AGO, MY SPIES TOLD ME THAT THOR WAS BANISHED FROM ASGARD AND HIS URU HAMMER MJOLNIR BROKEN.
AND YOU CARRY YOURSELF...DIFFERENTLY THAN ANY ASGARDIAN I HAVE EVER KNOWN.
OF COURSE. I AM THOR.
AND I ASSURE YOU, MY...HAMMER WORKS JUST FINE.
AHEM.
OH BROTHER.
THEN TO ASSUAGE ALL WHO DOUBT HIM...
...LET OUR GUEST AND SAVIOR PROVE HE IS WHO HE CLAIMS TO BE--
--OR PERISH IN THE CHALLENGES TO COME!

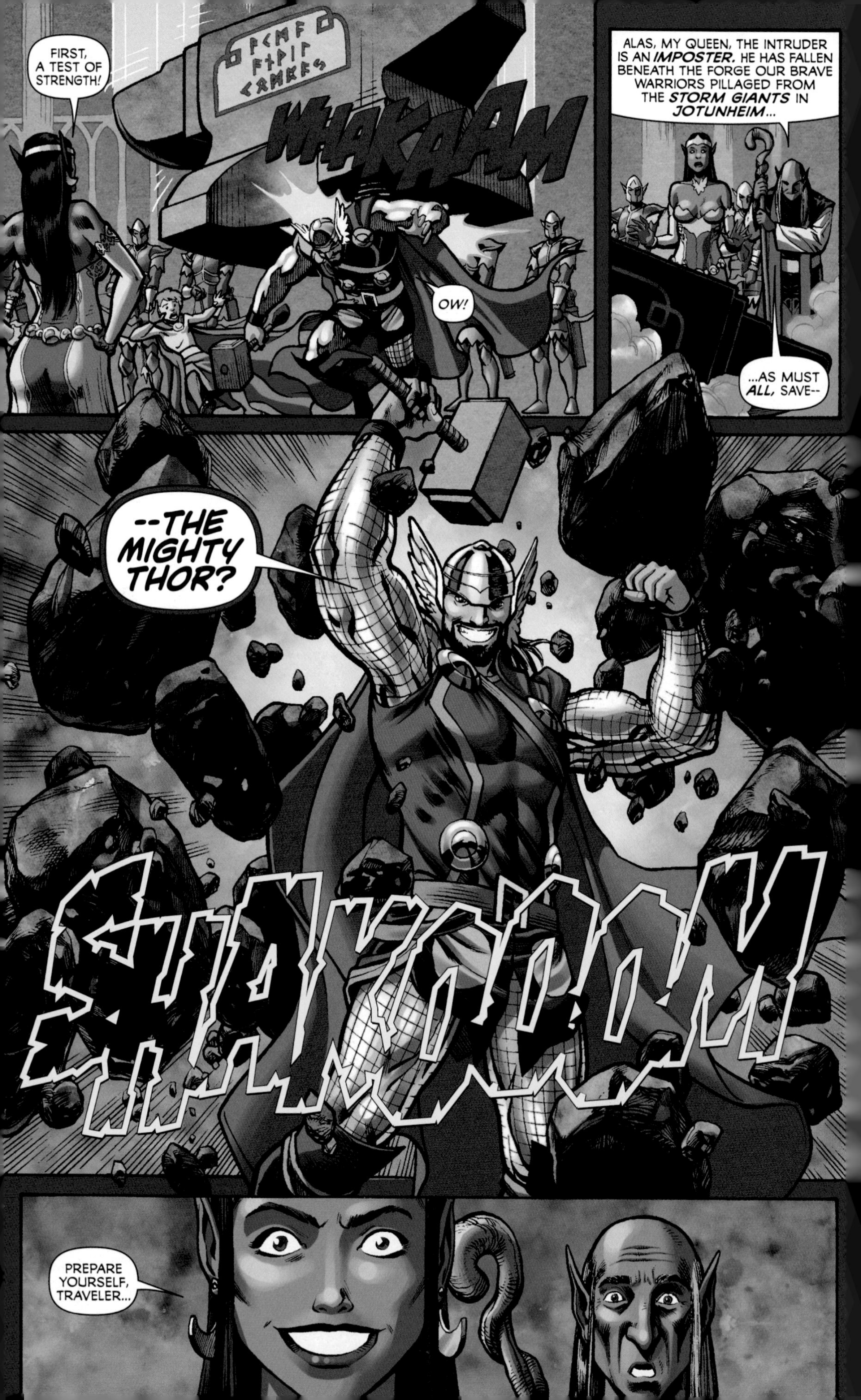
FIRST, A TEST OF STRENGTH!
WHAKAAM
OW!
ALAS, MY QUEEN, THE INTRUDER IS AN IMPOSTER. HE HAS FALLEN BENEATH THE FORGE OUR BRAVE WARRIORS PILLAGED FROM THE STORM GIANTS IN JOTUNHEIM...
...AS MUST ALL, SAVE--
--THE MIGHTY THOR?
PREPARE YOURSELF, TRAVELER...

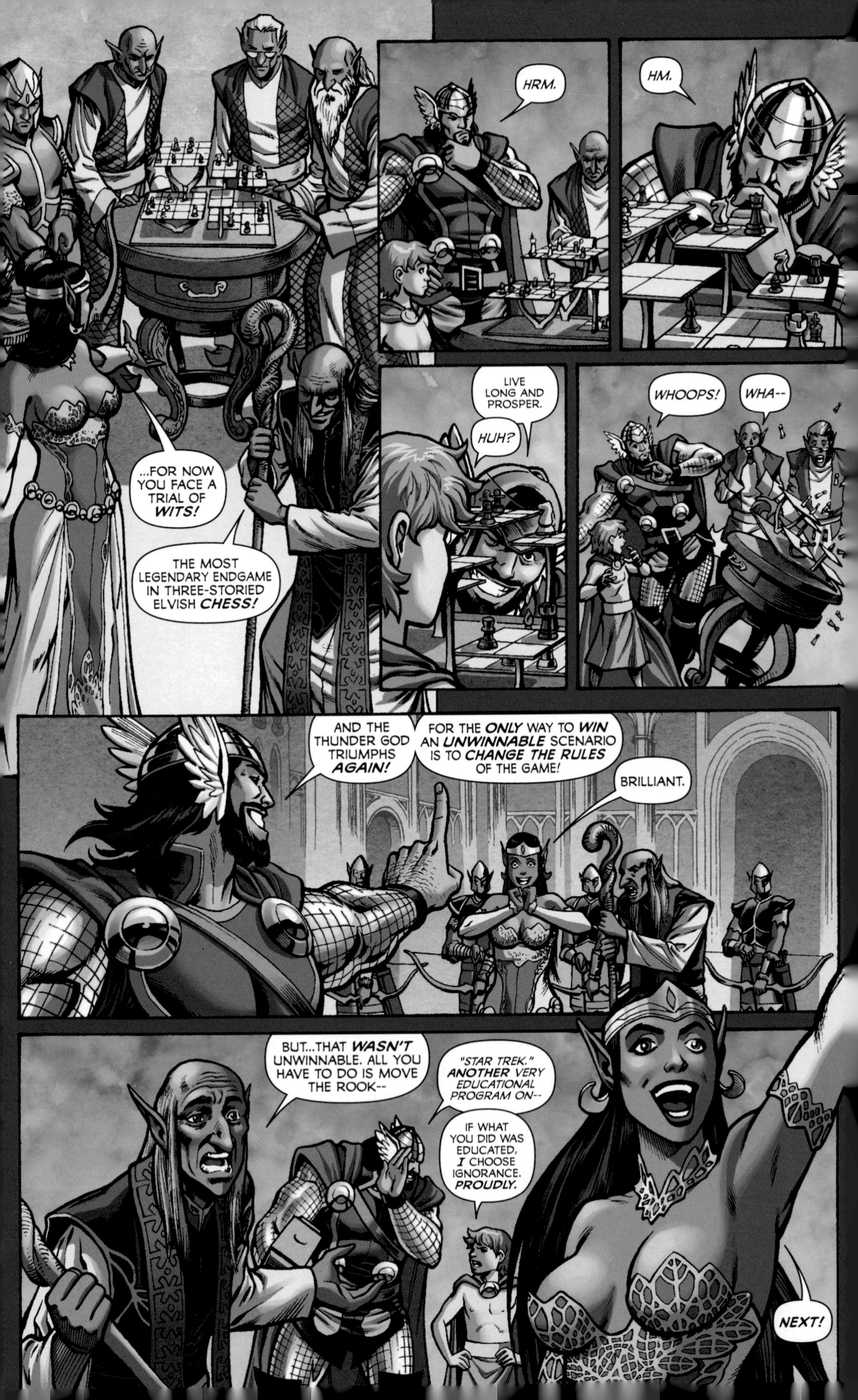
HRM.
HM.
...FOR NOW YOU FACE A TRIAL OF WITS!
THE MOST LEGENDARY ENDGAME IN THREE-STORIED ELVISH CHESS!
LIVE LONG AND PROSPER.
HUH?
WHOOPS!
WHA--
AND THE THUNDER GOD TRIUMPHS AGAIN!
FOR THE ONLY WAY TO WIN AN UNWINNABLE SCENARIO IS TO CHANGE THE RULES OF THE GAME!
BRILLIANT.
BUT...THAT WASN'T UNWINNABLE. ALL YOU HAVE TO DO IS MOVE THE ROOK--
"STAR TREK." ANOTHER VERY EDUCATIONAL PROGRAM ON--
IF WHAT YOU DID WAS EDUCATED, I CHOOSE IGNORANCE. PROUDLY.
NEXT!

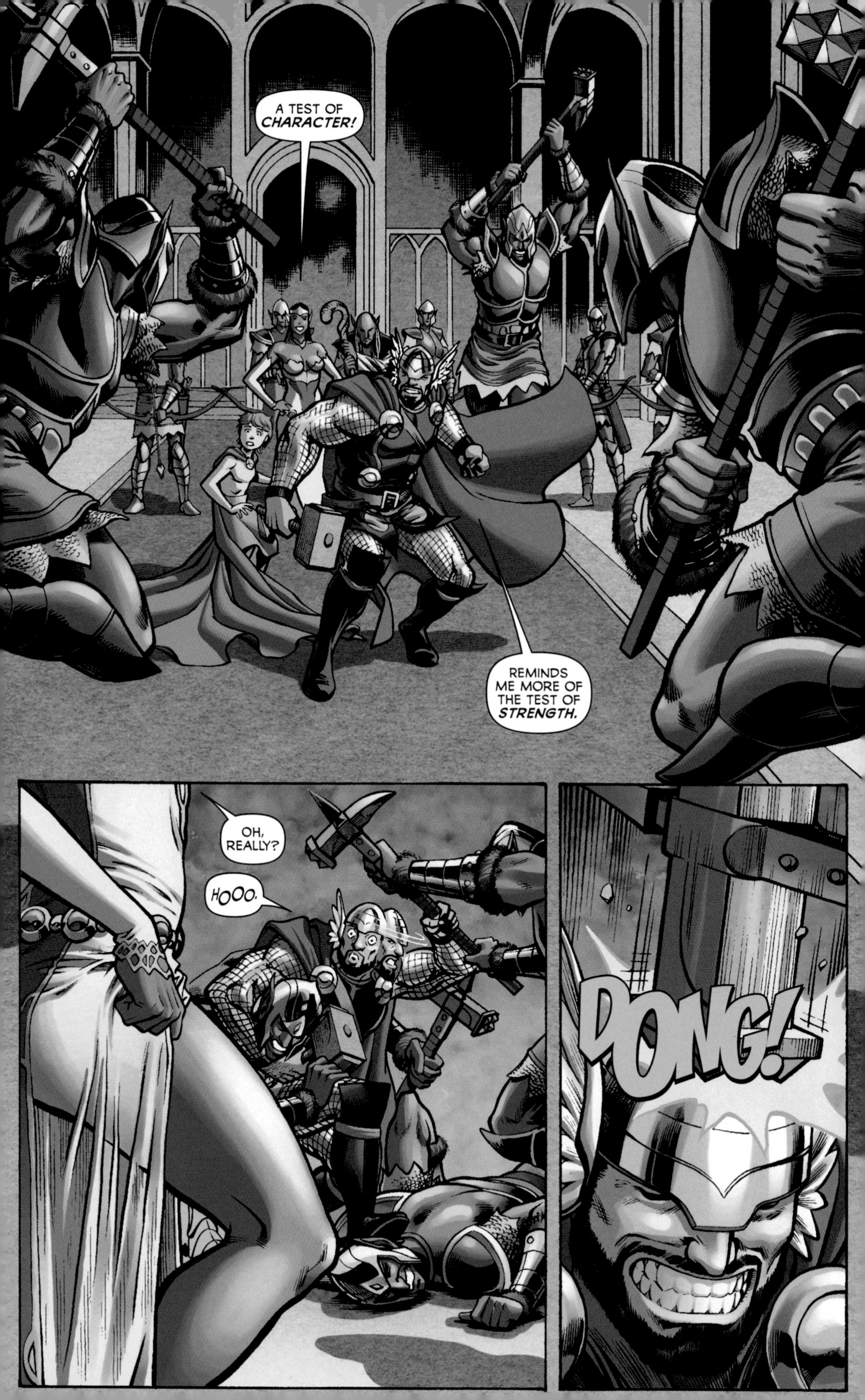
A TEST OF CHARACTER!
REMINDS ME MORE OF THE TEST OF STRENGTH.
OH, REALLY?
HOOO.
DONG!

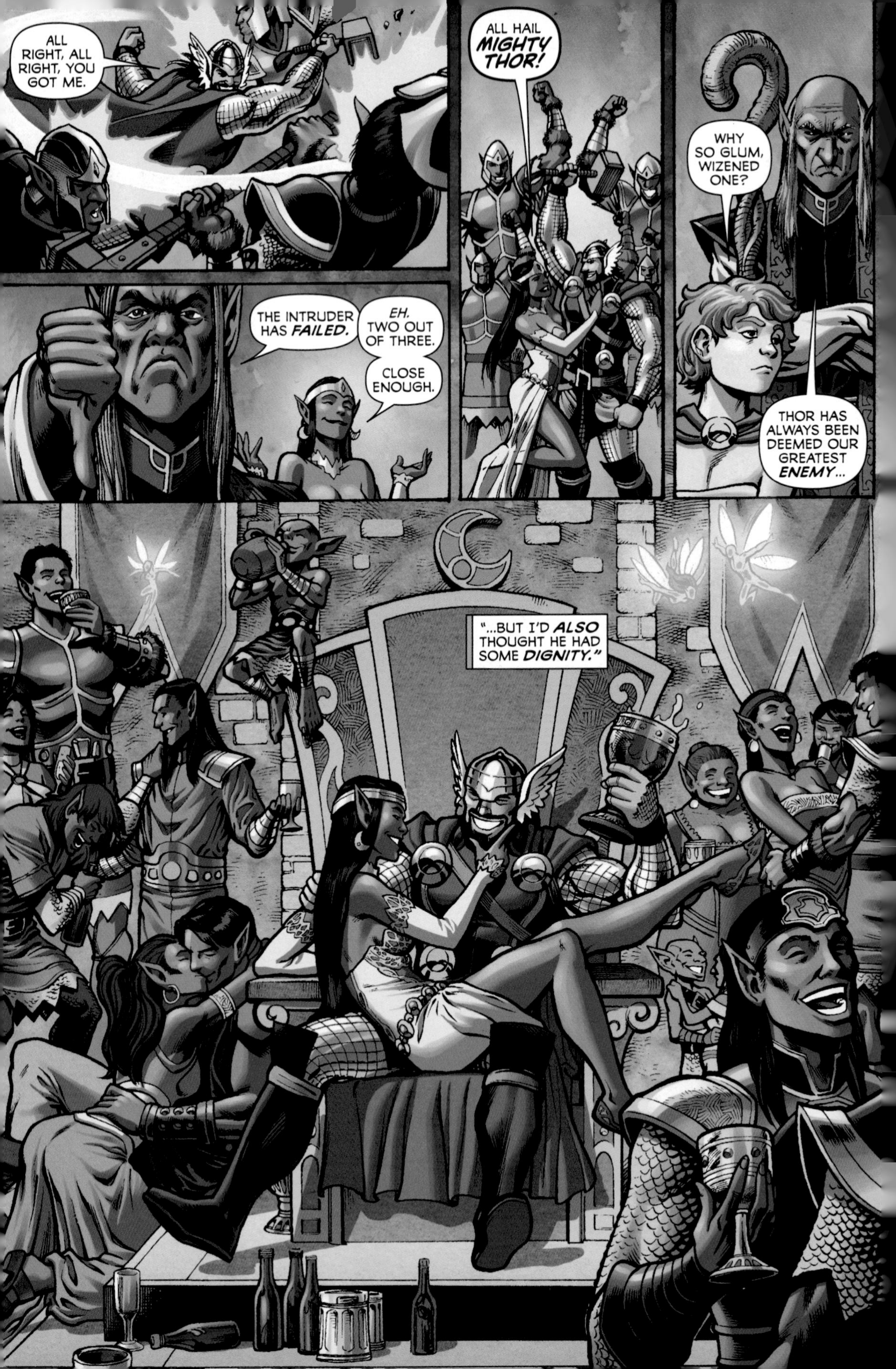
ALL RIGHT, ALL RIGHT, YOU GOT ME.
ALL HAIL *MIGHTY THOR!*
WHY SO GLUM, WIZENED ONE?
THE INTRUDER HAS *FAILED.*
EH. TWO OUT OF THREE.
CLOSE ENOUGH.
THOR HAS ALWAYS BEEN DEEMED OUR GREATEST *ENEMY*...
"...BUT I'D *ALSO* THOUGHT HE HAD SOME *DIGNITY.*"

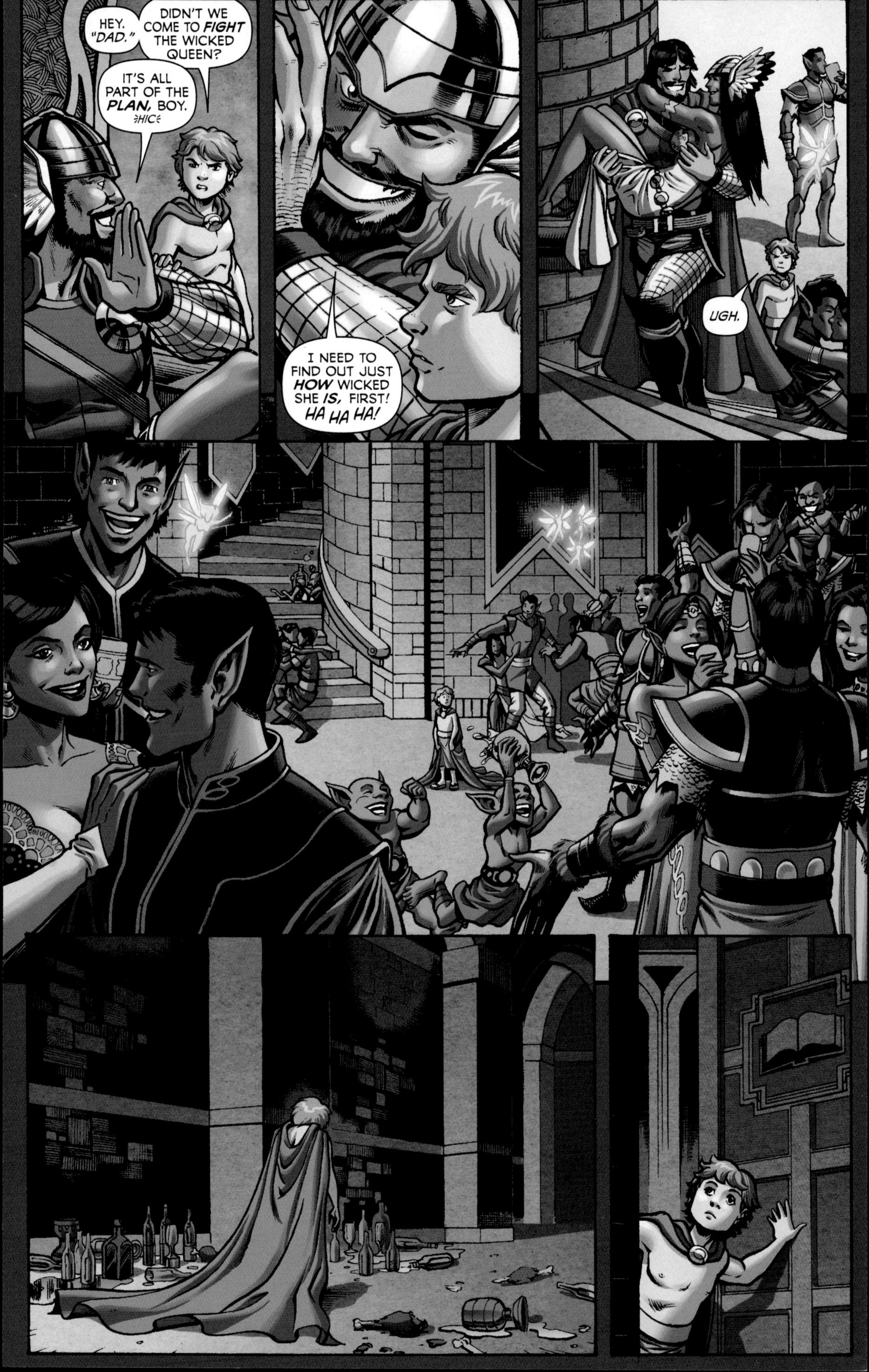
HEY. "DAD."
DIDN'T WE COME TO FIGHT THE WICKED QUEEN?
IT'S ALL PART OF THE PLAN, BOY. HIC
I NEED TO FIND OUT JUST HOW WICKED SHE IS, FIRST! HA HA HA!
UGH.

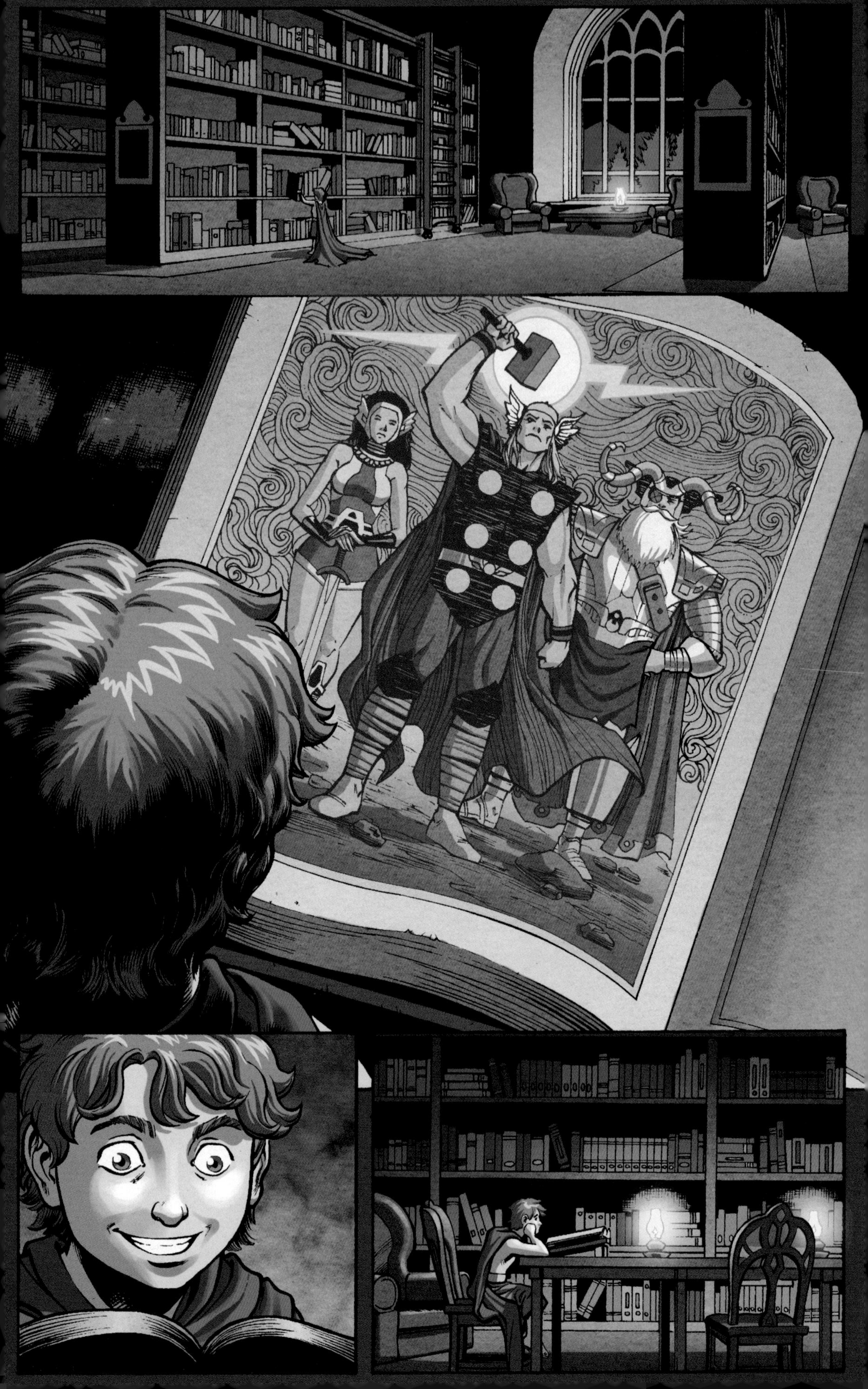

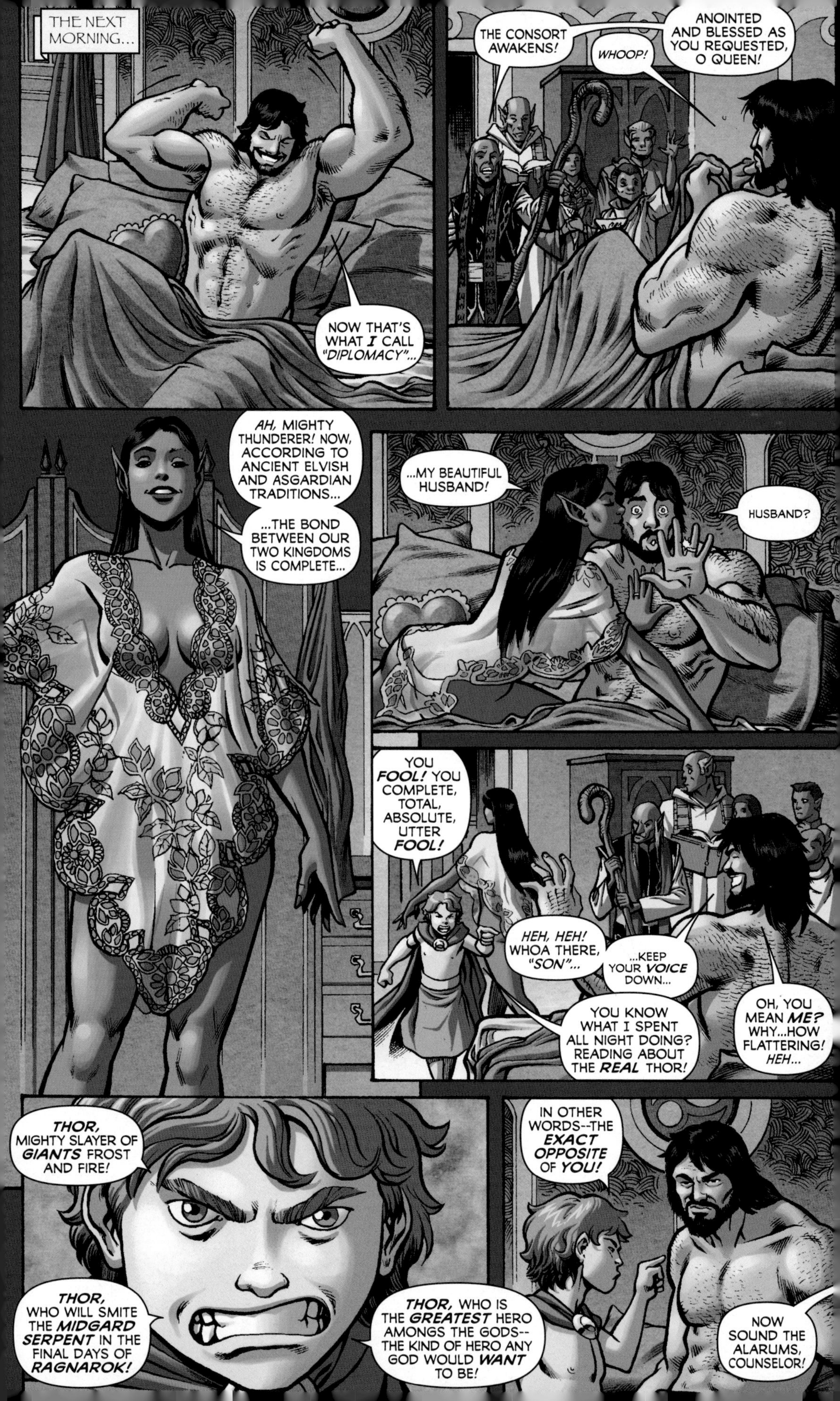
THE NEXT MORNING...
NOW THAT'S WHAT *I* CALL *"DIPLOMACY"*...
THE CONSORT AWAKENS!
WHOOP!
ANOINTED AND BLESSED AS YOU REQUESTED, O QUEEN!
AH, MIGHTY THUNDERER! NOW, ACCORDING TO ANCIENT ELVISH AND ASGARDIAN TRADITIONS...
...THE BOND BETWEEN OUR TWO KINGDOMS IS COMPLETE...
...MY BEAUTIFUL HUSBAND!
HUSBAND?
YOU ***FOOL!*** YOU COMPLETE, TOTAL, ABSOLUTE, UTTER ***FOOL!***
HEH, HEH! WHOA THERE, *"SON"*...
...KEEP YOUR ***VOICE*** DOWN...
YOU KNOW WHAT I SPENT ALL NIGHT DOING? READING ABOUT THE ***REAL*** THOR!
OH, YOU MEAN ***ME?*** WHY...HOW FLATTERING! *HEH...*
THOR, MIGHTY SLAYER OF ***GIANTS*** FROST AND FIRE!
THOR, WHO WILL SMITE THE ***MIDGARD SERPENT*** IN THE FINAL DAYS OF ***RAGNAROK!***
THOR, WHO IS THE ***GREATEST*** HERO AMONGS THE GODS-- THE KIND OF HERO ANY GOD WOULD ***WANT*** TO BE!
IN OTHER WORDS--THE ***EXACT OPPOSITE*** OF ***YOU!***
NOW SOUND THE ALARUMS, COUNSELOR!

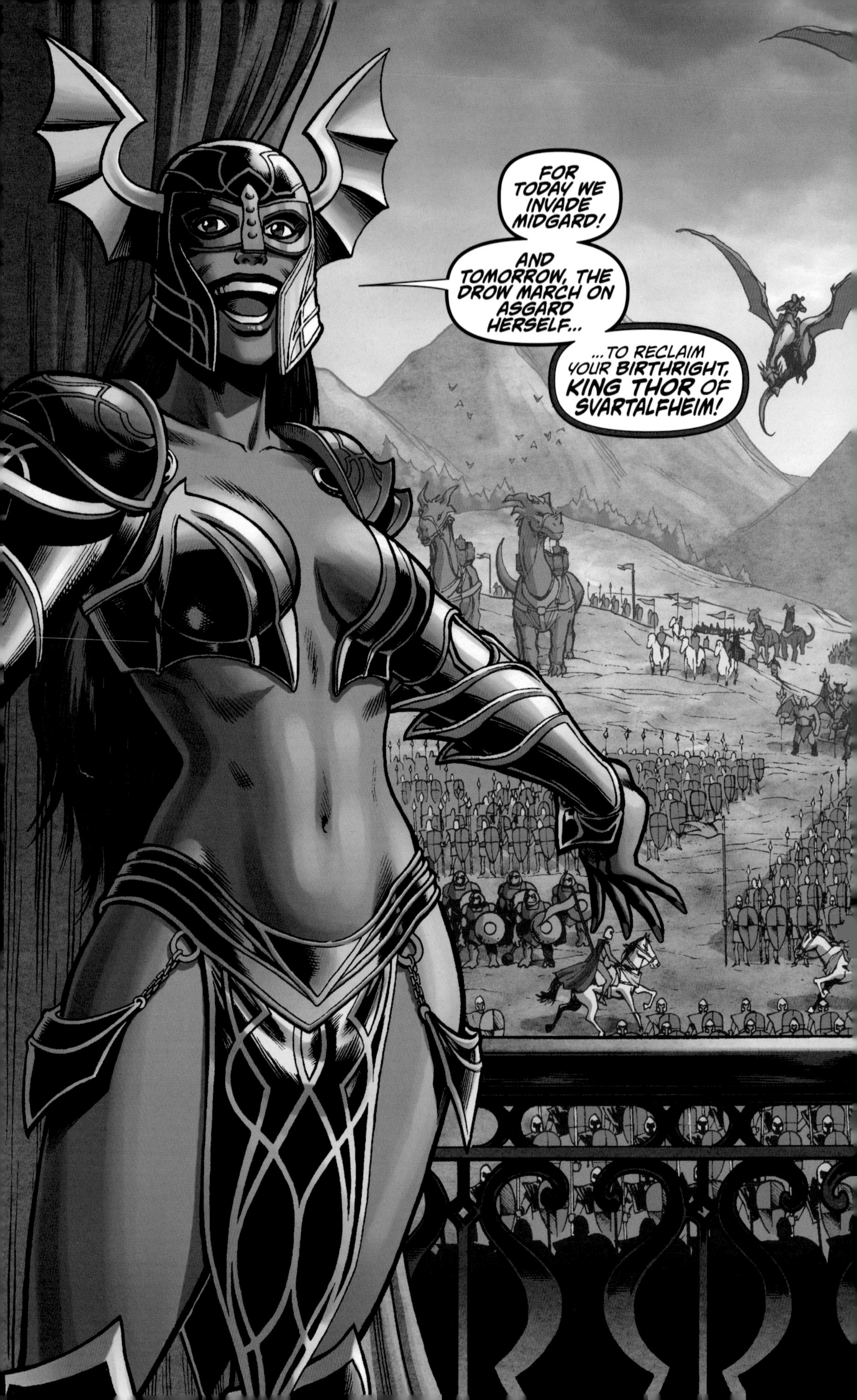
FOR TODAY WE INVADE MIDGARD!
AND TOMORROW, THE DROW MARCH ON ASGARD HERSELF...
...TO RECLAIM YOUR BIRTHRIGHT, KING THOR OF SVARTALFHEIM!

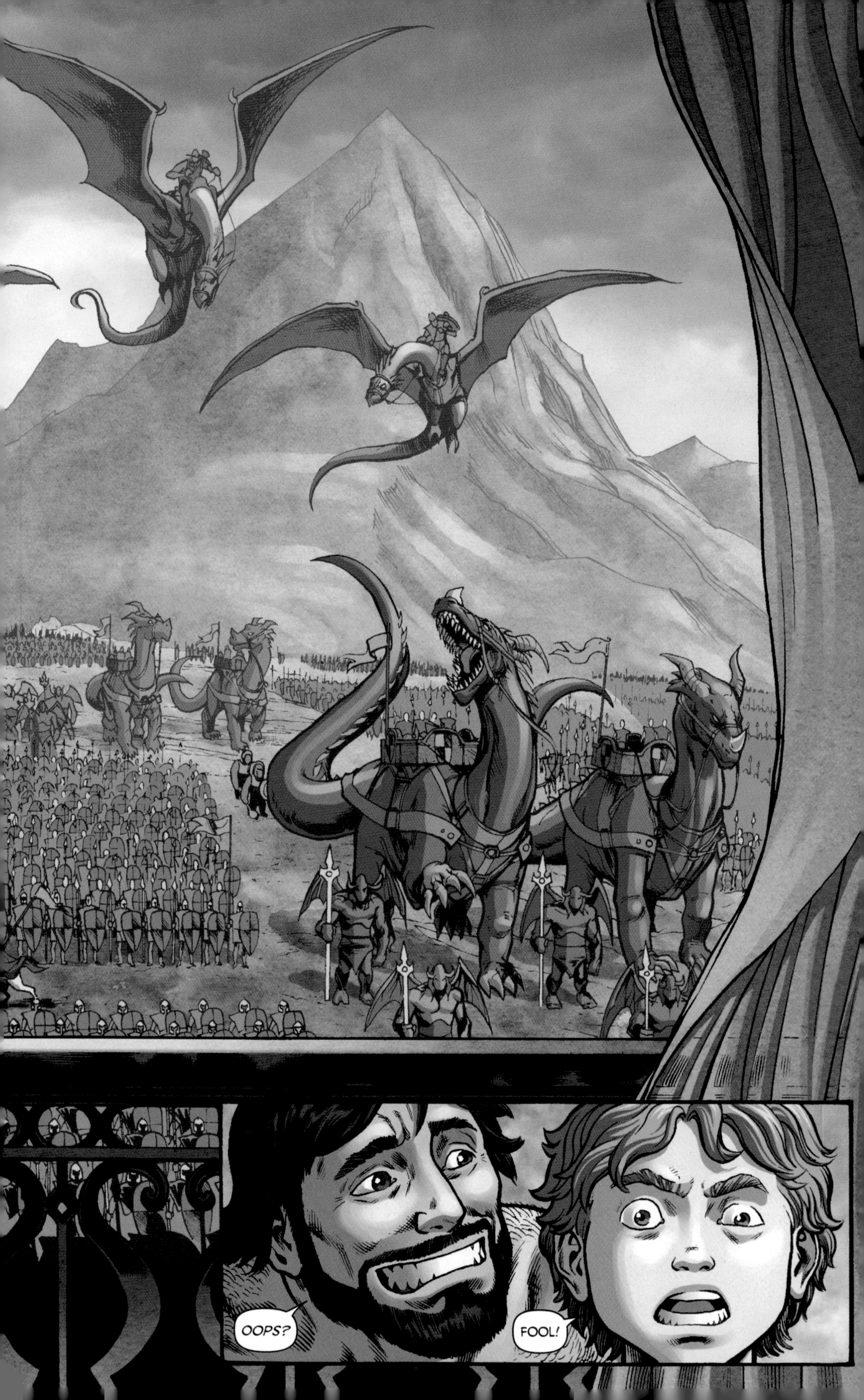
OOPS?
FOOL!

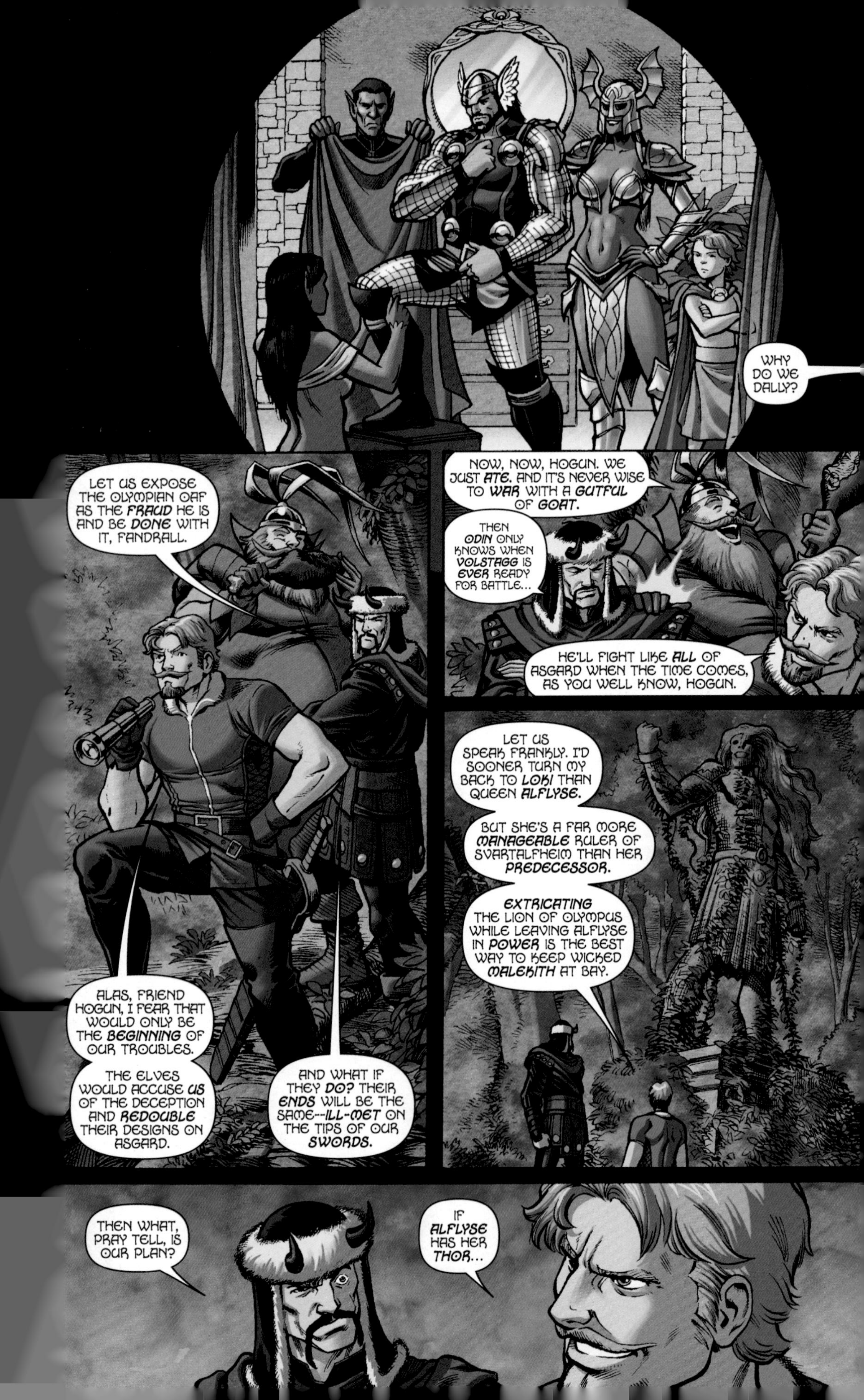
WHY DO WE DALLY?
LET US EXPOSE THE OLYMPIAN OAF AS THE FRAUD HE IS AND BE DONE WITH IT, FANDRALL.
NOW, NOW, HOGUN. WE JUST ATE. AND IT'S NEVER WISE TO WAR WITH A GUTFUL OF GOAT.
THEN ODIN ONLY KNOWS WHEN VOLSTAGG IS EVER READY FOR BATTLE...
HE'LL FIGHT LIKE ALL OF ASGARD WHEN THE TIME COMES, AS YOU WELL KNOW, HOGUN.
ALAS, FRIEND HOGUN, I FEAR THAT WOULD ONLY BE THE BEGINNING OF OUR TROUBLES.
THE ELVES WOULD ACCUSE US OF THE DECEPTION AND REDOUBLE THEIR DESIGNS ON ASGARD.
AND WHAT IF THEY DO? THEIR ENDS WILL BE THE SAME--ILL-MET ON THE TIPS OF OUR SWORDS.
LET US SPEAK FRANKLY. I'D SOONER TURN MY BACK TO LOKI THAN QUEEN ALFLYSE.
BUT SHE'S A FAR MORE MANAGEABLE RULER OF SVARTALFHEIM THAN HER PREDECESSOR.
EXTRICATING THE LION OF OLYMPUS WHILE LEAVING ALFLYSE IN POWER IS THE BEST WAY TO KEEP WICKED MALEKITH AT BAY.
THEN WHAT, PRAY TELL, IS OUR PLAN?
IF ALFLYSE HAS HER THOR...

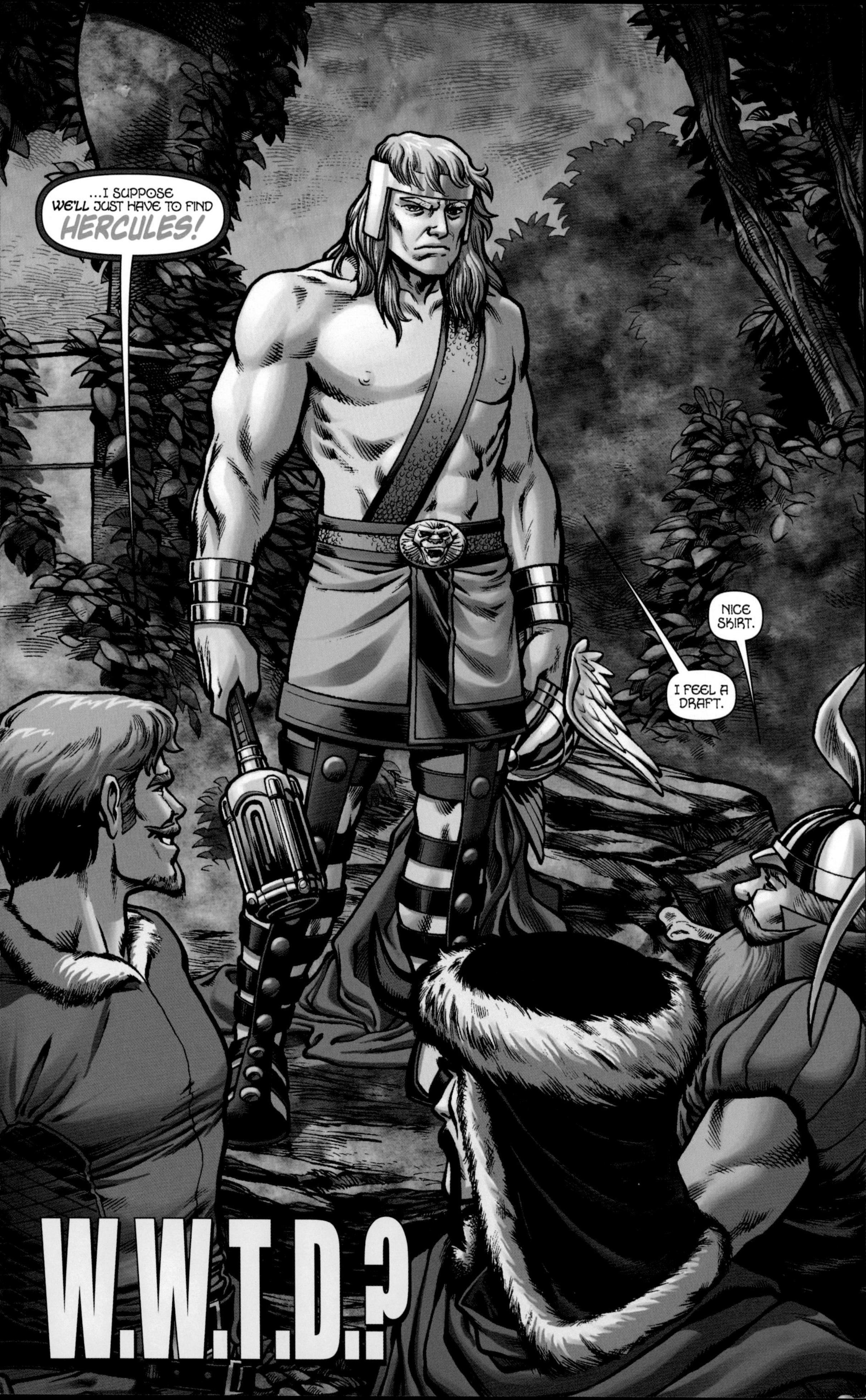
...I SUPPOSE WE'LL JUST HAVE TO FIND HERCULES!
NICE SKIRT.
I FEEL A DRAFT.
W.W.T.D.?

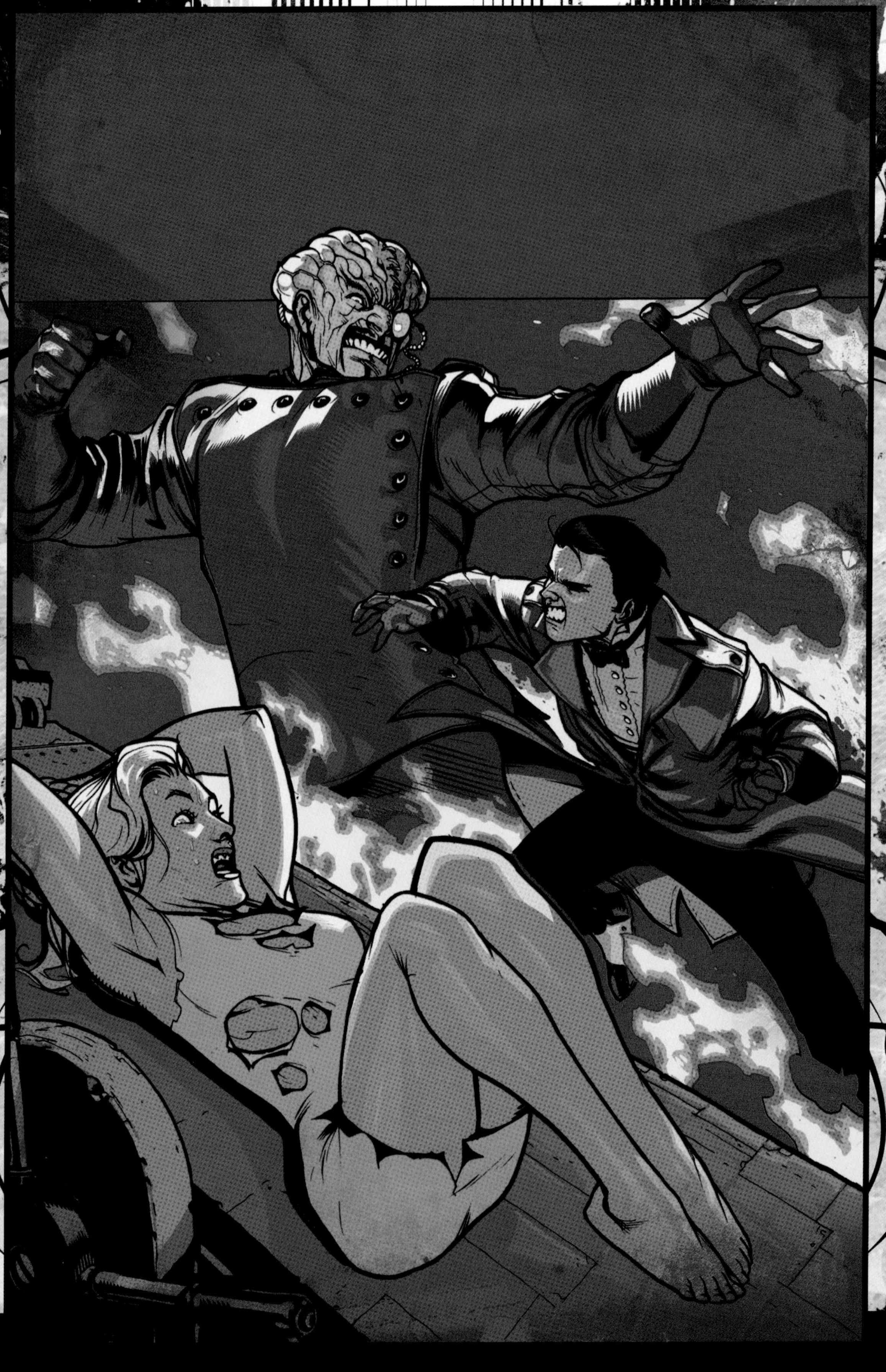

INCREDIBLE HERCULES #135

X1

BEGINNER MODULE

WELCOME TO THE MASTER MIND EXCELLO ROLEPLAYING GAME®!

Property of Amadeus Cho, 7th Smartest Person on Earth

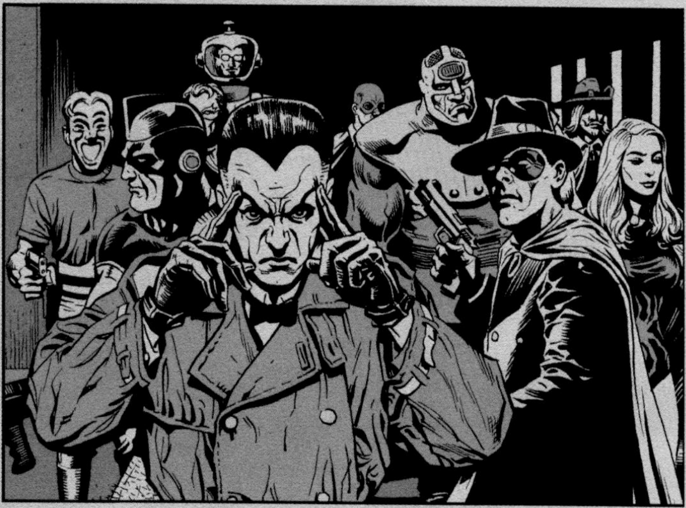

To Do:
- Ditch Hercules ✓
- travel to Excello, Utah ✓
- Battle Pythagoras Dupree
- find missing sister

INTRODUCTORY SOLO ADVENTURE

Come back with us now to the thrilling days of World War II, where you can become a fascist-fighting mystery man like everyone's favorite heroic super-genius, Carl Everett, the **MASTER MIND EXCELLO**™!

We here at **Pythagoras Dupree Games®** have included this short solo adventure for a single character — you can roll up one of your own or use one of the pre-generated PC's provided on page 246 of this **PLAYERS' GUIDE**™ — so you can learn the rules as you play, with no **Master Mind Mind-Master** (what some RPG's call "The Gamemaster") required. Grab a pencil, all seventeen kinds of dice provided in the box, as well as a calculator with keys for sine, cosine, and tangent, then LET THE ADVENTURE BEGIN!™

1: An Army Air Force Base on the southern coast of England. June 1944. You are playing twenty-five GI's in chess simultaneously in the base commissary and you have twenty-three of them one move away from checkmate (the other two you've already defeated).

Suddenly, the voice of **William "Wild Bill" Donovan**, head of the Office of Strategic Services, booms over the loudspeaker: "Master Mind Excello! Report at once to the Briefing Room for your next mission!"

If you decide to stay and finish your chess match(es), proceed to 2.
If you decide to go to the briefing, skip to 3.

2: The Nazis conquer the whole world because you are a selfish piece of garbage and you are the twelfth executed at Buchenwald, between Bucky (Captain America's sidekick) and that Destroyer guy. Nice job, Dumbass. *GAME OVER.*

3: You boldly make your way down the corridor until the hallway makes a T. You know the briefing room is down the left-hand hallway.

If you go left, continue to 4.
If you go right, jump to 5.

4: A German spy leaps out of the darkness with a knife as you turn down the hallway! Time to calculate "Initiative," or who goes first, in the following manner: Take your modifier from your AGILITY bonus and multiply it by the degree of SURPRISE inspired by this attack as rolled on a 1d8. The square root of that number is the "TARGET THROW" the spy must exceed on a 1d20 as modified by his own INSTINCTUAL ATTRIBUTE LEVEL, which is the average of his **Lurking in Shadows** and **Springing at Victim** skill percentiles, rounded down to the nearest tenth.

If you won the Initiative roll, skip to 6.
If you lost the Initiative roll, turn to 7.

5: The Nazis conquer the whole world because you are a lazy piece of garbage wandering randomly down hallways. You are the twelfth executed at Buchenwald, between Bucky (Captain America's sidekick) and that Destroyer guy. Nice job, Dumbass. *GAME OVER.*

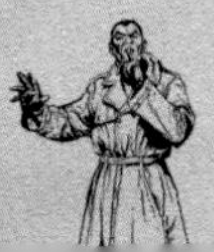

XLO Games
(a subsidiary of Excello Soap Co.)
POB 756
Excello, UT

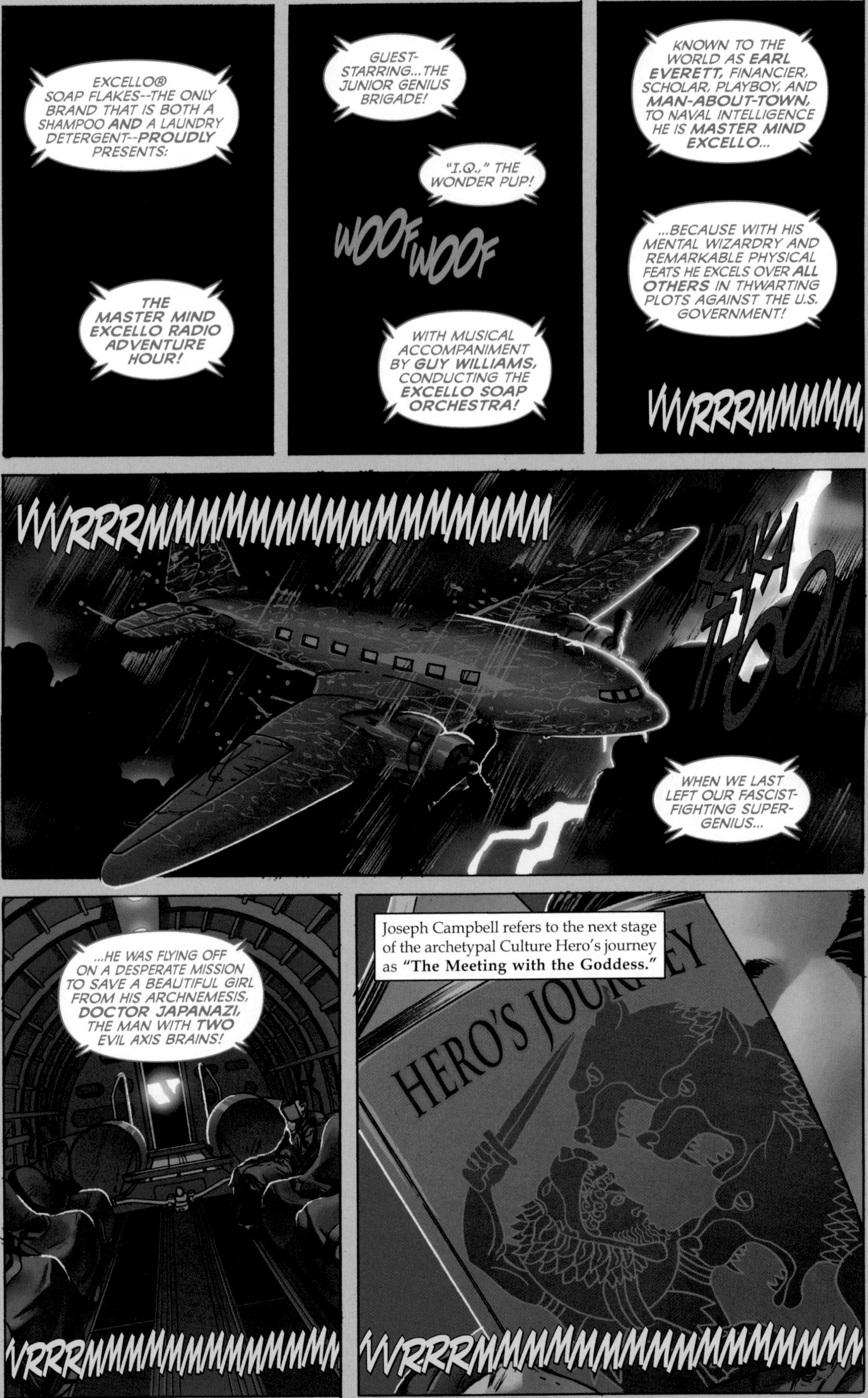

EXCELLO® SOAP FLAKES--THE ONLY BRAND THAT IS BOTH A SHAMPOO AND A LAUNDRY DETERGENT--PROUDLY PRESENTS:
THE MASTER MIND EXCELLO RADIO ADVENTURE HOUR!
GUEST-STARRING...THE JUNIOR GENIUS BRIGADE!
"I.Q.," THE WONDER PUP!
WOOF WOOF
WITH MUSICAL ACCOMPANIMENT BY GUY WILLIAMS, CONDUCTING THE EXCELLO SOAP ORCHESTRA!
KNOWN TO THE WORLD AS EARL EVERETT, FINANCIER, SCHOLAR, PLAYBOY, AND MAN-ABOUT-TOWN, TO NAVAL INTELLIGENCE HE IS MASTER MIND EXCELLO...
...BECAUSE WITH HIS MENTAL WIZARDRY AND REMARKABLE PHYSICAL FEATS HE EXCELS OVER ALL OTHERS IN THWARTING PLOTS AGAINST THE U.S. GOVERNMENT!
VVVRRRMMMMM
VVVRRRMMMMMMMMMMMMMMMMMMMMM
KRAKA THOOM
WHEN WE LAST LEFT OUR FASCIST-FIGHTING SUPER-GENIUS...
...HE WAS FLYING OFF ON A DESPERATE MISSION TO SAVE A BEAUTIFUL GIRL FROM HIS ARCHNEMESIS, DOCTOR JAPANAZI, THE MAN WITH TWO EVIL AXIS BRAINS!
VRRRMMMMMMMMMMMM
Joseph Campbell refers to the next stage of the archetypal Culture Hero's journey as **"The Meeting with the Goddess."**
HERO'S JOURNEY
VVVRRRMMMMMMMMMMMMMMMMMMMMM

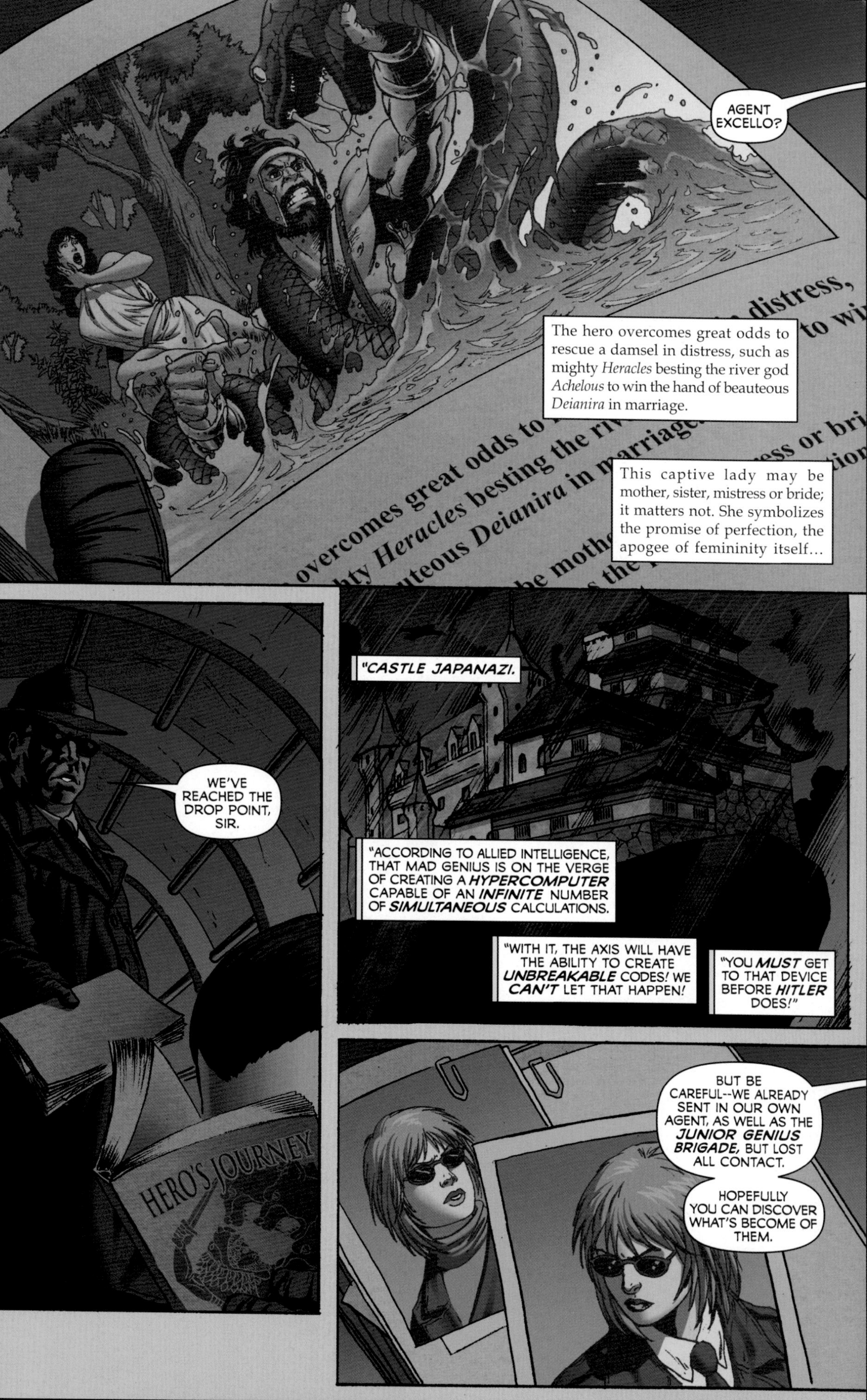
AGENT EXCELLO?
The hero overcomes great odds to rescue a damsel in distress, such as mighty *Heracles* besting the river god *Achelous* to win the hand of beauteous *Deianira* in marriage.
This captive lady may be mother, sister, mistress or bride; it matters not. She symbolizes the promise of perfection, the apogee of femininity itself...
WE'VE REACHED THE DROP POINT, SIR.
"CASTLE JAPANAZI.
"ACCORDING TO ALLIED INTELLIGENCE, THAT MAD GENIUS IS ON THE VERGE OF CREATING A HYPERCOMPUTER CAPABLE OF AN INFINITE NUMBER OF SIMULTANEOUS CALCULATIONS.
"WITH IT, THE AXIS WILL HAVE THE ABILITY TO CREATE UNBREAKABLE CODES! WE CAN'T LET THAT HAPPEN!
"YOU MUST GET TO THAT DEVICE BEFORE HITLER DOES!"
HERO'S JOURNEY
BUT BE CAREFUL--WE ALREADY SENT IN OUR OWN AGENT, AS WELL AS THE JUNIOR GENIUS BRIGADE, BUT LOST ALL CONTACT.
HOPEFULLY YOU CAN DISCOVER WHAT'S BECOME OF THEM.

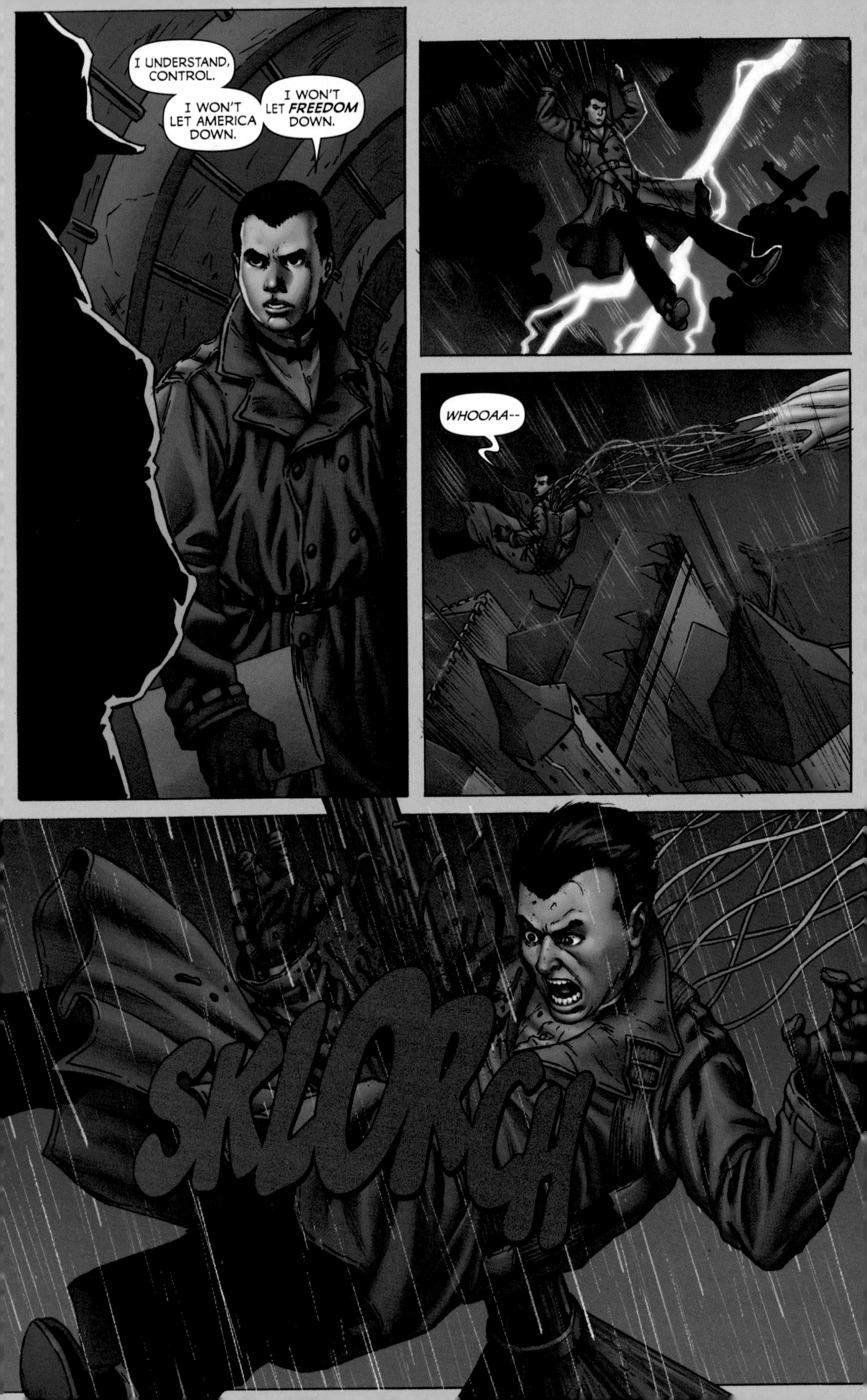
I UNDERSTAND, CONTROL.
I WON'T LET AMERICA DOWN.
I WON'T LET *FREEDOM* DOWN.
WHOOAA--
SKLORCH

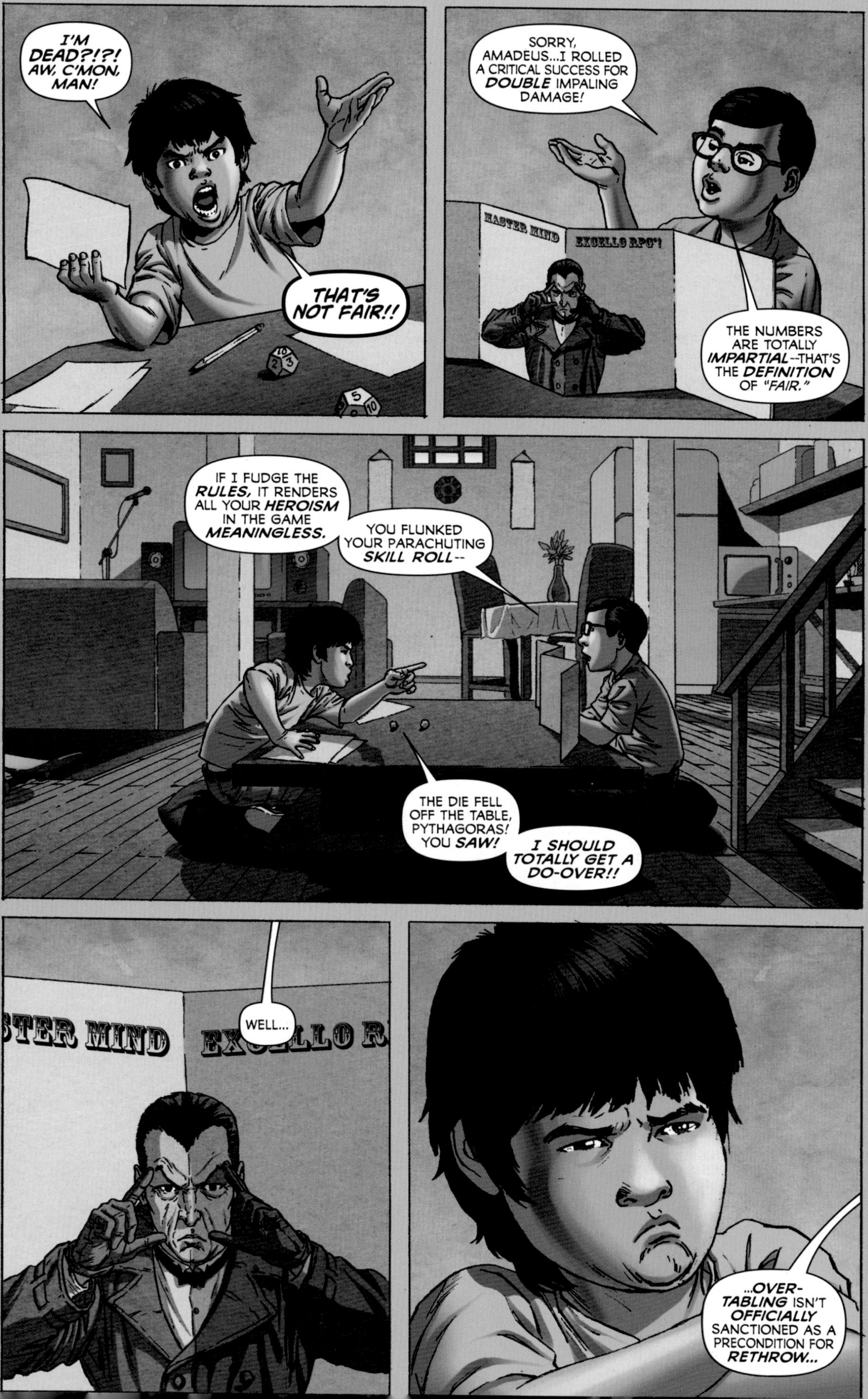
I'M DEAD?!?! AW, C'MON, MAN!
THAT'S NOT FAIR!!
SORRY, AMADEUS...I ROLLED A CRITICAL SUCCESS FOR DOUBLE IMPALING DAMAGE!
MASTER MIND
EXCELLO RPG
THE NUMBERS ARE TOTALLY IMPARTIAL--THAT'S THE DEFINITION OF "FAIR."
IF I FUDGE THE RULES, IT RENDERS ALL YOUR HEROISM IN THE GAME MEANINGLESS.
YOU FLUNKED YOUR PARACHUTING SKILL ROLL--
THE DIE FELL OFF THE TABLE, PYTHAGORAS! YOU SAW!
I SHOULD TOTALLY GET A DO-OVER!!
WELL...
...OVER-TABLING ISN'T OFFICIALLY SANCTIONED AS A PRECONDITION FOR RETHROW...

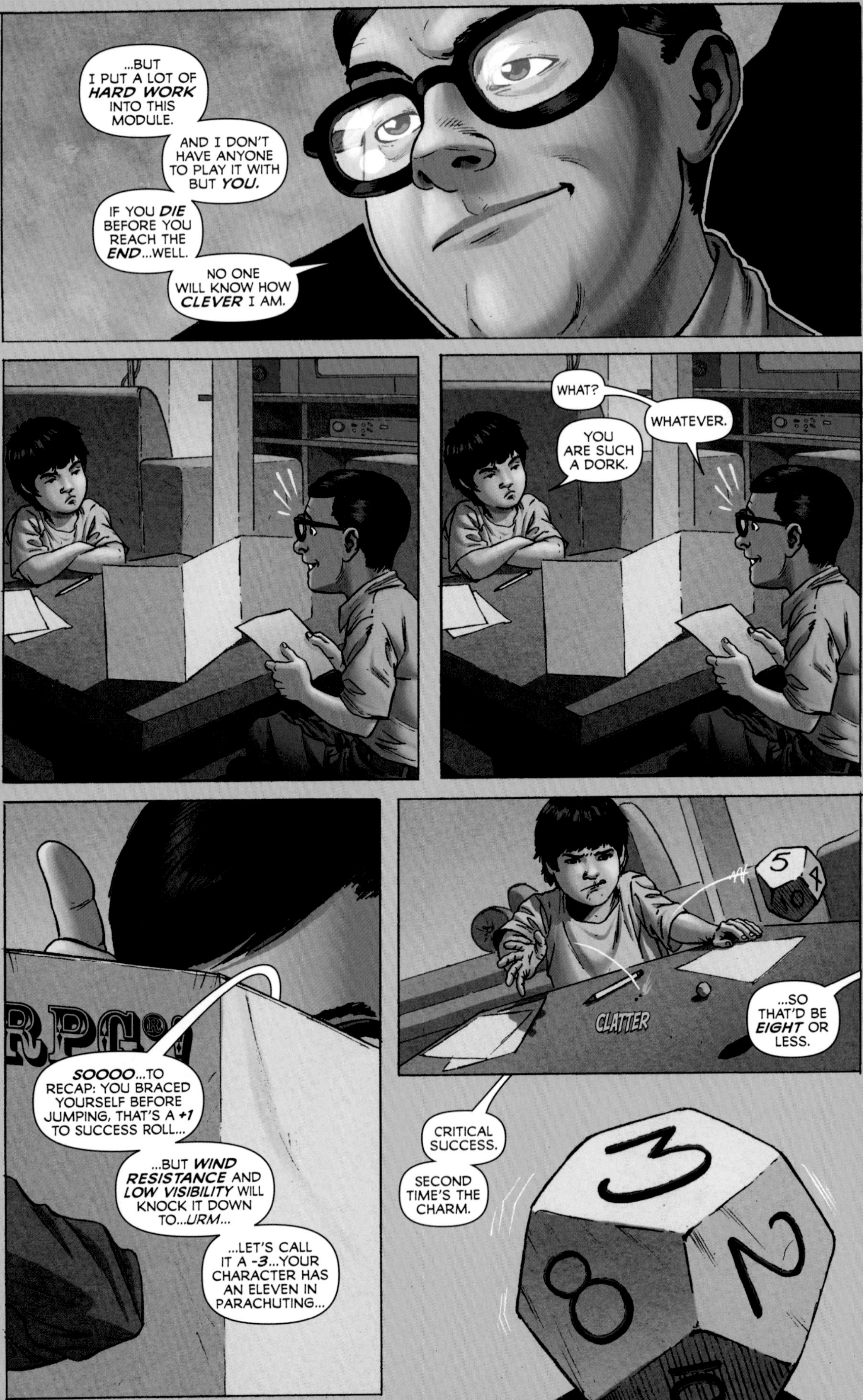
...BUT I PUT A LOT OF HARD WORK INTO THIS MODULE.
AND I DON'T HAVE ANYONE TO PLAY IT WITH BUT YOU.
IF YOU DIE BEFORE YOU REACH THE END...WELL.
NO ONE WILL KNOW HOW CLEVER I AM.
WHAT?
YOU ARE SUCH A DORK.
WHATEVER.
SOOOO...TO RECAP: YOU BRACED YOURSELF BEFORE JUMPING, THAT'S A +1 TO SUCCESS ROLL...
...BUT WIND RESISTANCE AND LOW VISIBILITY WILL KNOCK IT DOWN TO...URM...
...LET'S CALL IT A -3...YOUR CHARACTER HAS AN ELEVEN IN PARACHUTING...
...SO THAT'D BE EIGHT OR LESS.
CLATTER
CRITICAL SUCCESS.
SECOND TIME'S THE CHARM.

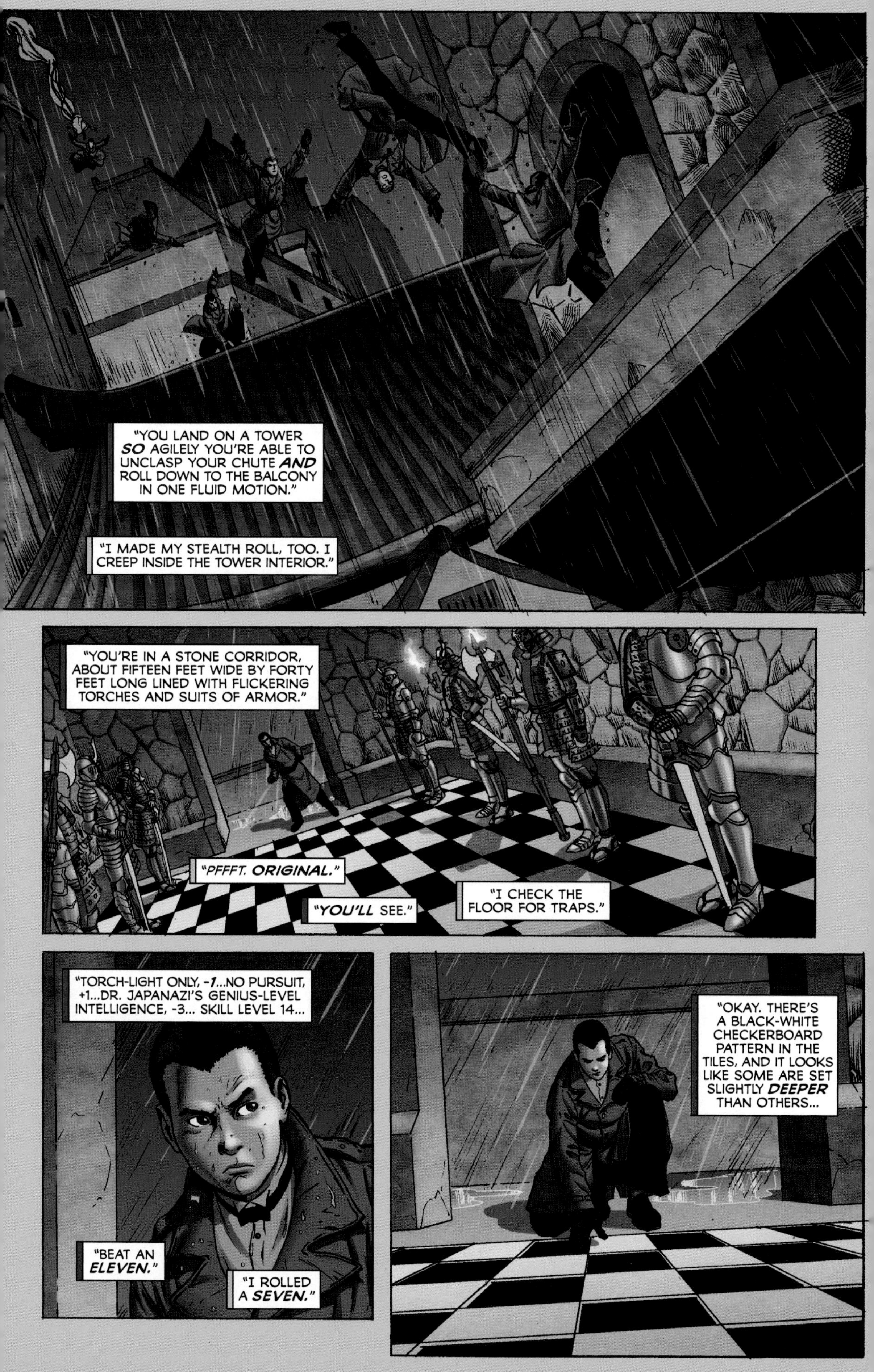
"YOU LAND ON A TOWER SO AGILELY YOU'RE ABLE TO UNCLASP YOUR CHUTE AND ROLL DOWN TO THE BALCONY IN ONE FLUID MOTION."
"I MADE MY STEALTH ROLL, TOO. I CREEP INSIDE THE TOWER INTERIOR."
"YOU'RE IN A STONE CORRIDOR, ABOUT FIFTEEN FEET WIDE BY FORTY FEET LONG LINED WITH FLICKERING TORCHES AND SUITS OF ARMOR."
"PFFFT. ORIGINAL."
"YOU'LL SEE."
"I CHECK THE FLOOR FOR TRAPS."
"TORCH-LIGHT ONLY, -1...NO PURSUIT, +1...DR. JAPANAZI'S GENIUS-LEVEL INTELLIGENCE, -3... SKILL LEVEL 14...
"BEAT AN ELEVEN."
"I ROLLED A SEVEN."
"OKAY. THERE'S A BLACK-WHITE CHECKERBOARD PATTERN IN THE TILES, AND IT LOOKS LIKE SOME ARE SET SLIGHTLY DEEPER THAN OTHERS...

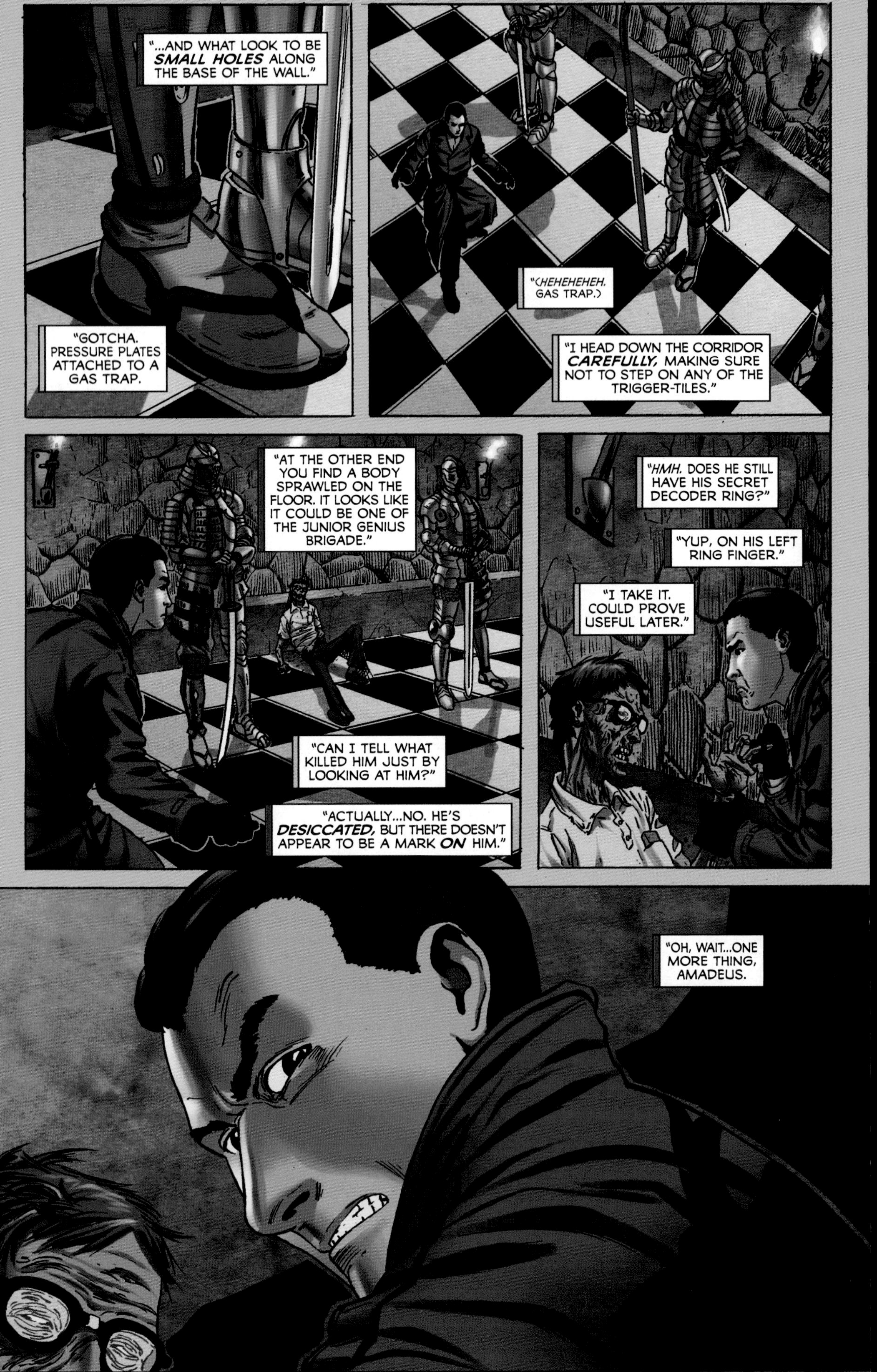
"...AND WHAT LOOK TO BE **SMALL HOLES** ALONG THE BASE OF THE WALL."
"GOTCHA. PRESSURE PLATES ATTACHED TO A GAS TRAP.
"(*HEHEHEHEH.* GAS TRAP.)
"I HEAD DOWN THE CORRIDOR ***CAREFULLY,*** MAKING SURE NOT TO STEP ON ANY OF THE TRIGGER-TILES."
"AT THE OTHER END YOU FIND A BODY SPRAWLED ON THE FLOOR. IT LOOKS LIKE IT COULD BE ONE OF THE JUNIOR GENIUS BRIGADE."
"CAN I TELL WHAT KILLED HIM JUST BY LOOKING AT HIM?"
"ACTUALLY...NO. HE'S ***DESICCATED,*** BUT THERE DOESN'T APPEAR TO BE A MARK **ON** HIM."
"*HMH.* DOES HE STILL HAVE HIS SECRET DECODER RING?"
"YUP, ON HIS LEFT RING FINGER."
"I TAKE IT. COULD PROVE USEFUL LATER."
"OH, WAIT...ONE MORE THING, AMADEUS.

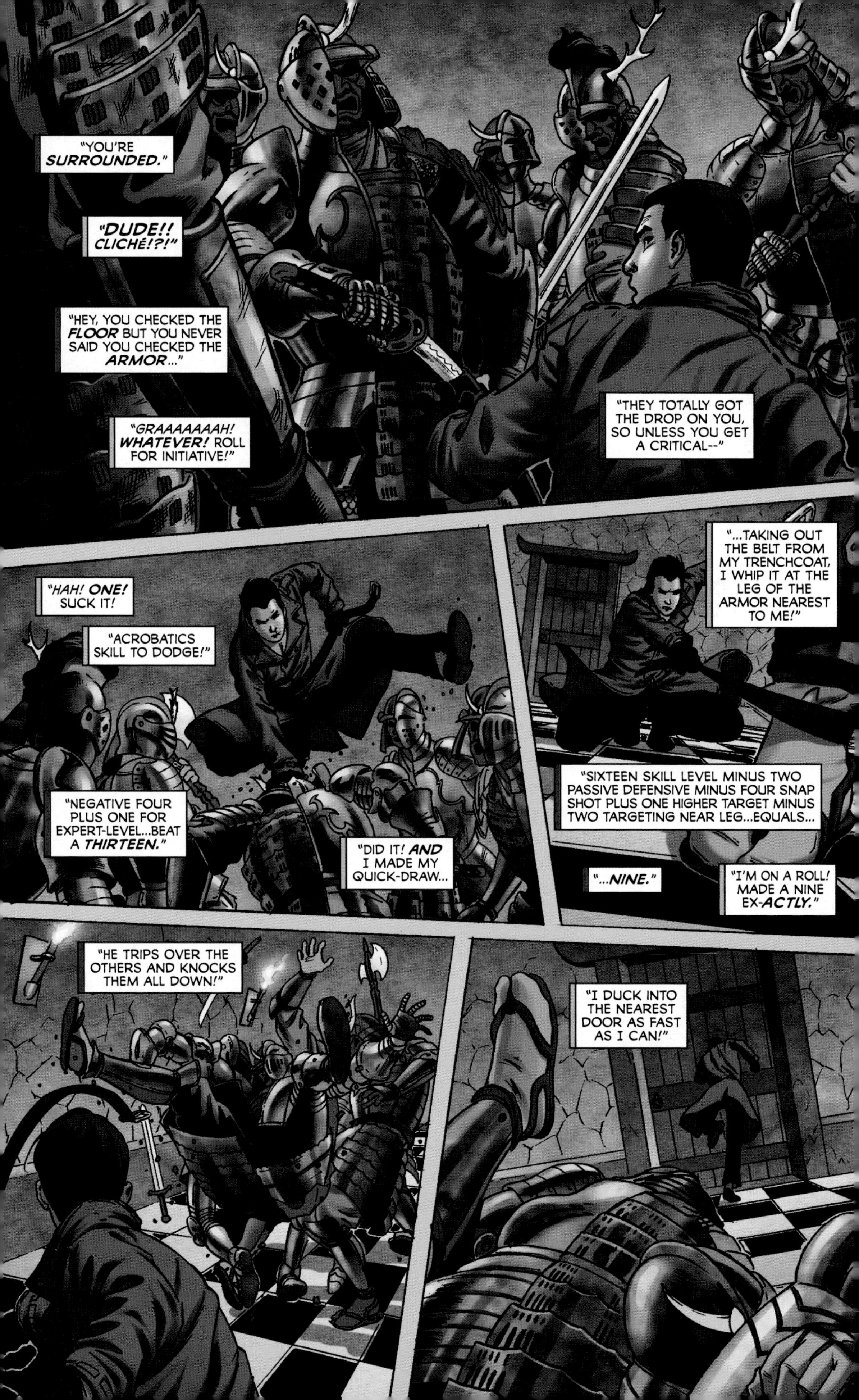
"YOU'RE *SURROUNDED.*"
"*DUDE!! CLICHÉ!?!*"
"HEY, YOU CHECKED THE ***FLOOR*** BUT YOU NEVER SAID YOU CHECKED THE ***ARMOR***..."
"THEY TOTALLY GOT THE DROP ON YOU, SO UNLESS YOU GET A CRITICAL--"
"*GRAAAAAAAH!* ***WHATEVER!*** ROLL FOR INITIATIVE!"
"*HAH!* ***ONE!*** SUCK IT*!*
"ACROBATICS SKILL TO DODGE*!*"
"NEGATIVE FOUR PLUS ONE FOR EXPERT-LEVEL...BEAT A ***THIRTEEN.***"
"DID IT*!* ***AND*** I MADE MY QUICK-DRAW...
"...TAKING OUT THE BELT FROM MY TRENCHCOAT, I WHIP IT AT THE LEG OF THE ARMOR NEAREST TO ME*!*"
"SIXTEEN SKILL LEVEL MINUS TWO PASSIVE DEFENSIVE MINUS FOUR SNAP SHOT PLUS ONE HIGHER TARGET MINUS TWO TARGETING NEAR LEG...EQUALS...
"...***NINE.***"
"I'M ON A ROLL*!* MADE A NINE EX-***ACTLY.***"
"HE TRIPS OVER THE OTHERS AND KNOCKS THEM ALL DOWN*!*"
"I DUCK INTO THE NEAREST DOOR AS FAST AS I CAN*!*"

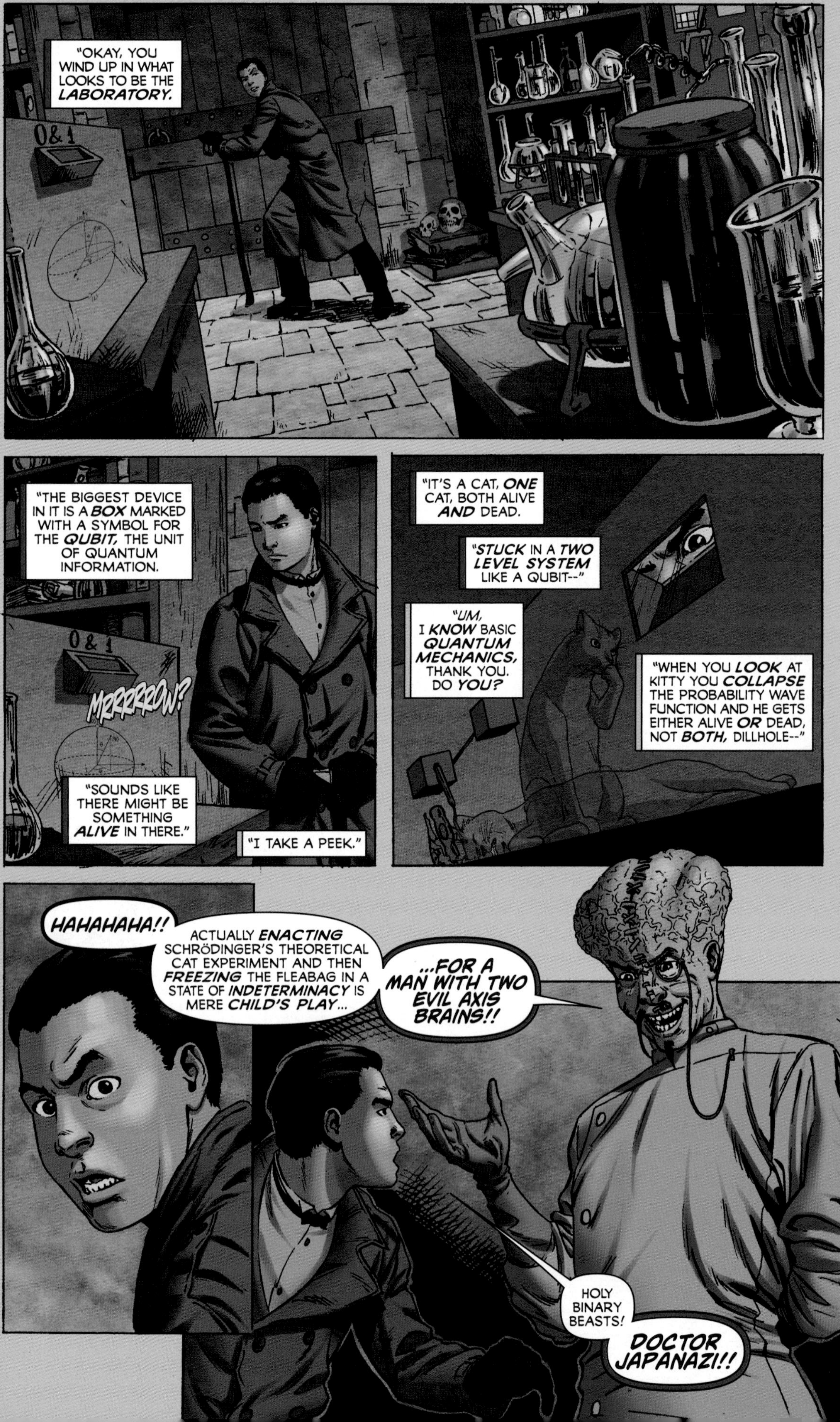
"OKAY, YOU WIND UP IN WHAT LOOKS TO BE THE *LABORATORY.*
0&1
"THE BIGGEST DEVICE IN IT IS A *BOX* MARKED WITH A SYMBOL FOR THE *QUBIT,* THE UNIT OF QUANTUM INFORMATION.
0 & 1
MRRRRROW?
"SOUNDS LIKE THERE MIGHT BE SOMETHING *ALIVE* IN THERE."
"I TAKE A PEEK."
"IT'S A CAT, *ONE* CAT, BOTH ALIVE *AND* DEAD.
"*STUCK* IN A *TWO LEVEL SYSTEM* LIKE A QUBIT--"
"*UM,* I *KNOW* BASIC *QUANTUM MECHANICS,* THANK YOU. DO *YOU?*
"WHEN YOU *LOOK* AT KITTY YOU *COLLAPSE* THE PROBABILITY WAVE FUNCTION AND HE GETS EITHER ALIVE *OR* DEAD, NOT *BOTH,* DILLHOLE--"
HAHAHAHA!!
ACTUALLY *ENACTING* SCHRÖDINGER'S THEORETICAL CAT EXPERIMENT AND THEN *FREEZING* THE FLEABAG IN A STATE OF *INDETERMINACY* IS MERE *CHILD'S PLAY...*
...FOR A MAN WITH TWO EVIL AXIS BRAINS!!
HOLY BINARY BEASTS!
DOCTOR JAPANAZI!!

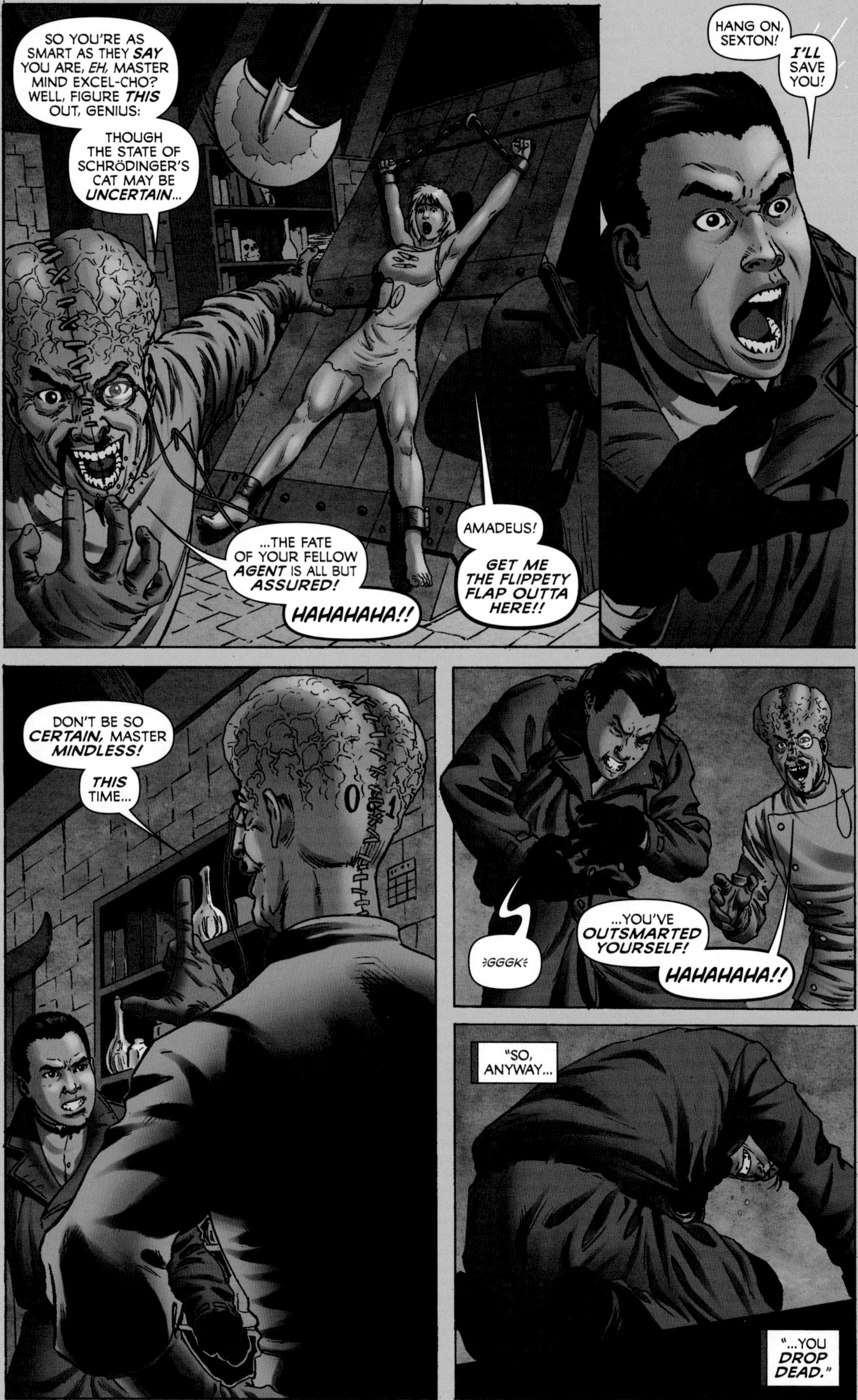

SO YOU'RE AS SMART AS THEY SAY YOU ARE, EH, MASTER MIND EXCEL-CHO? WELL, FIGURE THIS OUT, GENIUS:
THOUGH THE STATE OF SCHRÖDINGER'S CAT MAY BE UNCERTAIN...
...THE FATE OF YOUR FELLOW AGENT IS ALL BUT ASSURED!
HAHAHAHA!!
AMADEUS!
GET ME THE FLIPPETY FLAP OUTTA HERE!!
HANG ON, SEXTON!
I'LL SAVE YOU!
DON'T BE SO CERTAIN, MASTER MINDLESS!
THIS TIME...
0 1
...YOU'VE OUTSMARTED YOURSELF!
HAHAHAHA!!
GGGK
"SO, ANYWAY...
"...YOU DROP DEAD."

WHAT?!? THAT'S IT? THAT'S YOUR CLEVER PLOT TWIST?

I DROP DEAD? JUST LIKE THAT?

DON'T BLAME ME--IF YOU SPENT AS MUCH TIME LOOKING FOR CLUES AS BEING A WISEASS...

YOU DIDN'T CHECK THE ARMOR--OR THE TORCHES!

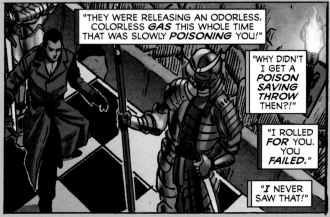

"THEY WERE RELEASING AN ODORLESS, COLORLESS GAS THIS WHOLE TIME THAT WAS SLOWLY POISONING YOU!"

"WHY DIDN'T I GET A POISON SAVING THROW THEN?!"

"I ROLLED FOR YOU. YOU FAILED."

"I NEVER SAW THAT!"

IT DOESN'T MATTER WHAT YOU SEE. I'M THE GAMEMASTER. IT'S MY OBSERVATIONS THAT DETERMINE THIS REALITY--

I CALL TOTAL B.S.!!

YOU GO ON AND ON ABOUT HOW IMPORTANT THE RULES ARE, BUT YOU CHANGE THEM WHENEVER YOU FEEL LIKE IT!

I'M NOT GONNA PLAY WITH YOU ANY--

--MORE...

YEAH.

GOOD LUCK WITH THAT.

WHERE...

WHERE DID THE STAIRS GO?

YOU SEE NOW, CHO? YOU SEE HOW MUCH SMARTER I AM?

I PROMISED I WOULD KILL YOU. THERE'S NO POSSIBLE SOLUTION TO ANY EQUATION YOU CAN CALCULATE...

...WHERE YOU DON'T DIE.

YOU'LL NEVER FIND THE HYPERCOMPUTER.

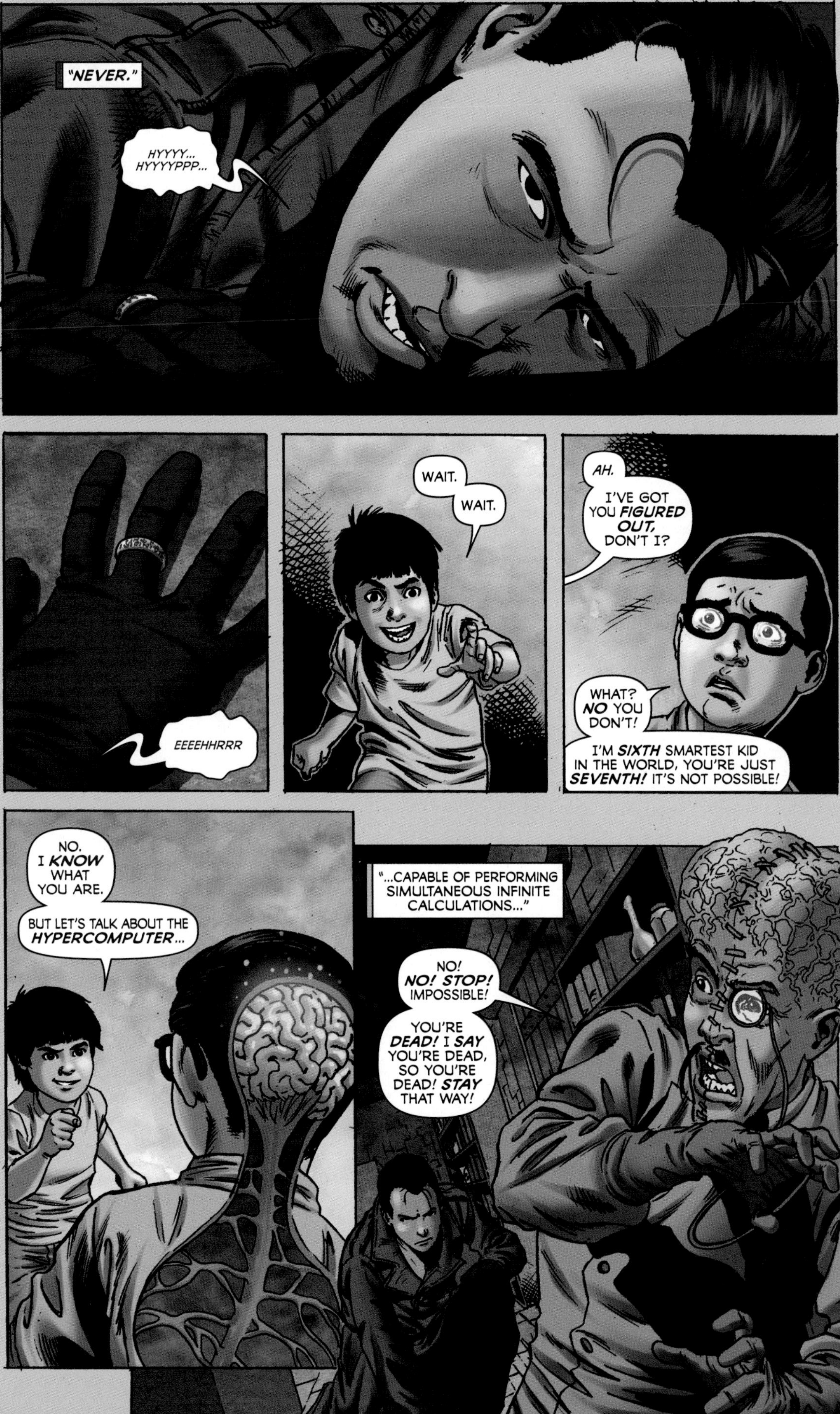
"NEVER."
HYYYY... HYYYYPPP...
EEEEHHRRR
WAIT.
WAIT.
AH.
I'VE GOT YOU FIGURED OUT, DON'T I?
WHAT? NO YOU DON'T!
I'M SIXTH SMARTEST KID IN THE WORLD, YOU'RE JUST SEVENTH! IT'S NOT POSSIBLE!
NO. I KNOW WHAT YOU ARE.
BUT LET'S TALK ABOUT THE HYPERCOMPUTER...
"...CAPABLE OF PERFORMING SIMULTANEOUS INFINITE CALCULATIONS..."
NO! NO! STOP! IMPOSSIBLE!
YOU'RE DEAD! I SAY YOU'RE DEAD, SO YOU'RE DEAD! STAY THAT WAY!

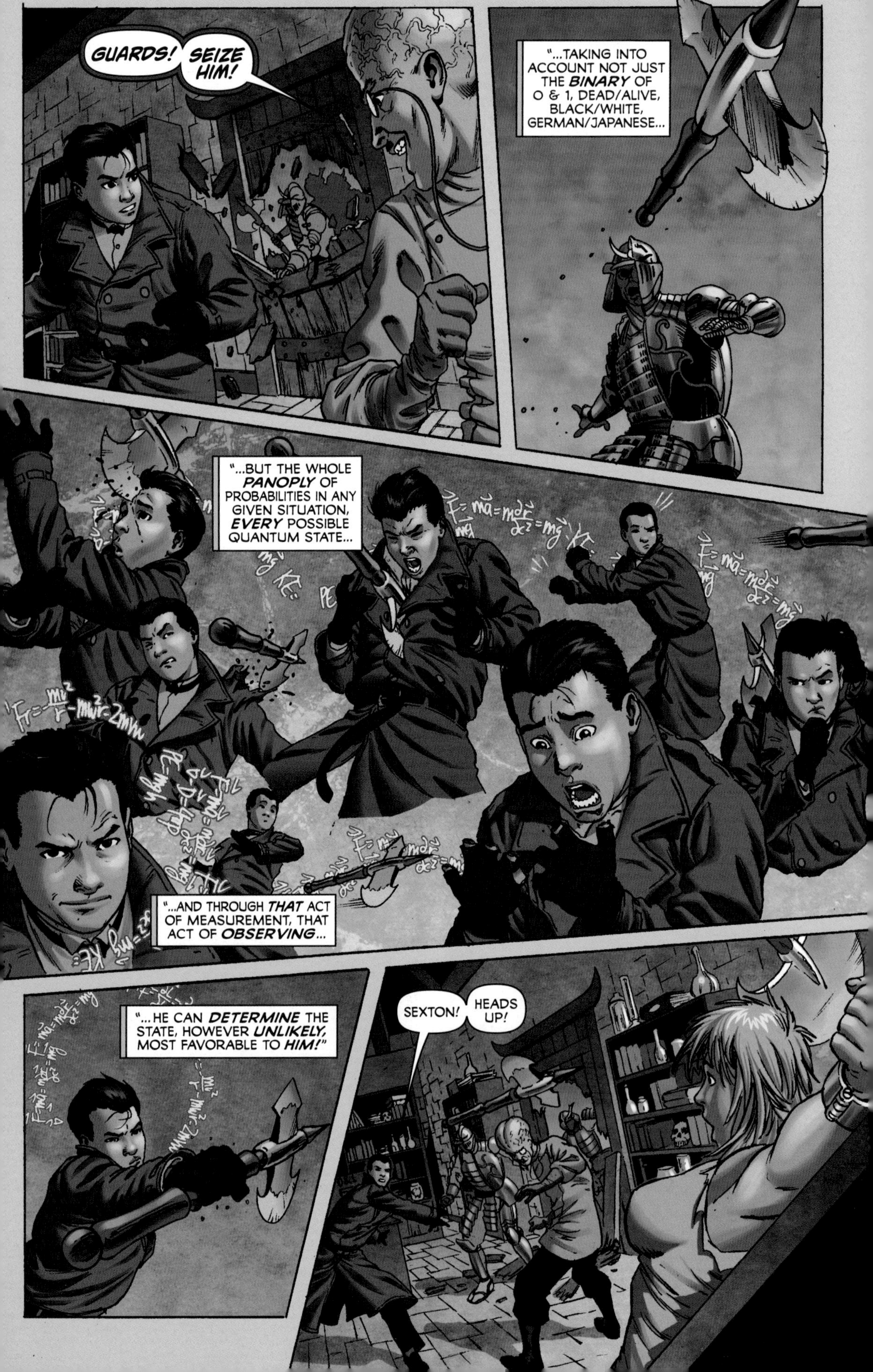
GUARDS!
SEIZE HIM!
"...TAKING INTO ACCOUNT NOT JUST THE BINARY OF O & 1, DEAD/ALIVE, BLACK/WHITE, GERMAN/JAPANESE...
"...BUT THE WHOLE PANOPLY OF PROBABILITIES IN ANY GIVEN SITUATION, EVERY POSSIBLE QUANTUM STATE...
"...AND THROUGH THAT ACT OF MEASUREMENT, THAT ACT OF OBSERVING...
"...HE CAN DETERMINE THE STATE, HOWEVER UNLIKELY, MOST FAVORABLE TO HIM!"
SEXTON!
HEADS UP!

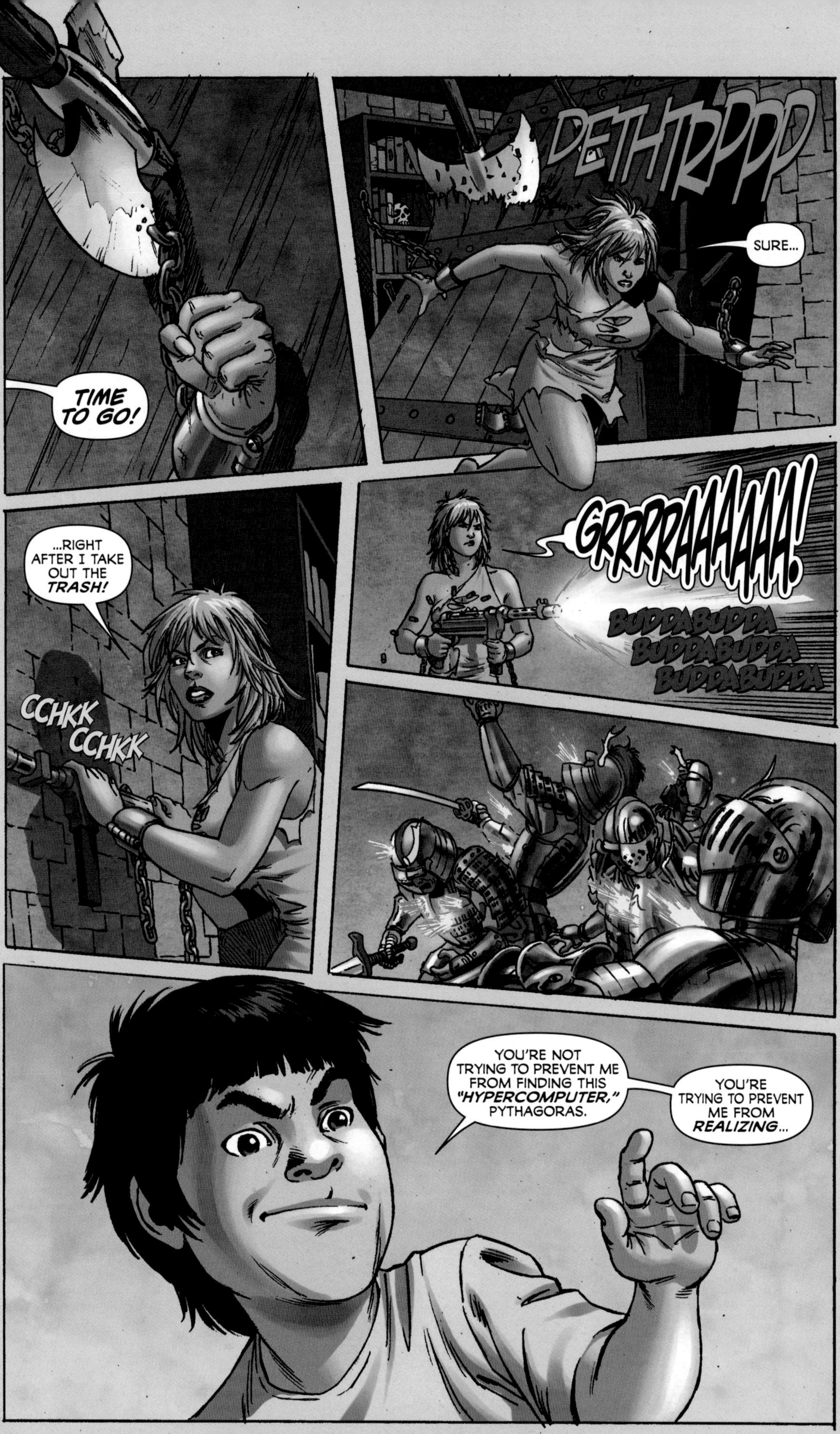
TIME TO GO!
DETHRPPPP
SURE...
...RIGHT AFTER I TAKE OUT THE TRASH!
CCHKK CCHKK
GRRRRAAAAAAA!
BUDDABUDDA BUDDABUDDA BUDDABUDDA
YOU'RE NOT TRYING TO PREVENT ME FROM FINDING THIS "HYPERCOMPUTER," PYTHAGORAS.
YOU'RE TRYING TO PREVENT ME FROM REALIZING...

...THAT THAT'S WHAT I NATURALLY AM.

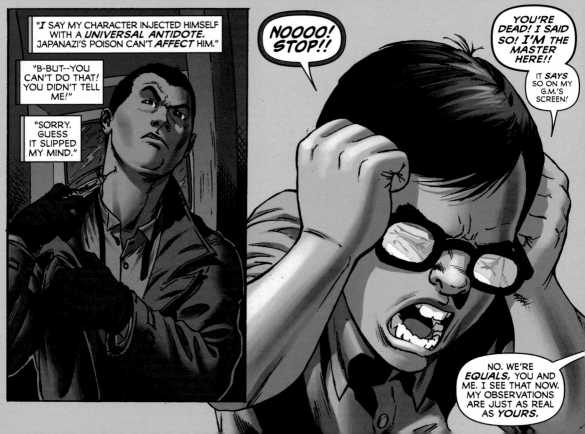

"I SAY MY CHARACTER INJECTED HIMSELF WITH A *UNIVERSAL ANTIDOTE.* JAPANAZI'S POISON CAN'T *AFFECT* HIM."

"B-BUT--YOU CAN'T DO THAT! YOU DIDN'T TELL ME!"

"SORRY. GUESS IT SLIPPED MY MIND."

NOOOO! STOP!!

YOU'RE DEAD! I SAID SO! I'M THE MASTER HERE!!

IT SAYS SO ON MY G.M.'S SCREEN!

NO. WE'RE *EQUALS,* YOU AND ME. I SEE THAT NOW. MY OBSERVATIONS ARE JUST AS REAL AS *YOURS.*

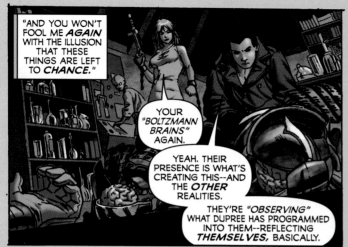

"AND YOU WON'T FOOL ME *AGAIN* WITH THE ILLUSION THAT THESE THINGS ARE LEFT TO *CHANCE*."

YOUR *"BOLTZMANN BRAINS"* AGAIN.

YEAH. THEIR PRESENCE IS WHAT'S CREATING THIS--AND THE *OTHER* REALITIES.

THEY'RE *"OBSERVING"* WHAT DUPREE HAS PROGRAMMED INTO THEM--REFLECTING *THEMSELVES*, BASICALLY.

YOU'LL NEVER TAKE ME *ALIVE*, AMERIKANER AND/OR GAIJIN *SWINE!*

LOOK OUT!

BUDDA BUDDA

WARNING. COUNTDOWN BEGUN.

KLAK

CASTLE JAPANAZI WILL SELF-DESTRUCT IN T-MINUS ONE MINUTE. HEIL HITLER. BANZAI.

BDOOOR

AW, ****.

HOLD ON. THIS IS NO TIME TO *PANIC.*

THIS ISN'T *PANIC.* THIS IS MOMENTARY *PARALYSIS* INCITED BY TOTAL *DESPAIR.*

LISTEN...FROM THE MOMENT WE ENTERED THE *TOWN* OF EXCELLO, DUPREE HAS TRAPPED US IN A *LABYRINTH* OF *"BUBBLE REALITIES"* OF HIS OWN CREATION...

...*FREEZING* US IN A *MULTIPLICITY* OF QUANTUM STATES LIKE THAT *CAT* IN DR. JAPANAZI'S BOX.

ARE YOU IN THIS REALITY TOO, SEXTON? SORRY...GETTING SLIGHTLY *MUDDLED...*

OH, SO ALL THIS STUFF IS AN *ILLUSION--*

NO, NO, IT'S QUITE REA--

OW!

YEAH, I WOULDN'T DO THAT.

THESE "BOLTZMANN BRAINS" ARE HIGHLY SOPHISTICATED *QUANTUM COMPUTERS.*

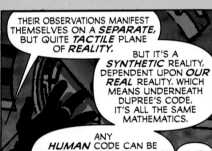

THEIR OBSERVATIONS MANIFEST THEMSELVES ON A *SEPARATE,* BUT QUITE *TACTILE* PLANE OF *REALITY.*

BUT IT'S A *SYNTHETIC* REALITY, DEPENDENT UPON *OUR REAL* REALITY. WHICH MEANS UNDERNEATH DUPREE'S CODE, IT'S ALL THE SAME MATHEMATICS.

ANY *HUMAN* CODE CAN BE *CRACKED...*ITS REDUNDANCIES ELIMINATED TO REVEAL THE TRUE MEANING *BEHIND* IT.

AND I CAN *DO* IT.

T-MINUS FIFTEEN SECONDS AND COUNTING.

I GET IT...*PATTERN RECOGNITION.*

FUNNY. SINCE THE LAST TIME I CONTACTED YOU, YOU'VE... *CHANGED.*

BEFORE YOU WERE JUST *COCKY,* AND NOW...

...NOW YOU'RE *CONFIDENT.*

LIKE YOU ACTUALLY *KNOW WHAT YOU'RE DOING* WITH THIS HERO STUFF.

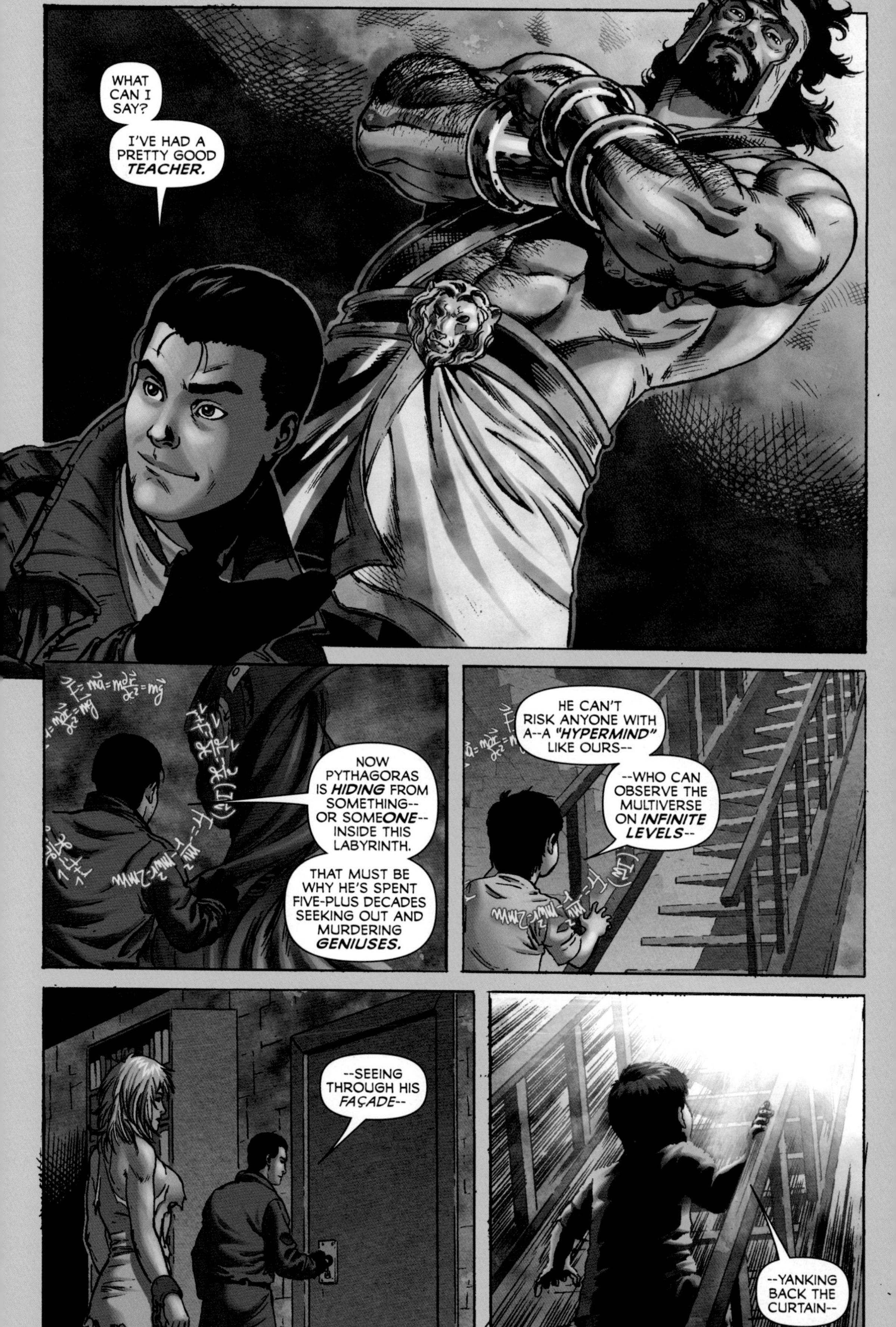
WHAT CAN I SAY?
I'VE HAD A PRETTY GOOD *TEACHER.*
NOW PYTHAGORAS IS *HIDING* FROM SOMETHING-- OR SOME*ONE*-- INSIDE THIS LABYRINTH.
THAT MUST BE WHY HE'S SPENT FIVE-PLUS DECADES SEEKING OUT AND MURDERING *GENIUSES.*
HE CAN'T RISK ANYONE WITH A--A *"HYPERMIND"* LIKE OURS--
--WHO CAN OBSERVE THE MULTIVERSE ON *INFINITE LEVELS*--
--SEEING THROUGH HIS *FAÇADE*--
--YANKING BACK THE CURTAIN--

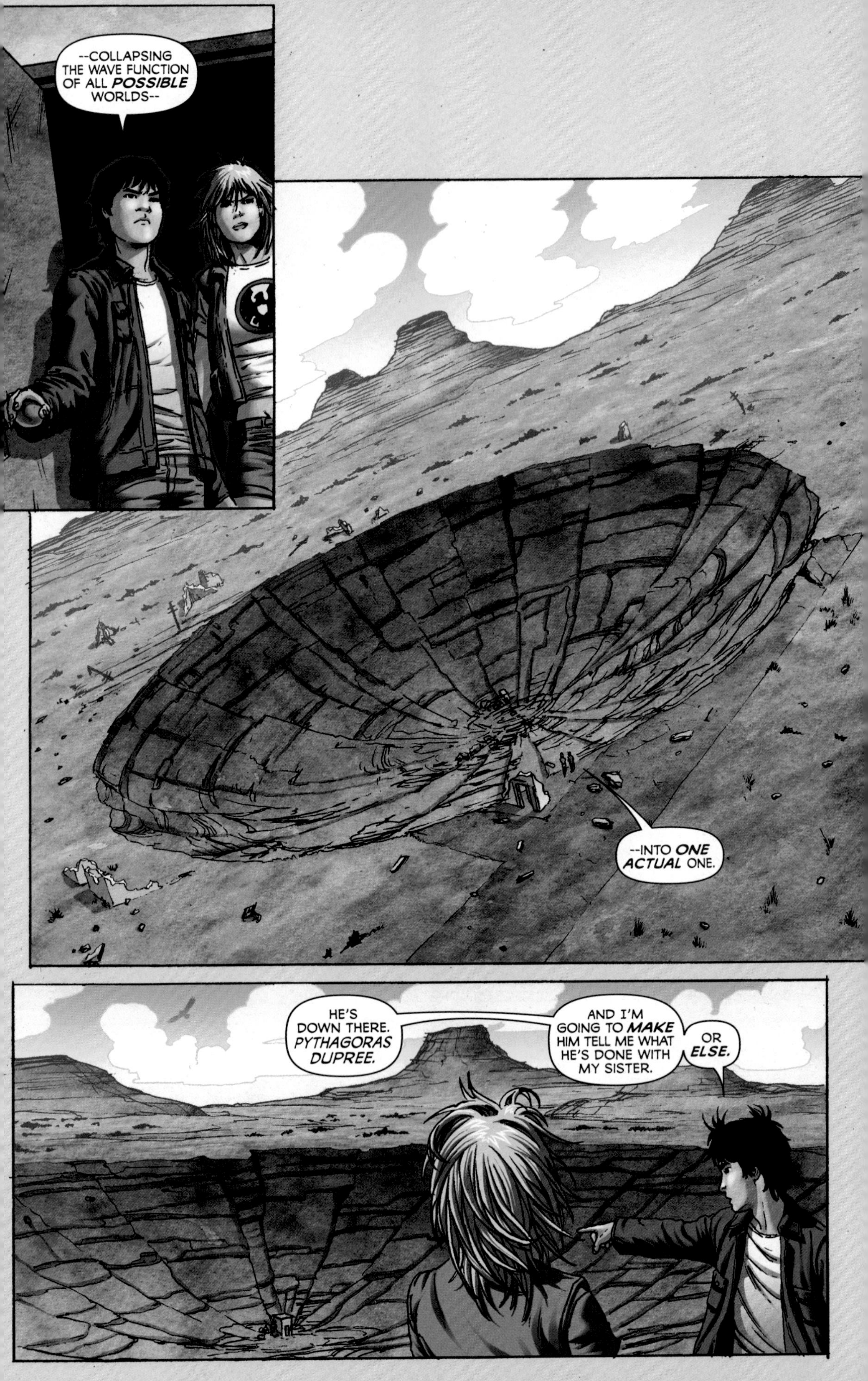
--COLLAPSING THE WAVE FUNCTION OF ALL *POSSIBLE* WORLDS--
--INTO *ONE ACTUAL* ONE.
HE'S DOWN THERE. *PYTHAGORAS DUPREE.*
AND I'M GOING TO *MAKE* HIM TELL ME WHAT HE'S DONE WITH MY SISTER.
OR *ELSE.*

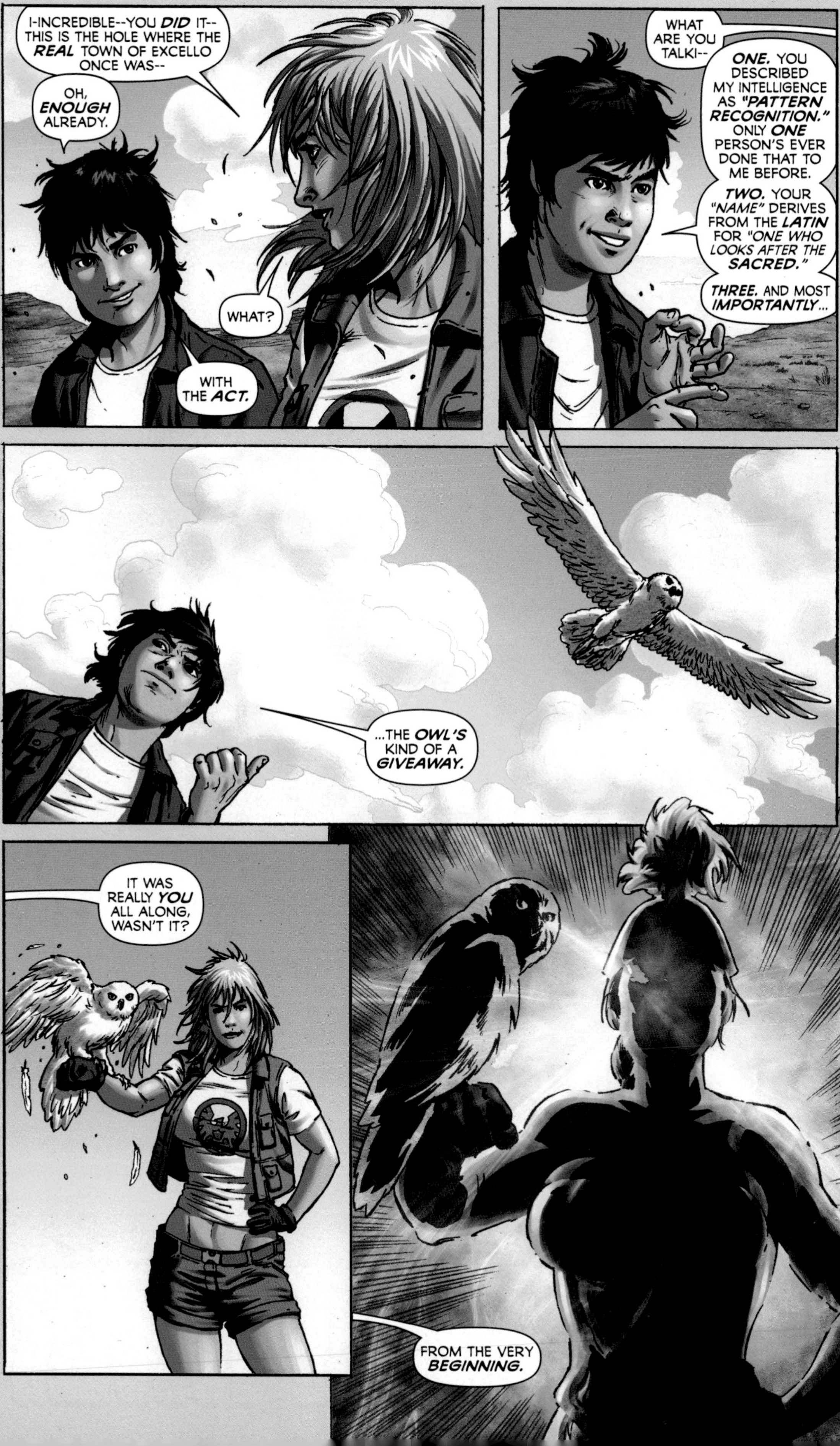
I-INCREDIBLE--YOU DID IT--THIS IS THE HOLE WHERE THE REAL TOWN OF EXCELLO ONCE WAS--
OH, ENOUGH ALREADY.
WHAT?
WITH THE ACT.
WHAT ARE YOU TALKI--
ONE. YOU DESCRIBED MY INTELLIGENCE AS "PATTERN RECOGNITION." ONLY ONE PERSON'S EVER DONE THAT TO ME BEFORE.
TWO. YOUR "NAME" DERIVES FROM THE LATIN FOR "ONE WHO LOOKS AFTER THE SACRED."
THREE. AND MOST IMPORTANTLY...
...THE OWL'S KIND OF A GIVEAWAY.
IT WAS REALLY YOU ALL ALONG, WASN'T IT?
FROM THE VERY BEGINNING.

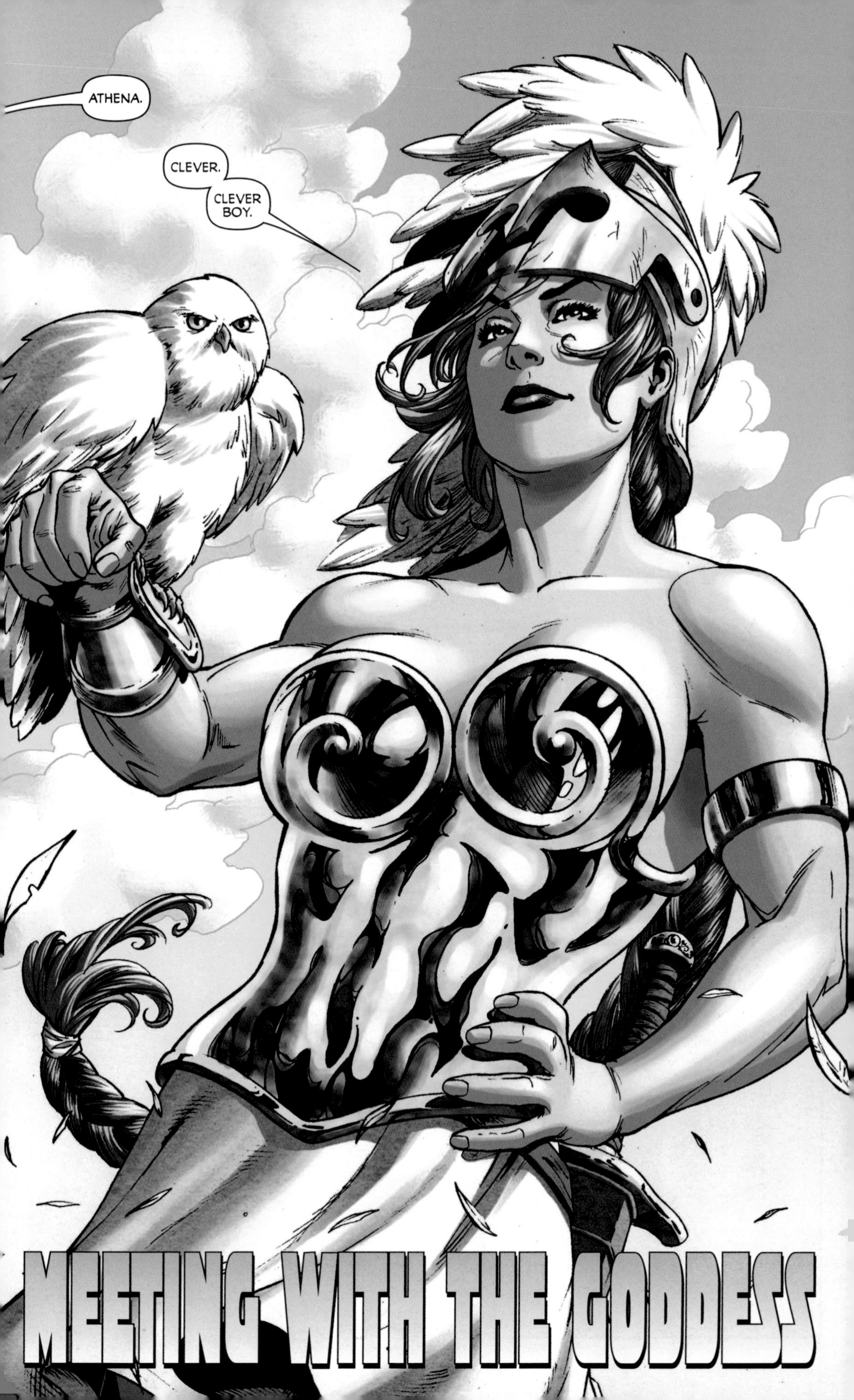
ATHENA.
CLEVER.
CLEVER BOY.
MEETING WITH THE GODDESS

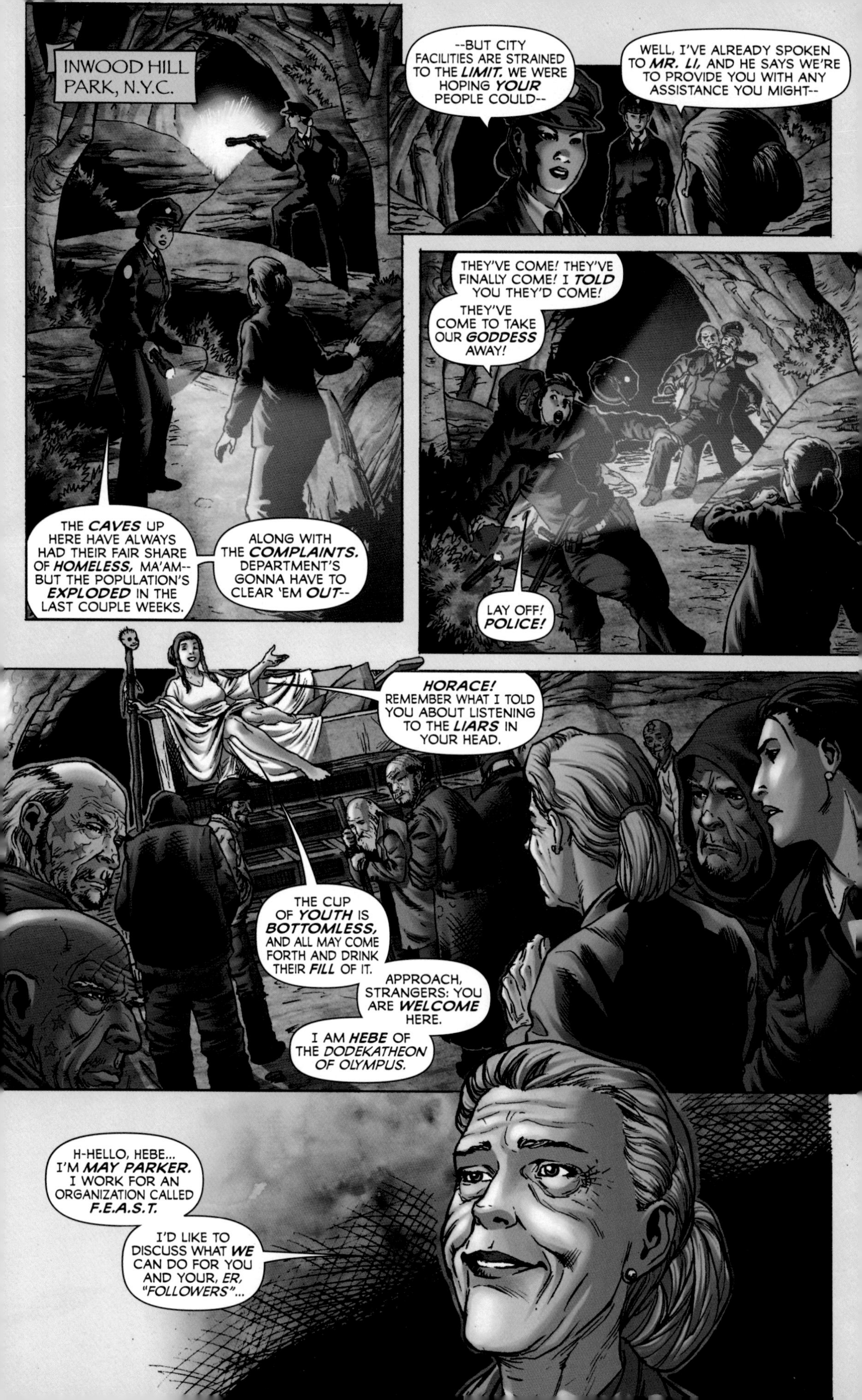
INWOOD HILL PARK, N.Y.C.
THE CAVES UP HERE HAVE ALWAYS HAD THEIR FAIR SHARE OF HOMELESS, MA'AM-- BUT THE POPULATION'S EXPLODED IN THE LAST COUPLE WEEKS.
ALONG WITH THE COMPLAINTS. DEPARTMENT'S GONNA HAVE TO CLEAR 'EM OUT--
--BUT CITY FACILITIES ARE STRAINED TO THE LIMIT. WE WERE HOPING YOUR PEOPLE COULD--
WELL, I'VE ALREADY SPOKEN TO MR. LI, AND HE SAYS WE'RE TO PROVIDE YOU WITH ANY ASSISTANCE YOU MIGHT--
THEY'VE COME! THEY'VE FINALLY COME! I TOLD YOU THEY'D COME!
THEY'VE COME TO TAKE OUR GODDESS AWAY!
LAY OFF! POLICE!
HORACE! REMEMBER WHAT I TOLD YOU ABOUT LISTENING TO THE LIARS IN YOUR HEAD.
THE CUP OF YOUTH IS BOTTOMLESS, AND ALL MAY COME FORTH AND DRINK THEIR FILL OF IT.
APPROACH, STRANGERS: YOU ARE WELCOME HERE.
I AM HEBE OF THE DODEKATHEON OF OLYMPUS.
H-HELLO, HEBE... I'M MAY PARKER. I WORK FOR AN ORGANIZATION CALLED F.E.A.S.T.
I'D LIKE TO DISCUSS WHAT WE CAN DO FOR YOU AND YOUR, ER, "FOLLOWERS"...

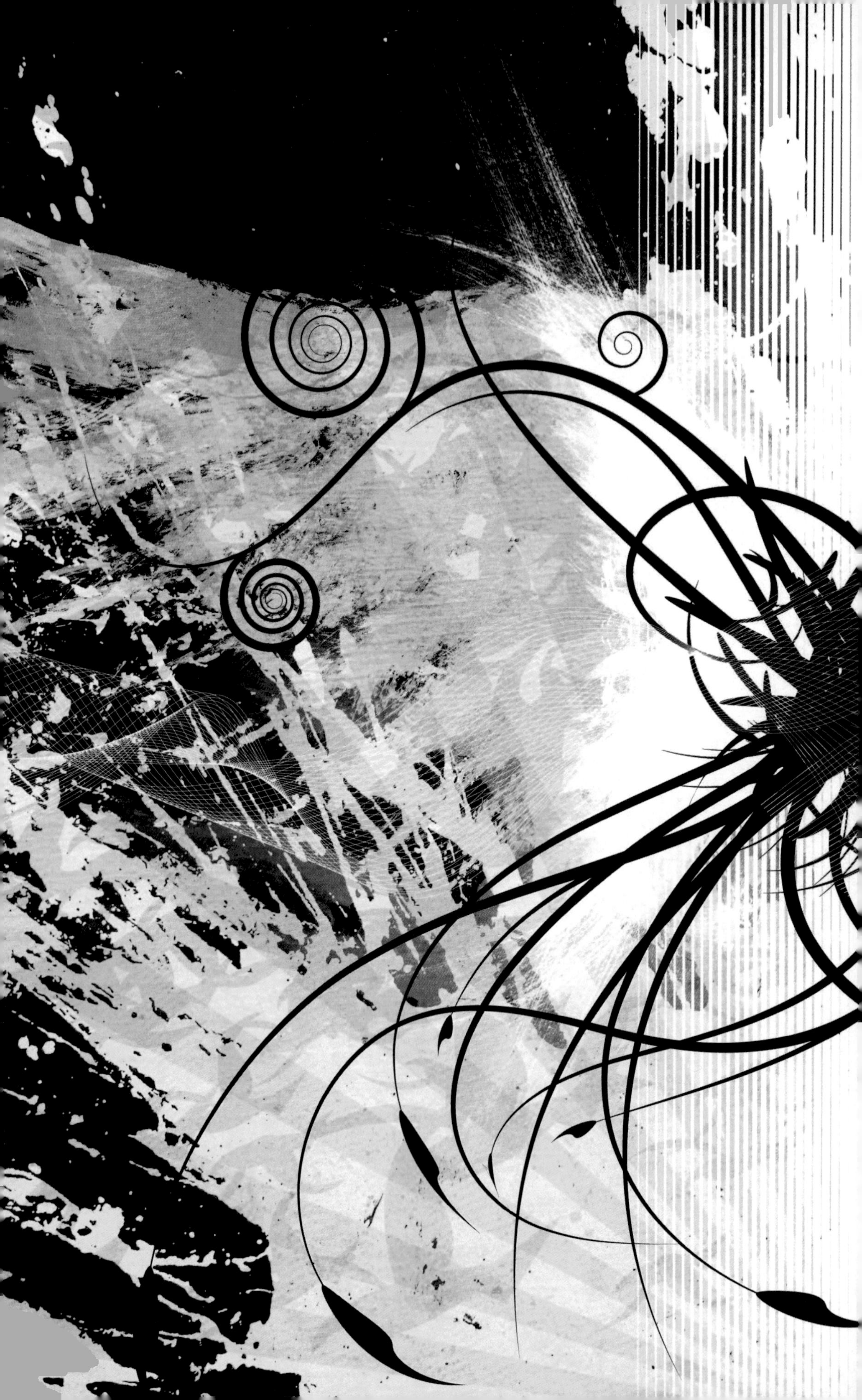

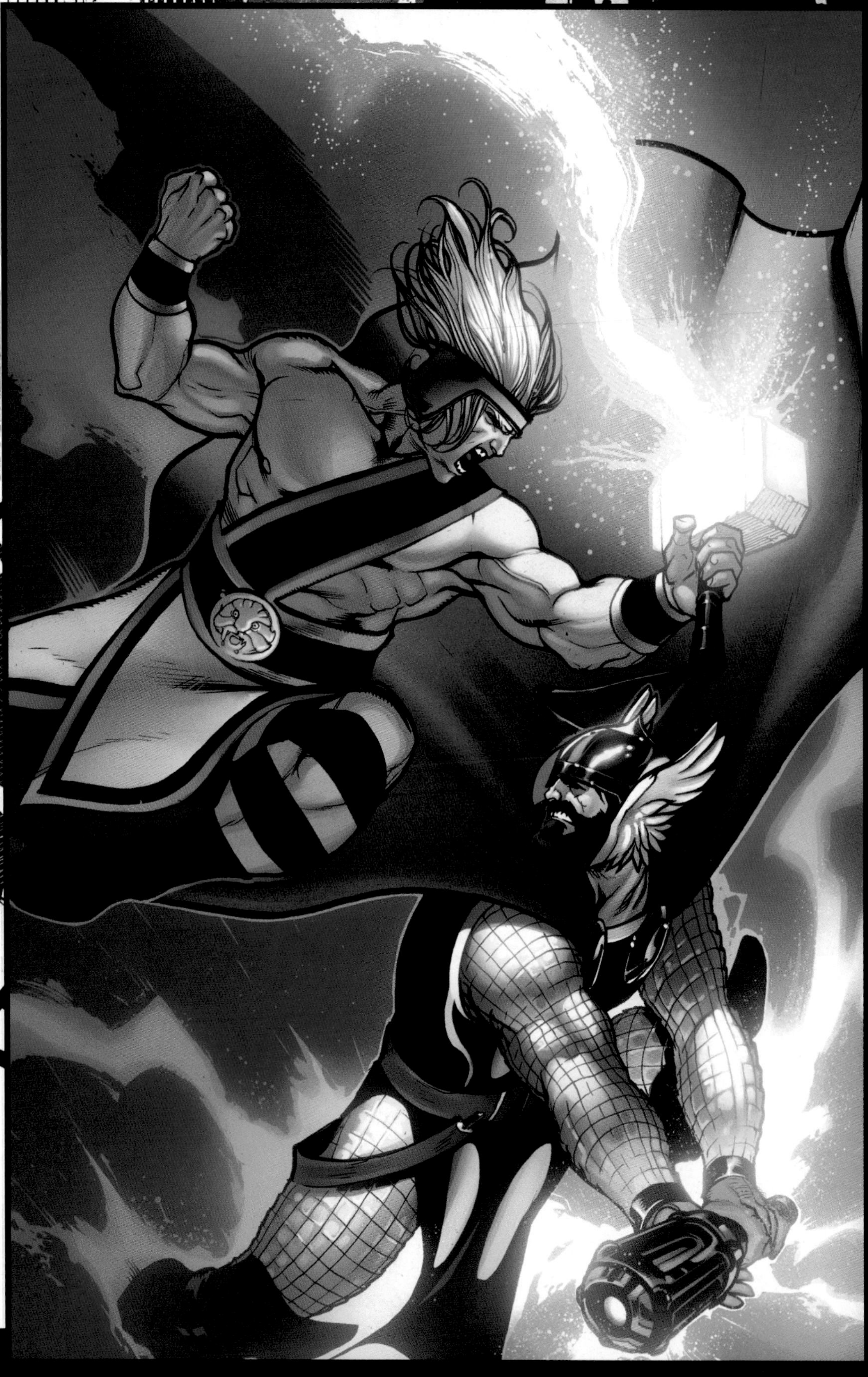

INCREDIBLE HERCULES #136

WHEN TITANS CLASH!
THOR vs. HERCULES!
THE CLASSIC CLASH CLARIFIED BY *THE MIGHTY THOR*

Panel 1: BUT, I MUST SEEK A WAY *BACK* TO THE GOLDEN CITY! I SHALL CROSS THAT CRUDE BRIDGE AND SEEK INFORMATION FROM THE ONE WHO STANDS THUS BOLDLY!

HOLD! COME NO FURTHER! YOU MAY CROSS YON BRIDGE ONLY AFTER *HERCULES* HAS DONE SO!

Panel 2: FIRST, I CATCH YOUR WRIST ON MY HAMMER'S *THONGS,* HURLING YOU OFF-BALANCE AS EASILY AS I MIGHT SNAP A TWIG!

Panel 3: AND THEN, WITH ONE SINGLE, SMASHING BLOW, THE THUNDER GOD DOES WHAT NO LIVING BEING HAS EVER DONE BEFORE... HE BATTERS HERCULES OFF HIS FEET!!

WHHOP!

YES, *THIS* IS THE SOURCE OF OUR ENMITY— MR. *IMPATIENT* HAD TO GO FIRST.

I ONLY WISH HERCULES HIMSELF HAD WORN E'EN A THONG. 'TWAS NOT A VIEW I RELISHED.

MAYHAP, IF THE PRINCE OF POWER SPENT MORE TIME BATTLING AND LESS TIME WITH FEMALE DISTRACTIONS, HE WOULD BEST ME NOW AND AGAIN.

BUT, SEE HOW I FORCE *BACK* THAT ARM, AND HURL THEE BACKWARDS TO THE GROUND!

YIELD, HERCULES!! YIELD TO *THOR,* GOD OF THUNDER... PRINCE OF VIKINGS... SON OF ODIN!

NEVER!!

WE MEET, WE BRAWL, HERCULES EATS DIRT. A PATTERN EMERGES.

YET THE STUBBORN OAF RETURNS FOR MORE... AND MORE...

AND NOW THE BUFFOON WEARS MY RAIMENT AND SPURS A WAR IN MY NAME? TWO CAN PLAY AT THIS GAME...

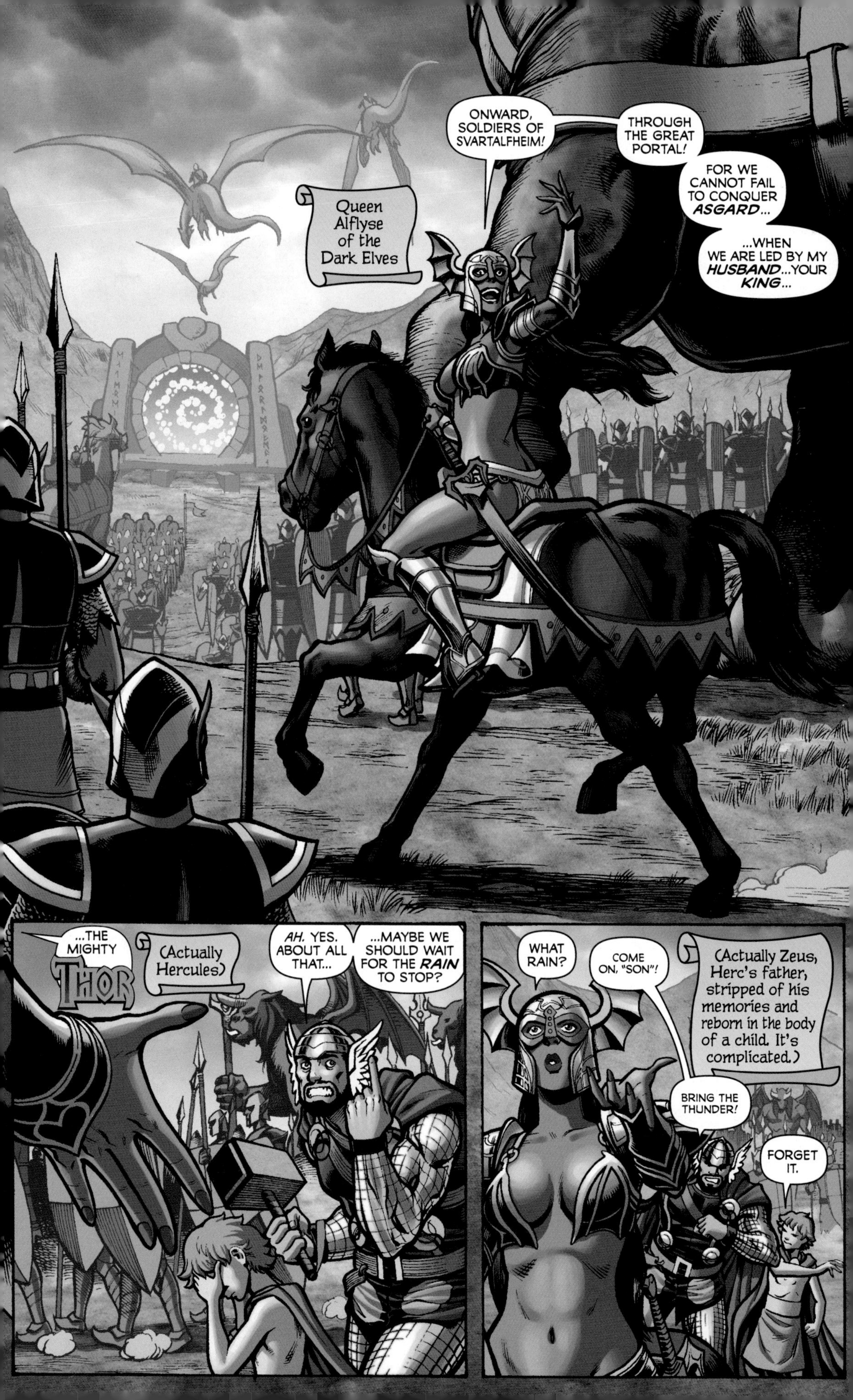
ONWARD, SOLDIERS OF SVARTALFHEIM!
THROUGH THE GREAT PORTAL!
FOR WE CANNOT FAIL TO CONQUER ASGARD...
...WHEN WE ARE LED BY MY HUSBAND...YOUR KING...
Queen Alflyse of the Dark Elves
...THE MIGHTY THOR
(Actually Hercules)
AH. YES. ABOUT ALL THAT...
...MAYBE WE SHOULD WAIT FOR THE RAIN TO STOP?
WHAT RAIN?
COME ON, "SON"!
(Actually Zeus, Herc's father, stripped of his memories and reborn in the body of a child. It's complicated.)
BRING THE THUNDER!
FORGET IT.

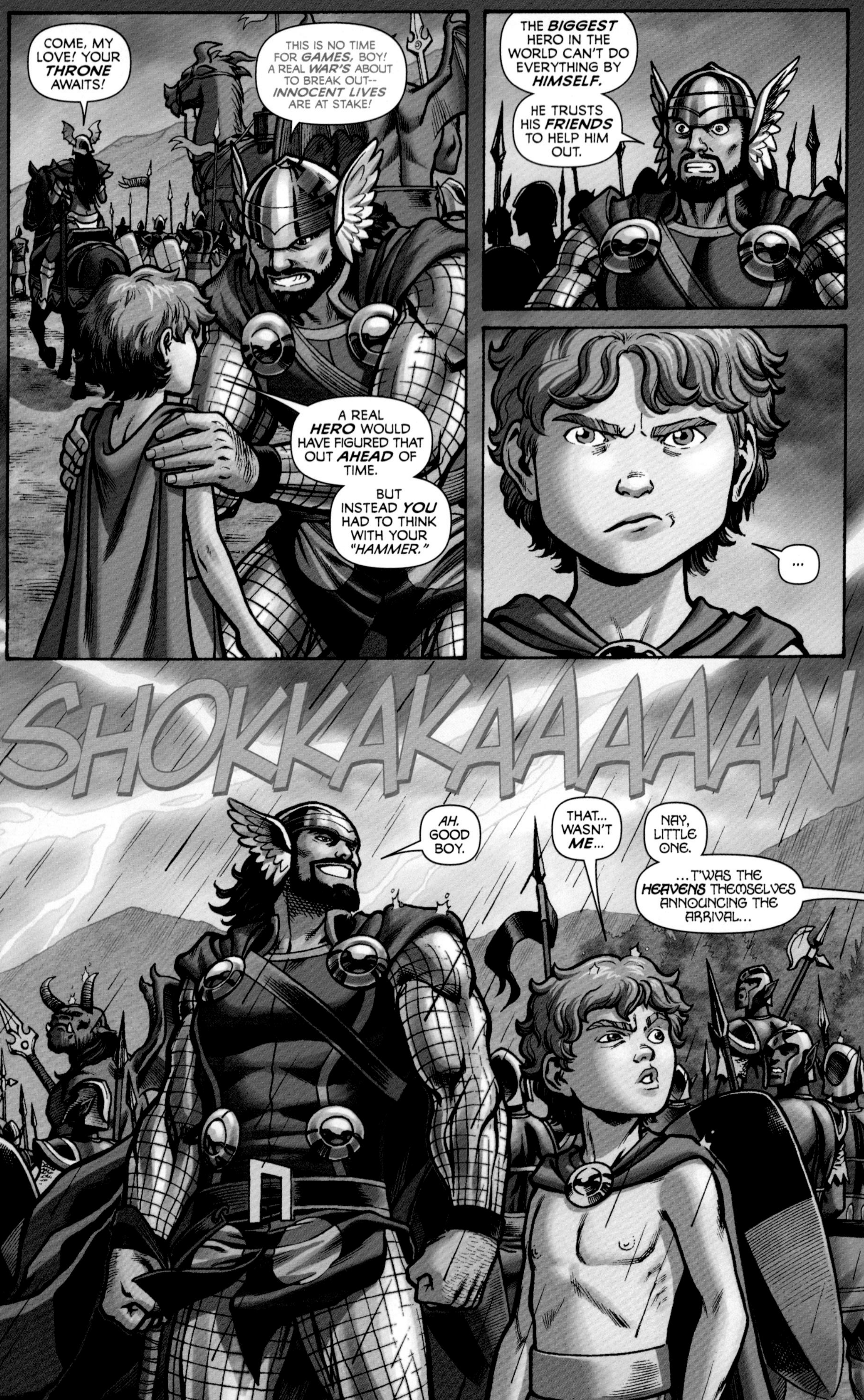
COME, MY LOVE! YOUR THRONE AWAITS!
THIS IS NO TIME FOR GAMES, BOY! A REAL WAR'S ABOUT TO BREAK OUT-- INNOCENT LIVES ARE AT STAKE!
A REAL HERO WOULD HAVE FIGURED THAT OUT AHEAD OF TIME.
BUT INSTEAD YOU HAD TO THINK WITH YOUR "HAMMER."
THE BIGGEST HERO IN THE WORLD CAN'T DO EVERYTHING BY HIMSELF.
HE TRUSTS HIS FRIENDS TO HELP HIM OUT.
...
SHOKKAKAAAAAAN
AH. GOOD BOY.
THAT... WASN'T ME...
NAY, LITTLE ONE.
...T'WAS THE HEAVENS THEMSELVES ANNOUNCING THE ARRIVAL...

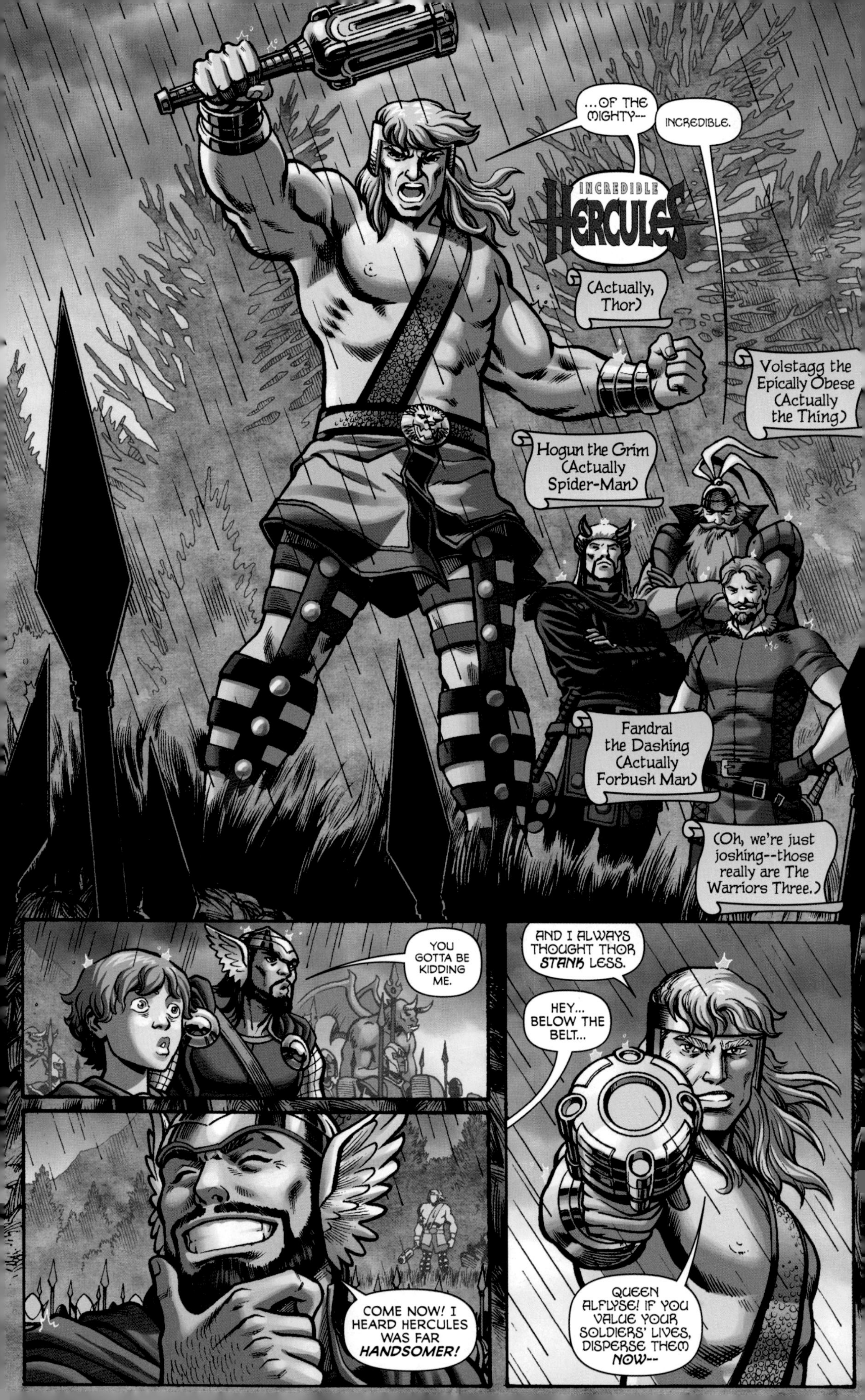

...OF THE MIGHTY--
INCREDIBLE HERCULES
INCREDIBLE.
(Actually, Thor)
Volstagg the Epically Obese (Actually the Thing)
Hogun the Grim (Actually Spider-Man)
Fandral the Dashing (Actually Forbush Man)
(Oh, we're just joshing--those really are The Warriors Three.)
YOU GOTTA BE KIDDING ME.
COME NOW! I HEARD HERCULES WAS FAR HANDSOMER!
AND I ALWAYS THOUGHT THOR STANK LESS.
HEY... BELOW THE BELT...
QUEEN ALFLYSE! IF YOU VALUE YOUR SOLDIERS' LIVES, DISPERSE THEM NOW--

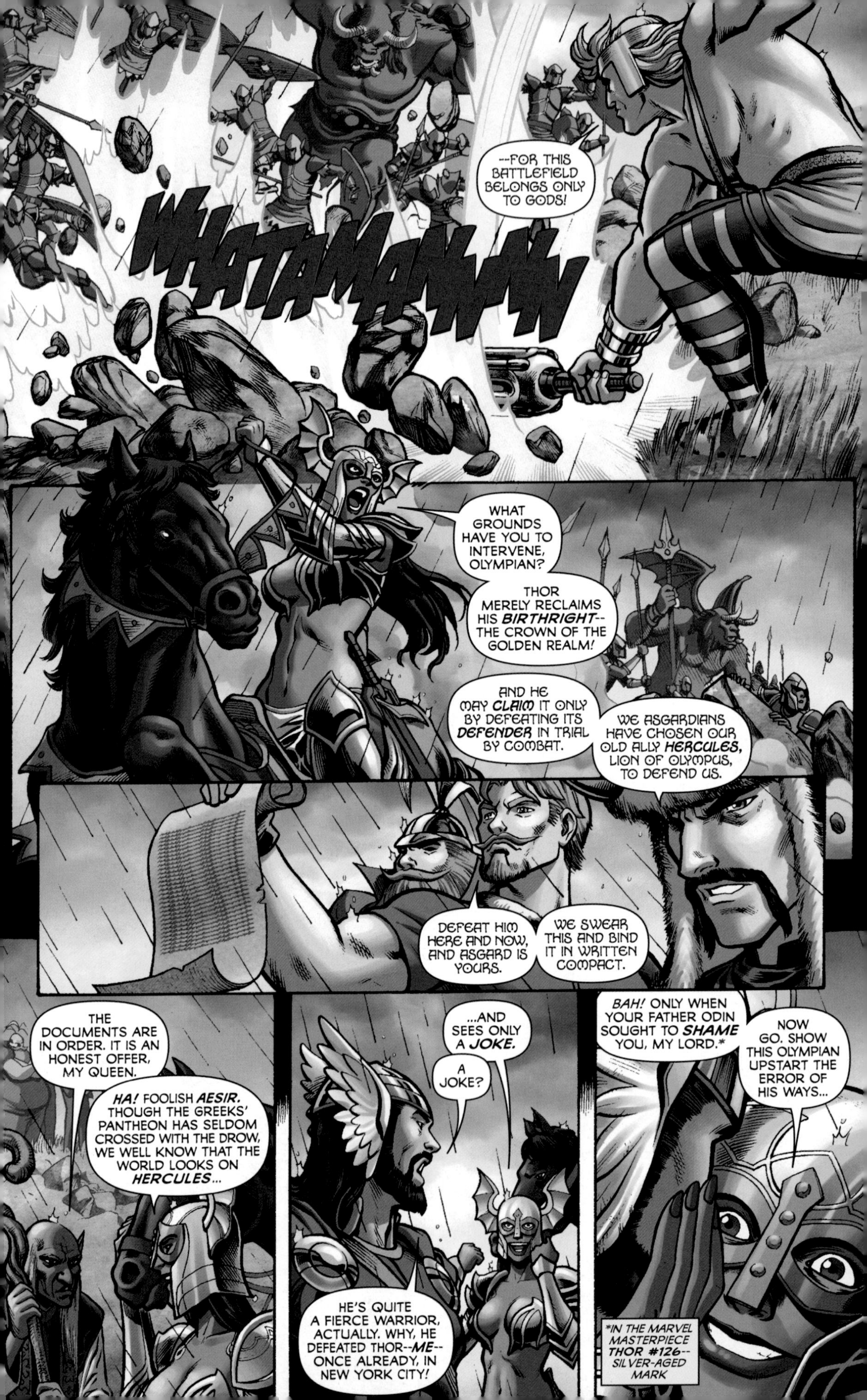
--FOR THIS BATTLEFIELD BELONGS ONLY TO GODS!
WHATAMANWAN
WHAT GROUNDS HAVE YOU TO INTERVENE, OLYMPIAN?
THOR MERELY RECLAIMS HIS BIRTHRIGHT-- THE CROWN OF THE GOLDEN REALM!
AND HE MAY CLAIM IT ONLY BY DEFEATING ITS DEFENDER IN TRIAL BY COMBAT.
WE ASGARDIANS HAVE CHOSEN OUR OLD ALLY HERCULES, LION OF OLYMPUS, TO DEFEND US.
DEFEAT HIM HERE AND NOW, AND ASGARD IS YOURS.
WE SWEAR THIS AND BIND IT IN WRITTEN COMPACT.
THE DOCUMENTS ARE IN ORDER. IT IS AN HONEST OFFER, MY QUEEN.
HA! FOOLISH AESIR. THOUGH THE GREEKS' PANTHEON HAS SELDOM CROSSED WITH THE DROW, WE WELL KNOW THAT THE WORLD LOOKS ON HERCULES...
...AND SEES ONLY A JOKE.
A JOKE?
HE'S QUITE A FIERCE WARRIOR, ACTUALLY. WHY, HE DEFEATED THOR--ME-- ONCE ALREADY, IN NEW YORK CITY!
BAH! ONLY WHEN YOUR FATHER ODIN SOUGHT TO SHAME YOU, MY LORD.*
NOW GO. SHOW THIS OLYMPIAN UPSTART THE ERROR OF HIS WAYS...
*IN THE MARVEL MASTERPIECE THOR #126-- SILVER-AGED MARK

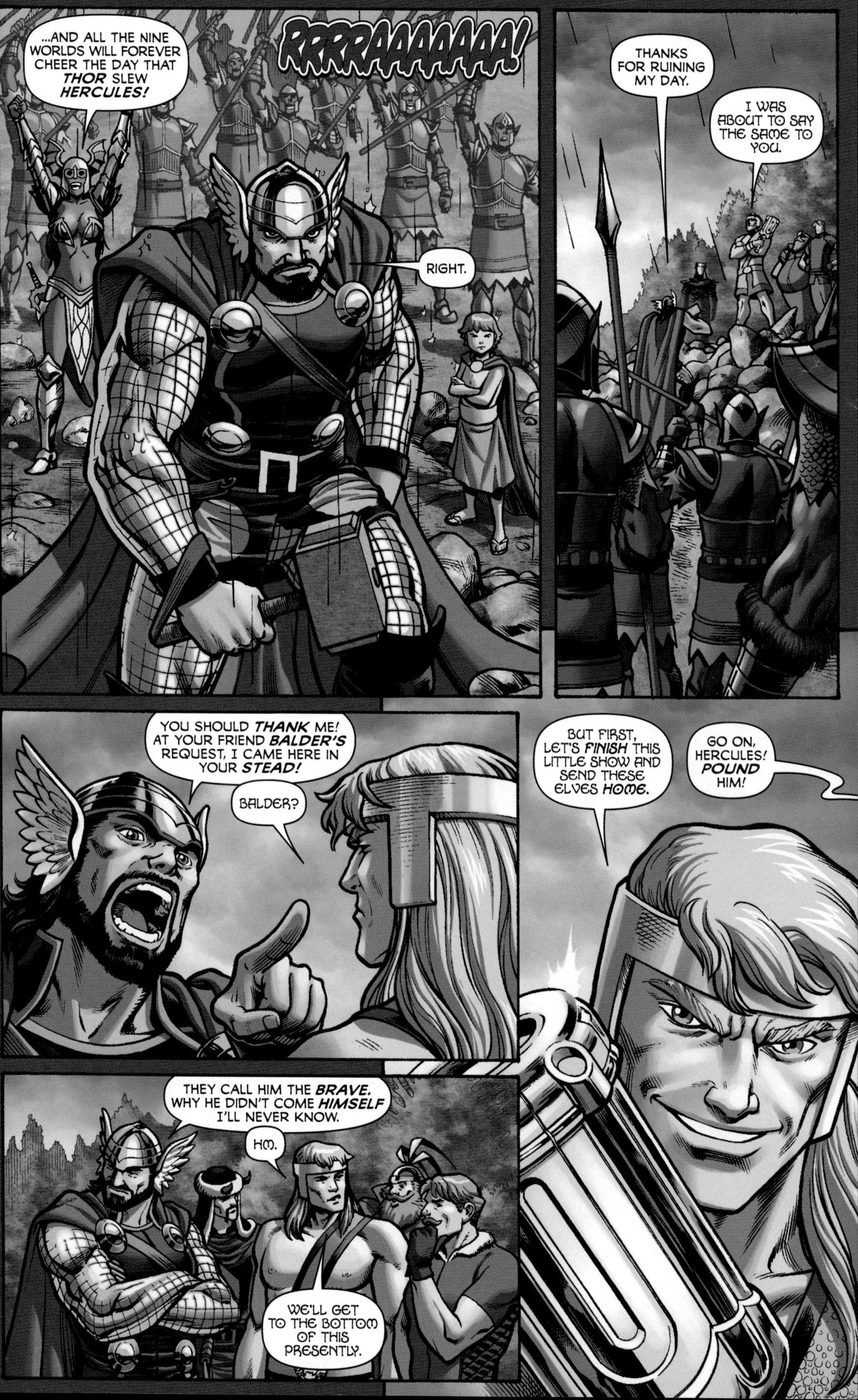
...AND ALL THE NINE WORLDS WILL FOREVER CHEER THE DAY THAT THOR SLEW HERCULES!
RRRRAAAAAAA!
RIGHT.
THANKS FOR RUINING MY DAY.
I WAS ABOUT TO SAY THE SAME TO YOU.
YOU SHOULD THANK ME! AT YOUR FRIEND BALDER'S REQUEST, I CAME HERE IN YOUR STEAD!
BALDER?
THEY CALL HIM THE BRAVE. WHY HE DIDN'T COME HIMSELF I'LL NEVER KNOW.
HM.
WE'LL GET TO THE BOTTOM OF THIS PRESENTLY.
BUT FIRST, LET'S FINISH THIS LITTLE SHOW AND SEND THESE ELVES HOME.
GO ON, HERCULES! POUND HIM!

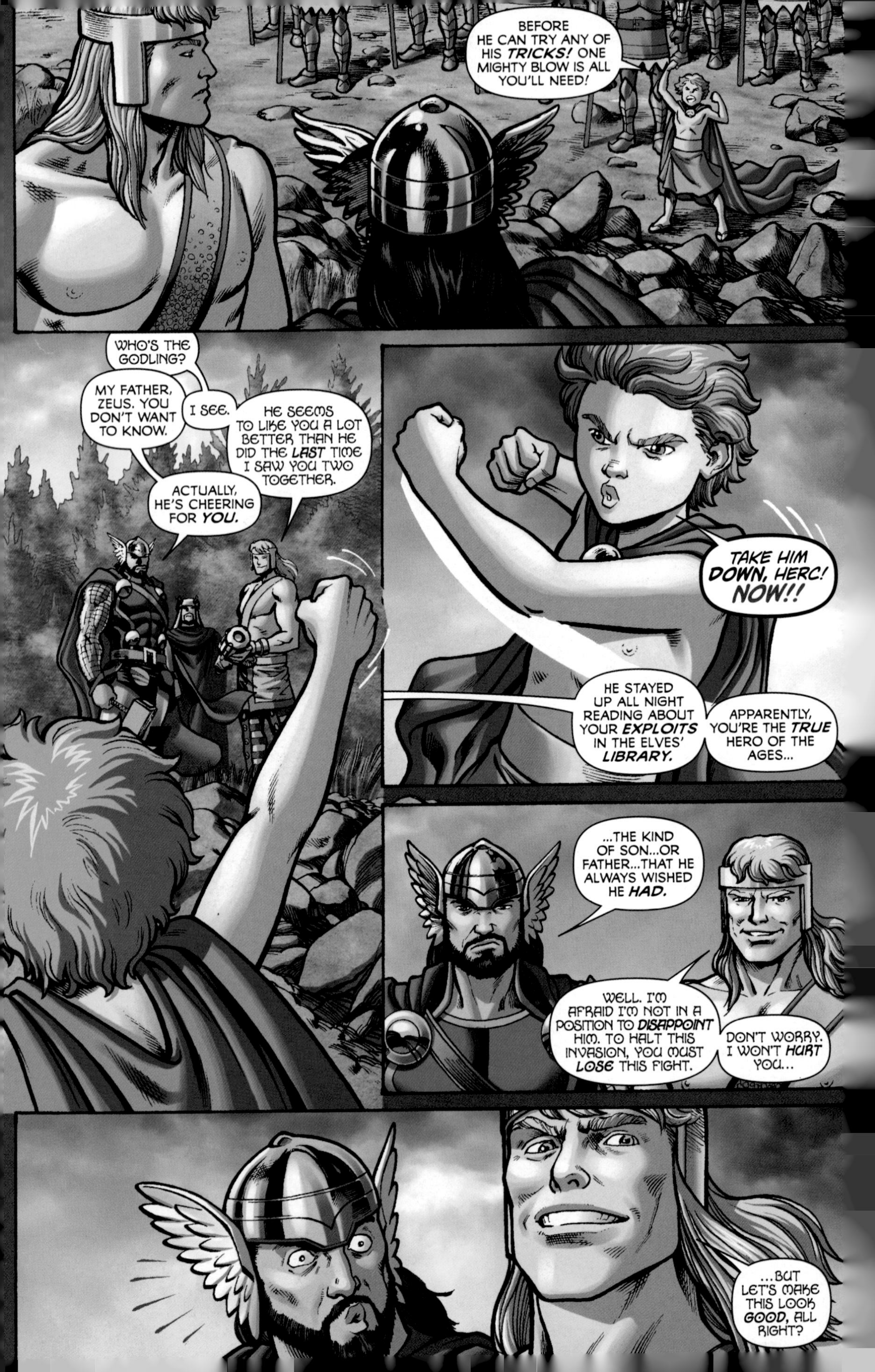
BEFORE HE CAN TRY ANY OF HIS TRICKS! ONE MIGHTY BLOW IS ALL YOU'LL NEED!
WHO'S THE GODLING?
MY FATHER, ZEUS. YOU DON'T WANT TO KNOW.
I SEE.
HE SEEMS TO LIKE YOU A LOT BETTER THAN HE DID THE LAST TIME I SAW YOU TWO TOGETHER.
ACTUALLY, HE'S CHEERING FOR YOU.
TAKE HIM DOWN, HERC! NOW!!
HE STAYED UP ALL NIGHT READING ABOUT YOUR EXPLOITS IN THE ELVES' LIBRARY.
APPARENTLY, YOU'RE THE TRUE HERO OF THE AGES...
...THE KIND OF SON...OR FATHER...THAT HE ALWAYS WISHED HE HAD.
WELL. I'M AFRAID I'M NOT IN A POSITION TO DISAPPOINT HIM. TO HALT THIS INVASION, YOU MUST LOSE THIS FIGHT.
DON'T WORRY. I WON'T HURT YOU...
...BUT LET'S MAKE THIS LOOK GOOD, ALL RIGHT?

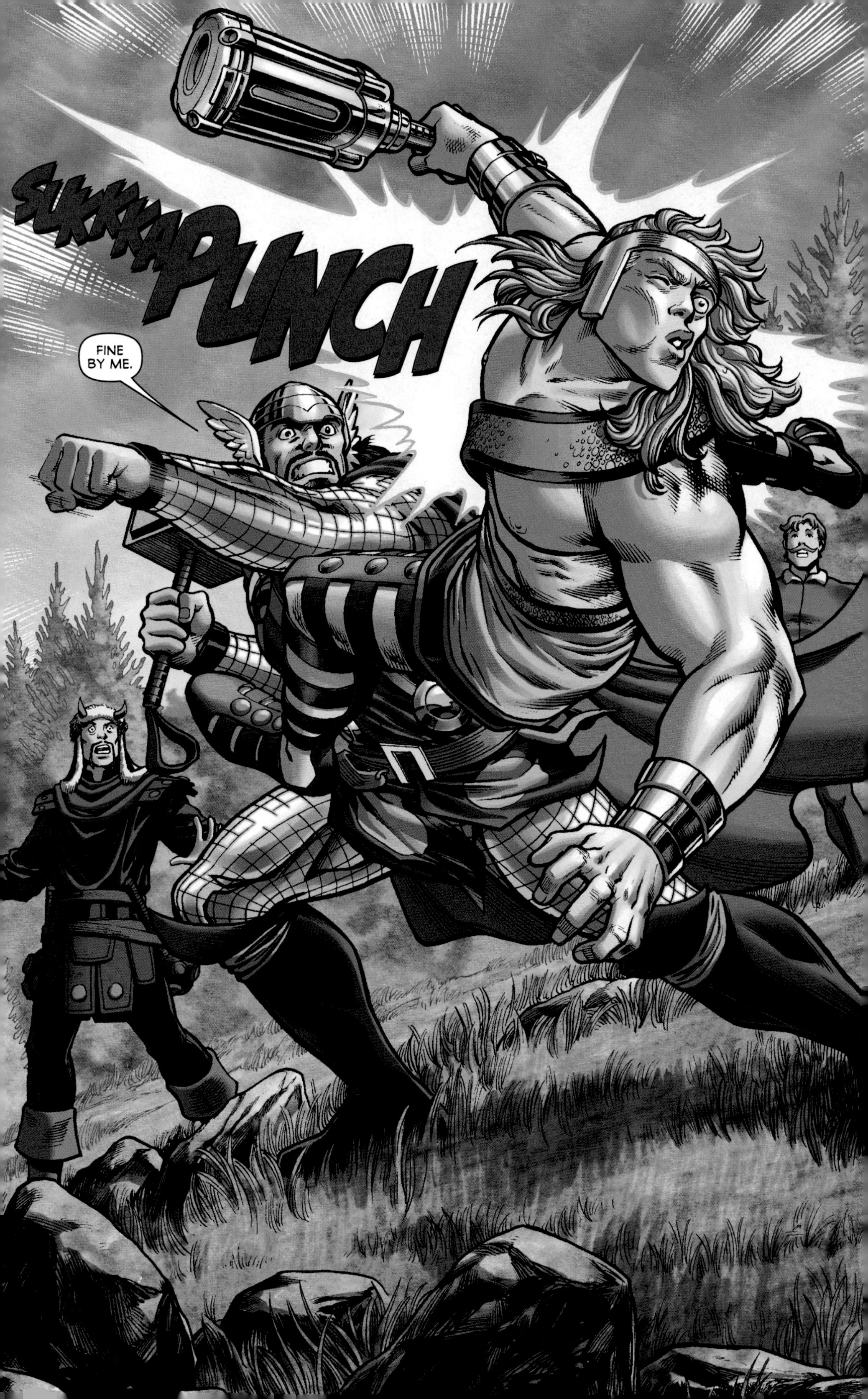
SUKKKAPUNCH
FINE BY ME.

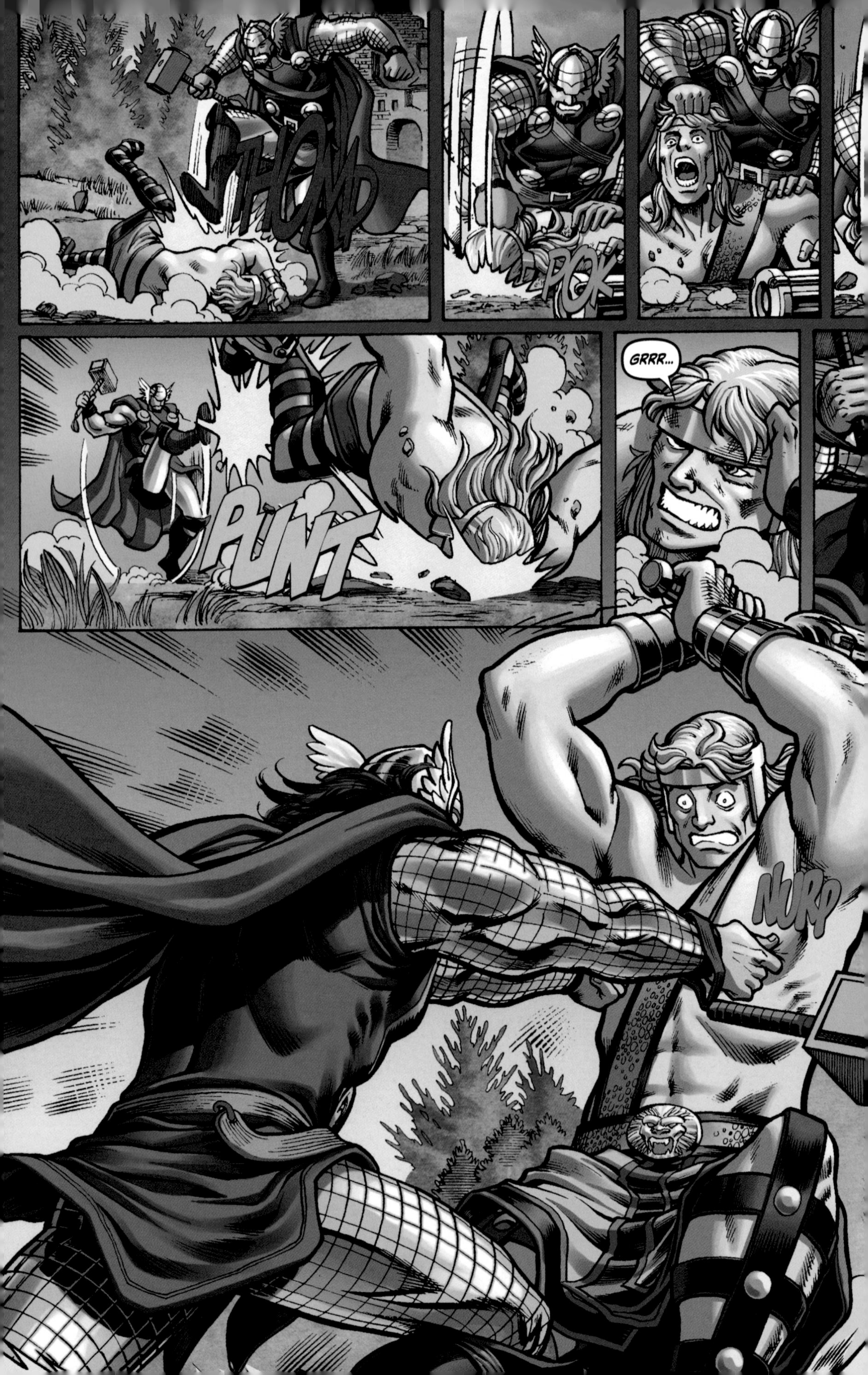
THOMP
POK
PUNT
GRRR...
NURP

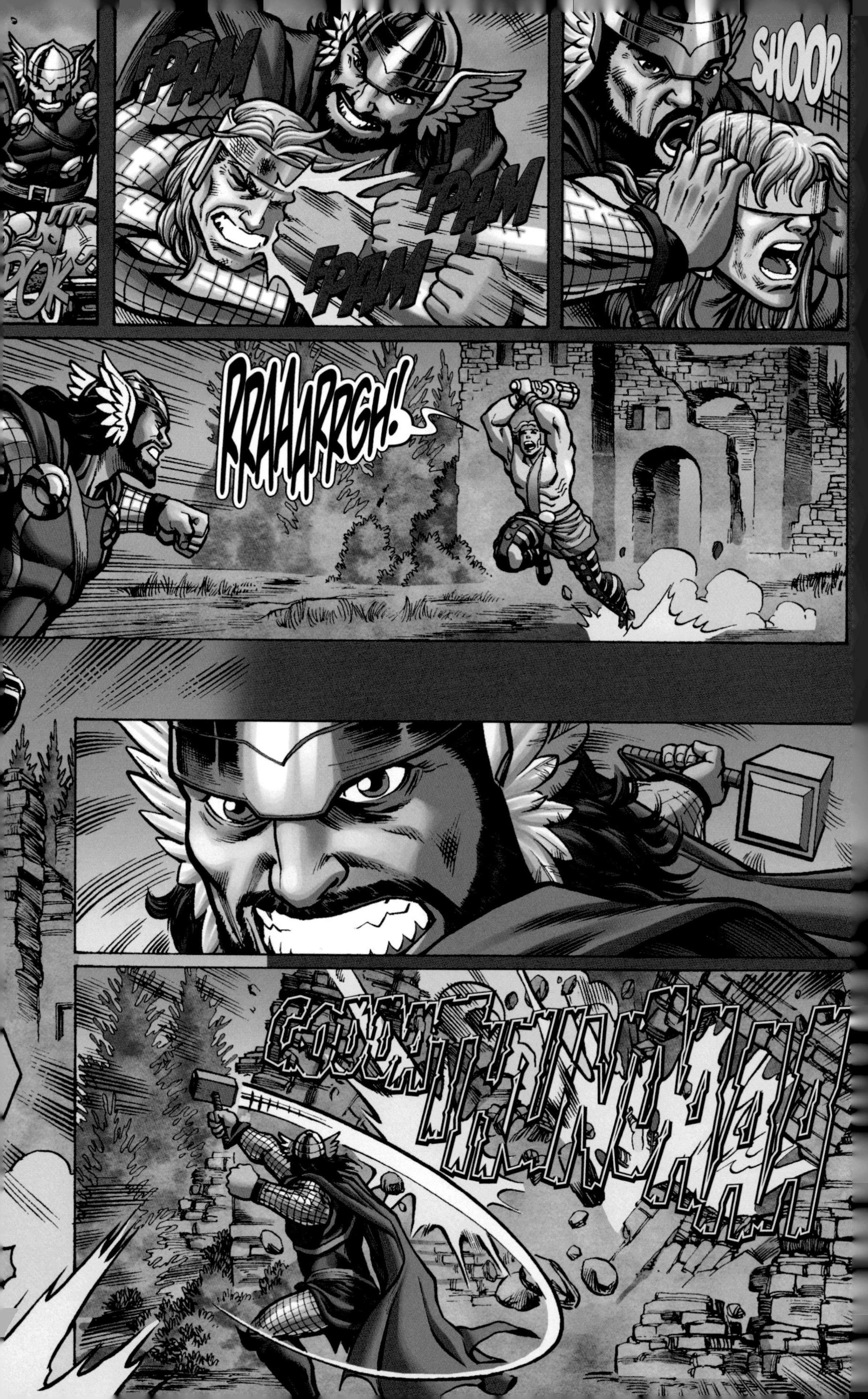
FPAM
FPAM
FPAM
SHOOP
RRAAARRGH!

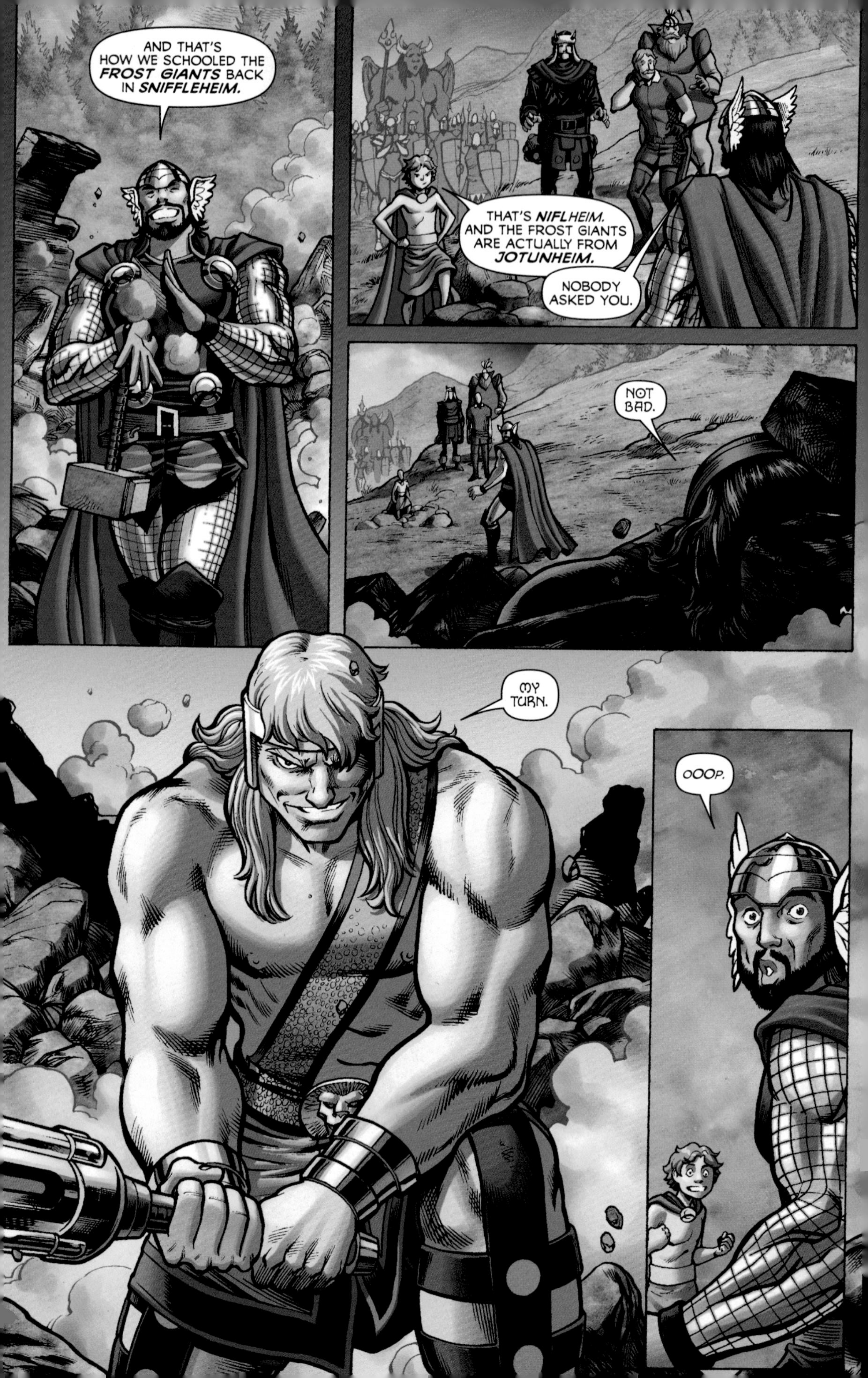

AND THAT'S HOW WE SCHOOLED THE *FROST GIANTS* BACK IN *SNIFFLEHEIM.*
THAT'S *NIFLHEIM.* AND THE FROST GIANTS ARE ACTUALLY FROM *JOTUNHEIM.*
NOBODY ASKED YOU.
NOT BAD.
MY TURN.
OOOP.

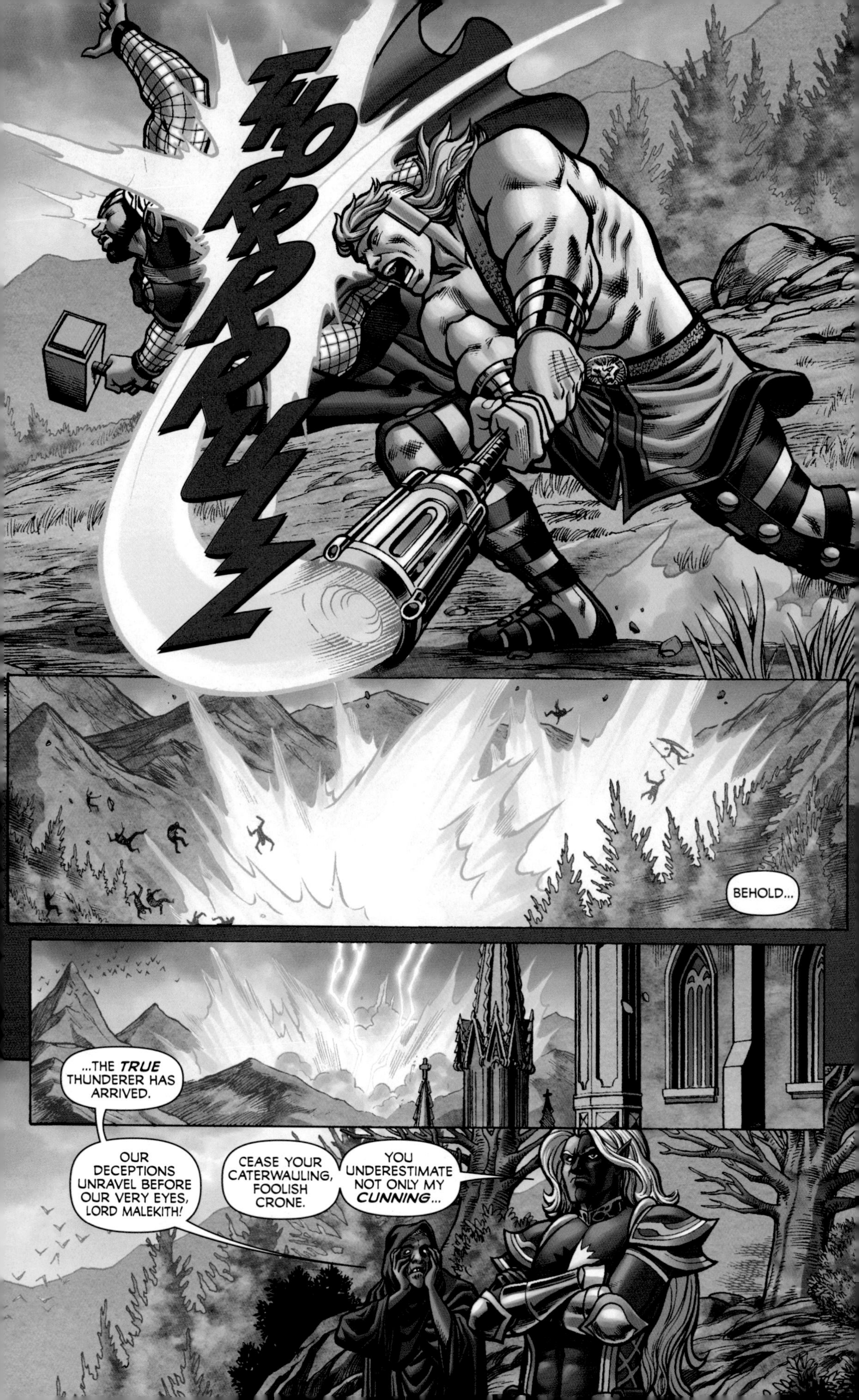
THOOOMRRRRRUUM
BEHOLD...
...THE TRUE THUNDERER HAS ARRIVED.
OUR DECEPTIONS UNRAVEL BEFORE OUR VERY EYES, LORD MALEKITH!
CEASE YOUR CATERWAULING, FOOLISH CRONE.
YOU UNDERESTIMATE NOT ONLY MY CUNNING...

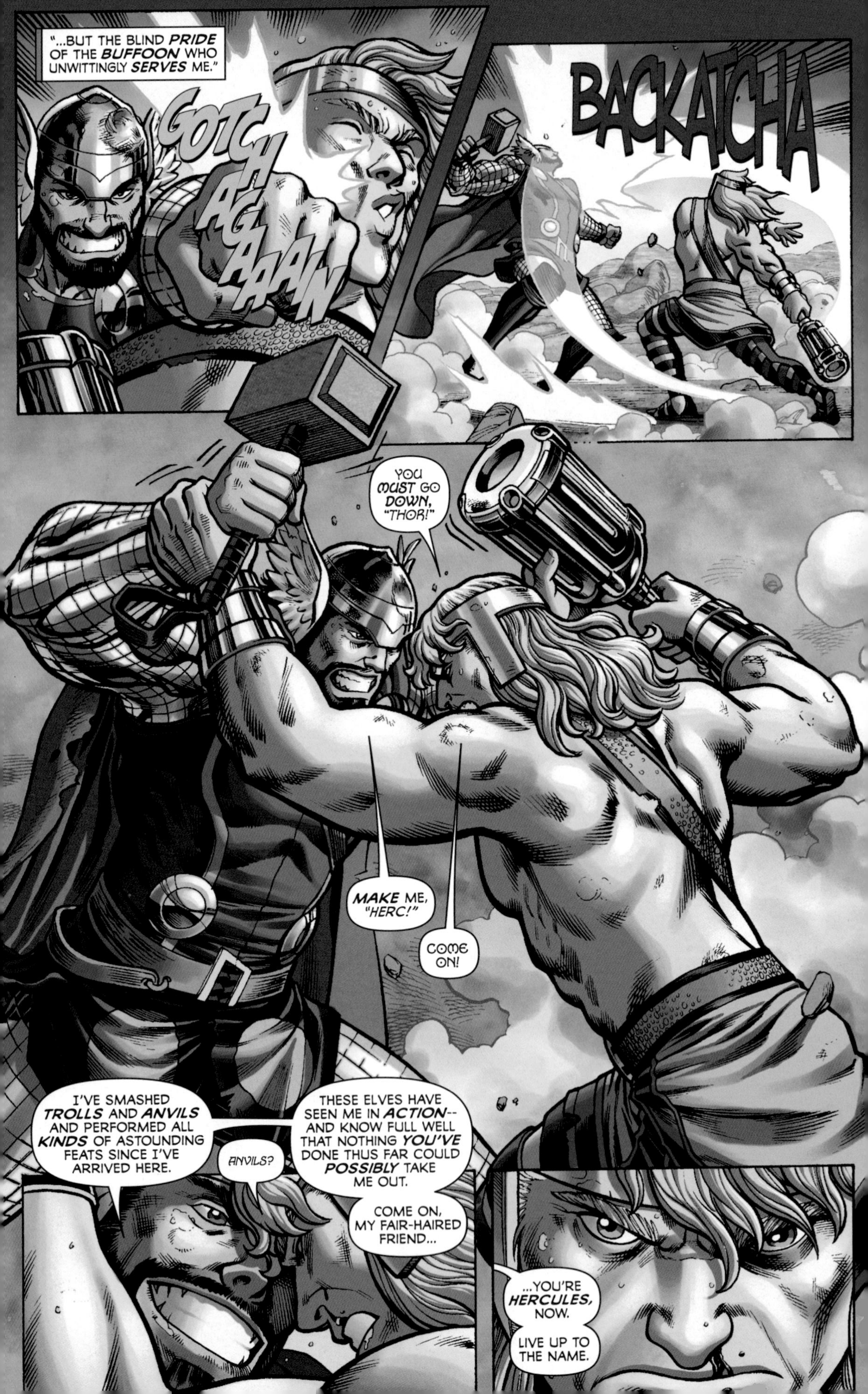
"...BUT THE BLIND PRIDE OF THE BUFFOON WHO UNWITTINGLY SERVES ME."
GOTCHA AGAAAIN
BACKATCHA
YOU MUST GO DOWN, "THOR!"
MAKE ME, "HERC!"
COME ON!
I'VE SMASHED TROLLS AND ANVILS AND PERFORMED ALL KINDS OF ASTOUNDING FEATS SINCE I'VE ARRIVED HERE.
ANVILS?
THESE ELVES HAVE SEEN ME IN ACTION-- AND KNOW FULL WELL THAT NOTHING YOU'VE DONE THUS FAR COULD POSSIBLY TAKE ME OUT.
COME ON, MY FAIR-HAIRED FRIEND...
...YOU'RE HERCULES, NOW.
LIVE UP TO THE NAME.

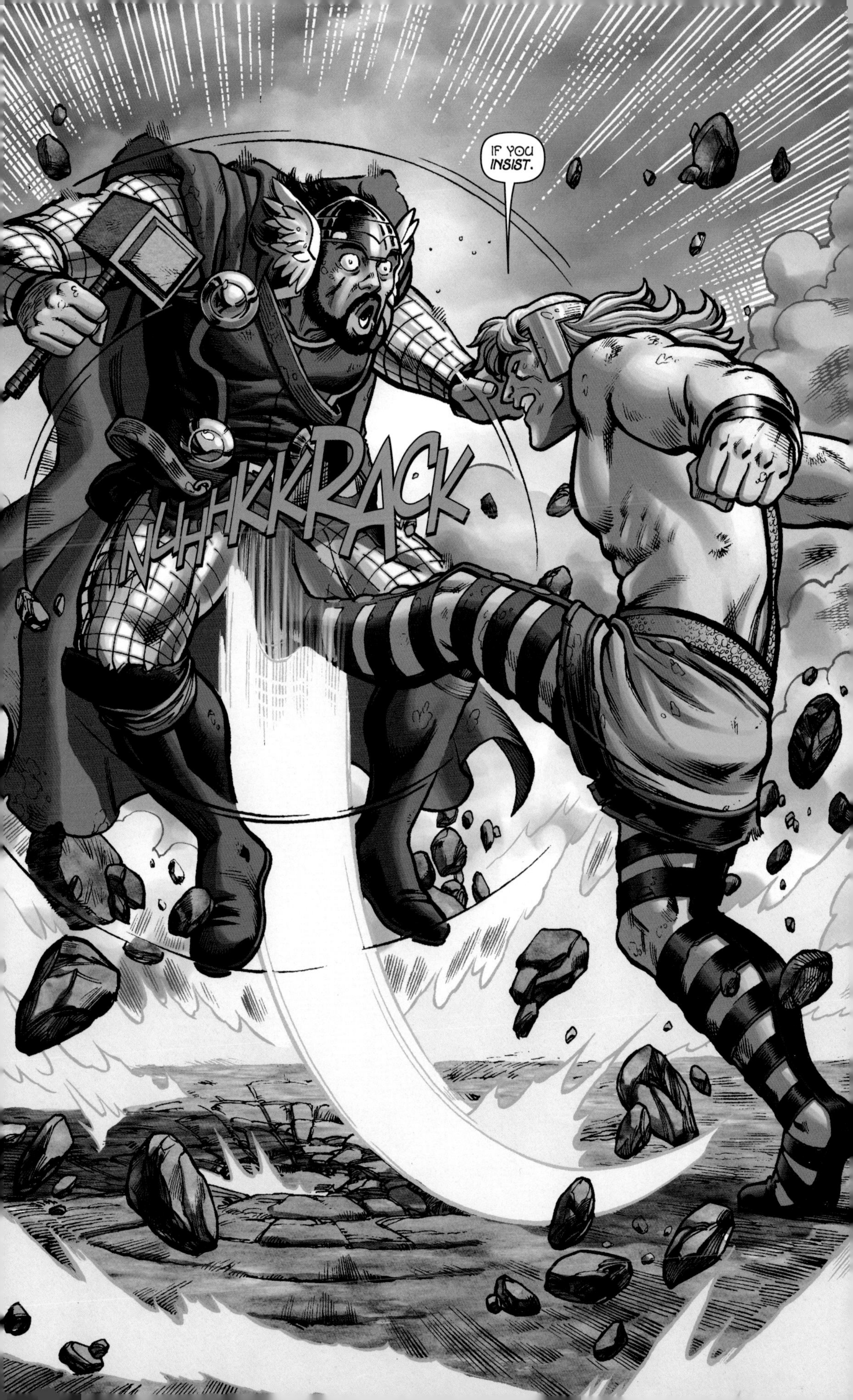
IF YOU INSIST.
NUHHKKRACK

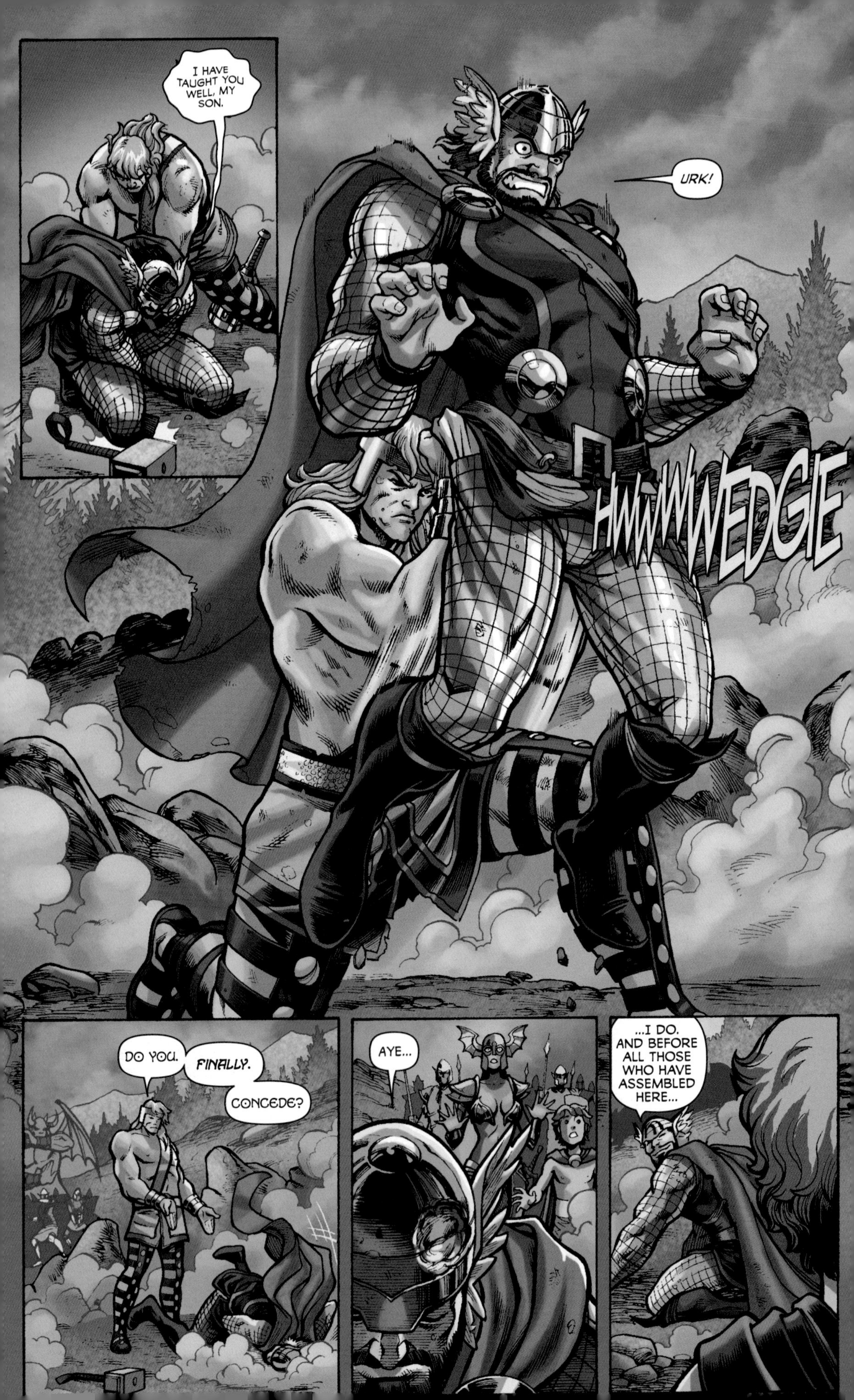
I HAVE TAUGHT YOU WELL, MY SON.
URK!
HWWWWEDGIE
DO YOU.
FINALLY.
CONCEDE?
AYE...
...I DO. AND BEFORE ALL THOSE WHO HAVE ASSEMBLED HERE...

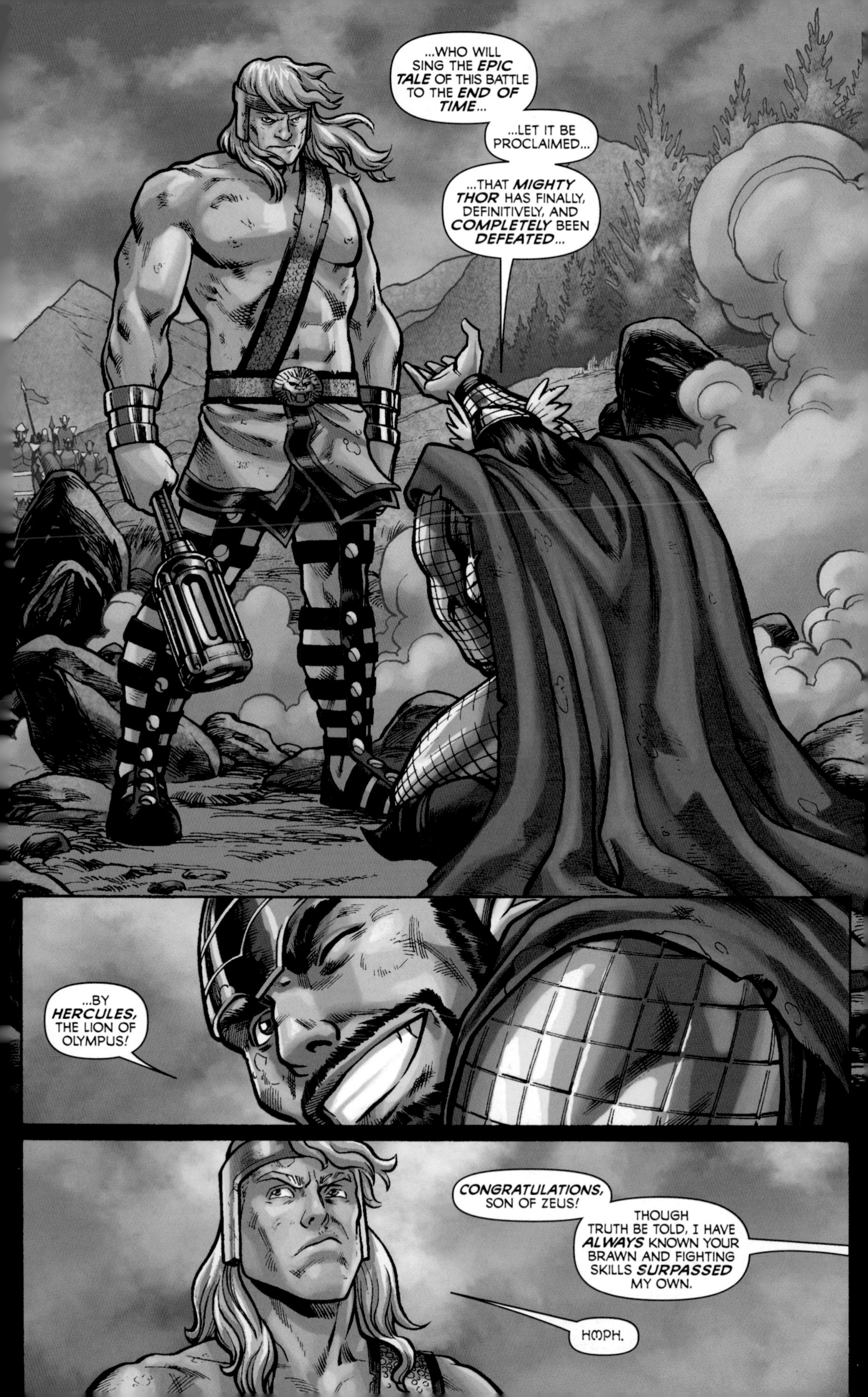
...WHO WILL SING THE EPIC TALE OF THIS BATTLE TO THE END OF TIME...
...LET IT BE PROCLAIMED...
...THAT MIGHTY THOR HAS FINALLY, DEFINITIVELY, AND COMPLETELY BEEN DEFEATED...
...BY HERCULES, THE LION OF OLYMPUS!
CONGRATULATIONS, SON OF ZEUS!
THOUGH TRUTH BE TOLD, I HAVE ALWAYS KNOWN YOUR BRAWN AND FIGHTING SKILLS SURPASSED MY OWN.
HMPH.

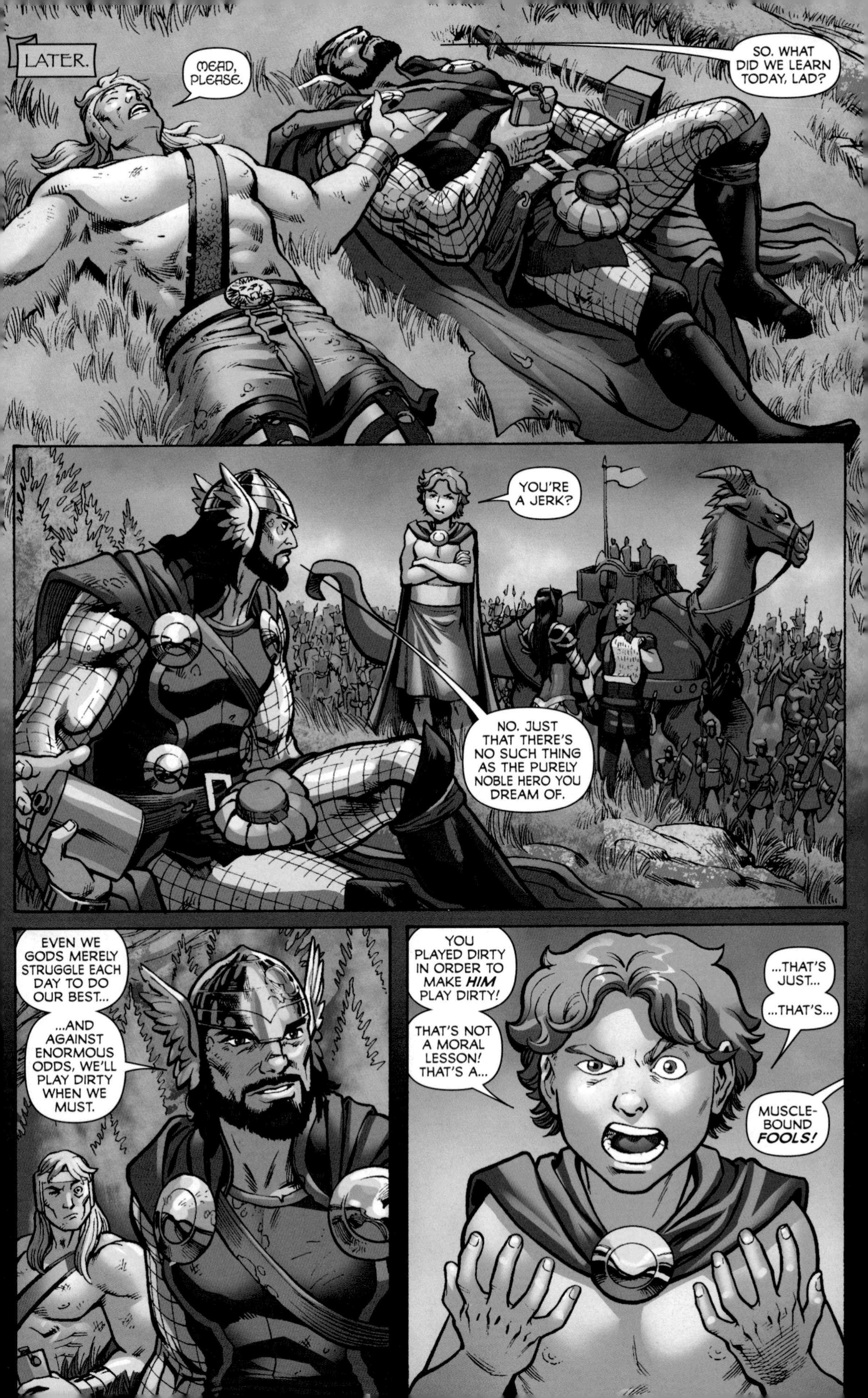
LATER.
MEAD, PLEASE.
SO. WHAT DID WE LEARN TODAY, LAD?
YOU'RE A JERK?
NO. JUST THAT THERE'S NO SUCH THING AS THE PURELY NOBLE HERO YOU DREAM OF.
EVEN WE GODS MERELY STRUGGLE EACH DAY TO DO OUR BEST...
...AND AGAINST ENORMOUS ODDS, WE'LL PLAY DIRTY WHEN WE MUST.
YOU PLAYED DIRTY IN ORDER TO MAKE *HIM* PLAY DIRTY!
THAT'S NOT A MORAL LESSON! THAT'S A...
...THAT'S JUST...
...THAT'S...
MUSCLE-BOUND *FOOLS!*

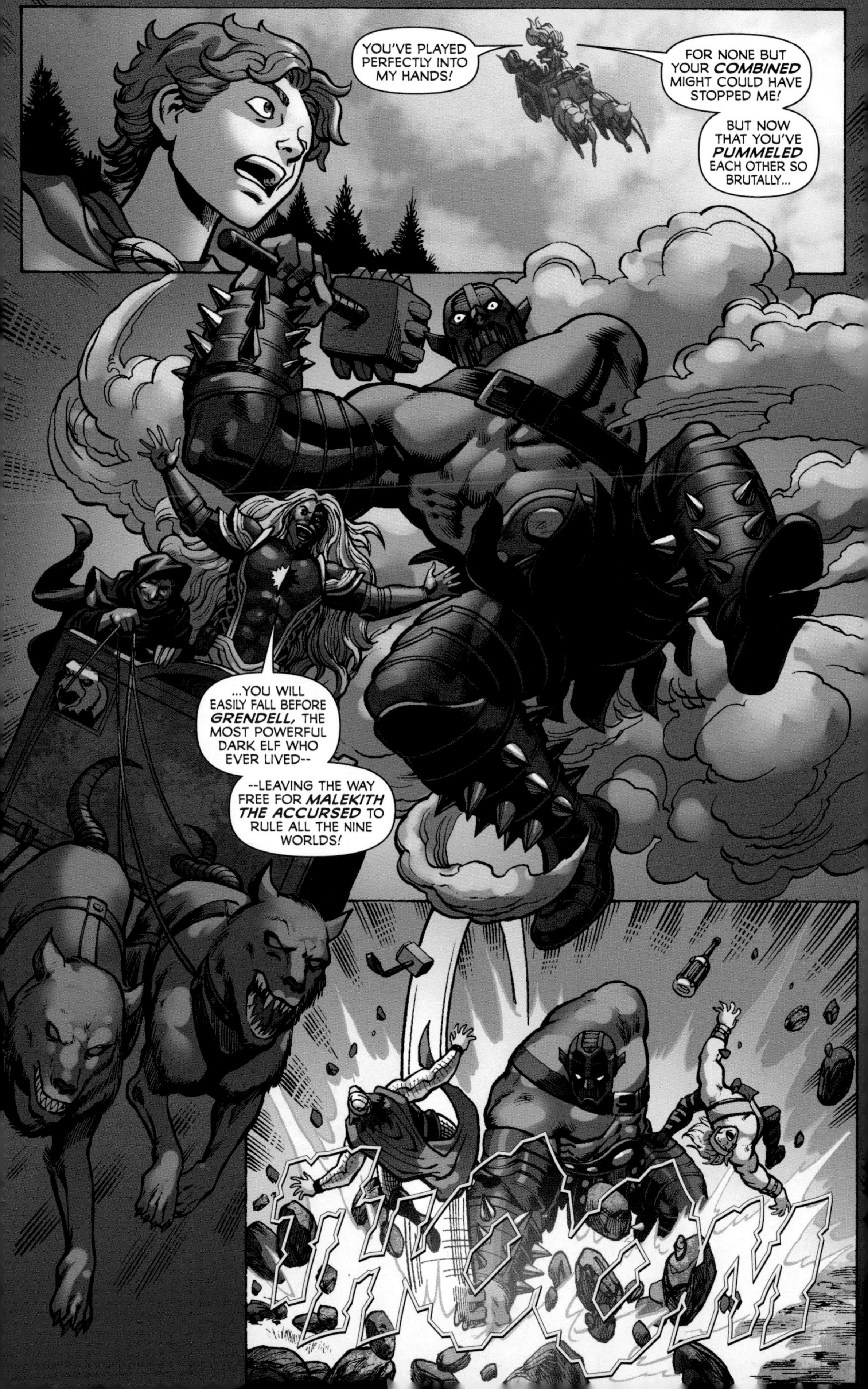
YOU'VE PLAYED PERFECTLY INTO MY HANDS!
FOR NONE BUT YOUR COMBINED MIGHT COULD HAVE STOPPED ME!
BUT NOW THAT YOU'VE PUMMELED EACH OTHER SO BRUTALLY...
...YOU WILL EASILY FALL BEFORE GRENDELL, THE MOST POWERFUL DARK ELF WHO EVER LIVED--
--LEAVING THE WAY FREE FOR MALEKITH THE ACCURSED TO RULE ALL THE NINE WORLDS!

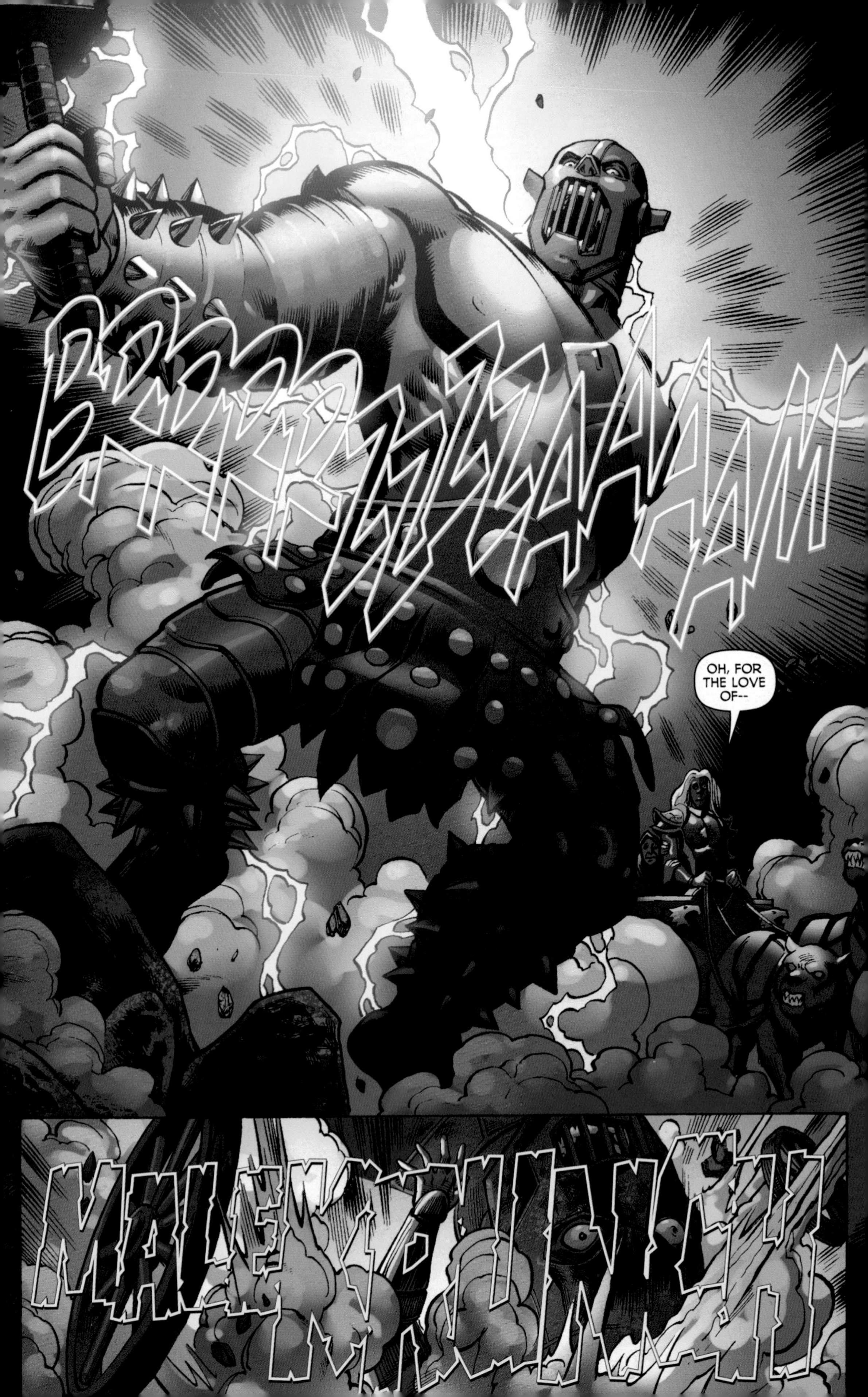
OH, FOR THE LOVE OF--
MALEKITH!!

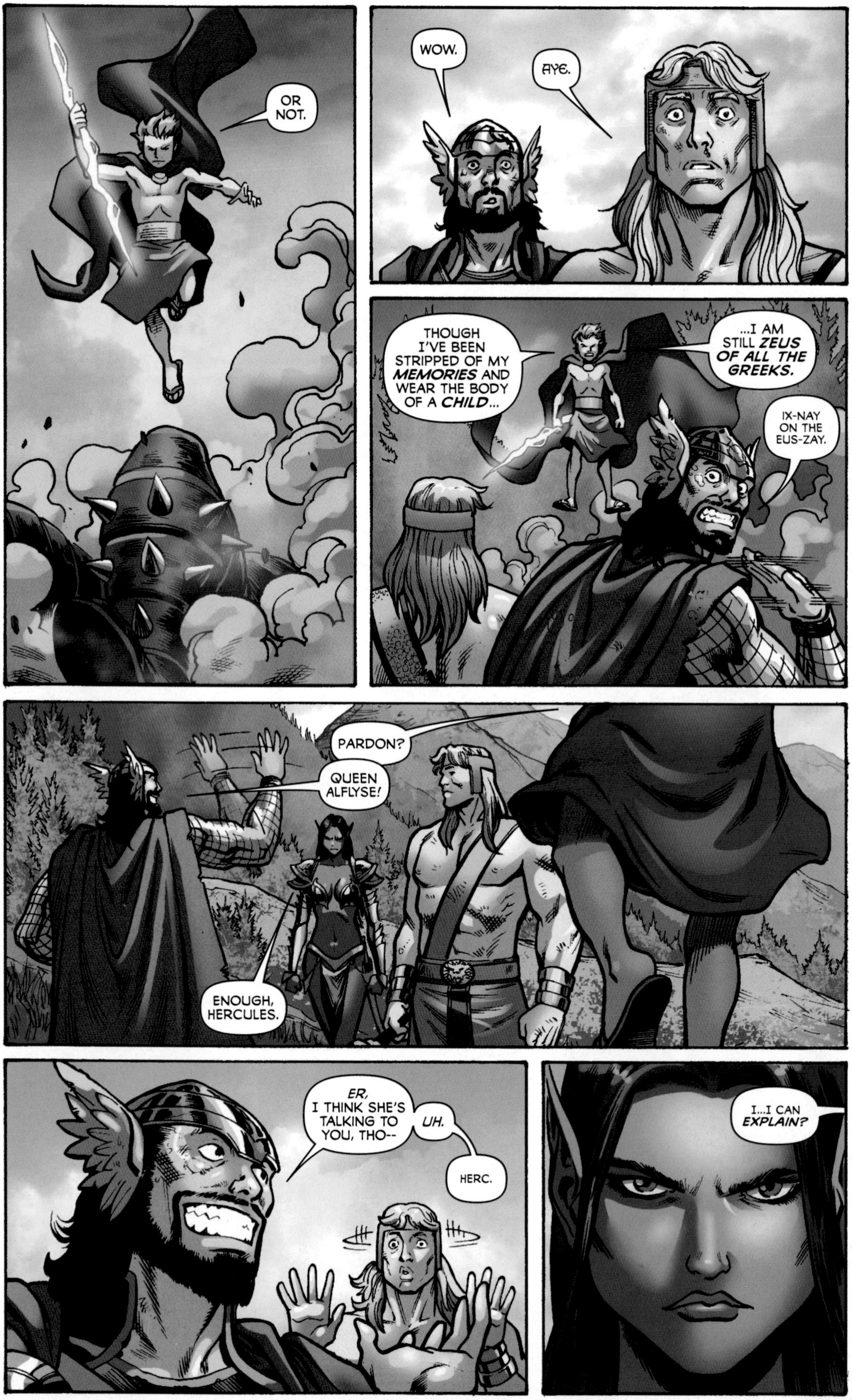
OR NOT.
WOW.
AYE.
THOUGH I'VE BEEN STRIPPED OF MY MEMORIES AND WEAR THE BODY OF A CHILD...
...I AM STILL ZEUS OF ALL THE GREEKS.
IX-NAY ON THE EUS-ZAY.
PARDON?
QUEEN ALFLYSE!
ENOUGH, HERCULES.
ER, I THINK SHE'S TALKING TO YOU, THO--
UH.
HERC.
I...I CAN EXPLAIN?

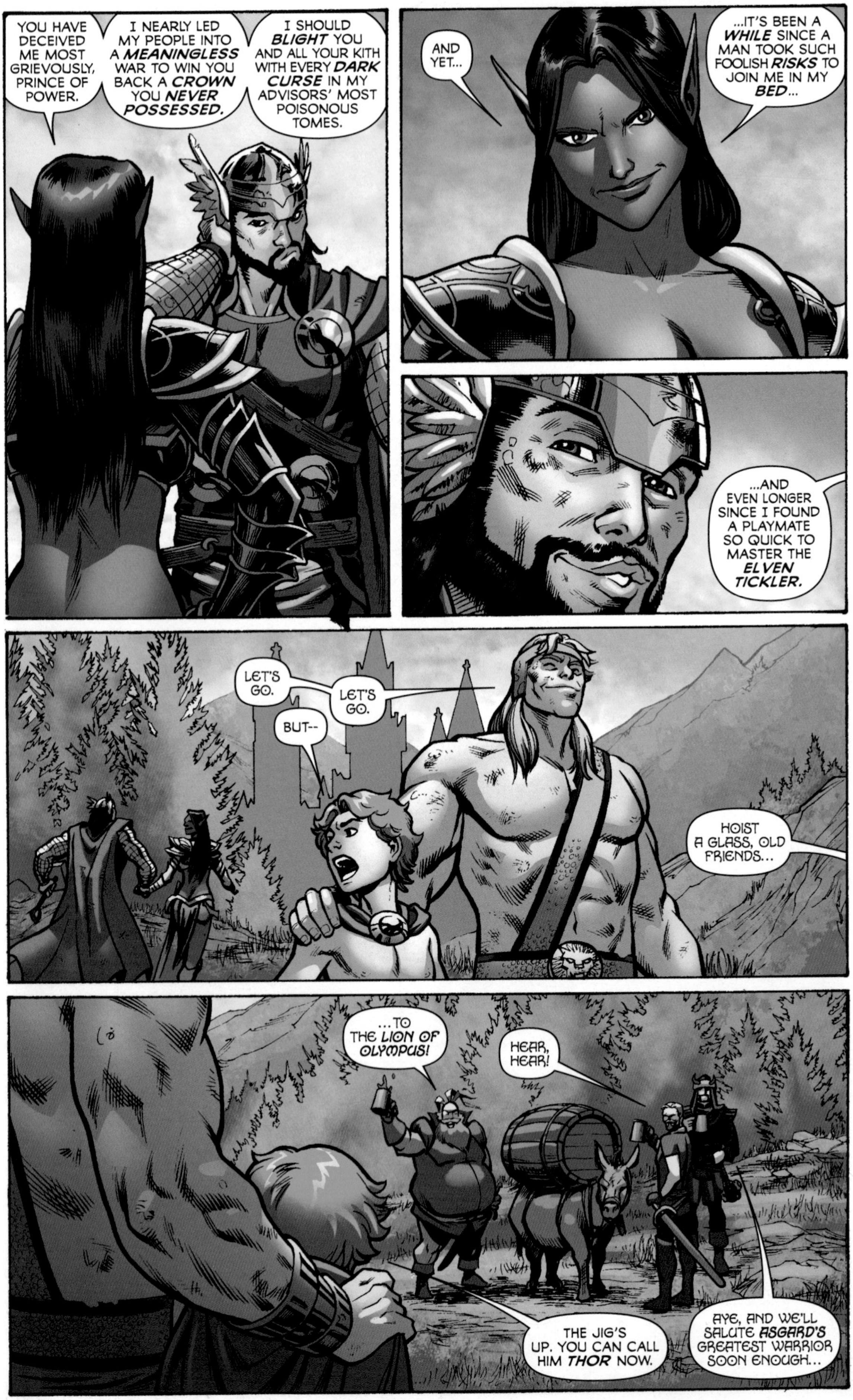
YOU HAVE DECEIVED ME MOST GRIEVOUSLY, PRINCE OF POWER.
I NEARLY LED MY PEOPLE INTO A MEANINGLESS WAR TO WIN YOU BACK A CROWN YOU NEVER POSSESSED.
I SHOULD BLIGHT YOU AND ALL YOUR KITH WITH EVERY DARK CURSE IN MY ADVISORS' MOST POISONOUS TOMES.
AND YET...
...IT'S BEEN A WHILE SINCE A MAN TOOK SUCH FOOLISH RISKS TO JOIN ME IN MY BED...
...AND EVEN LONGER SINCE I FOUND A PLAYMATE SO QUICK TO MASTER THE ELVEN TICKLER.
LET'S GO.
LET'S GO.
BUT--
HOIST A GLASS, OLD FRIENDS...
...TO THE LION OF OLYMPUS!
HEAR, HEAR!
THE JIG'S UP. YOU CAN CALL HIM THOR NOW.
AYE, AND WE'LL SALUTE ASGARD'S GREATEST WARRIOR SOON ENOUGH...

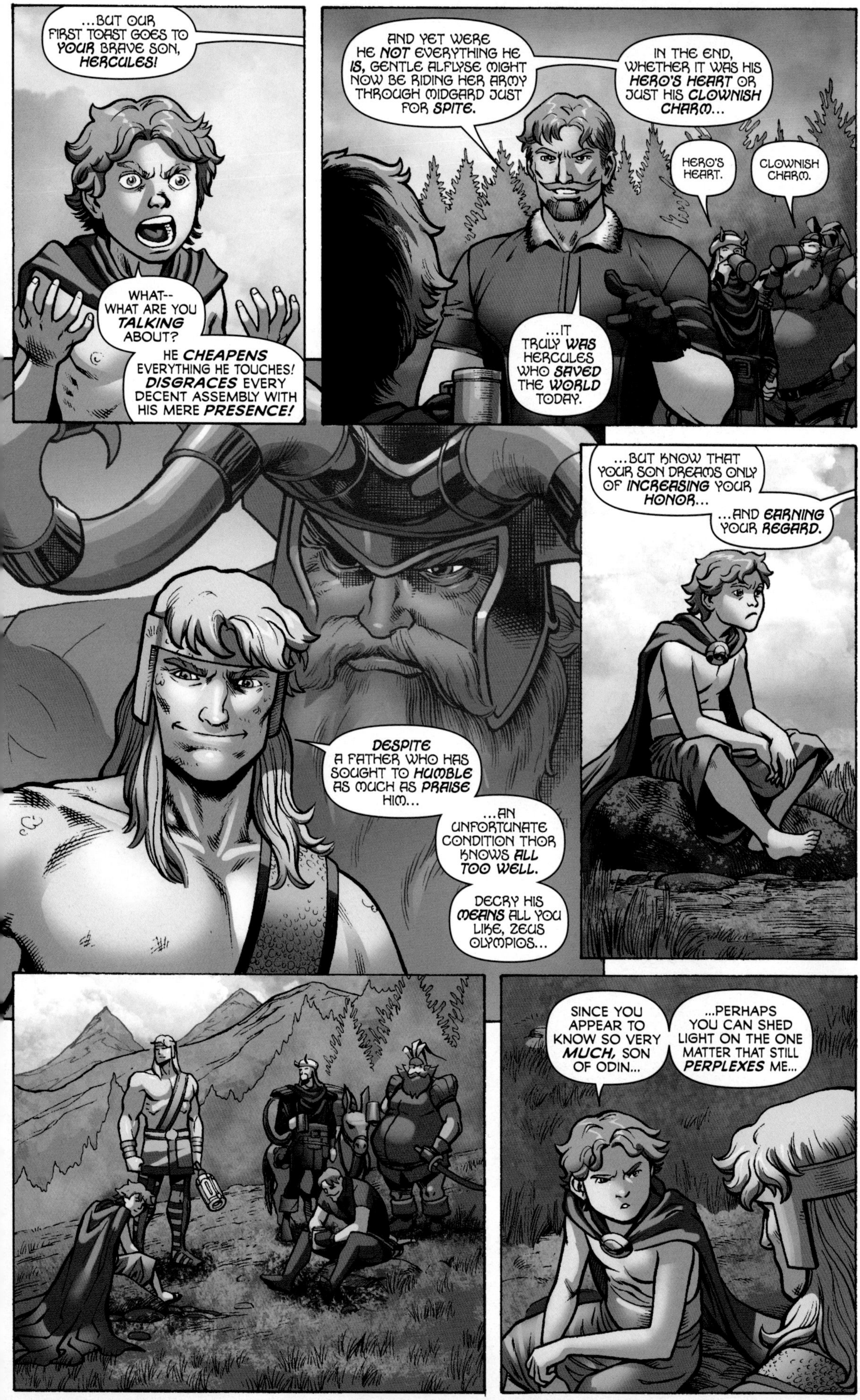
...BUT OUR FIRST TOAST GOES TO YOUR BRAVE SON, HERCULES!
WHAT--WHAT ARE YOU TALKING ABOUT?
HE CHEAPENS EVERYTHING HE TOUCHES! DISGRACES EVERY DECENT ASSEMBLY WITH HIS MERE PRESENCE!
AND YET WERE HE NOT EVERYTHING HE IS, GENTLE ALFLYSE MIGHT NOW BE RIDING HER ARMY THROUGH MIDGARD JUST FOR SPITE.
IN THE END, WHETHER IT WAS HIS HERO'S HEART OR JUST HIS CLOWNISH CHARM...
HERO'S HEART.
CLOWNISH CHARM.
...IT TRULY WAS HERCULES WHO SAVED THE WORLD TODAY.
DESPITE A FATHER WHO HAS SOUGHT TO HUMBLE AS MUCH AS PRAISE HIM...
...AN UNFORTUNATE CONDITION THOR KNOWS ALL TOO WELL.
DECRY HIS MEANS ALL YOU LIKE, ZEUS OLYMPIOS...
...BUT KNOW THAT YOUR SON DREAMS ONLY OF INCREASING YOUR HONOR...
...AND EARNING YOUR REGARD.
SINCE YOU APPEAR TO KNOW SO VERY MUCH, SON OF ODIN...
...PERHAPS YOU CAN SHED LIGHT ON THE ONE MATTER THAT STILL PERPLEXES ME...

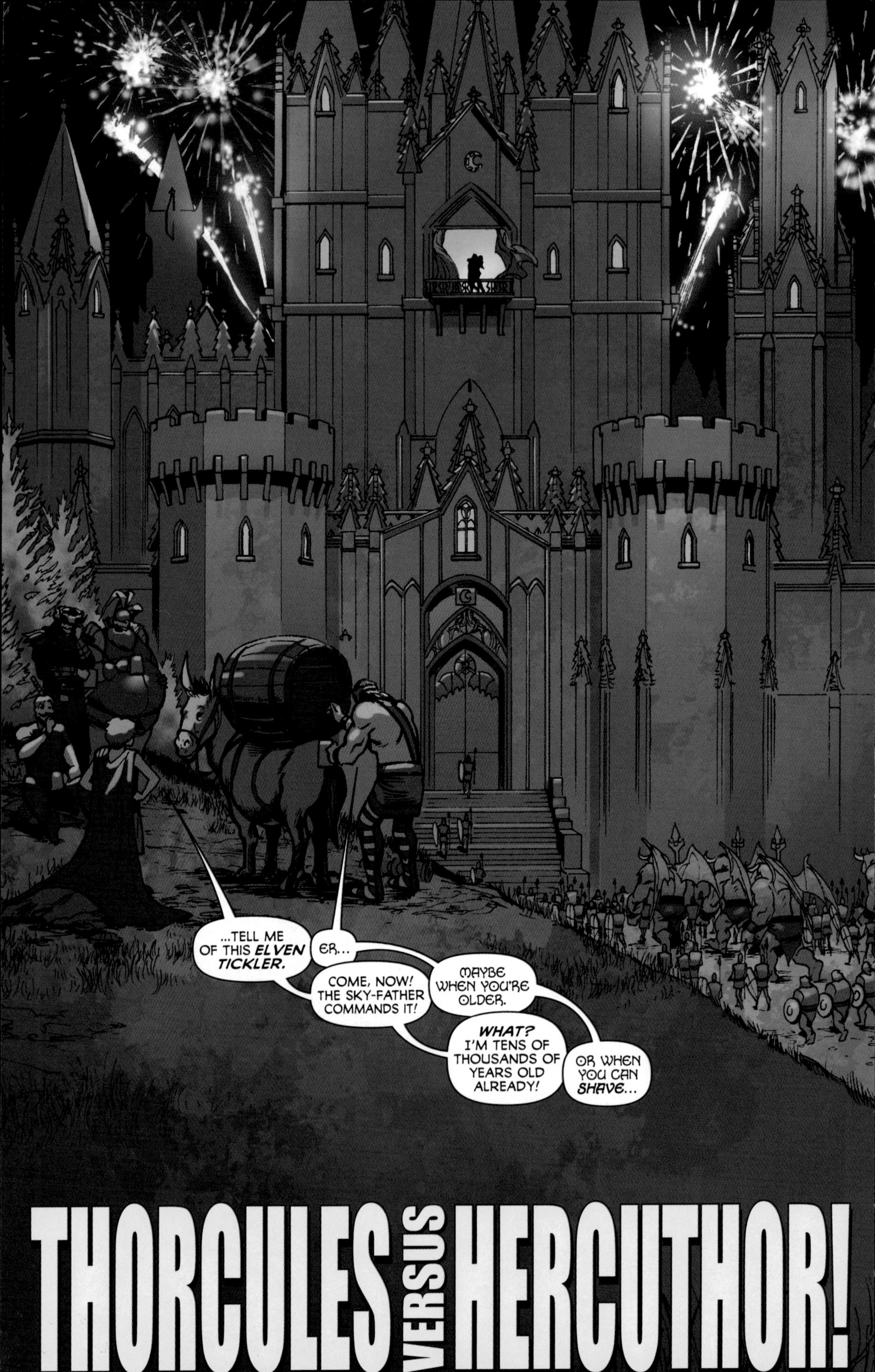
...TELL ME OF THIS *ELVEN TICKLER.*
ER...
COME, NOW! THE SKY-FATHER COMMANDS IT!
MAYBE WHEN YOU'RE OLDER.
WHAT? I'M TENS OF THOUSANDS OF YEARS OLD ALREADY!
OR WHEN YOU CAN *SHAVE*...
THORCULES VERSUS HERCUTHOR!

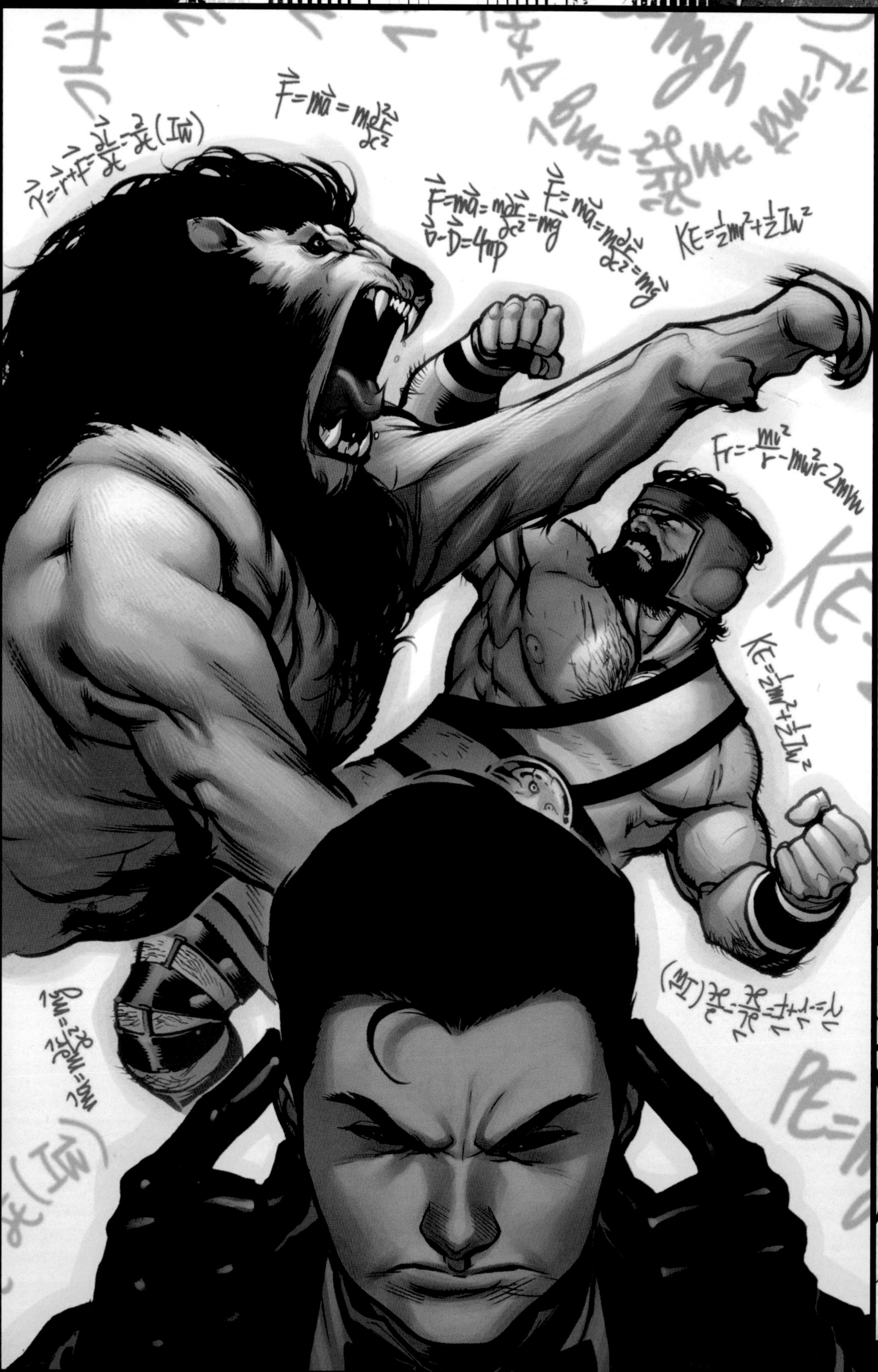

INCREDIBLE HERCULES #137

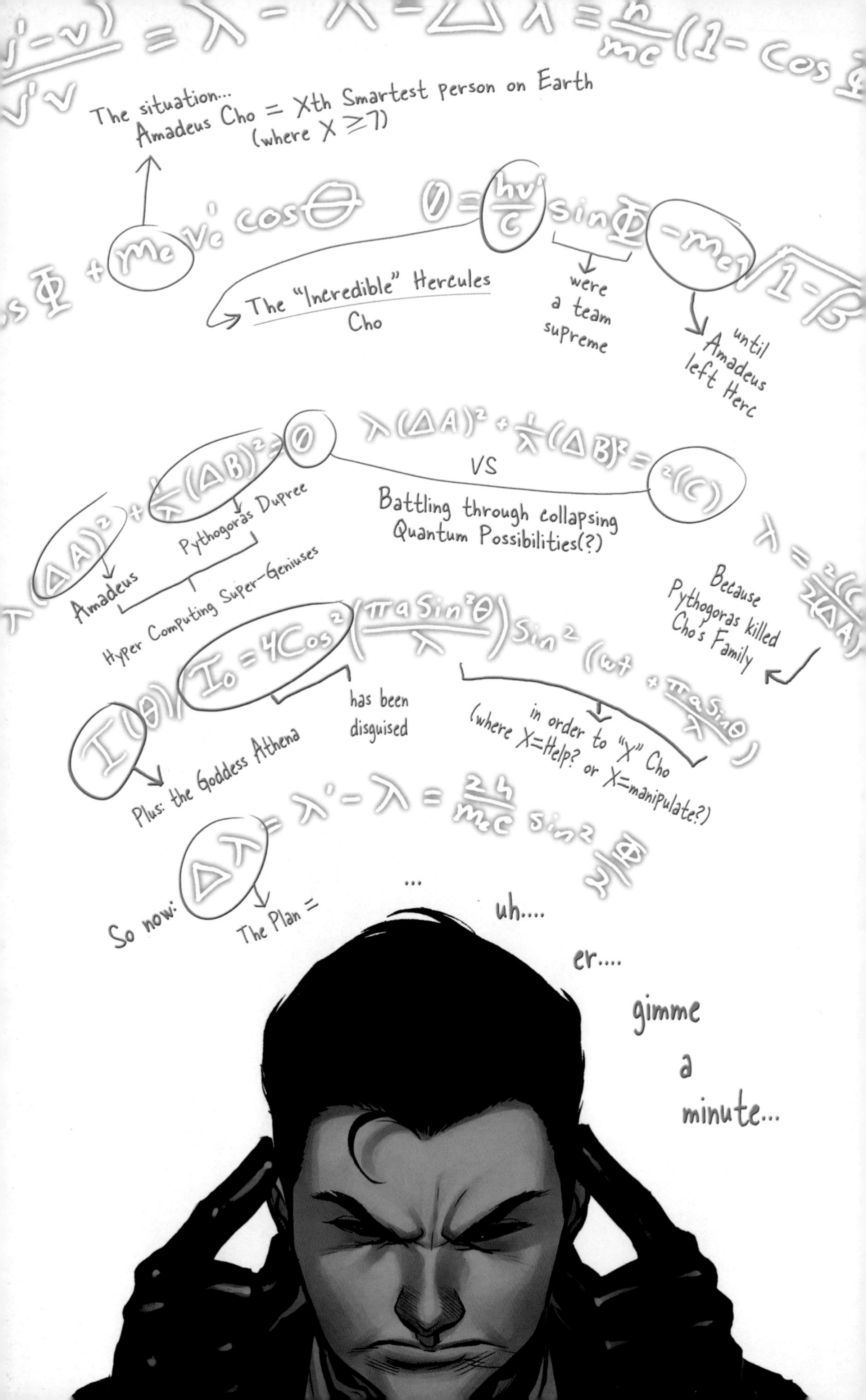

The situation...
Amadeus Cho = Xth Smartest person on Earth
(where X ≥ 7)
The "Incredible" Hercules
Cho
were a team supreme
until Amadeus left Herc
Amadeus
Pythogoras Dupree
Hyper Computing Super-Geniuses
VS
Battling through collapsing Quantum Possibilities(?)
Because Pythogoras killed Cho's Family
Plus: the Goddess Athena
has been disguised
in order to "X" Cho
(where X=Help? or X=manipulate?)
So now:
The Plan =
...
uh....
er....
gimme a minute...

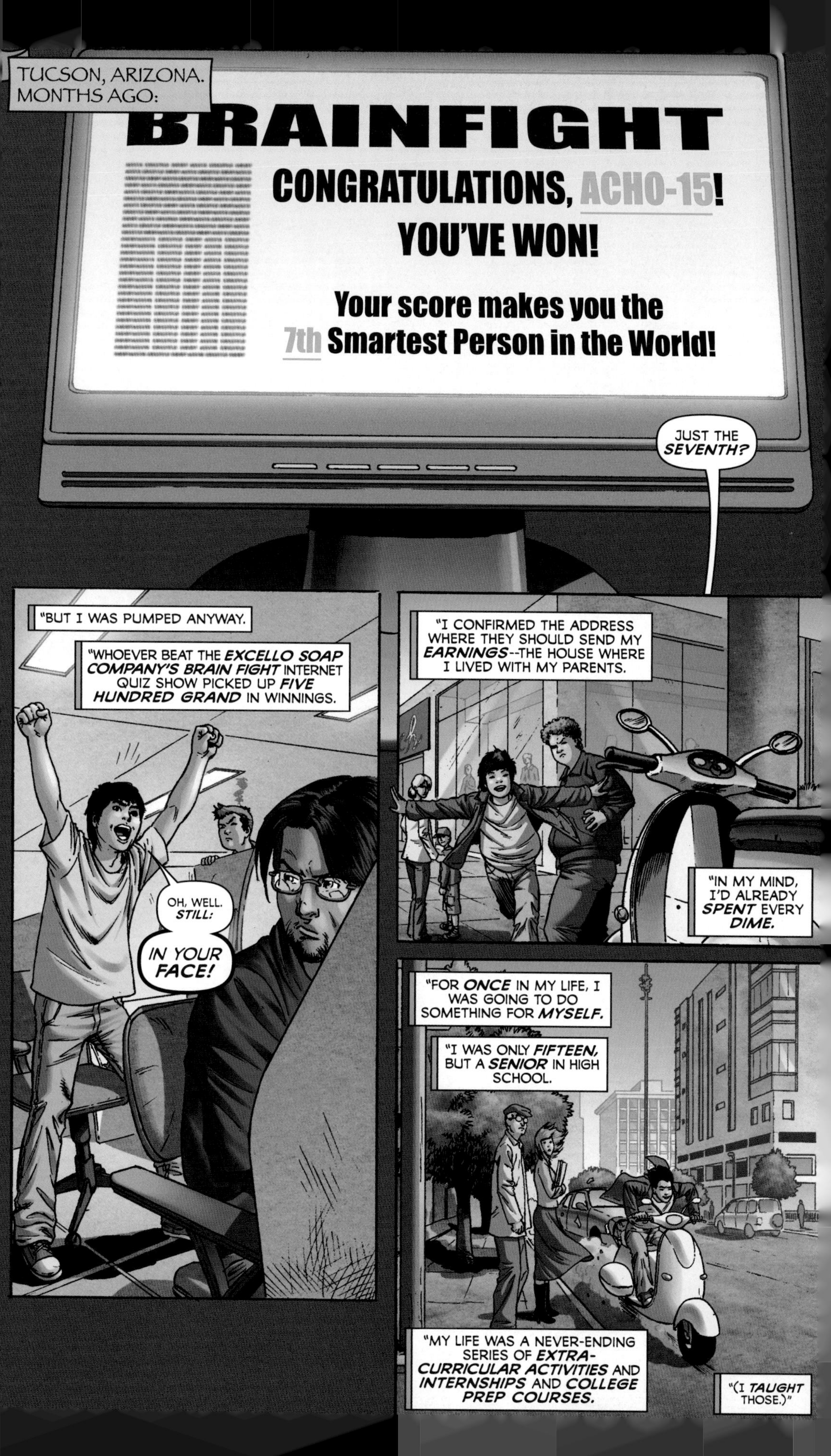
TUCSON, ARIZONA. MONTHS AGO:
BRAINFIGHT
CONGRATULATIONS, ACHO-15!
YOU'VE WON!
Your score makes you the 7th Smartest Person in the World!
JUST THE SEVENTH?
"BUT I WAS PUMPED ANYWAY.
"WHOEVER BEAT THE EXCELLO SOAP COMPANY'S BRAIN FIGHT INTERNET QUIZ SHOW PICKED UP FIVE HUNDRED GRAND IN WINNINGS.
OH, WELL. STILL:
IN YOUR FACE!
"I CONFIRMED THE ADDRESS WHERE THEY SHOULD SEND MY EARNINGS--THE HOUSE WHERE I LIVED WITH MY PARENTS.
"IN MY MIND, I'D ALREADY SPENT EVERY DIME.
"FOR ONCE IN MY LIFE, I WAS GOING TO DO SOMETHING FOR MYSELF.
"I WAS ONLY FIFTEEN, BUT A SENIOR IN HIGH SCHOOL.
"MY LIFE WAS A NEVER-ENDING SERIES OF EXTRA-CURRICULAR ACTIVITIES AND INTERNSHIPS AND COLLEGE PREP COURSES.
"(I TAUGHT THOSE.)"

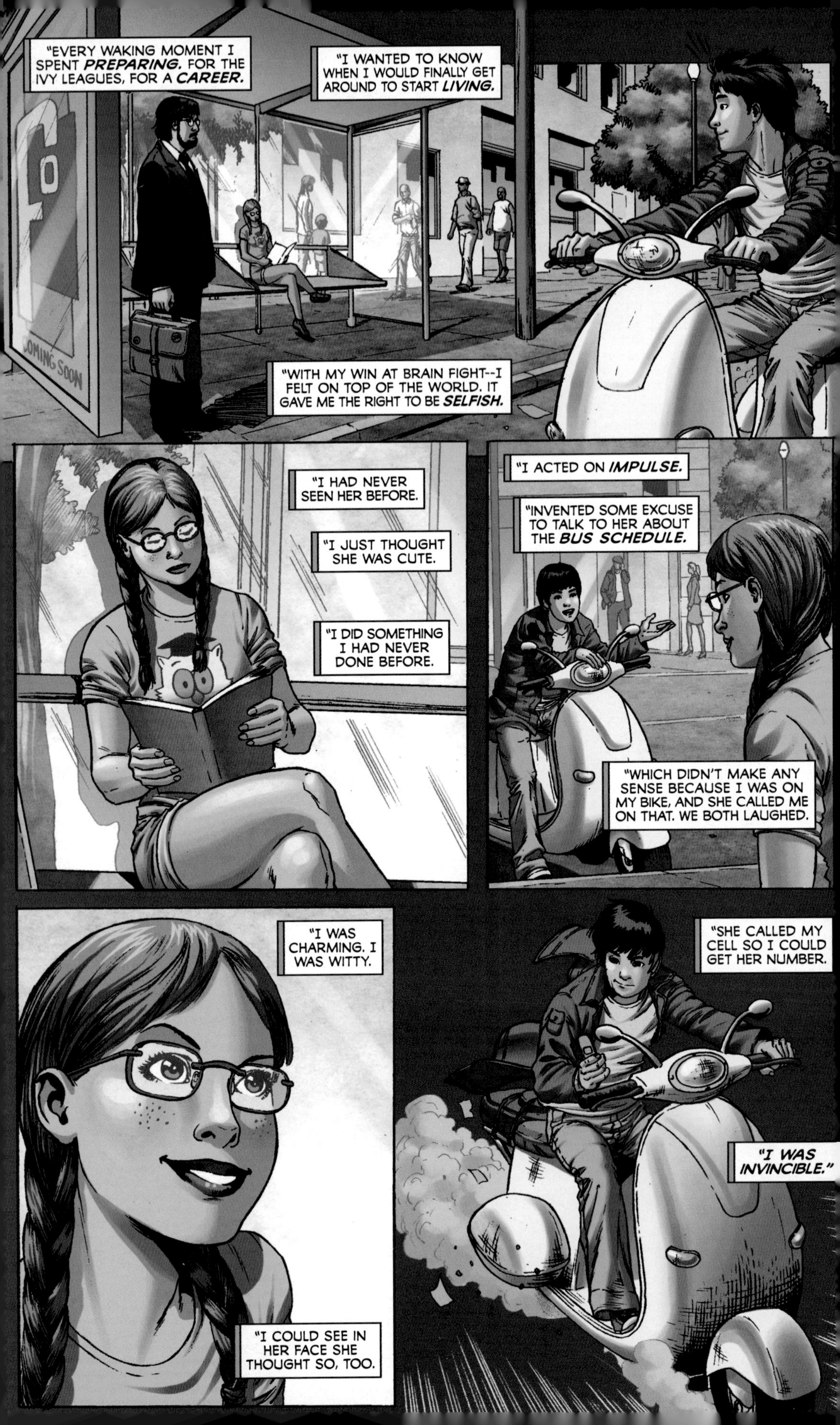
"EVERY WAKING MOMENT I SPENT PREPARING. FOR THE IVY LEAGUES, FOR A CAREER.
"I WANTED TO KNOW WHEN I WOULD FINALLY GET AROUND TO START LIVING.
COMING SOON
"WITH MY WIN AT BRAIN FIGHT--I FELT ON TOP OF THE WORLD. IT GAVE ME THE RIGHT TO BE SELFISH.
"I HAD NEVER SEEN HER BEFORE.
"I JUST THOUGHT SHE WAS CUTE.
"I DID SOMETHING I HAD NEVER DONE BEFORE.
"I ACTED ON IMPULSE.
"INVENTED SOME EXCUSE TO TALK TO HER ABOUT THE BUS SCHEDULE.
"WHICH DIDN'T MAKE ANY SENSE BECAUSE I WAS ON MY BIKE, AND SHE CALLED ME ON THAT. WE BOTH LAUGHED.
"I WAS CHARMING. I WAS WITTY.
"I COULD SEE IN HER FACE SHE THOUGHT SO, TOO.
"SHE CALLED MY CELL SO I COULD GET HER NUMBER.
"I WAS INVINCIBLE."

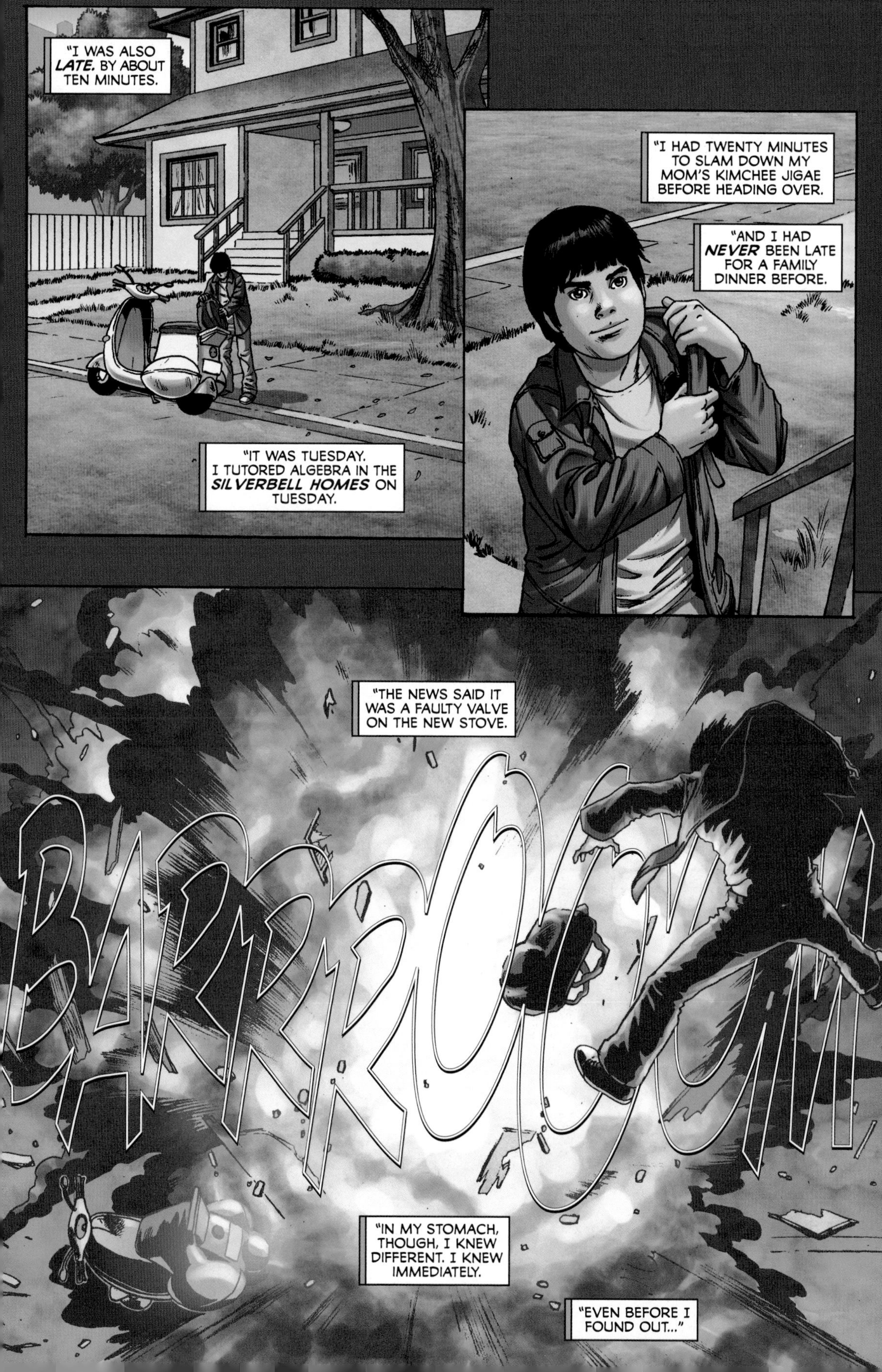
"I WAS ALSO *LATE.* BY ABOUT TEN MINUTES.
"IT WAS TUESDAY. I TUTORED ALGEBRA IN THE *SILVERBELL HOMES* ON TUESDAY.
"I HAD TWENTY MINUTES TO SLAM DOWN MY MOM'S KIMCHEE JIGAE BEFORE HEADING OVER.
"AND I HAD *NEVER* BEEN LATE FOR A FAMILY DINNER BEFORE.
"THE NEWS SAID IT WAS A FAULTY VALVE ON THE NEW STOVE.
BARRROOOM
"IN MY STOMACH, THOUGH, I KNEW DIFFERENT. I KNEW IMMEDIATELY.
"EVEN BEFORE I FOUND OUT..."

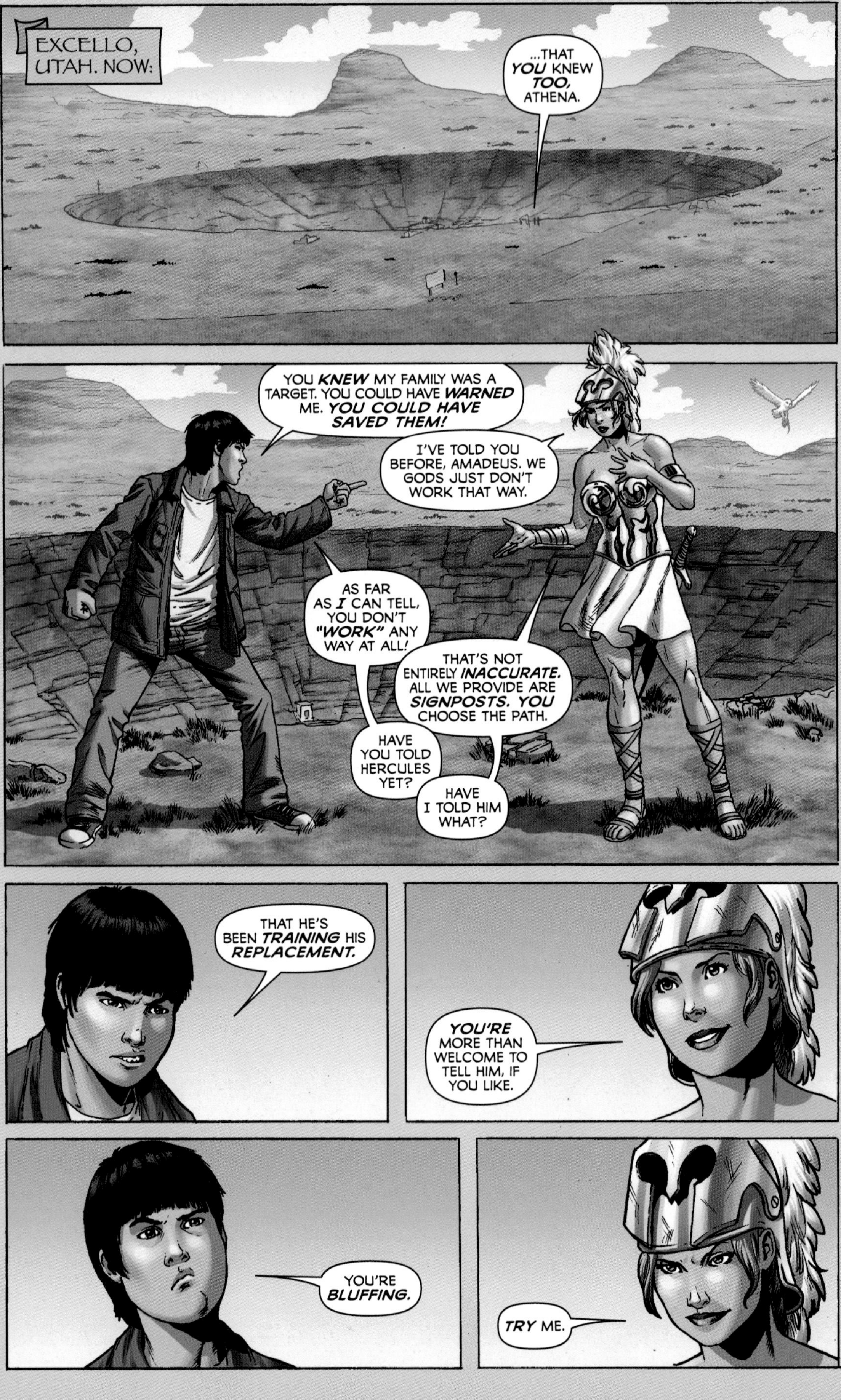
EXCELLO, UTAH. NOW:
...THAT *YOU* KNEW *TOO,* ATHENA.
YOU *KNEW* MY FAMILY WAS A TARGET. YOU COULD HAVE *WARNED* ME. *YOU COULD HAVE SAVED THEM!*
I'VE TOLD YOU BEFORE, AMADEUS. WE GODS JUST DON'T WORK THAT WAY.
AS FAR AS *I* CAN TELL, YOU DON'T *"WORK"* ANY WAY AT ALL!
THAT'S NOT ENTIRELY *INACCURATE.* ALL WE PROVIDE ARE *SIGNPOSTS. YOU* CHOOSE THE PATH.
HAVE YOU TOLD HERCULES YET?
HAVE I TOLD HIM WHAT?
THAT HE'S BEEN *TRAINING* HIS *REPLACEMENT.*
YOU'RE MORE THAN WELCOME TO TELL HIM, IF YOU LIKE.
YOU'RE *BLUFFING.*
TRY ME.

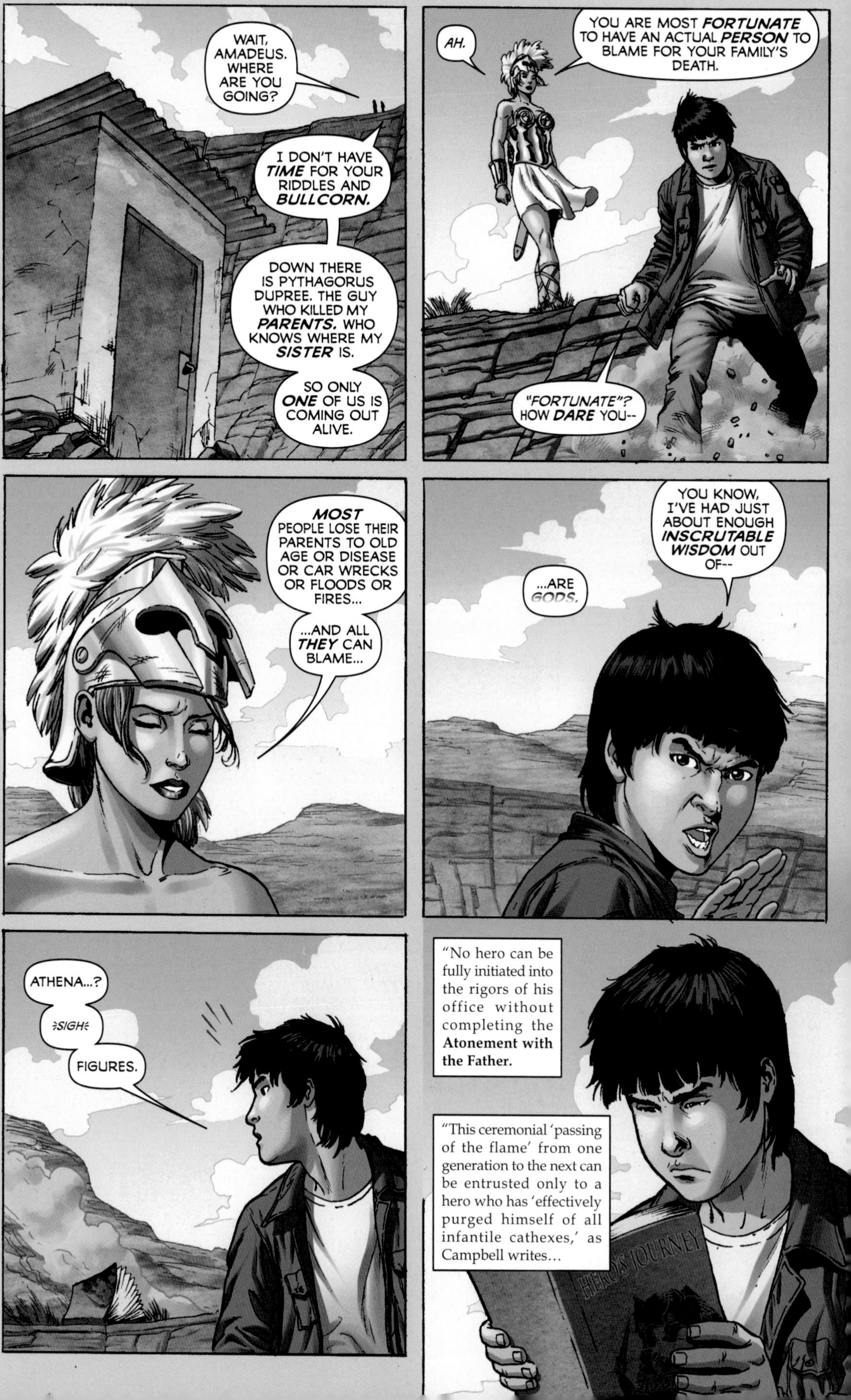

WAIT, AMADEUS. WHERE ARE YOU GOING?
I DON'T HAVE *TIME* FOR YOUR RIDDLES AND *BULLCORN.*
DOWN THERE IS PYTHAGORUS DUPREE. THE GUY WHO KILLED MY *PARENTS.* WHO KNOWS WHERE MY *SISTER* IS.
SO ONLY *ONE* OF US IS COMING OUT ALIVE.
AH.
YOU ARE MOST *FORTUNATE* TO HAVE AN ACTUAL *PERSON* TO BLAME FOR YOUR FAMILY'S DEATH.
"FORTUNATE"? HOW *DARE* YOU--
MOST PEOPLE LOSE THEIR PARENTS TO OLD AGE OR DISEASE OR CAR WRECKS OR FLOODS OR FIRES...
...AND ALL *THEY* CAN BLAME...
YOU KNOW, I'VE HAD JUST ABOUT ENOUGH *INSCRUTABLE WISDOM* OUT OF--
...ARE *GODS.*
ATHENA...?
SIGH
FIGURES.
"No hero can be fully initiated into the rigors of his office without completing the **Atonement with the Father.**
"This ceremonial 'passing of the flame' from one generation to the next can be entrusted only to a hero who has 'effectively purged himself of all infantile cathexes,' as Campbell writes…
HERO'S JOURNEY

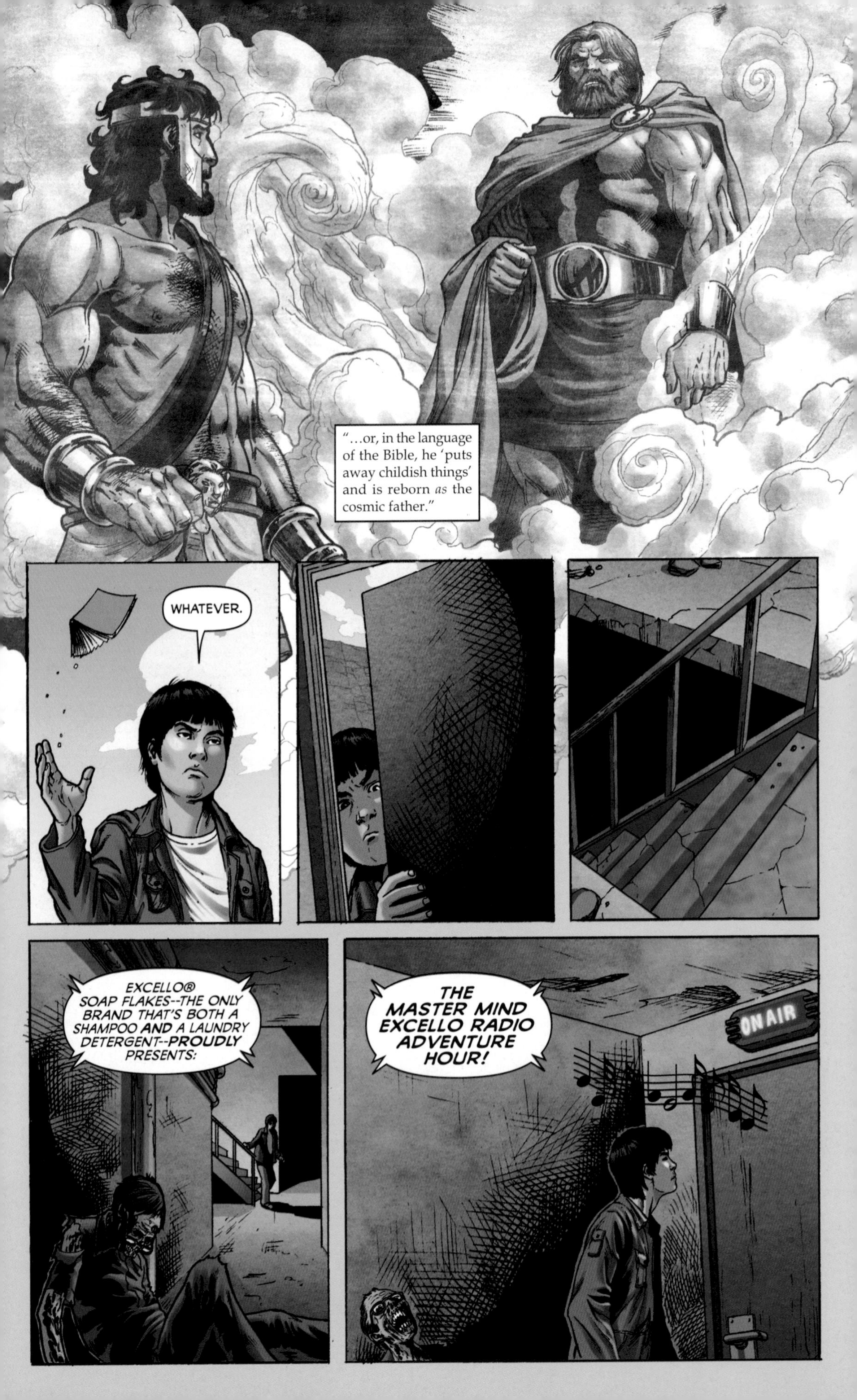
"…or, in the language of the Bible, he 'puts away childish things' and is reborn *as* the cosmic father."
WHATEVER.
EXCELLO® SOAP FLAKES--THE ONLY BRAND THAT'S BOTH A SHAMPOO **AND** A LAUNDRY DETERGENT--**PROUDLY** PRESENTS:
THE MASTER MIND EXCELLO RADIO ADVENTURE HOUR!
ON AIR

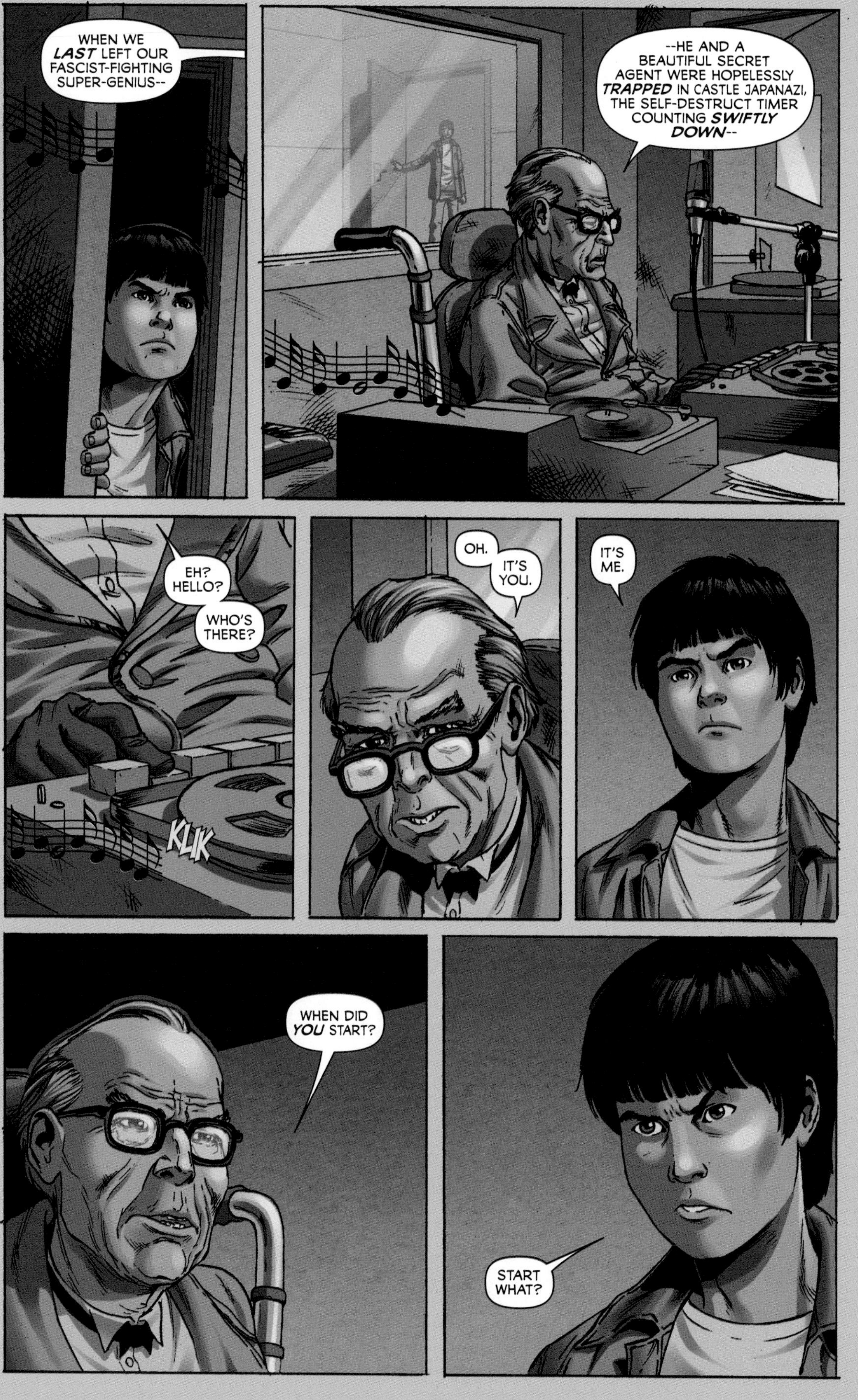
WHEN WE LAST LEFT OUR FASCIST-FIGHTING SUPER-GENIUS--
--HE AND A BEAUTIFUL SECRET AGENT WERE HOPELESSLY TRAPPED IN CASTLE JAPANAZI, THE SELF-DESTRUCT TIMER COUNTING SWIFTLY DOWN--
EH? HELLO?
WHO'S THERE?
KLIK
OH.
IT'S YOU.
IT'S ME.
WHEN DID YOU START?
START WHAT?

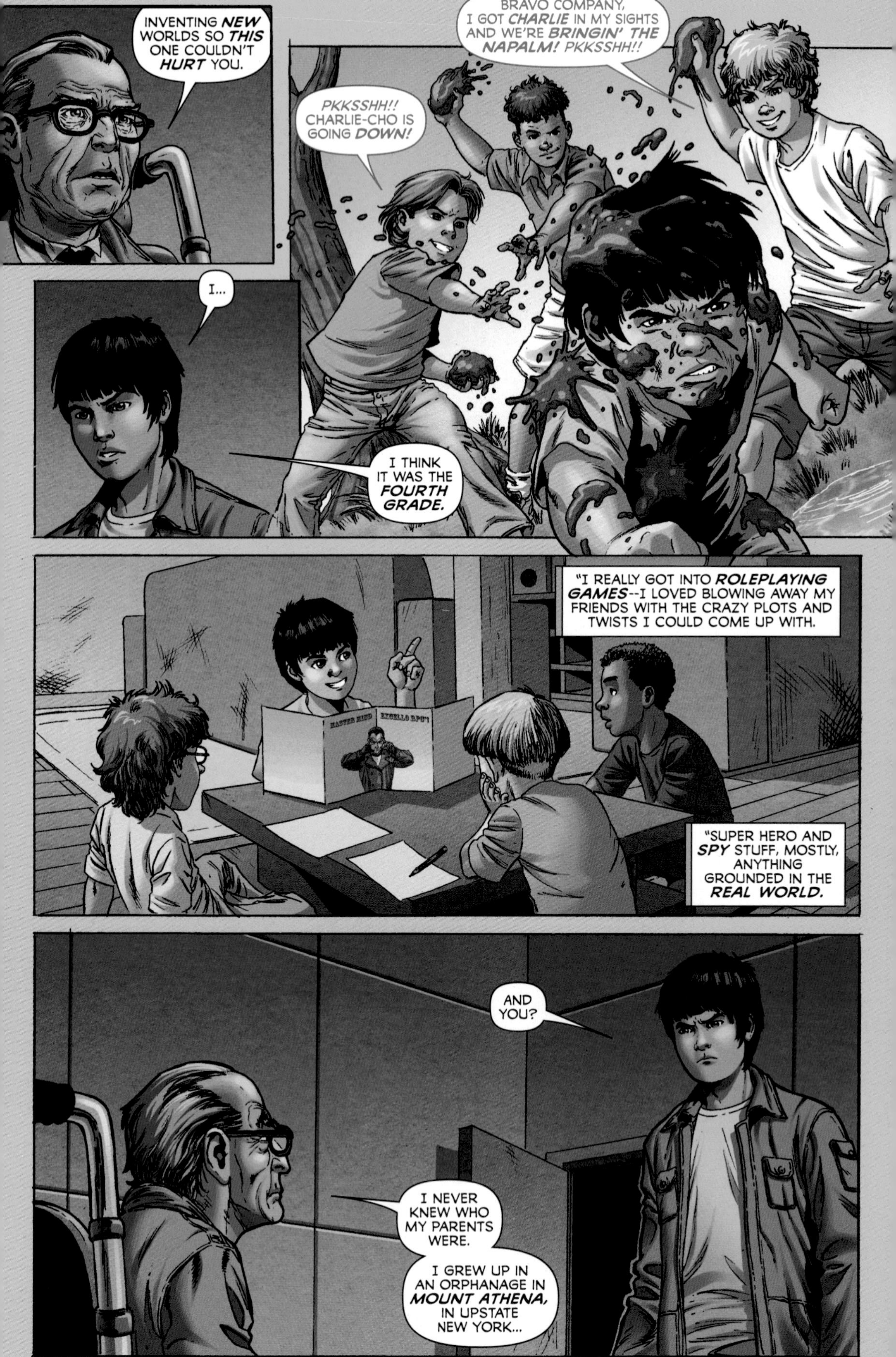
INVENTING *NEW* WORLDS SO *THIS* ONE COULDN'T *HURT* YOU.
BRAVO COMPANY, I GOT *CHARLIE* IN MY SIGHTS AND WE'RE *BRINGIN' THE NAPALM!* PKKSSHH!!
PKKSSHH!! CHARLIE-CHO IS GOING *DOWN!*
I...
I THINK IT WAS THE *FOURTH GRADE.*
"I REALLY GOT INTO *ROLEPLAYING GAMES*--I LOVED BLOWING AWAY MY FRIENDS WITH THE CRAZY PLOTS AND TWISTS I COULD COME UP WITH.
"SUPER HERO AND *SPY* STUFF, MOSTLY, ANYTHING GROUNDED IN THE *REAL WORLD.*
AND YOU?
I NEVER KNEW WHO MY PARENTS WERE.
I GREW UP IN AN ORPHANAGE IN *MOUNT ATHENA,* IN UPSTATE NEW YORK...

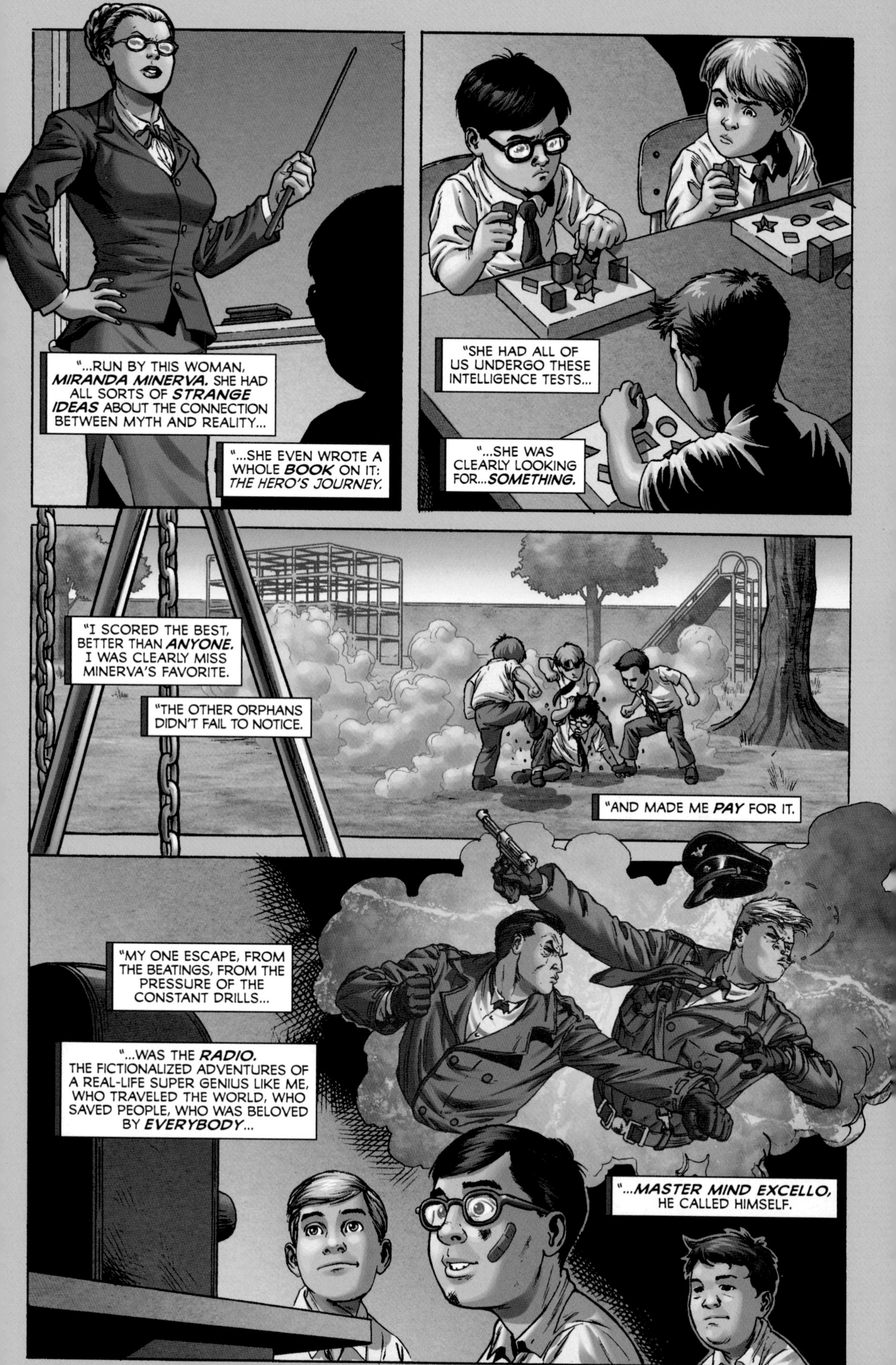

"...RUN BY THIS WOMAN, **MIRANDA MINERVA.** SHE HAD ALL SORTS OF **STRANGE IDEAS** ABOUT THE CONNECTION BETWEEN MYTH AND REALITY...
"...SHE EVEN WROTE A WHOLE **BOOK** ON IT: *THE HERO'S JOURNEY.*
"SHE HAD ALL OF US UNDERGO THESE INTELLIGENCE TESTS...
"...SHE WAS CLEARLY LOOKING FOR...**SOMETHING.**
"I SCORED THE BEST, BETTER THAN **ANYONE.** I WAS CLEARLY MISS MINERVA'S FAVORITE.
"THE OTHER ORPHANS DIDN'T FAIL TO NOTICE.
"AND MADE ME **PAY** FOR IT.
"MY ONE ESCAPE, FROM THE BEATINGS, FROM THE PRESSURE OF THE CONSTANT DRILLS...
"...WAS THE **RADIO.** THE FICTIONALIZED ADVENTURES OF A REAL-LIFE SUPER GENIUS LIKE ME, WHO TRAVELED THE WORLD, WHO SAVED PEOPLE, WHO WAS BELOVED BY **EVERYBODY**...
"...**MASTER MIND EXCELLO,** HE CALLED HIMSELF.

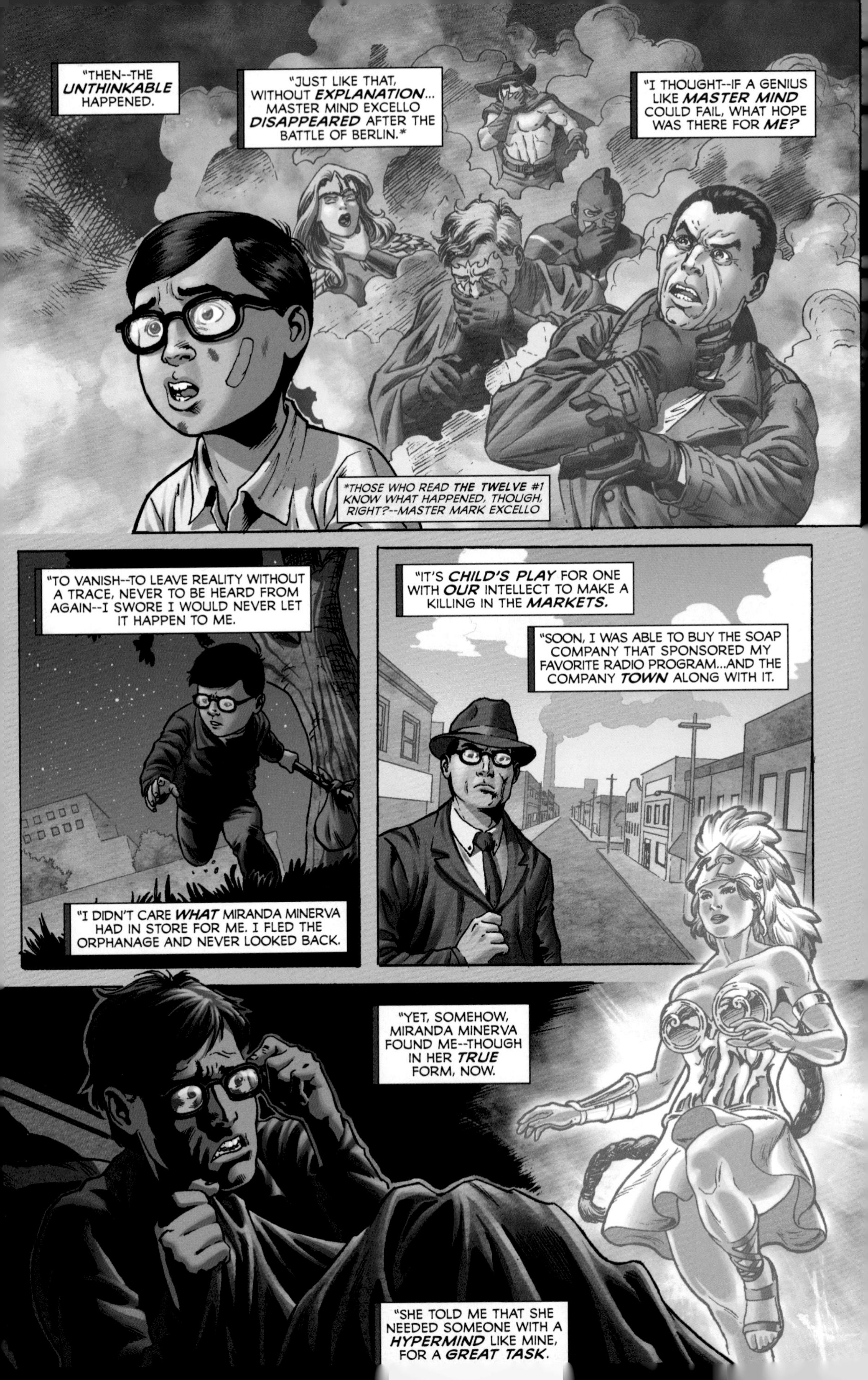
"THEN--THE UNTHINKABLE HAPPENED.
"JUST LIKE THAT, WITHOUT EXPLANATION... MASTER MIND EXCELLO DISAPPEARED AFTER THE BATTLE OF BERLIN.*
"I THOUGHT--IF A GENIUS LIKE MASTER MIND COULD FAIL, WHAT HOPE WAS THERE FOR ME?
*THOSE WHO READ THE TWELVE #1 KNOW WHAT HAPPENED, THOUGH, RIGHT?--MASTER MARK EXCELLO
"TO VANISH--TO LEAVE REALITY WITHOUT A TRACE, NEVER TO BE HEARD FROM AGAIN--I SWORE I WOULD NEVER LET IT HAPPEN TO ME.
"I DIDN'T CARE WHAT MIRANDA MINERVA HAD IN STORE FOR ME. I FLED THE ORPHANAGE AND NEVER LOOKED BACK.
"IT'S CHILD'S PLAY FOR ONE WITH OUR INTELLECT TO MAKE A KILLING IN THE MARKETS.
"SOON, I WAS ABLE TO BUY THE SOAP COMPANY THAT SPONSORED MY FAVORITE RADIO PROGRAM...AND THE COMPANY TOWN ALONG WITH IT.
"YET, SOMEHOW, MIRANDA MINERVA FOUND ME--THOUGH IN HER TRUE FORM, NOW.
"SHE TOLD ME THAT SHE NEEDED SOMEONE WITH A HYPERMIND LIKE MINE, FOR A GREAT TASK.

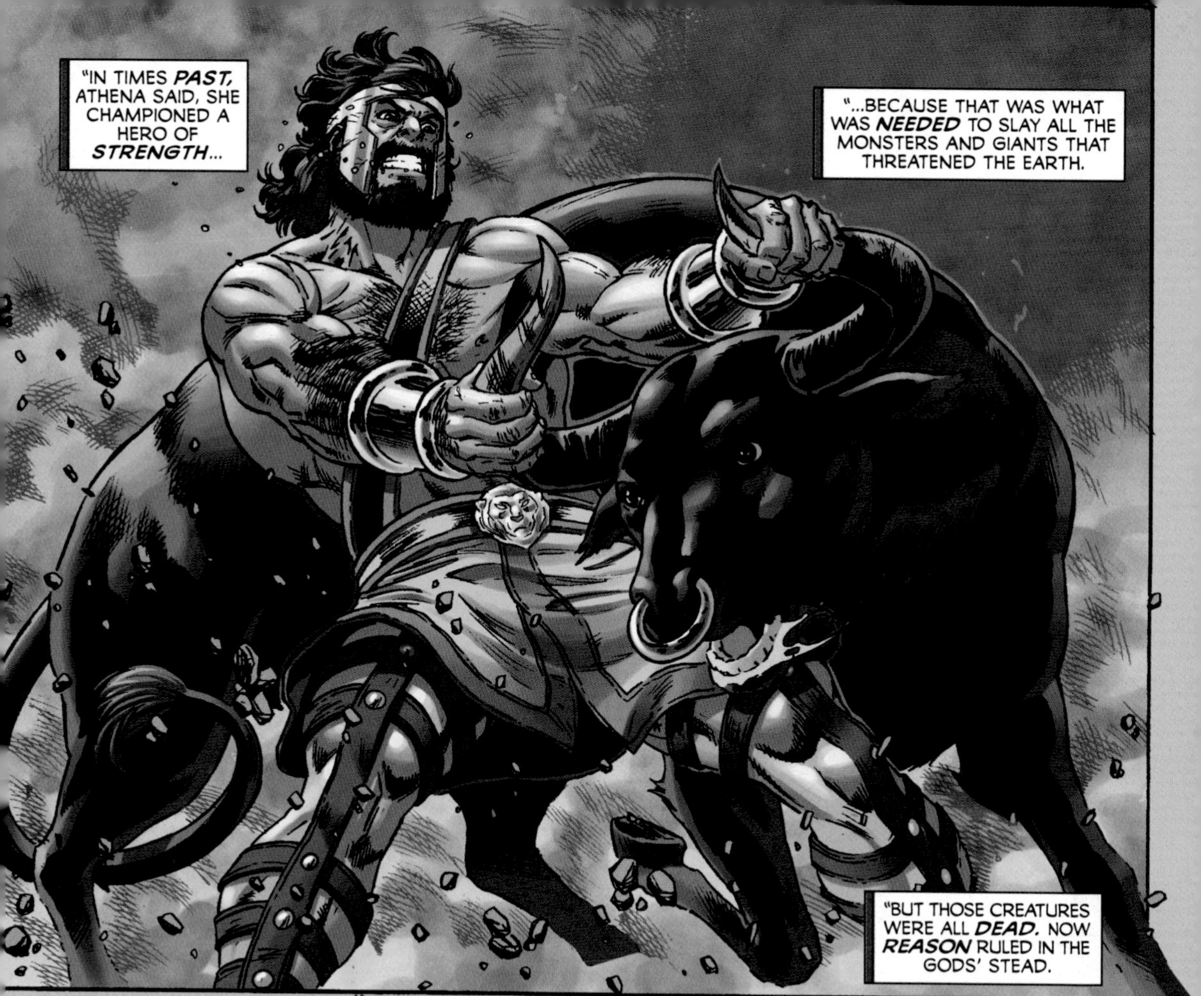
"IN TIMES PAST, ATHENA SAID, SHE CHAMPIONED A HERO OF STRENGTH...
"...BECAUSE THAT WAS WHAT WAS NEEDED TO SLAY ALL THE MONSTERS AND GIANTS THAT THREATENED THE EARTH.
"BUT THOSE CREATURES WERE ALL DEAD. NOW REASON RULED IN THE GODS' STEAD.

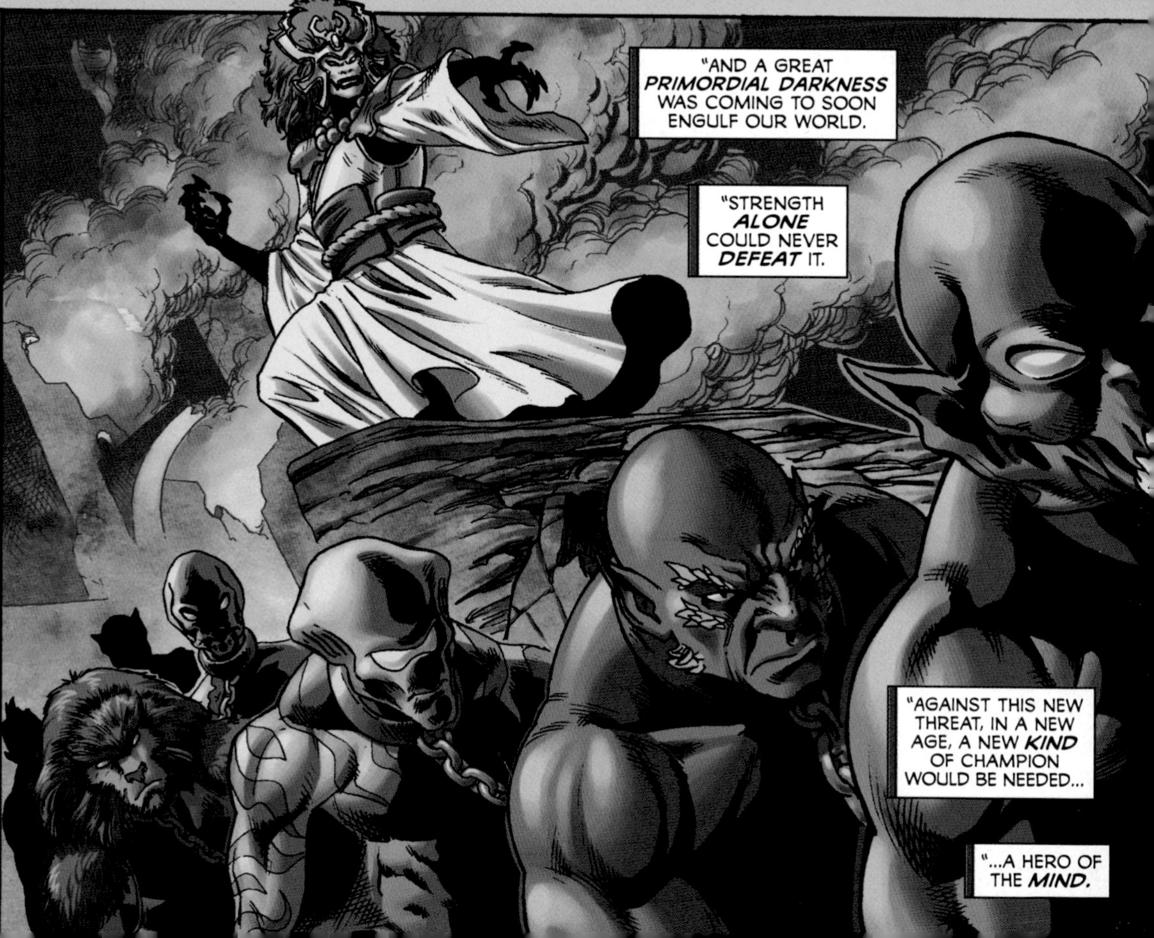
"AND A GREAT PRIMORDIAL DARKNESS WAS COMING TO SOON ENGULF OUR WORLD.
"STRENGTH ALONE COULD NEVER DEFEAT IT.
"AGAINST THIS NEW THREAT, IN A NEW AGE, A NEW KIND OF CHAMPION WOULD BE NEEDED...
"...A HERO OF THE MIND.

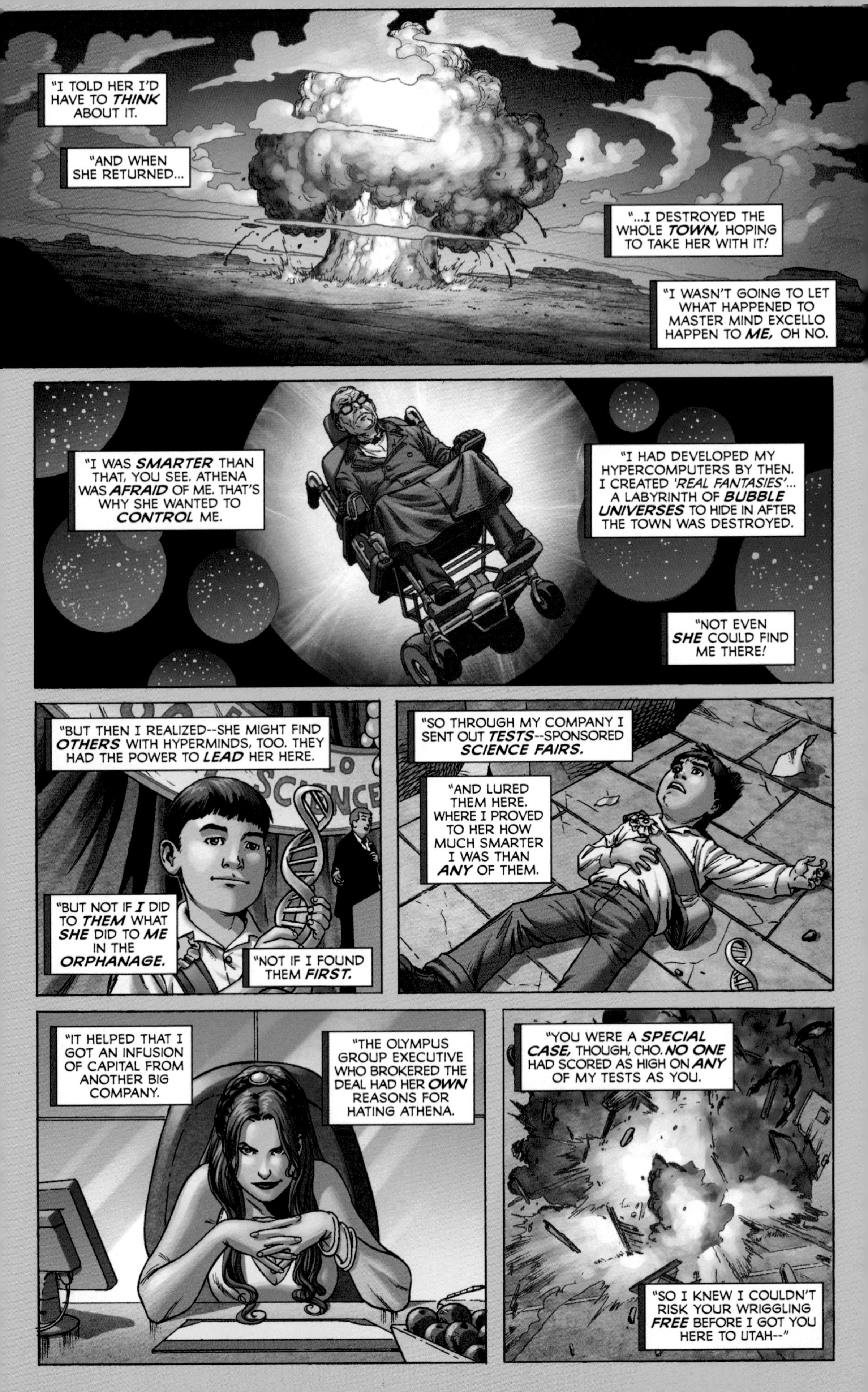
"I TOLD HER I'D HAVE TO THINK ABOUT IT.
"AND WHEN SHE RETURNED...
"...I DESTROYED THE WHOLE TOWN, HOPING TO TAKE HER WITH IT!
"I WASN'T GOING TO LET WHAT HAPPENED TO MASTER MIND EXCELLO HAPPEN TO ME, OH NO.
"I WAS SMARTER THAN THAT, YOU SEE. ATHENA WAS AFRAID OF ME. THAT'S WHY SHE WANTED TO CONTROL ME.
"I HAD DEVELOPED MY HYPERCOMPUTERS BY THEN. I CREATED 'REAL FANTASIES'... A LABYRINTH OF BUBBLE UNIVERSES TO HIDE IN AFTER THE TOWN WAS DESTROYED.
"NOT EVEN SHE COULD FIND ME THERE!
"BUT THEN I REALIZED--SHE MIGHT FIND OTHERS WITH HYPERMINDS, TOO. THEY HAD THE POWER TO LEAD HER HERE.
SCIENCE
"BUT NOT IF I DID TO THEM WHAT SHE DID TO ME IN THE ORPHANAGE.
"NOT IF I FOUND THEM FIRST.
"SO THROUGH MY COMPANY I SENT OUT TESTS--SPONSORED SCIENCE FAIRS.
"AND LURED THEM HERE. WHERE I PROVED TO HER HOW MUCH SMARTER I WAS THAN ANY OF THEM.
"IT HELPED THAT I GOT AN INFUSION OF CAPITAL FROM ANOTHER BIG COMPANY.
"THE OLYMPUS GROUP EXECUTIVE WHO BROKERED THE DEAL HAD HER OWN REASONS FOR HATING ATHENA.
"YOU WERE A SPECIAL CASE, THOUGH, CHO. NO ONE HAD SCORED AS HIGH ON ANY OF MY TESTS AS YOU.
"SO I KNEW I COULDN'T RISK YOUR WRIGGLING FREE BEFORE I GOT YOU HERE TO UTAH--"

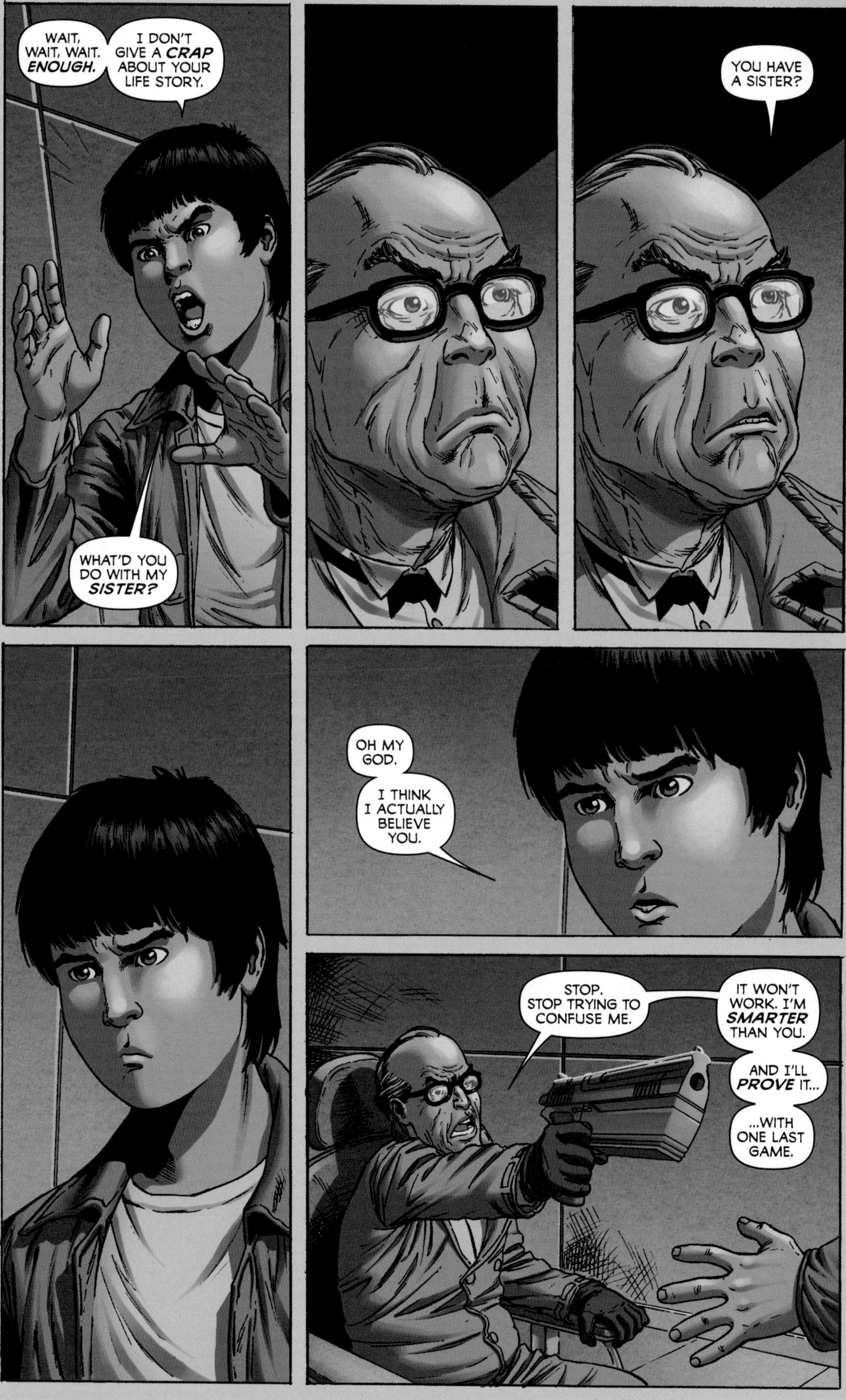
WAIT, WAIT, WAIT. ENOUGH.
I DON'T GIVE A CRAP ABOUT YOUR LIFE STORY.
WHAT'D YOU DO WITH MY SISTER?
YOU HAVE A SISTER?
OH MY GOD.
I THINK I ACTUALLY BELIEVE YOU.
STOP. STOP TRYING TO CONFUSE ME.
IT WON'T WORK. I'M SMARTER THAN YOU.
AND I'LL PROVE IT...
...WITH ONE LAST GAME.

IT'S SIMPLE, REALLY.

LIKE RUSSIAN ROULETTE.

BUT FOR HYPERMINDS.

YOU'LL CALCULATE EXACTLY *WHEN* AND *WHERE* I'M GOING TO FIRE.

AND YOU'RE NOT GOING TO *BE THERE* WHEN THE BULLET ARRIVES.

UNLESS...

...I CALCULATE EXACTLY WHERE *YOU'RE* GOING TO MOVE.

THEN, AT THE LAST NANOSECOND, I FIRE *THERE* INSTEAD.

YOU SEE? TWO OPTIONS. *BINARY.* JUST LIKE SCHRÖDINGER'S CAT.

ALIVE. OR DEAD.

IF I HIT YOU, IT'LL BE THROUGH THE *BRAIN.* AND YOU WILL DIE.

BUT IF I MISS...

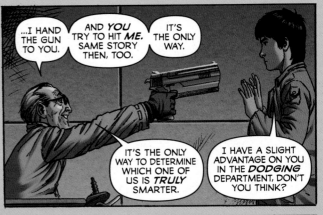

...I HAND THE GUN TO YOU.

AND *YOU* TRY TO HIT *ME.* SAME STORY THEN, TOO.

IT'S THE ONLY WAY.

IT'S THE ONLY WAY TO DETERMINE WHICH ONE OF US IS *TRULY* SMARTER.

I HAVE A SLIGHT ADVANTAGE ON YOU IN THE *DODGING* DEPARTMENT, DON'T YOU THINK?

NO.

NOT REALLY.

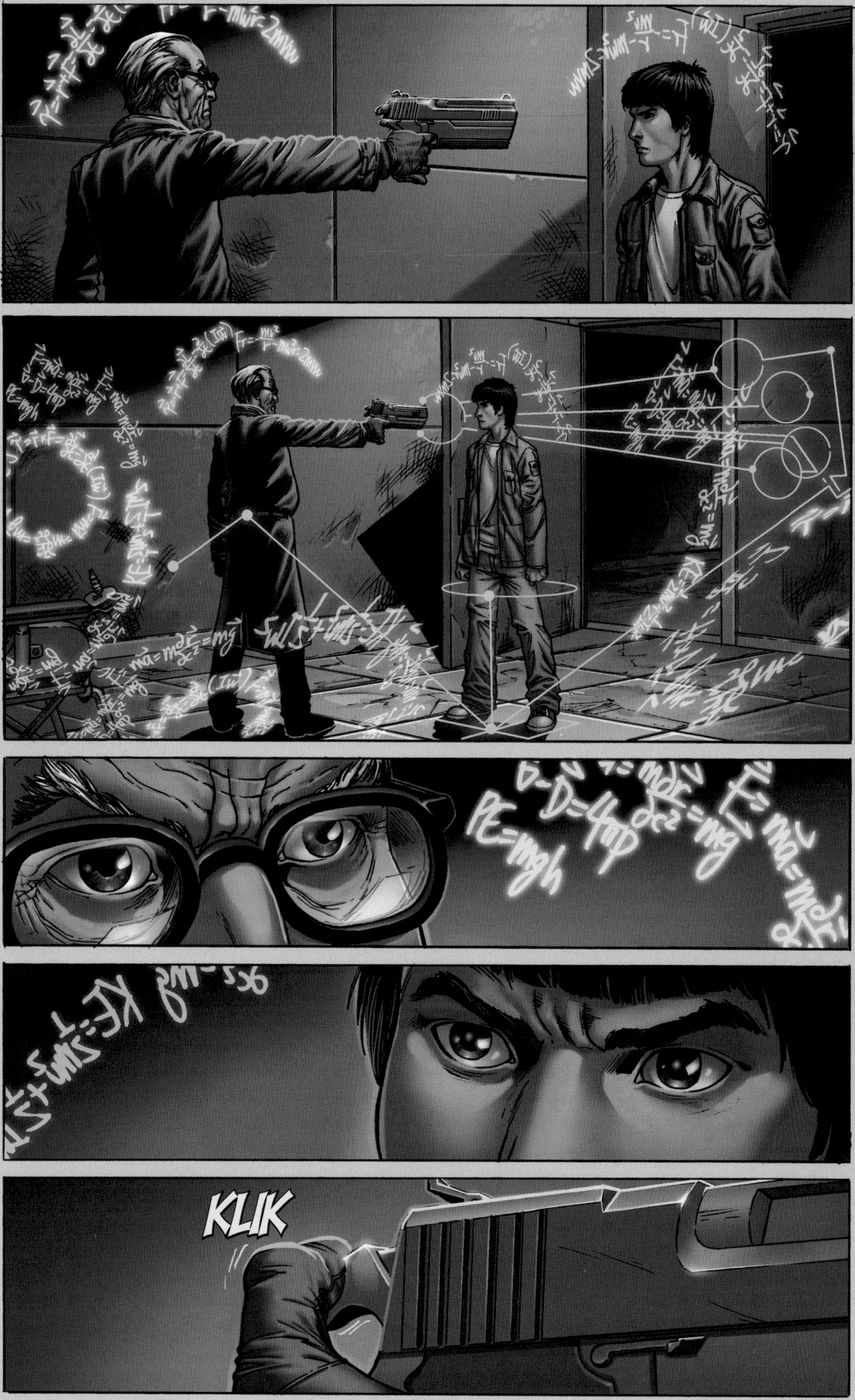
KLIK

PFT.

WHAT?

WAIT, WHAT ARE YOU--

WHERE ARE YOU--

I CAN'T *LOSE* IF I DON'T *PLAY*.

DON'T NEED TO BE A *GENIUS* TO FIGURE *THAT*.

YOU--YOU *CAN'T*! WE'LL NEVER KNOW WHICH ONE OF US IS REALLY SMARTER!

COULDN'T CARE LESS. I CAME HERE TO FIND MADDY. YOU DON'T KNOW WHERE SHE IS.

SO I'M LEAVING.

BUT-- I *KILLED* YOUR *PARENTS*!

YOU CAN PUNISH ME!

I *AM* GOING TO PUNISH YOU.

I'M GOING TO *LIVE MY LIFE*.

I'M GOING TO FORGET ALL *ABOUT* YOU.

YOU'LL *DISAPPEAR*.

LIKE YOU *NEVER EXISTED AT ALL*.

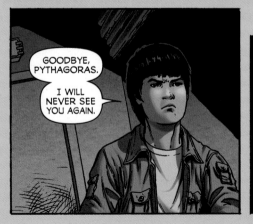

GOODBYE, PYTHAGORAS.

I WILL NEVER SEE YOU AGAIN.

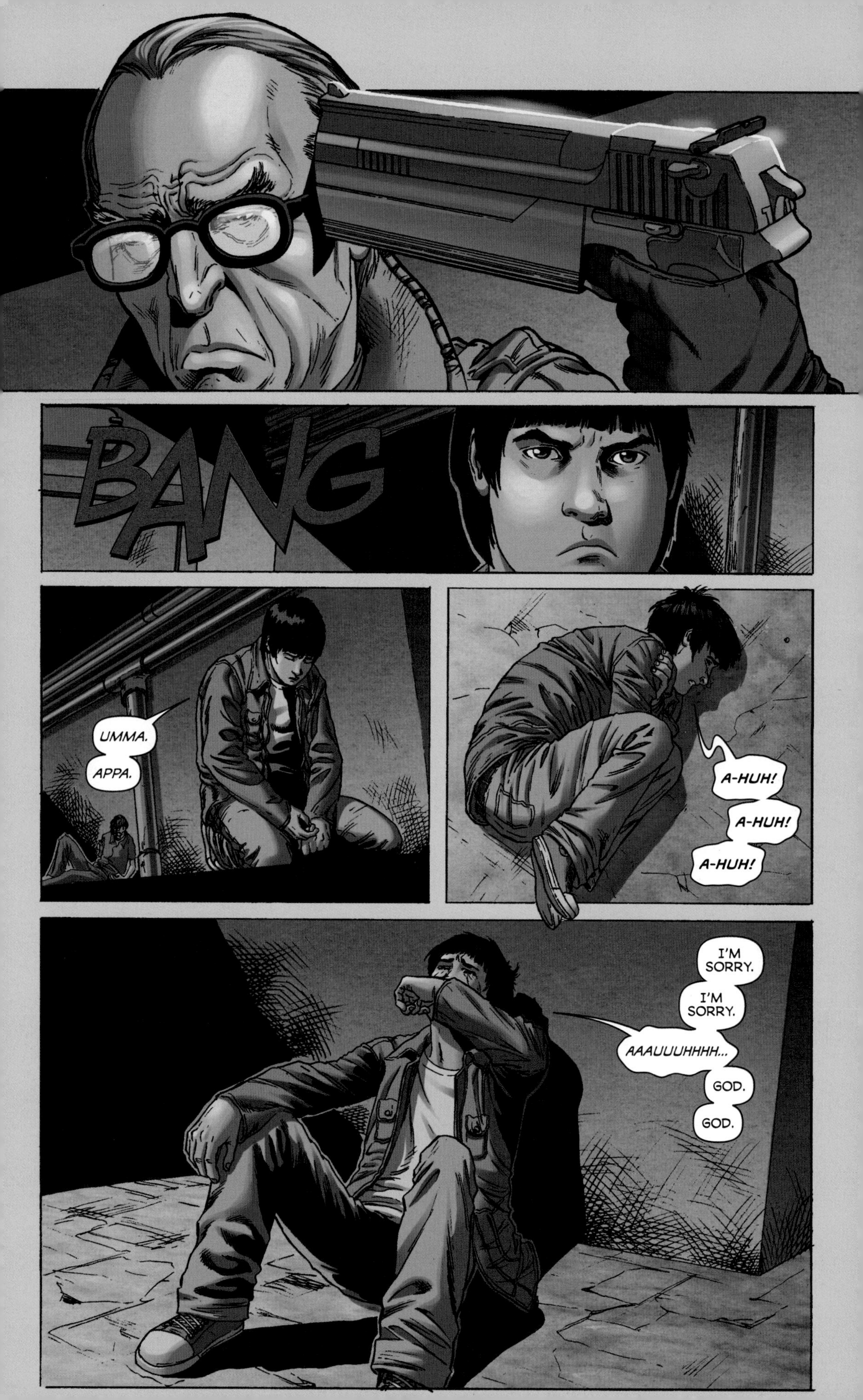
BANG
UMMA.
APPA.
A-HUH!
A-HUH!
A-HUH!
I'M SORRY.
I'M SORRY.
AAAUUUHHHH...
GOD.
GOD.

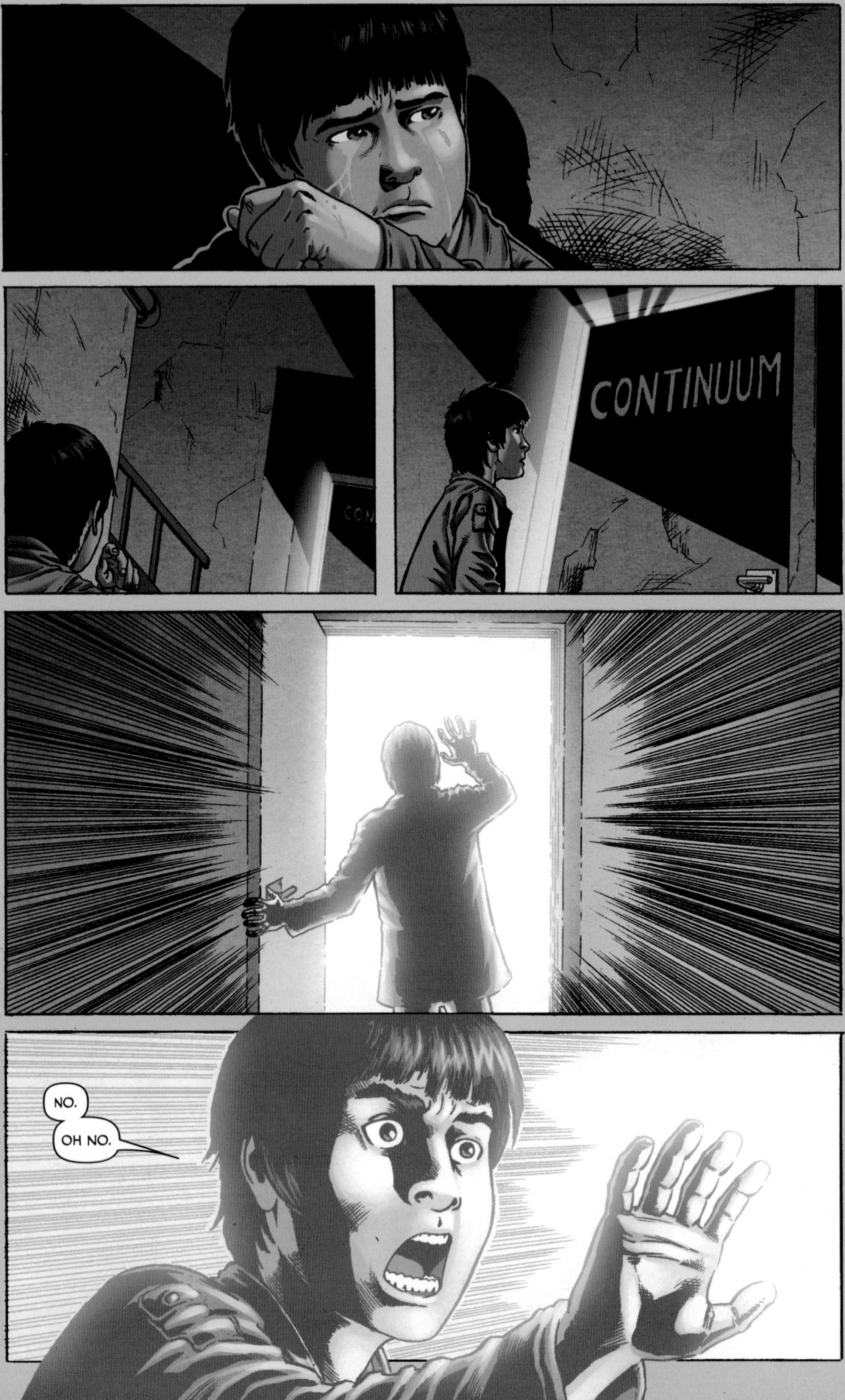
CONTINUUM
NO.
OH NO.

SO. YOU CHOSE NOT TO KILL THE MAN WHO KILLED YOUR PARENTS.

NO.

AND WHY NOT?

BECAUSE...

...REVENGE IS A *CHILDISH* EMOTION.

AND I'VE CHOSEN TO *PUT AWAY* CHILDISH THINGS.

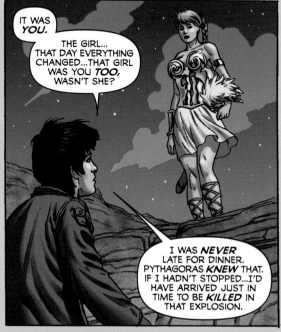

IT WAS *YOU.*

THE GIRL... THAT DAY EVERYTHING CHANGED...THAT GIRL WAS YOU *TOO,* WASN'T SHE?

I WAS *NEVER* LATE FOR DINNER. PYTHAGORAS *KNEW* THAT. IF I HADN'T STOPPED...I'D HAVE ARRIVED JUST IN TIME TO BE *KILLED* IN THAT EXPLOSION.

"YOU... YOU SAVED MY *LIFE,* ATHENA."

YOU SAVED *YOURSELF.*

PYTHAGORAS WAS THE *TEST RUN.* WITH HIM I...*ERRED.*

I PUT TOO *MUCH* ON HIM, TOO *QUICKLY.*

THE NEW CHAMPION WOULD NEED A...*DIFFERENT* SORT OF MENTOR THAN *ME.*

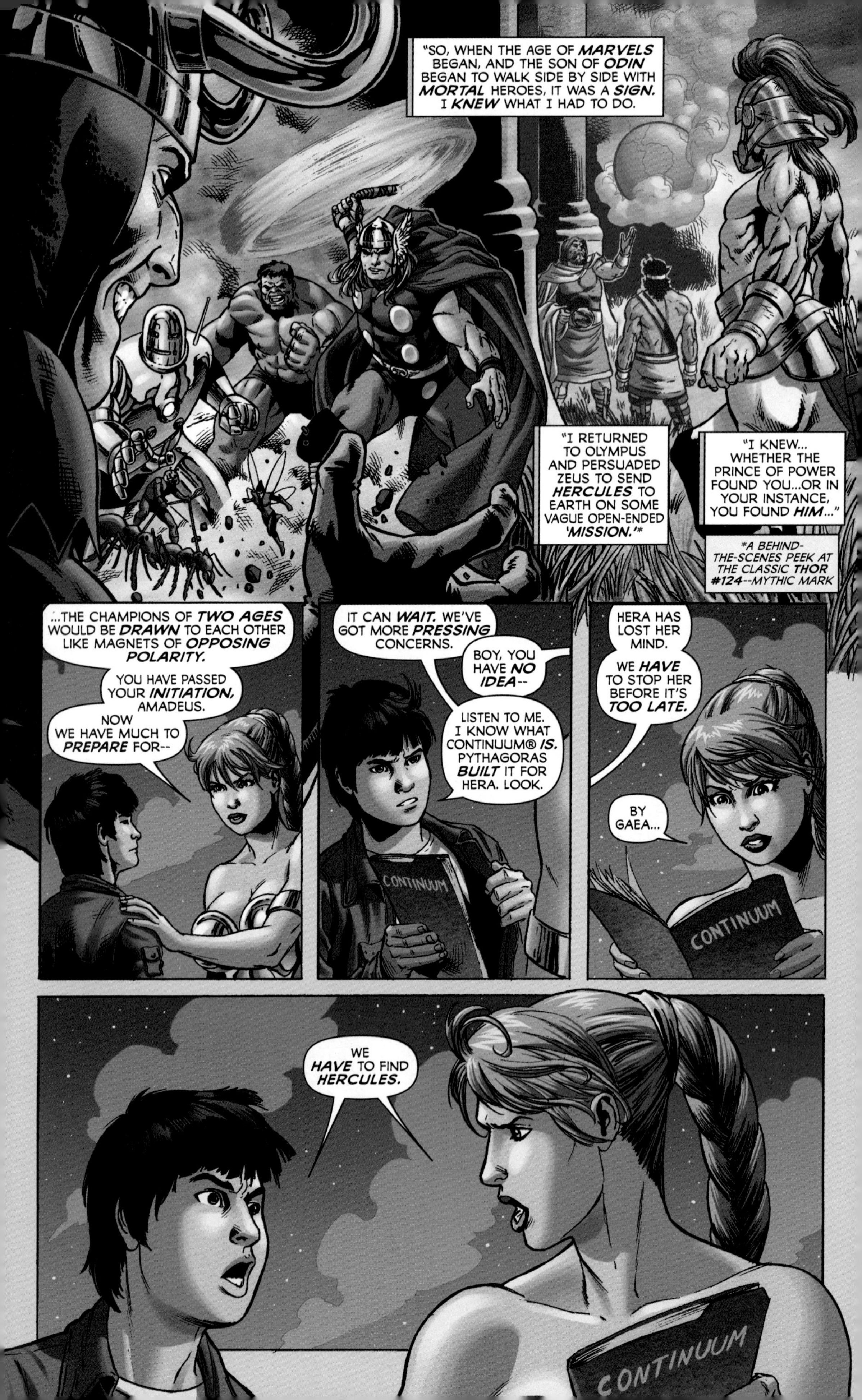
"SO, WHEN THE AGE OF MARVELS BEGAN, AND THE SON OF ODIN BEGAN TO WALK SIDE BY SIDE WITH MORTAL HEROES, IT WAS A SIGN. I KNEW WHAT I HAD TO DO.
"I RETURNED TO OLYMPUS AND PERSUADED ZEUS TO SEND HERCULES TO EARTH ON SOME VAGUE OPEN-ENDED 'MISSION.'*
"I KNEW... WHETHER THE PRINCE OF POWER FOUND YOU...OR IN YOUR INSTANCE, YOU FOUND HIM..."
*A BEHIND-THE-SCENES PEEK AT THE CLASSIC THOR #124--MYTHIC MARK
...THE CHAMPIONS OF TWO AGES WOULD BE DRAWN TO EACH OTHER LIKE MAGNETS OF OPPOSING POLARITY.
YOU HAVE PASSED YOUR INITIATION, AMADEUS.
NOW WE HAVE MUCH TO PREPARE FOR--
IT CAN WAIT. WE'VE GOT MORE PRESSING CONCERNS.
BOY, YOU HAVE NO IDEA--
LISTEN TO ME. I KNOW WHAT CONTINUUM® IS. PYTHAGORAS BUILT IT FOR HERA. LOOK.
CONTINUUM
HERA HAS LOST HER MIND.
WE HAVE TO STOP HER BEFORE IT'S TOO LATE.
BY GAEA...
CONTINUUM
WE HAVE TO FIND HERCULES.
CONTINUUM

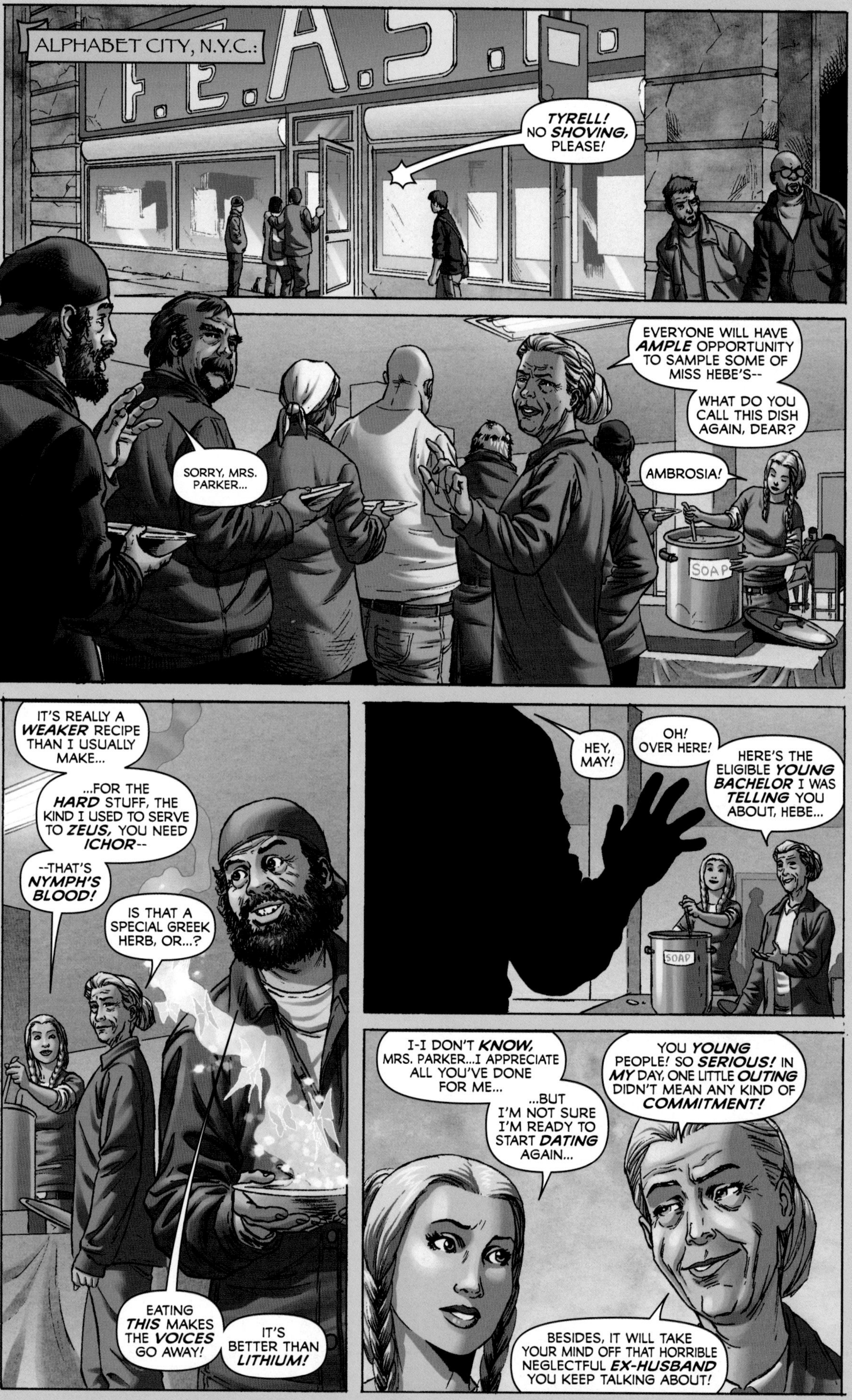

ALPHABET CITY, N.Y.C.:
TYRELL! NO SHOVING, PLEASE!
SORRY, MRS. PARKER...
EVERYONE WILL HAVE AMPLE OPPORTUNITY TO SAMPLE SOME OF MISS HEBE'S--
WHAT DO YOU CALL THIS DISH AGAIN, DEAR?
AMBROSIA!
SOAP
IT'S REALLY A WEAKER RECIPE THAN I USUALLY MAKE...
...FOR THE HARD STUFF, THE KIND I USED TO SERVE TO ZEUS, YOU NEED ICHOR--
--THAT'S NYMPH'S BLOOD!
IS THAT A SPECIAL GREEK HERB, OR...?
EATING THIS MAKES THE VOICES GO AWAY!
IT'S BETTER THAN LITHIUM!
HEY, MAY!
OH! OVER HERE!
HERE'S THE ELIGIBLE YOUNG BACHELOR I WAS TELLING YOU ABOUT, HEBE...
SOAP
I-I DON'T KNOW, MRS. PARKER...I APPRECIATE ALL YOU'VE DONE FOR ME...
...BUT I'M NOT SURE I'M READY TO START DATING AGAIN...
YOU YOUNG PEOPLE! SO SERIOUS! IN MY DAY, ONE LITTLE OUTING DIDN'T MEAN ANY KIND OF COMMITMENT!
BESIDES, IT WILL TAKE YOUR MIND OFF THAT HORRIBLE NEGLECTFUL EX-HUSBAND YOU KEEP TALKING ABOUT!

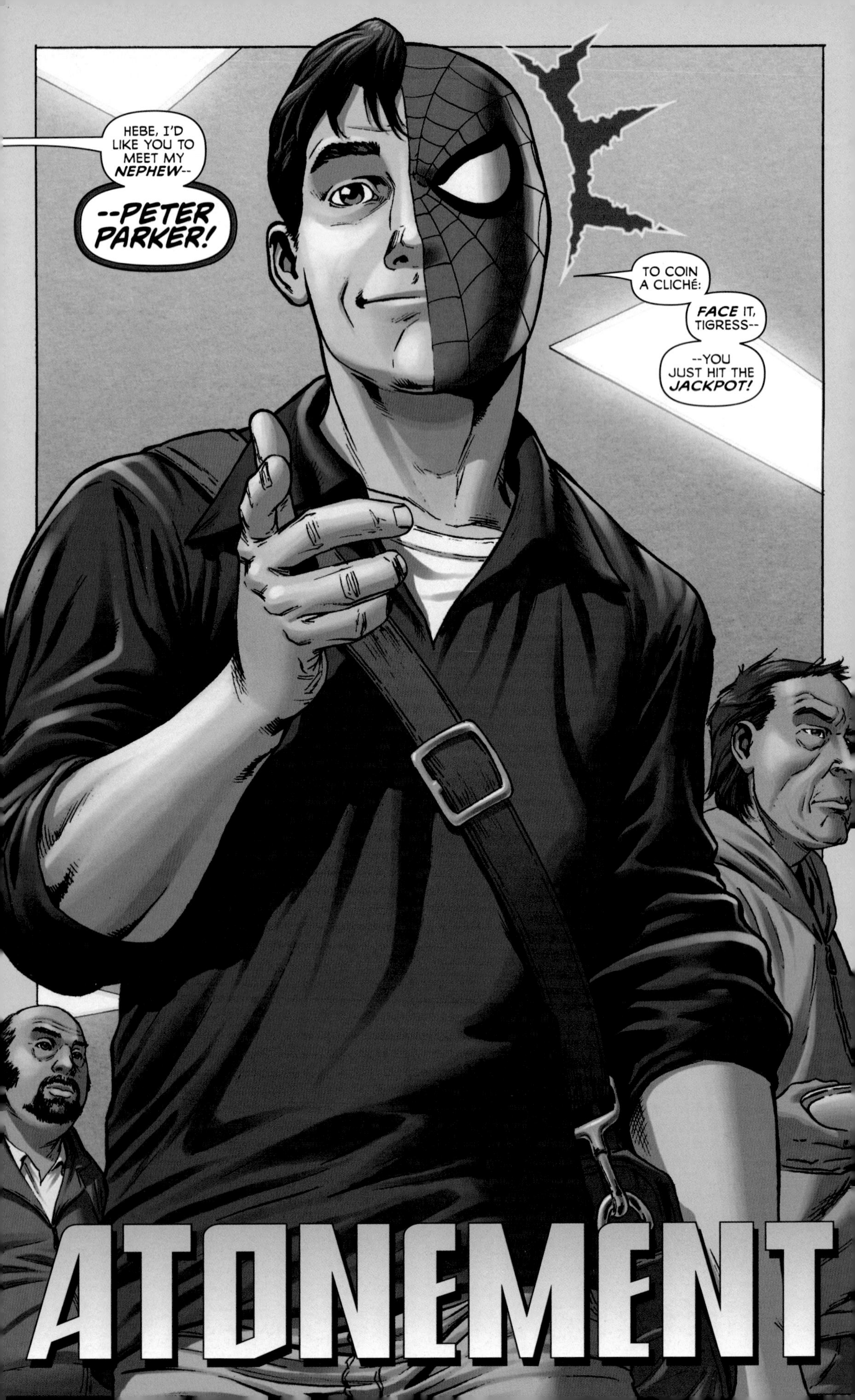
HEBE, I'D LIKE YOU TO MEET MY NEPHEW--
--PETER PARKER!
TO COIN A CLICHÉ:
FACE IT, TIGRESS--
--YOU JUST HIT THE JACKPOT!
ATONEMENT

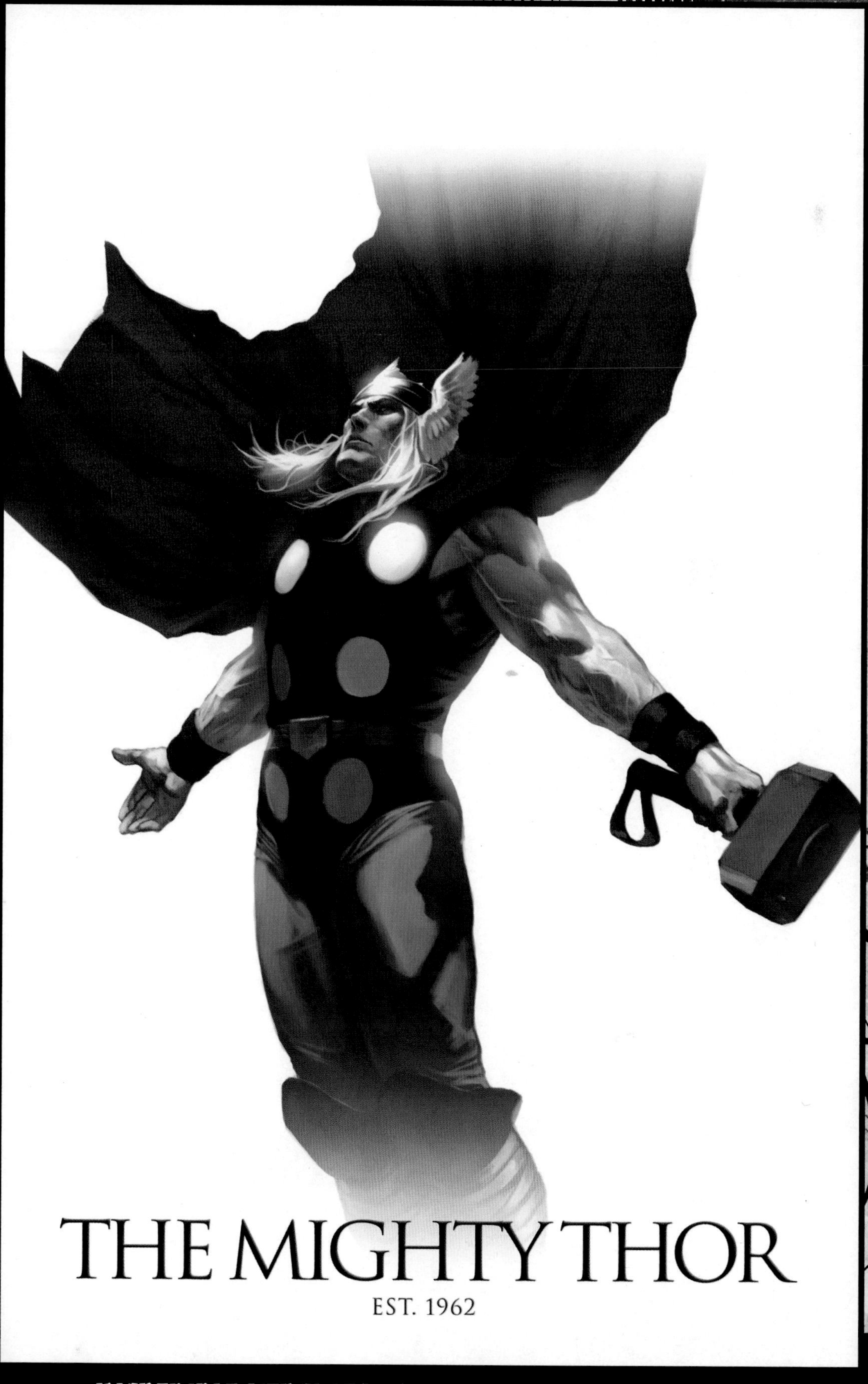
THE MIGHTY THOR
EST. 1962

INCREDIBLE HERCULES #132 70TH ANNIVERSARY VARIANT

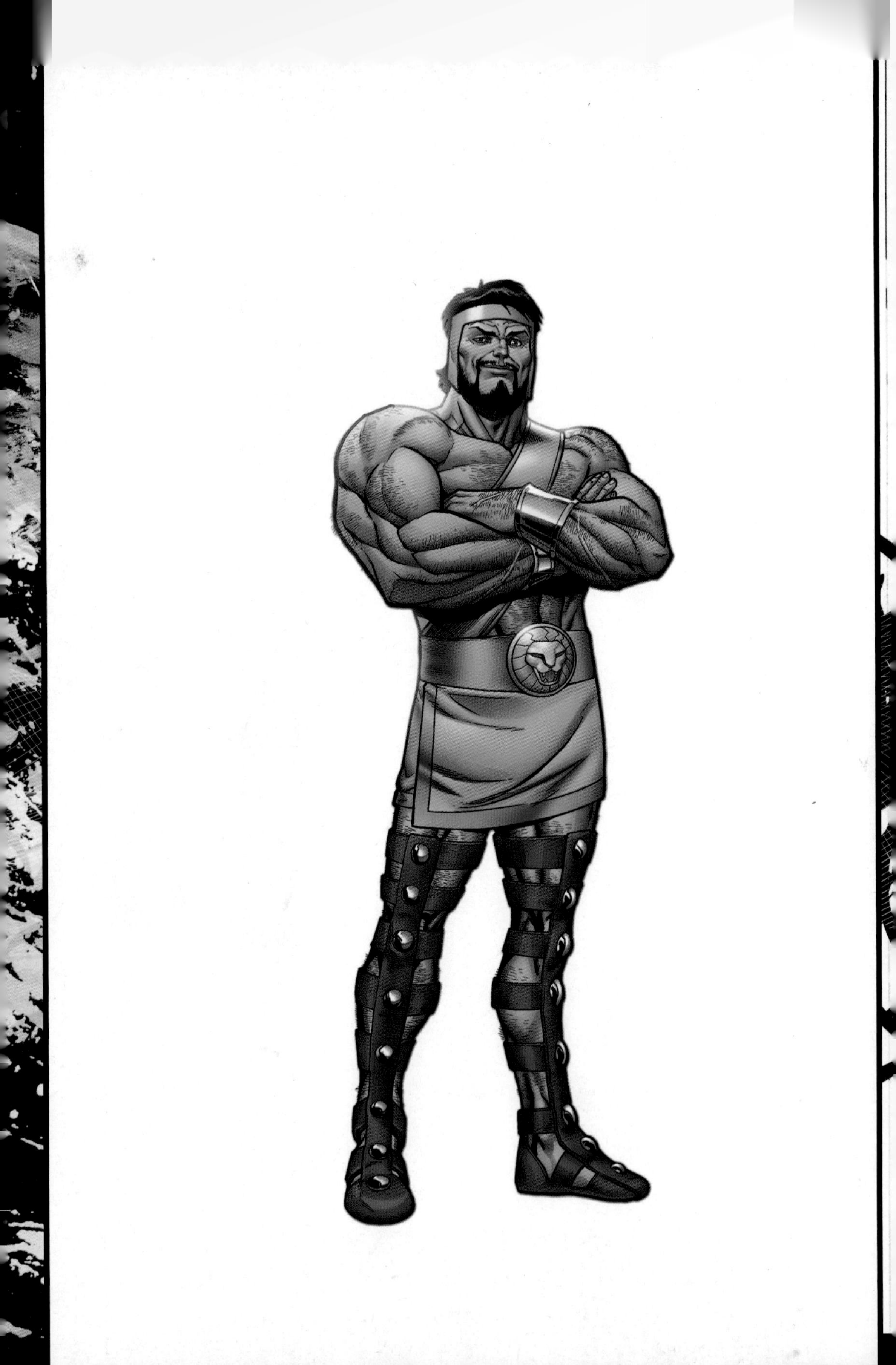

INCREDIBLE HERCULES #133 70TH ANNIVERSARY FRAME VARIANT

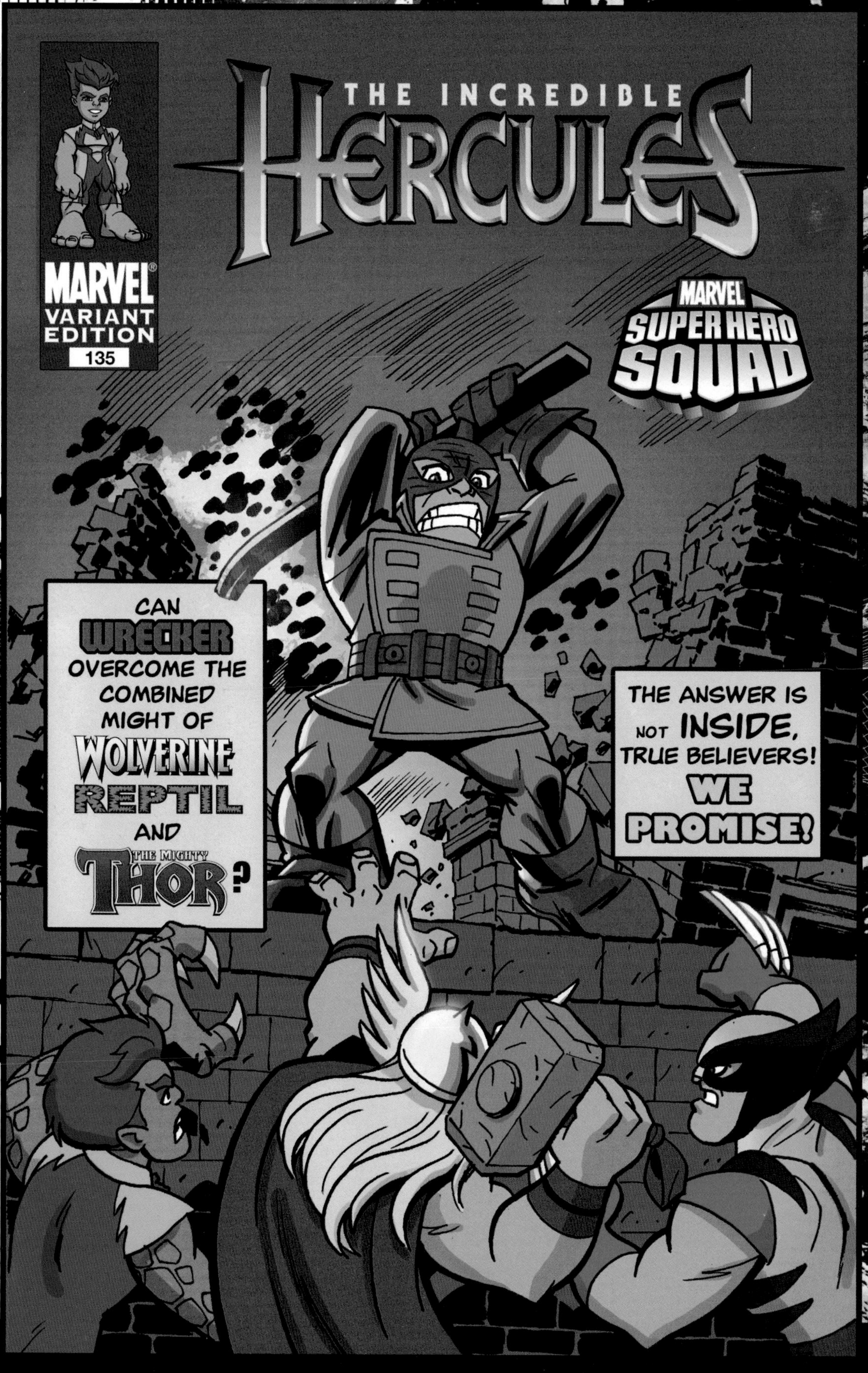

THE INCREDIBLE
HERCULES
MARVEL
VARIANT EDITION
135
MARVEL
SUPER HERO SQUAD
CAN
WRECKER
OVERCOME THE
COMBINED
MIGHT OF
WOLVERINE
REPTIL
AND
THE MIGHTY
THOR?
THE ANSWER IS
NOT INSIDE,
TRUE BELIEVERS!
WE
PROMISE!

INCREDIBLE HERCULES #135 SHS VARIANT

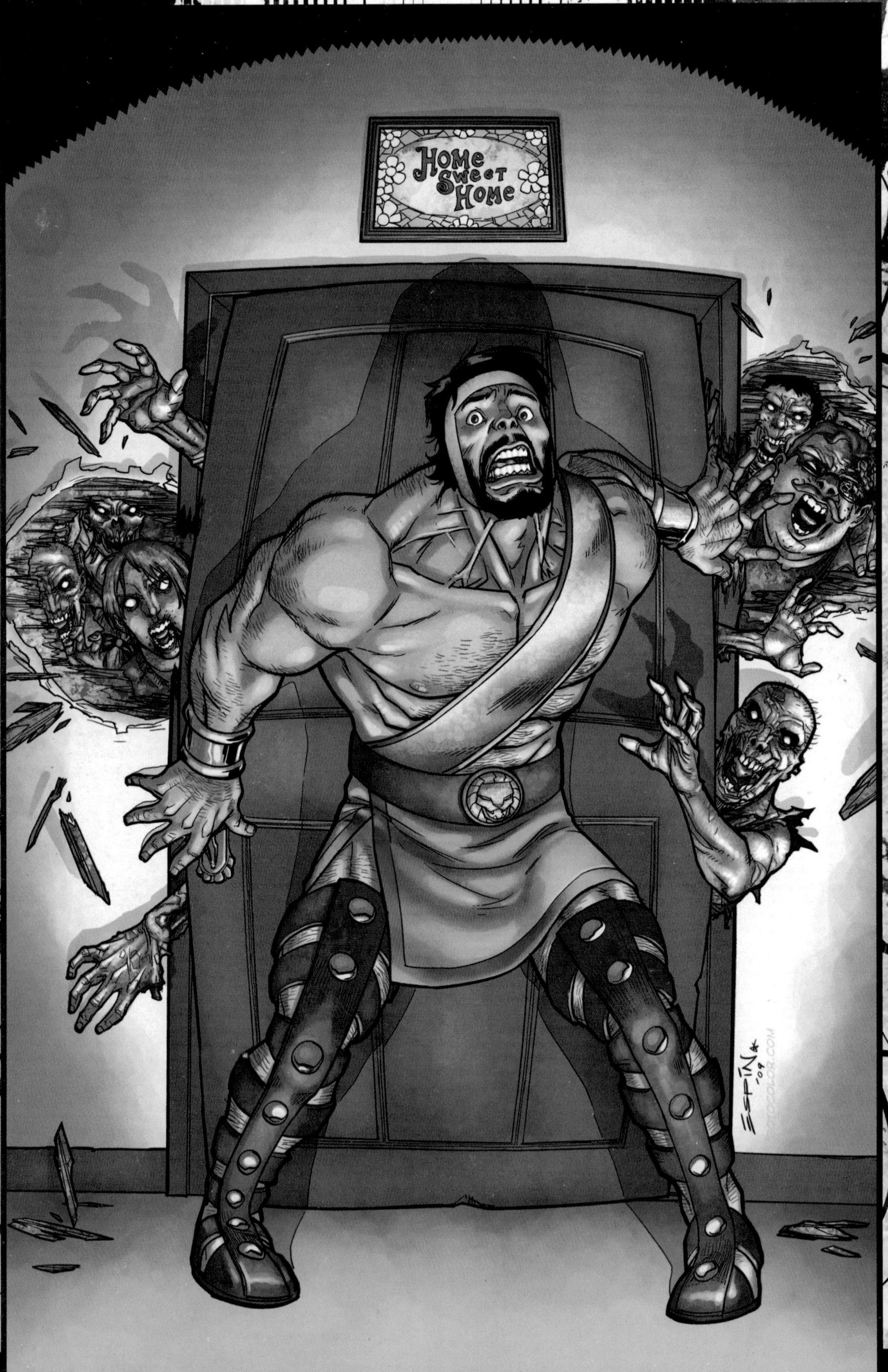
HOME SWEET HOME